Elaine Leeder
Editor

Inside and Out:
Women, Prison, and Therapy

Inside and Out: Women, Prison, and Therapy has been co-published simultaneously as *Women & Therapy*, Volume 29, Numbers 3/4 2006.

Pre-publication
REVIEWS,
COMMENTARIES,
EVALUATIONS . . .

"Valuable first because US prisons and gender, race and class are major issues at this time in history. . . . Her authors identify many meaningful dimensions, human rights, the failure of prisons, the sociocultural and global involvement. These complicated interconnections are the stuff of social action and feminist therapy today. The book is valuable secondly because it represents a range of perspectives and standpoints. . . . Finally the book is valuable because it presents a strong example of interdisciplinary and inter-perspective collaboration. I believe the text OFFERS A MODEL OF COLLABORATION THAT FORESHADOWS THE FUTURE OF PROGRESSIVE PEOPLES."

Mary Ballou, PhD
Professor
Department of Counseling and
Applied Educational Psychology
Northeastern University

Inside and Out:
Women, Prison, and Therapy

Inside and Out: Women, Prison, and Therapy has been co-published simultaneously as *Women & Therapy*, Volume 29, Numbers 3/4 2006.

Monographs from *Women & Therapy*™

For additional information on these and other Haworth Press titles, including descriptions, tables of contents, reviews, and prices, use the QuickSearch catalog at http://www.HaworthPress.com.

1. *Current Feminist Issues in Psychotherapy,* edited by The New England Association for Women in Psychology (Vol. 1, No. 3, 1983). *Addresses depression, displaced homemakers, sibling incest, and body image from a feminist perspective.*

2. *Women Changing Therapy: New Assessments, Values, and Strategies in Feminist Therapy,* edited by Joan Hamerman Robbins and Rachel Josefowitz Siegel, MSW (Vol. 2, No. 2/3, 1983). *"An excellent collection to use in teaching therapists that reflection and resolution in treatment do not simply lead to adaptation, but to an active inner process of judging." (News for Women in Psychiatry)*

3. *Women and Mental Health: New Directions for Change,* edited by Carol T. Mowbray, PhD, Susan Lanir, MA, and Marilyn Hulce, MSW, ACSW (Vol. 3, No. 3/4, 1985). *"The overview of sex differences in disorders is clear and sensitive, as is the review of sexual exploitation of clients by therapists. . . . Mandatory reading for all therapists who work with women." (British Journal of Medical Psychology and The British Psychological Society)*

4. *Another Silenced Trauma: Twelve Feminist Therapists and Activists Respond to One Woman's Recovery from War,* edited by Esther D. Rothblum, PhD, and Ellen Cole, PhD (Vol. 5, No. 1, 1986). *"A milestone. In it, twelve women pay very close attention to a woman who has been deeply wounded by war." (The World)*

5. *A Guide to Dynamics of Feminist Therapy,* edited by Doris Howard (Vol. 5, No. 2/3, 1987). *"A comprehensive treatment of an important and vexing subject." (Australian Journal of Sex, Marriage and Family)*

6. *Women, Power, and Therapy: Issues for Women,* edited by Marjorie Braude, MD (Vol. 6, No. 1/2, 1987). *"Raise[s] therapists' consciousness about the importance of considering gender-based power in therapy . . . welcome contribution." (Australian Journal of Psychology)*

7. *Treating Women's Fear of Failure,* edited by Esther D. Rothblum, PhD, and Ellen Cole, PhD (Vol. 6, No. 3, 1988). *"Should be recommended reading for all mental health professionals, social workers, educators, and vocational counselors who work with women." (The Journal of Clinical Psychiatry)*

8. *The Psychopathology of Everyday Racism and Sexism,* edited by Lenora Fulani, PhD (Vol. 6, No. 4, 1988). *In this enlightening book, women of color eloquently and honestly articulate the impact of racism, sexism, and poverty on their personal lives and on the histories of people.*

9. *Women and Sex Therapy: Closing the Circle of Sexual Knowledge,* edited by Ellen Cole, PhD, and Esther D. Rothblum, PhD (Vol. 7, No. 2/3, 1989). *"Adds immeasurably to the feminist therapy literature that dispels male paradigms of pathology with regard to women." (Journal of Sex Education & Therapy)*

10. *Loving Boldly: Issues Facing Lesbians,* edited by Esther D. Rothblum, PhD, and Ellen Cole, PhD. (Vol. 8, No. 1/2, 1989). *"Covers virtually every aspect of lesbian life. . . . This book merits reading by everyone concerned with treating and helping lesbians." (American Journal of Psychotherapy)*

11. *Overcoming Fear of Fat,* edited by Laura S. Brown, PhD, and Esther D. Rothblum, PhD (Vol. 8, No. 3, 1990). *"Challenges many traditional beliefs about being fat . . . A refreshing new perspective for approaching and thinking about issues related to weight." (Association for Women in Psychology Newsletter)*

12. *Diversity and Complexity in Feminist Therapy,* edited by Laura Brown, PhD, ABPP, and Maria P. P. Root, PhD (Vol. 9, No. 1/2, 1990). *"A most convincing discussion and illustration of the*

importance of adopting a multicultural perspective for theory building in feminist therapy. . . . This book is a must for therapists and should be included on psychology of women syllabi." (Association for Women in Psychology Newsletter)

13. **Woman-Defined Motherhood,** edited by Jane Price Knowles, MD, and Ellen Cole, PhD (Vol. 10, No. 1/2, 1990). *"Provides some enlightening perspectives. . . . It is worth the time of both male and female readers."* (Contemporary Psychology)

14. **Women's Mental Health in Africa,** edited by Esther D. Rothblum, PhD, and Ellen Cole, PhD (Vol. 10, No. 3, 1990). *"A valuable contribution and will be of particular interest to scholars in women's studies, mental health, and cross-cultural psychology."* (Contemporary Psychology)

15. **Jewish Women in Therapy: Seen But Not Heard,** edited by Rachel Josefowitz Siegel, MSW, and Ellen Cole, PhD (Vol. 10, No. 4, 1991). *"A varied collection of prose and poetry, first-person stories, and accessible theoretical pieces that can help Jews and non-Jews, women and men, therapists and patients, and general readers to grapple with questions of Jewish women's identities and diversity."* (Canadian Psychology)

16. **Professional Training for Feminist Therapists: Personal Memoirs,** edited by Esther D. Rothblum, PhD, and Ellen Cole, PhD (Vol. 11, No. 1, 1991). *"Exciting, interesting, and filled with the angst and the energies that directed these women to develop an entirely different approach to counseling."* (Science Books & Films)

17. **Women, Girls and Psychotherapy: Reframing Resistance,** edited by Carol Gilligan, PhD, Annie Rogers, PhD, and Deborah Tolman, EdD (Vol. 11, No. 3/4, 1991). *"Of use to educators, psychotherapists, and parents–in short, to any person who is directly involved with girls at adolescence."* (Harvard Educational Review)

18. **Refugee Women and Their Mental Health: Shattered Societies, Shattered Lives,** edited by Ellen Cole, PhD, Oliva M. Espin, PhD, and Esther D. Rothblum, PhD (Vol. 13, No. 1/2/3, 1992). *"The ideas presented are rich and the perspectives varied, and the book is an important contribution to understanding refugee women in a global context."* (Contemporary Psychology)

19. **Faces of Women and Aging,** edited by Nancy D. Davis, MD, Ellen Cole, PhD, and Esther D. Rothblum, PhD (Vol. 14, No. 1/2, 1993). *"This uplifting, helpful book is of great value not only for aging women, but also for women of all ages who are interested in taking active control of their own lives."* (New Mature Woman)

20. **Women with Disabilities: Found Voices,** edited by Mary Willmuth, PhD, and Lillian Holcomb, PhD (Vol. 14, No. 3/4, 1994). *"These powerful chapters often jolt the anti-disability consciousness and force readers to contend with the ways in which disability has been constructed, disguised, and rendered disgusting by much of society."* (Academic Library Book Review)

21. **Bringing Ethics Alive: Feminist Ethics in Psychotherapy Practice,** edited by Nanette K. Gartrell, MD (Vol. 15, No. 1, 1994). *"Examines the theoretical and practical issues of ethics in feminist therapies. From the responsibilities of training programs to include social issues ranging from racism to sexism to practice ethics, this outlines real questions and concerns."* (Midwest Book Review)

22. **Wilderness Therapy for Women: The Power of Adventure,** edited by Ellen Cole, PhD, Eve Erdman, MEd, MLS, and Esther D. Rothblum, PhD (Vol. 15, No. 3/4, 1994). *"There's an undeniable excitement in these pages about the thrilling satisfaction of meeting challenges in the physical world, the world outside our cities that is unfamiliar, uneasy territory for many women. If you're interested at all in the subject, this book is well worth your time."* (Psychology of Women Quarterly)

23. **Psychopharmacology from a Feminist Perspective,** edited by Jean A. Hamilton, MD, Margaret Jensvold, MD, Esther D. Rothblum, PhD, and Ellen Cole, PhD (Vol. 16, No. 1, 1995). *"Challenges readers to increase their sensitivity and awareness of the role of sex and gender in response to and acceptance of pharmacologic therapy."* (American Journal of Pharmaceutical Education)

24. **Women's Spirituality, Women's Lives,** edited by Judith Ochshorn, PhD, and Ellen Cole, PhD (Vol. 16, No. 2/3, 1995). *"A delightful and complex book on spirituality and sacredness in women's lives."* (Joan Clingan, MA, Spiritual Psychology, Graduate Advisor, Prescott College Master of Arts Program)

25. *Feminist Foremothers in Women's Studies, Psychology, and Mental Health,* edited by Phyllis Chesler, PhD, Esther D. Rothblum, PhD, and Ellen Cole, PhD (Vol. 17, No. 1/2/3/4, 1995). *"A must for feminist scholars and teachers . . . These women's personal experiences are poignant and powerful." (Women's Studies International Forum)*

26. *Lesbian Therapists and Their Therapy: From Both Sides of the Couch,* edited by Nancy D. Davis, MD, Ellen Cole, PhD, and Esther D. Rothblum, PhD (Vol. 18, No. 2, 1996). *"Highlights the power and boundary issues of psychotherapy from perspectives that many readers may have neither considered nor experienced in their own professional lives." (Psychiatric Services)*

27. *Classism and Feminist Therapy: Counting Costs,* edited by Marcia Hill, EdD, and Esther D. Rothblum, PhD (Vol. 18, No. 3/4, 1996). *"Educates, challenges, and questions the influence of classism on the clinical practice of psychotherapy with women." (Kathleen P. Gates, MA, Certified Professional Counselor, Center for Psychological Health, Superior, Wisconsin)*

28. *A Feminist Clinician's Guide to the Memory Debate,* edited by Susan Contratto, PhD, and M. Janice Gutfreund, PhD (Vol. 19, No. 1, 1996). *"Unites diverse scholars, clinicians, and activists in an insightful and useful examination of the issues related to recovered memories." (Feminist Bookstore News)*

29. *Couples Therapy: Feminist Perspectives,* edited by Marcia Hill, EdD, and Esther D. Rothblum, PhD (Vol. 19, No. 3, 1996). *Addresses some of the inadequacies, omissions, and assumptions in traditional couples' therapy to help you face the issues of race, ethnicity, and sexual orientation in helping couples today.*

30. *Sexualities,* edited by Marny Hall, PhD, LCSW (Vol. 19, No. 4, 1997). *"Explores the diverse and multifaceted nature of female sexuality, covering topics including sadomasochism in the therapy room, sexual exploitation in cults, and genderbending in cyberspace." (Feminist Bookstore News)*

31. *More than a Mirror: How Clients Influence Therapists' Lives,* edited by Marcia Hill, EdD (Vol. 20, No. 1, 1997). *"Courageous, insightful, and deeply moving. These pages reveal the scrupulous self-examination and self-reflection of conscientious therapists at their best. An important contribution to feminist therapy literature and a book worth reading by therapists and clients alike." (Rachel Josefowitz Siegal, MSW, retired feminist therapy practitioner; Co-Editor,* Women Changing Therapy; *and* Celebrating the Lives of Jewish Women: Patterns in a Feminist Sampler)

32. *Children's Rights, Therapists' Responsibilities: Feminist Commentaries,* edited by Gail Anderson, MA, and Marcia Hill, EdD (Vol. 20, No. 2, 1997). *"Addresses specific practice dimensions that will help therapists organize and resolve conflicts about working with children, adolescents, and their families in therapy." (Feminist Bookstore News)*

33. *Breaking the Rules: Women in Prison and Feminist Therapy,* edited by Judy Harden, PhD, and Marcia Hill, EdD (Vol. 20, No. 4 & Vol. 21, No. 1, 1998). *"Fills a long-recognized gap in the psychology of women curricula, demonstrating that feminist theory can be made relevant to the practice of feminism, even in prison." (Suzanne J. Kessler, PhD, Professor of Psychology and Women's Studies, State University of New York at Purchase)*

34. *Feminist Therapy as a Political Act,* edited by Marcia Hill, EdD (Vol. 21, No. 2, 1998). *"A real contribution to the field. . . . A valuable tool for feminist therapists and those who want to learn about feminist therapy." (Florence L. Denmark, PhD, Robert S. Pace, Distinguished Professor of Psychology and Chair, Psychology Department, Pace University, New York, New York)*

35. *Learning from Our Mistakes: Difficulties and Failures in Feminist Therapy,* edited by Marcia Hill, EdD, and Esther D. Rothblum, PhD (Vol. 21, No. 3, 1998). *"A courageous and fundamental step in evolving a well-grounded body of theory and of investigating the assumptions that, unexamined, lead us to error." (Teresa Bernardez, MD, Training and Supervising Analyst, The Michigan Psychoanalytic Council)*

36. *Assault on the Soul: Women in the Former Yugoslavia,* edited by Sara Sharratt, PhD, and Ellyn Kaschak, PhD (Vol. 22, No. 1, 1999). *Explores the applications and intersections of feminist therapy, activism and jurisprudence with women and children in the former Yugoslavia.*

37. ***Beyond the Rule Book: Moral Issues and Dilemmas in the Practice of Psychotherapy,*** edited by Ellyn Kaschak, PhD, and Marcia Hill, EdD (Vol. 22, No. 2, 1999). *"The authors in this important and timely book tackle the difficult task of working through . . . conflicts, sharing their moral struggles and real life solutions in working with diverse populations and in a variety of clinical settings. . . . Will provide psychotherapists with a thought-provoking source for the stimulating and essential discussion of our own and our profession's moral bases." (Carolyn C. Larsen, PhD, Senior Counsellor Emeritus, University of Calgary, Partner in private practice, Alberta Psychological Resources Ltd., Calgary, and Co-Editor,* Ethical Decision Making in Therapy: Feminist Perspectives)

38. ***For Love or Money: The Fee in Feminist Therapy,*** edited by Marcia Hill, EdD, and Ellyn Kaschak, PhD (Vol. 22, No. 3, 1999). *"Recommended reading for both new and seasoned professionals. . . . An exciting and timely book about 'the last taboo.' . . ." (Carolyn C. Larsen, PhD, Senior Counsellor Emeritus, University of Calgary; Partner, Alberta Psychological Resources Ltd., Calgary, and Co-Editor,* Ethical Decision Making in Therapy: Feminist Perspectives)

39. ***Minding the Body: Psychotherapy in Cases of Chronic and Life-Threatening Illness,*** edited by Ellyn Kaschak, PhD (Vol. 23, No. 1, 2001). *Being diagnosed with cancer, lupus, or fibromyalgia is a traumatic event. All too often, women are told their disease is "all in their heads" and, therefore, both "unreal and insignificant" by a medical profession that dismisses emotions and scorns mental illness. Combining personal narratives and theoretical views of illness,* Minding the Body *offers an alternative approach to the mind-body connection. This book shows the reader how to deal with the painful and difficult emotions that exacerbate illness, while learning the emotional and spiritual lessons illness can teach.*

40. ***The Next Generation: Third Wave Feminist Psychotherapy,*** edited by Ellyn Kaschak, PhD (Vol. 23, No. 2, 2001). *Discusses the issues young feminists face, focusing on the implications for psychotherapists of the false sense that feminism is no longer necessary.*

41. ***Intimate Betrayal: Domestic Violence in Lesbian Relationships,*** edited by Ellyn Kaschak, PhD (Vol. 23, No. 3, 2001). *"A groundbreaking examination of a taboo and complex subject. Both scholarly and down to earth, this superbly edited volume is an indispensable resource for clinicians, researchers, and lesbians caught up in the cycle of domestic violence." (Dr. Marny Hall, Psychotherapist; Author of* The Lesbian Love Companion, *Co-Author of* Queer Blues)

42. ***A New View of Women's Sexual Problems,*** edited by Ellyn Kaschak, PhD, and Leonore Tiefer, PhD (Vol. 24, No. 1/2, 2001). *"This useful, complex, and valid critique of simplistic notions of women's sexuality will be especially valuable for women's studies and public health courses. An important compilation representing many diverse individuals and groups of women." (Judy Norsigian and Jane Pincus, Co-Founders, Boston Women's Health Collective; Co-Authors,* Our Bodies, Ourselves for the New Century)

43. ***The Invisible Alliance: Psyche and Spirit in Feminist Therapy,*** edited by Ellyn Kaschak, PhD (Vol. 24, No. 3/4, 2001). *"The richness of this volume is reflected in the diversity of the collected viewpoints, perspectives, and practices. Each chapter challenges us to move out of the confines of our traditional training and reflect on the importance of spirituality. This book also brings us back to the original meaning of psychology–the study and knowledge of the soul." (Stephanie S. Covington, PhD, LCSW, Co-Director, Institute for Relational Development, La Jolla, California; Author,* A Woman's Way Through the Twelve Steps)

44. ***Exercise and Sport in Feminist Therapy: Constructing Modalities and Assessing Outcomes,*** edited by Ruth L. Hall, PhD, and Carole A. Oglesby, PhD (Vol. 25, No. 2, 2002). *Explores the healing use of exercise and sport as a helpful adjunct to feminist therapy.*

45. ***Violence in the Lives of Black Women: Battered, Black, and Blue,*** edited by Carolyn M. West, PhD (Vol. 25, No. 3/4, 2002). *Helps break the silence surrounding Black women's experiences of violence.*

46. ***Women with Visible and Invisible Disabilities: Multiple Intersections, Multiple Issues, Multiple Therapies,*** edited by Martha E. Banks, PhD, and Ellyn Kaschak, PhD (Vol. 26, No. 1/2/3/4, 2003). *"Bravo . . . provides powerful and direct answers to the questions, concerns, and challenges all women with disability experience. The voices in this book are speaking loud and clear to a wide range of readers and audiences. . . . Centered on the core principle that quality of life revolves around one's mental health, a sense of strength, and resiliency." (Theresa M. Rankin, BA, NCE,*

National Community Educator, Brain Injury Services, Inc.; MidAtlantic Traumatic Brain Injury Consortium; Fairhaven Institute for Brain Injury/University of Wisconsin-Scott)

47. **Biracial Women in Therapy: Between the Rock of Gender and the Hard Place of Race,** edited by Angela R. Gillem, PhD, and Cathy A. Thompson, PhD (Vol. 27, No. 1/2, 2004). *"A must-read. . . . Compelling and poignant. . . . Enhances our understanding of what it means to be biracial and female in society dominated by monoracial notions of identity and sexualized notions of biracial women. . . . Delves insightfully into a variety of biracial women's experiences." (Lisa Bowleg, PhD, Assistant Professor, Department of Psychology, University of Rhode Island)*

48. **From Menarche to Menopause: The Female Body in Feminist Therapy,** edited by Joan C. Chrisler, PhD (Vol. 27, No. 3/4, 2004). *"A definitive resource on women's reproductive health. . . . Brings this topic out of the closet. . . . The coverage is excellent, spanning the adolescent experience of menarche and moving from pregnancy issues to menopause and beyond. The chapter authors are clearly experts on their topics, and this edited book is admirable in its philosophical coherence. Feminist therapists working with young girls, women in their reproductive years, and older women will find clear information about how to understand and affirm their clients' experiences." (Maryka Biaggio, PhD, Professor and Director of Research on Feminist Issues, Department of Professional Psychiatry, Pacific University)*

49. **Therapeutic and Legal Issues for Therapists Who Have Survived a Client Suicide: Breaking the Silence,** edited by Kayla Miriyam Weiner, PhD (Vol. 28, No. 1, 2005). *"This book offers resources, understanding, and most importantly, company for therapists living with or worrying about the nightmare of client suicide." (Marcia Hill, EdD, psychologist in private practice; author of* Diary of a Country Therapist)

50. **The Foundation and Future of Feminist Therapy,** edited by Marcia Hill, EdD, and Mary Ballou, PhD (Vol. 28, No. 3/4, 2005). *"This insider's chronicle offers an intimate portrait of feminist therapy from the 1970s to today and the vibrant and courageous women who created it. The book celebrates the idealism, fierce determination, and innovative thinking of these therapists. It provides a map of the past, but more important, it gives us a moral compass for the future." (Jeanne Marecek, PhD, Professor of Psychology, Swarthmore College)*

51. **Inside and Out: Women, Prison, and Therapy,** edited by Elaine Leeder, PhD (Vol. 29, No. 3/4, 2006). *Valuable first because US prisons and gender, race and class are major issues at this time in history. . . . Her authors identify many meaningful dimensions, human rights, the failure of prisons, the sociocultural and global involvement. These complicated interconnections are the stuff of social action and feminist therapy today. The book is valuable secondly because it represents a range of perspectives and standpoints. . . . Finally the book is valuable because it presents a strong example of interdisciplinary and inter-perspective collaboration. I believe the text offers a model of collaboration that foreshadows the future of progressive peoples." (Mary Ballou, PhD, Professor, Department of Counseling and Applied Educational Psychology, Northeastern University)*

Inside and Out:
Women, Prison, and Therapy

Elaine Leeder

Editor

Inside and Out: Women, Prison, and Therapy has been co-published simultaneously as *Women & Therapy*, Volume 29, Numbers 3/4 2006.

The Haworth Press, Inc.

New York • London • Victoria (AU)
www.HaworthPress.com

Inside and Out: Women, Prison, and Therapy has been co-published simultaneously as *Women & Therapy*, Volume 29, Numbers 3/4 2006.

The Haworth Press, Inc., 10 Alice Street, Binghamton, NY 13904-1580 USA

Cover design by Kerry E. Mack

Library of Congress Cataloging-in-Publication Data

Inside and out : women, prison, and therapy / Elaine Leeder, editor.
     p. cm.
"Inside and out : women, prison, and therapy has been co-published simultaneously as Women & Therapy, Volume 29, Numbers 3/4 2006."
    Includes bibliographical references and index.
    ISBN-13: 978-0-7890-3429-8 (hard cover : alk. paper)
    ISBN-10: 0-7890-3429-8 (hard cover : alk. paper)
    ISBN-13: 978-0-7890-3430-4 (soft cover : alk. paper)
    ISBN-10: 0-7890-3430-1 (soft cover : alk. paper)
    1. Women prisoners–Mental health–United States. 2. Women prisoners–United States–Family relationships. 3. Women prisoners–Counseling of–United States. I. Leeder, Elaine J.
RC451.4.P68I48 2006
365'.66–dc22
2006013351

This section provides you with a list of major indexing & abstracting services and other tools for bibliographic access. That is to say, each service began covering this periodical during the the year noted in the right column. Most Websites which are listed below have indicated that they will either post, disseminate, compile, archive, cite or alert their own Website users with research-based content from this work. (This list is as current as the copyright date of this publication.)

Abstracting, Website/Indexing Coverage . . . . Year When Coverage Began

- **Academic ASAP (Thomson Gale)** 1992
- **Academic Search Premier (EBSCO)**
  <http://www.epnet.com/academic/acasearchprem.asp> 1994
- **CINAHL Plus (EBSCO)** 2006
- **CINAHL (Cumulative Index to Nursing & Allied Health Literature) (EBSCO)** <http://www.cinahl.com> 2001
- **Current Contents/Social & Behavioral Sciences (Thomson Scientific)** <http://www.isinet.com> 1995
- **Expanded Academic ASAP (Thomson Gale)** 1992
- **Expanded Academic Index (Thomson Gale)** 1993
- **InfoTrac Custom (Thomson Gale)** 1996
- **InfoTrac OneFile (Thomson Gale)** 1992
- **Journal Citation Reports/Social Sciences Edition (Thomson Scientific** <http://www.isinet.com> . . ./ 2005
- **ProQuest Academic Research Library**
  <http://www.proquest.com> 1992
- **Psychological Abstracts (PsycINFO)** <http://www.apa.org> . . . 1982
- **Research Library (ProQuest)** <http://www.proquest.com> 2006
- **Social Sciences Citation Index (Thomson Scientific)**
  <http://www.isinet.com> 1995
- **Social Scisearch (Thomson Scientific)** <http://www.isinet.com> 1995

(continued)

(continued)

(continued)

*Exact start date to come.

Bibliographic Access

- *Cabell's Directory of Publishing Opportunities in Psychology*
  <http://www.cabells.com>

- *Magazines for Libraries (Katz)*

- *MediaFinder (Bibliographic Access) <http://www.mediafinder.com/>*

- *Ulrich's Periodicals Directory: International Periodicals*
  Information Since 1932 <http://www.Bowkerlink.com>

*Special Bibliographic Notes related to special journal issues
(separates) and indexing/abstracting:*

- indexing/abstracting services in this list will also cover material in any "separate" that is co-published simultaneously with Haworth's special thematic journal issue or DocuSerial. Indexing/abstracting usually covers material at the article/chapter level.
- monographic co-editions are intended for either non-subscribers or libraries which intend to purchase a second copy for their circulating collections.
- monographic co-editions are reported to all jobbers/wholesalers/approval plans. The source journal is listed as the "series" to assist the prevention of duplicate purchasing in the same manner utilized for books-in-series.
- to facilitate user/access services all indexing/abstracting services are encouraged to utilize the co-indexing entry note indicated at the bottom of the first page of each article/chapter/contribution.
- this is intended to assist a library user of any reference tool (whether print, electronic, online, or CD-ROM) to locate the monographic version if the library has purchased this version but not a subscription to the source journal.
- individual articles/chapters in any Haworth publication are also available through the Haworth Document Delivery Service (HDDS).

As part of Haworth's continuing committment to better serve our library patrons, we are proud to be working with the following electronic services:

AGGREGATOR SERVICES

EBSCOhost

Ingenta

J-Gate

Minerva

OCLC FirstSearch

Oxmill

SwetsWise

MINERVA

FirstSearch

Oxmill Publishing

SwetsWise

LINK RESOLVER SERVICES

1Cate (Openly Informatics)

CrossRef

Gold Rush (Coalliance)

LinkOut (PubMed)

LINKplus (Atypon)

LinkSolver (Ovid)

LinkSource with A-to-Z (EBSCO)

Resource Linker (Ulrich)

SerialsSolutions (ProQuest)

SFX (Ex Libris)

Sirsi Resolver (SirsiDynix)

Tour (TDnet)

Vlink (Extensity, *formerly Geac*)

WebBridge (Innovative Interfaces)

1cate

CrossRef

Gold Rush

LinkOut. LINKING TO A WORLD OF RESOURCES

atypon

A to Z EBSCO

OVID LinkSolver

ULRICH'S RESOURCE LINKER

S·F·X

SerialsSolutions

SirsiDynix

TOUR

extensity

WebBridge

ABOUT THE EDITOR

Elaine Leeder is Professor of Sociology and Dean of the School of Social Sciences, Sonoma State University. She is the author of three other books, including *The Gentle General: Rose Pesotta, Anarchist and Labor Organizer*; *Treating Abuse in Families: A Feminist and Community Approach*; and *The Family in Global Perspective: A Gendered Journey*. She has written a number of articles on topics related to lesbian battering, the treatment of Munchhausen Syndrome, and radical women's history. Leeder is a member of the Feminist Therapy Institute and served on its steering committee for a number of years. Having received numerous awards for scholarship and teaching, she was a visiting scholar at the United States Holocaust Memorial Museum, and a National Endowment for the Humanities awardee. She was a practicing feminist therapist for twenty-five years and is currently the chair of the board of United Against Sexual Assault of Sonoma County (California) as well as a member of the editorial board of *Women & Therapy*. She is at work on another co-edited book entitled *Beyond the Gates of Knowledge: College Teaching in Prison*. Leeder traveled around the world twice on Semester at Sea and is interested in global feminist issues.

Inside and Out:
Women, Prison, and Therapy

CONTENTS

Inside and Out:
Women, Prison and Therapy:
A Feminist Dialogue
on Challenging Correctional Discourse

Elaine Leeder

One does not come to the study of women in prison easily. For me it was an indirect route, from the study of violence against women, to the study of perpetrators, to the study of the prisons where perpetrators were incarcerated, and finally to the study of women inside prisons. Years ago a group of my students asked to visit a maximum-security penitentiary in upstate New York. I was wary of accommodating them, since I maintained the usual stereotypes of prisoners. But I also knew of the racist nature of the criminal justice system and wanted the students to see firsthand how virulent the prison-industrial-complex had grown in the last decade. After that simple trip I transformed my academic focus.

Elaine Leeder, MSW, MPH, PhD, is Professor of Sociology and Dean of the School of Social Sciences at Sonoma State University.

Author note: I would like to thank Zoë Sodja for her editing and formatting of this issue, as well as Linda Evans and Eve Goldberg for their suggestions on title and editing. Gratitude also to Jonathan Laskowitz, Sandra Feldman and Myrna Goodman. Thanks to Ellyn Kaschak for suggesting that I work on this issue and her excellent editorial suggestions. Appreciation to Iain Twaddle and his colleagues for the subtitle of this essay. This book is dedicated to my students at San Quentin.

[Haworth co-indexing entry note]: "Inside and Out: Women, Prison and Therapy: A Feminist Dialogue on Challenging Correctional Discourse." Leeder, Elaine. Co-published simultaneously in *Women & Therapy* (The Haworth Press, Inc.) Vol. 29, No. 3/4, 2006, pp. 1-8; and: *Inside and Out: Women, Prison, and Therapy* (ed: Elaine Leeder) The Haworth Press, Inc., 2006, pp. 1-8. Single or multiple copies of this article are available for a fee from The Haworth Document Delivery Service [1-800-HAWORTH, 9:00 a.m. - 5:00 p.m. (EST). E-mail address: docdelivery@haworthpress.com].

Available online at http://wt.haworthpress.com
doi:10.1300/J015v29n03_01

Soon after that visit, I began a program of higher education for prisoners, offering a class taught by volunteer faculty members including me, and sponsored for credit by Ithaca College. I was shocked to find such brilliant students, and I could see that the street smarts of many could be transformed into excellent academic skills. I kept that program running until I left in 2001. Soon after my move to California I found a similar program in existence at San Quentin. It was far more sophisticated and better organized. Since 2003 I have been teaching in that program, volunteering and consulting with lifers at San Quentin, helping others with their issues of reentry and adjustment to the larger society. While working with prisoners I have become quite familiar with both men's and women's issues. My reading and experience have led me to the editing of this journal. Feminist therapists must become aware of the problems for incarcerated women, their children and families. Given the growth of the numbers of women in prison, many therapists encounter either ex-prisoners or their children, often without the awareness of their specific problems and strengths. Also crucial for therapists to understand are the global, economic, and political underpinnings of the work in which they are engaged so that they try not to accept the dominant ideology about prisoners.

In 1970 there were 5,600 women incarcerated. By June of 2001 there were over 160 thousand women held in U.S. prisons and jails. That means there was a 2,800 percent increase in thirty years (Sudbury, 2005). Presently there are over 2 million people incarcerated in the U.S. Women make up 9 percent of those incarcerated nationally.

The rate of population growth for women in prison surpasses that of men (Sudbury, 2005). Most women are imprisoned for non-violent crimes. They are there because of the changing drug laws, which disproportionately impact people of color and account for the increasing number of women going to prison. Although there are no available statistics for all women of color in prison, in 2003 there were 35,000 black women who were incarcerated nationally (Wright, 2005). Women who are incarcerated are multiply victimized because of their color, the violence done to them inside the prison and by the criminal justice system which incarcerates them at higher rates than white women (Davis, 2003).

As a society we like to deposit our "undesirable" populations in out-of-the-way places and forget about them (Davis, 2003). We do not want to think about what goes on behind those walls, unless it is on some network TV show or Hollywood movie that idealize and glamorize prison life. Life inside is not glamorous. It is harsh, cold, and a difficult existence. Yet most are not aware of the problem and many who are aware choose to ignore the reality of 2 million prisoners' daily tragedies in our American prisons.

Angela Davis (2003) argues that prison life is a form of slavery, a contemporary manifestation of the racialized disparities that many of us believe were abolished in 1865. African Americans make up the majority of the increase in the prison population. Between 1990 and 2003 the number of blacks in prison jumped from 360,000 to 621,300, an increase of 76.2 percent (Wright, 2005). Now 3.5 percent of all black males are in prison and, in the 25-29 age groups, more than 10 percent of black males are in prison (Wright, 316). The argument made by those in the prison reform movement is that the incarceration rate of people of color reflects a move toward warehousing of surplus populations (Sudbury, 2005). It further reflects a shift from rehabilitation and reform to incapacitation of people whose crimes were once dealt with by other means.

According to feminist scholars of the prison system, for women, prisons are a form of gendered servitude (Sudbury, 2005). Women are often seen as more culpable for committing the same crimes as men. And, as feminists, we know that often women are viewed as mentally ill when they engage in deviant behaviors (Davis, 2003). Male deviance is often seen as "normal," while female deviance is considered crazy. When men are incarcerated, their prison experience is one of punishment. When women are incarcerated, they are punished and encouraged to engage in domestic activities. According to Sudbury (2005) we must move beyond the micro-level of analysis of women's imprisonment and begin to see that incarceration of women is a part of a political economy which is benefited by warehousing the labor of the global economy and creates profits for the companies that service prisons. Through their experience with the guards, who benefit financially through the increase in jobs by incarceration, women are demeaned or sexually assaulted, thereby encouraged into compliance. They are also taught through prison classes to take on domestic service activities, like hospital aides or hotel maids, upon release. Little is offered in prison training beside these kinds of jobs. This is a racialized and gendered difference, preparing poor women, and black and brown skinned people for a continued class-based set of inequities (Sudbury, 2003).

For those involved in the prison movement there is also a move toward "decarceration." Finding a more humane way to imprison people is not the answer (Davis, 2003). Decarceration is a belief that alternatives to incarceration, restorative justice and reconciliation are more

appropriate methods for dealing with people in trouble. Some criminologists argue that crime is caused by economic disparities and lack of
opportunity structures for those who are forced to engage in seek any way
they can to meet their needs (Cloward & Ohlin, 1960). If our society
sought solutions to poverty, apartheid in the schools, and criminalization
of drugs we would be moving toward thinking of decarceration as a way
of life. These are not the usual ways of thinking, and yet without such
thinking, we maintain the status quo and continue the inequities of the
prison system.

The articles in this volume provide a method for feminist therapists to
begin the dialogue in our field focusing on the ways we work to sustain
the injustices of the criminal justice system and the roles we might play
in deconstructing and demystifying women prisoners' lives. This volume might also help us find clear steps in the process towards decarceration and alternatives to prisons. The volume falls into five parts. The
first is a macro analysis of ways of looking at gender and criminality;
the second assesses issues of violence and abuse of women; the third
highlights women as mothers and the impact of incarceration on the
children; the fourth looks closely at treatment approaches in programs
developed for women prisoners; and the final section outlines what
women need when leaving prison life.

The first article, by Stephanie Covington and Barbara Bloom, two activist scholars noted for their groundbreaking analysis of the specific
need for a gendered responsive treatment for women prisoners, argues
that as correction supervision increases there is a growing awareness of
the differences between women offenders and their male counterparts.
The authors take a "pathways" approach to women's entry into crime
and argue that gender matters in the treatment of incarcerated women.
The pathways model says that often women enter crime as a result of
personal abuse, mental illness, substance abuse and addiction, economic and social marginality, homelessness and intimate relationships.
To understand women in prison one needs to understand relational theory, trauma theory, and addiction theory. Program elements built on
these theories can lead to gender specific treatments that individualize
women's needs.

The second article in the first section, by MaDonna Maidment from
Canada, argues that we who work with women prisoners must realize
that the discourse surrounding women's incarceration portrays women
as psychologically deficient and marginalizes these disenfranchised
women. Arguing that Canada takes an androcentric, neoliberal approach to pathologizing women, Maidment maintains that the criminal

justice system further marginalizes women and individualizes what is clearly a social and structural problem. Maidment deconstructs the language of incarceration and challenges us to get beyond this way of thinking, to realize that the women we are working with are "not all that criminal."

The third article in the first section, by Zoë Sodja, asks us to think of the plight of women in prison as a human rights issue. Sodja has visited women's prisons, particularly looking at the manner in which women's health is being handled. She finds that the very minimum standards for the treatment of prisoners based on the Universal Declaration of Human Rights are not being maintained in U.S. women's prisons and gives us case examples of women whose lives have been lost because of that mistreatment. Sodja argues that the U.S. has a long way to go in applying these standards domestically and urges us to become educated to the abuses that occur, challenging us to show our true commitment to human rights by defending the human rights of our most disempowered people.

The first article in the second section of the book, which focuses on violence, is by Kolleen Duley, a member of the organization Free Battered Women. In a compelling and well-reasoned piece she points out that the prison expansion is a racialized, classed, and gendered process that must really be viewed in a transnational, feminist context. She argues that immigration, violence against women, trafficking of women, and globalization are all part of a global system of control, and to understand women's abuse one must see the web that unites all of these women in a structural and systemic connective whole. These complex systems of state and interpersonal violence are teased out for us and allow us an overview of why women prisoners come from poor and minority populations.

Melanie Bliss, Sarah Cook, and Nadine Kaslow present an ecological approach to incarcerated women's response to abuse by studying 85 women prisoners using a regression analysis to explain interpersonal violence responses. By studying a broad range of strategic responses to violence, the authors evaluate childhood, intimate relationships and individual impact of abuse, and community social support to determine that women who experience violence against them do seek help and engage in coping strategies, as do non-incarcerated victims of domestic violence. By studying a disenfranchised group of women, prisoners, the authors argue that when women are released from incarceration it is important that they be taught anger and stress management, problem solving in relationships and receive individual mental health counseling.

Shoshana Pollack and Kerry Brezina address sexual abuse counseling with imprisoned women. Working with women in prison in Canada, the authors note that being in prison re-traumatizes once sexually abused women. Feminist therapists want to diminish the power and control inequities in our work, and yet working in a setting that by its very nature is created to maintain punishment and control, a prison setting, contradicts our intentions. The authors present methods by which those contradictions can be diminished.

The next section of articles focuses on women prisoners as mothers and the impact of their imprisonment on parenthood and the children. Angela Moe and Kathleen Ferraro use qualitative life histories with 30 women to understand the ways that motherhood is included in the women's self-perceptions, their motivation for crime, and how it impacts therapeutic programs in prison. Through the women's own voices, we hear about the importance of being mothers, the symbolic nature of motherhood in their self-perceptions, and the need for an assets-based approach to therapy with incarcerated women.

Rivka Greenberg, a therapist who has worked with incarcerated women in Oakland, California, suggests that children of these women are at high risk developmentally, psychologically, emotionally, and economically. She argues that the risk factors can be countered and using a resiliency approach can enhance the children's mental health. By presenting the recently issued *Children of Incarcerated Parents Bill of Rights*, Greenberg argues that families must remain connected, even with a parent inside a prison, to assure that the children are supported to help build upon their resiliency.

The fourth section of the book is devoted to specific treatment approaches that have been employed or critiqued by the authors. Vanessa Alleyne focuses on addiction treatment for incarcerated women. Eighty percent of all crimes are committed with drug involvement, and most women in prison are untreated substance abusers. Because prisons are not equipped to deal with this level of addiction, the women are placed in a double bind, being incarcerated and untreated for their addictions. She presents case studies to illustrate the failings of our system as it (dis)serves these women and suggests steps to overcome these failings.

Abigail Leeder and Colleen Wimmer worked with incarcerated women using drama therapy and vividly describe their efforts to assist the women in overcoming internalized oppressive beliefs. Using writing exercises, performances, and group drama as tools for prisoner therapy, these therapists movingly present their successes and provide a hopeful alternative to the sad truths surrounding incarceration.

Iain Twaddle and his colleagues developed a feminist support group for women prisoners in a substance abuse program in Guam and present us with a success story which illustrates the ways they helped these women deal with trauma, addiction, and incarceration. Nonetheless transition back to the community remained a challenge to their clients, with 23% sent back to prison for parole violations. By reminding us that dealing with individual women and their problems is only part of the solution, they urge that we challenge social, structural conditions of injustice and that the public be educated about the real blame for social problems, rather than blaming the "criminals."

The final article in this section, by Julie Beck, is the most provocative. Using ethnographic data at a drug treatment program, she shows how the language of recovery recapitulates racist, classist, and gendered ideologies, further marginalizing the marginalized. The social, structural inequalities and the power of state authority train these women for "good citizenship." Beck suggests that this is just another manifestation of social control. By using the words "family" the therapeutic community reproduces the operations of the patriarchal state. She argues that drug treatment must be severed from the penal system, and that women need protection while in treatment and thereafter. Beck provides us with a challenge in our understanding of what "treatment" really is.

The final section covers reemergence into the community after incarceration. Patricia O'Brien and Nancy Lee suggest a holistic approach to transition from prison in which economic and self-sustainability, beyond mere social services, are what is called for. Using case studies, they argue that there need to be programs inside to prepare women for release, concrete assistance must be made available, and that the use of a ladder to develop goals that are attainable could be a useful tool. The challenge is to find out what is needed and to provide it to help women "make it" once outside.

Linda Evans, formerly of the Weather Underground and an incarcerated woman for 16 years at federal penitentiaries, details for us the vivid connections and closeness of women's communities inside and out. She helps us see the ways the discrimination women face, once released, makes it hard to reenter society. It can lead to discouragement, further disenfranchisement, and community impoverishment. Barriers must be removed so that there is a civil and human rights movement to provide alternatives to incarceration. Prisons help no one, not our communities, not the victims, nor the prisoners. Evans closes this book with a call for social change, new social policies, and a more creative way to look at the prison industrial complex that has taken over our country.

It is with pleasure that I present this volume as a challenge to feminist therapists to become involved in doing clinical work with women prisoners and their children. The fight to end prisons, as we know them, is an important contemporary movement for social change and is as invigorating as the early stages in the women's movement, when all things were possible. As feminist therapists we have something to add to that movement, by providing treatment while not replicating the very system that has created the problem.

REFERENCES

Cloward, R. & Ohlin, L. (1960). *Delinquency and opportunity: A theory of delinquent gangs.* New York: Free Press.
Davis, A. (2003). *Are prisons obsolete?* New York: Seven Stories Press.
Sudbury, J. (editor) (2005). *Global lockdown: Race, gender and the prison-industrial complex.* New York: Routledge.
Wright, J. (editor) (2006). *The New York Times almanac: The almanac of record.* New York: Penguin Reference.

doi:10.1300/J015v29n03_01

Gender Responsive Treatment and Services in Correctional Settings

Stephanie S. Covington
Barbara E. Bloom

SUMMARY. As the number of women under correctional supervision continues to increase, there is an emerging awareness that women offenders present different issues than their male counterparts. This paper addresses the importance of gender in terms of program design and delivery and describes the context for the development of effective gender-responsive programming for women. Using the pathways theory of women's criminality, the elements that should be considered in women's treatment and services are addressed, such as: program environment/culture, staff competencies, theoretical foundation, treatment modalities, reentry issues, and collaboration. The content of gender-responsive programming that integrates substance abuse and trauma services is also discussed. doi:10.1300/J015v29n03_02 *[Article copies available for a fee from The Haworth Document Delivery Service: 1-800-HAWORTH. E-mail*

Stephanie S. Covington, PhD, LCSW, is Co-Director of the Center for Gender and Justice located in La Jolla, CA.

Barbara E. Bloom, MSW, PhD, is Associate Professor in the Department of Criminology and Criminal Justice at Sonoma State University in Rohnert Park, CA.

Address correspondence to: Stephanie Covington and Barbara Bloom, Center for Gender & Justice, 7946 Ivanhoe Ave., Suite 201 B, La Jolla, CA 92037 (E-mail: sscird@aol.com; bloom@sonoma.edu).

[Haworth co-indexing entry note]: "Gender Responsive Treatment and Services in Correctional Settings." Covington, Stephanie S., and Barbara E. Bloom. Co-published simultaneously in *Women & Therapy* (The Haworth Press, Inc.) Vol. 29, No. 3/4, 2006, pp. 9-33; and: *Inside and Out: Women, Prison, and Therapy* (ed: Elaine Leeder) The Haworth Press, Inc., 2006, pp. 9-33. Single or multiple copies of this article are available for a fee from The Haworth Document Delivery Service [1-800-HAWORTH, 9:00 a.m. - 5:00 p.m. (EST). E-mail address: docdelivery@haworthpress.com].

Available online at http://wt.haworthpress.com
doi:10.1300/J015v29n03_02

address: <docdelivery@haworthpress.com> Website: <http://www.HaworthPress. com> © 2006 by The Haworth Press, Inc. All rights reserved.]

KEYWORDS. Gender-responsive, women offenders, trauma, addiction, treatment

INTRODUCTION

In recent decades, the number of women under criminal justice supervision in the United States has risen dramatically. In 1990, there were approximately 600,000 women in prisons or jails, on probation, or on parole. By 2001, the figure had reached over one million. Although the rate of incarceration for women remains lower than the rate for men, (62 sentenced female prisoners per 100,000 women versus 915 sentenced male prisoners per 100,000), the number of women imprisoned in the U.S. since 1980 has escalated at a rate double the rate for men. This increase–fueled primarily by stringent drug laws–has prompted a re-examination of correctional policy in order to establish the most effective way to respond to women offenders.

The story behind these numbers begins with an understanding of women's pathways into criminality as well as the unique issues women confront as a result of their race, class, and gender. Research confirms that women offenders differ significantly from their male counterparts in terms of their personal histories and how they enter into crime (Belknap, 2001). For example, female offenders are more likely to share a history of physical and/or sexual abuse; they are often the primary caretakers of young children at the time of arrest and they have separate, distinctive physical and mental needs (for more on pathways, see Pathways Theory). Their involvement in crime is often economically motivated, driven by poverty and/or substance abuse. Women are also less likely to be convicted of a violent offense, and their risk to society is much less than that of men. In other words, women offenders face gender-specific adversities–namely sexual abuse, sexual assault, domestic violence, and poverty.

Why the Need for Gender-Specific Treatment?

Research shows that addiction for women is a multi-dimensional issue involving complex environmental and psychosocial challenges.

Addiction comprises a piece of a larger mosaic that includes a woman's individual background and the social, economic, political, and cultural forces that shape the context of her life. Recent studies confirm that gender differences exist among men and women substance abusers regarding their relationships with family members; for example, women substance abusers tend to have severe family and social problems coupled with minimal family support upon entering treatment (Grella et al., 2003). In essence, gender differences are critical considerations when developing substance abuse programs for women. According to research, clinical services for addiction treatment that focus on women's specific issues and needs are more effective for women than traditional programs originally designed for men (Grella, 1999; Nelson-Zlupko, Dore, Kauffman & Kalterbach, 1996). Unfortunately, services available to women in correctional settings are rarely designed to match the specific needs of female offenders. Therefore, in conceptualizing treatment programs for addicted women, it is essential that providers ground theory and practice in a multi-dimensional perspective. Increased sensitivity to women's needs is necessary in order to design effective programs over the long term.

PROFILE OF WOMEN IN THE CRIMINAL JUSTICE SYSTEM

In order to design system-wide services that match the specific strengths and needs of women, it is important to consider the demographics and history of the female offender population, as well as how various life factors impact women's patterns of offending. A basic principle of clinical work is to know who the client is and what she brings into the treatment setting.

Most women in the criminal justice system are poor, undereducated, and unskilled, and they are disproportionately women of color. Many come from impoverished urban environments, were raised by single mothers, or were in foster-care placement. Women are more likely than men to have committed crimes in order to obtain money to purchase drugs. While some female addicts engage in prostitution as a way to support a drug habit, it is also common for them to engage in property crimes. In summary, a national profile of women offenders describes the following characteristics:

- Disproportionately women of color
- In their early-to-mid-thirties

- Most likely to have been convicted of a drug or drug-related offense
- Fragmented family histories, with other family members also involved with the criminal justice system
- Survivors of physical and/or sexual abuse as children and adults
- Significant substance abuse problems
- Multiple physical and mental health problems
- Unmarried mothers of minor children
- High school degree/GED, but limited vocational training and sporadic work histories (Bloom, Owen, & Covington, 2003)

When designing treatment and services, it is essential to program providers to have a foundation upon which to ground their practice. The following guiding principles were developed to serve as a blueprint for gender-responsive treatment and services.

FUNDAMENTALS OF GENDER-RESPONSIVE SERVICES

The National Institute of Corrections Gender-Responsive Strategies: Research, Practice and Guiding Principles for Women Offenders (Bloom, Owen & Covington, 2003) report documents the need for a new vision for the criminal justice system, one that recognizes the behavioral and social differences between female and male offenders that have specific implications for gender-responsive policy and practice.

Principles

Theoretically based evidence drawn from a variety of disciplines and effective practice suggests that addressing the realities of women's lives through gender-responsive policy and programs is fundamental to improved outcomes at all criminal justice phases. The guiding principles that follow are designed to address system concerns about the management, supervision, and treatment of women offenders in the criminal justice system. These guiding principles provide a blueprint for a gender-responsive approach to the development of criminal justice services.

Guiding Principle 1: Acknowledge That Gender Makes a Difference. The foremost principle in responding appropriately to women is to acknowledge the implications of gender throughout the criminal justice system. The criminal justice field has been dominated by the rule of parity, with equal treatment to be provided to everyone. However, this does not necessarily mean that the exact same treatment is appropriate for both women and men. The data are very clear concerning the distinguishing aspects of female and male offenders. They come into the criminal justice system via different pathways; respond to supervision and custody differently; exhibit differences in terms of substance abuse, trauma, mental illness, parenting responsibilities, and employment histories; and represent different levels of risk within both the institution and the community. To successfully develop and deliver services, supervision, and treatment for women offenders, we must first acknowledge these gender differences.

Guiding Principle 2: Create an Environment Based on Safety, Respect, and Dignity. Research from a range of disciplines (e.g., health, mental health, and substance abuse) has shown that safety, respect, and dignity are fundamental to behavioral change. To improve behavioral outcomes for women, it is critical to provide a safe and supportive setting for all services. A profile of women in the criminal justice system indicates that many have grown up in less than optimal family and community environments. In their interactions with women offenders, criminal justice professionals must be aware of the significant pattern of emotional, physical, and sexual abuse that many of these women have experienced. Every precaution must be taken to ensure that the criminal justice setting does not recreate the abusive environment that many women offenders have experienced in their lives. A safe, consistent, and supportive environment is the cornerstone of a corrective process. Because of their lower levels of violent crime and their low risk to public safety, women offenders should, whenever possible, be supervised and provided services with the minimal restrictions required to meet public safety interests.

Guiding Principle 3: Develop Policies, Practices, and Programs That Are Relational and Promote Healthy Connections to Children, Family, Significant Others, and the Community. Understanding the role of relationships in women's lives is fundamental because the theme of connections and relationships threads throughout the lives of female offenders. When the concept of relationship is incorporated into policies, practices, and programs, the effectiveness of the system or agency is enhanced. This concept is critical when addressing the following:

- Reasons why women commit crimes
- Impact of interpersonal violence on women's lives

- Importance of children in the lives of female offenders
- Relationships between women in an institutional setting
- Process of women's psychological growth and development
- Environmental context needed for programming
- Challenges involved in reentering the community

Guiding Principle 4: Address Substance Abuse, Trauma, and Mental Health Issues Through Comprehensive, Integrated, and Culturally Relevant Services and Appropriate Supervision. Substance abuse, trauma, and mental health are three critical, interrelated issues in the lives of women offenders. These issues have a major impact on both women's programming needs and successful reentry. Although they are therapeutically linked, these issues have historically been treated separately. One of the most important developments in health care over the past several decades is the recognition that a substantial proportion of women have a history of serious traumatic experiences that play a vital and often unrecognized role in the evolution of a woman's physical and mental health problems.

Guiding Principle 5: Provide Women with Opportunities to Improve Their Socioeconomic Conditions. Addressing both the social and material realities of women offenders is an important aspect of correctional intervention. The female offender's life is shaped by her socioeconomic status; her experience with trauma and substance abuse; and her relationships with partners, children, and family. Most women offenders are disadvantaged economically, and this reality is compounded by their trauma and substance abuse histories. Improving socioeconomic outcomes for women requires providing opportunities through education and training so they can support themselves and their children.

Guiding Principle 6: Establish a System of Community Supervision and Reentry with Comprehensive, Collaborative Services. Women offenders face specific challenges as they reenter the community from jail or prison. Women on probation also face challenges in their communities. In addition to the female offender stigma, they may carry additional burdens such as single motherhood, decreased economic potential, lack of services and programs targeted for women, responsibilities to multiple agencies, and a general lack of community support. Navigating through a myriad of systems that often provide fragmented services and conflicting requirements can interfere with supervision and successful reintegration. There is a need for wraparound services–that is, a holistic and culturally sensitive plan for each woman that draws on a coordinated range of services within her community.

Types of organizations that should work as partners in assisting women who are reentering the community include the following:

- Mental health systems
- Alcohol and other drug programs
- Programs for survivors of family and sexual violence
- Family service agencies
- Emergency shelter, food, and financial assistance programs
- Educational organizations
- Vocational and employment services
- Health care
- The child welfare system, child care, and other children's services
- Transportation
- Self-help groups
- Consumer-advocacy groups
- Organizations that provide leisure and recreation options
- Faith-based organizations
- Community service clubs

THEORETICAL PERSPECTIVES

In order to develop gender-responsive treatment and services for women, it is essential to have a theoretical framework of thought. This is the knowledge base that also creates the foundation upon which programs are developed. Four fundamental theories for creating women's services include: pathways theory, relational theory, trauma theory, and addiction theory.

Pathways Theory

Research on women's pathways into crime indicates that gender matters. Steffensmeier and Allen note how the "profound differences" between the lives of women and men shape their patterns of criminal offending (Steffensmeier & Allen, 1998). Many women on the social and economic margins struggle to survive outside legitimate enterprises, which brings them into contact with the criminal justice system. Because of their gender, women are also at greater risk for experiences such as sexual abuse, sexual assault, and domestic violence. As mentioned earlier, among women, the most common pathways to crime are based on survival (of abuse and poverty) and substance abuse. Pollock points out that women offenders have histories of sexual and/or physical abuse that appear to be major roots of subsequent delinquency, addiction, and criminality (Pollock, 1998).

Pathway research has identified such key issues in producing and sustaining female criminality as histories of personal abuse, mental illness tied to early life experiences, substance abuse and addiction, economic and social marginality, homelessness, and relationships.

Relational Theory

Theories that focus on female development, such as the relational model, posit that the primary motivation for women throughout life is the establishment of a strong sense of connection with others. Relational theory developed from an increased understanding of gender differences and, specifically, of the different ways in which women and men develop psychologically. According to relational theory, females develop a sense of self and self-worth when their actions arise out of, and lead back into, connections with others. Connection, not separation, is thus the guiding principle of growth for girls and women.

The importance of understanding relational theory is reflected in the recurring themes of relationship and family seen in the lives of female offenders. Disconnection and violation rather than growth-fostering relationships characterize the childhood experiences of most women in the criminal justice system. Females are far more likely than males to be motivated by relational concerns. For example, women offenders who cite drug abuse as self-medication often discuss personal relationships as the cause of their pain. The relational aspects of addiction are also evident in the research that indicates that women are more likely than men to turn to drugs in the context of relationships with drug-abusing partners in order to feel connected. A relational context is critical to successfully addressing the reasons why women commit crimes, the motivations behind their behaviors, the ways they can change their behavior, and their reintegration into the community.

Trauma and Addiction Theories

Trauma and addiction are interrelated issues in the lives of women offenders. Although they are therapeutically linked, these issues have historically been treated separately. Trauma and addiction theories provide a critical element in the integration of and foundation for gender-responsive services in the criminal justice system (Covington, 1999).

Trauma Theory. The terms violence, trauma, abuse, and PTSD (post-traumatic stress disorder) are often used interchangeably. One way to clarify these terms is to think of trauma as a response to violence. Trauma is both an event and a particular response to an overwhelming event. The response is one of overwhelming fear, helplessness, or horror. PTSD is one type of disorder that results from trauma. Women have different responses to violence and abuse. Some may respond without trauma, due to coping skills that may be effective for a specific event. Sometimes, however, trauma has occurred but may not be recognized immediately, because the violent event may have been perceived by the individual as normal.

As the understanding of traumatic experiences has increased, mental health conceptualizations and practice have changed accordingly. It is now considered necessary for all service providers to become "trauma informed" if they want to be effective. Trauma-informed services are services that are provided for problems other than trauma but require knowledge concerning violence against women and the impact of trauma. Trauma-informed services:

- take the trauma into account;
- avoid triggering trauma reactions and/or retraumatizing the individual;
- adjust the behavior of counselors, other staff, and the organization to support the individual's coping capacity; and
- allow survivors to manage their trauma symptoms successfully so that they are able to access, retain, and benefit from these services. (Harris & Fallot, 2001)

Becoming trauma-informed is particularly important for the criminal justice system. The standard operating practices (searches, seclusion, and restraint) may traumatize/retraumatize women. Abusive families and battering relationships are major themes in the lives of female offenders (Chesney-Lind, 1997; Owen & Bloom, 1995). Frequently, women have their first encounters with the justice system as juveniles who have run away from home to escape situations involving violence and sexual or physical abuse. Prostitution, property crime, and drug use can then become a way of life.

The high rates of severe childhood maltreatment, as well as the high rates of physical and sexual abuse in adolescence and adult life, underscore the importance of understanding the process of trauma. This is a critical step in the rehabilitation of women (Covington, 2003).

Addiction Theory. Historically, addiction research and treatment have been focused on men, even though women's addictions span a wide scope, ranging from alcohol and other types of drug dependence to smoking, gambling, sex, eating disorders, and shopping (Straussner & Brown, 2002).

The holistic health model of addiction, with the inclusion of the environmental and sociopolitical aspects of disease, is the theoretical framework recommended for the development of women's services (Covington, 1999; 2002). This is consistent with information from the National Institute on Drug Abuse (NIDA) and the Center for Substance Abuse Treatment (CSAT):

- The reality, based on twenty-five years of research, is that drug addiction is a brain disease, one that disrupts the mechanisms responsible for generating, modulating, and controlling cognitive, emotional, and social behavior (NIDA, 1998).
- Alcohol and drug use disorder, or addiction, is a progressive disease, with increasing severity of biological, psychological, and social problems over time (CSAT, 1994).

Although the addiction treatment field considers addiction a "chronic, progressive disease," its treatment methods are more closely aligned to those of the emergency-medicine specialist than the chronic-disease specialist (White, Boyle, & Loveland, 2002). Recent articles assert that treating severe and chronic substance use disorders through screening, assessment, admission, and brief treatment, followed by discharge and minimal aftercare, is ineffective and results in shaming and punishing clients for failing to respond to an intervention design that is inherently flawed.

An alternative to the acute intervention model is behavioral health recovery management (BHRM). This concept grew out of and shares much in common with "disease management" approaches to other chronic health problems, but BHRM focuses on quality-of-life outcomes as defined by the individual and family. It also offers a broader range of services earlier and extends treatment well beyond traditional treatment services. BHRM models extend the current continuum of care for addiction by including: (1) pretreatment (recovery-priming) services, (2) recovery mentoring through primary treatment, and (3) sustained post-treatment recovery-support services (White et al., 2002).

Although the debate over models will continue, this updated and expanded disease perspective offers a more helpful approach to the treatment of addiction for women because it is comprehensive and meets the requirements for a multidimensional framework. The holistic health model allows clinicians to treat addiction as the primary problem while also addressing the complexity of issues that women bring to treatment: genetic predisposition, health consequences, shame, isolation, and a history of abuse, or a combination of these. For example, while some women may have a genetic predisposition to addiction, it is important in treatment to acknowledge that many have grown up in environments in which drug dealing, substance abuse, and addiction are ways of life. In sum, when addiction has been a core part of the multiple aspects of a woman's life, the treatment process requires a holistic, multidimensional approach.

The link between female criminality and drug use is very strong, with research indicating that women who use drugs are more likely to be involved in crime (Merlo & Pollock, 1995). Approximately 80 percent of women in state prisons have substance-abuse problems (CSAT, 1997), and about 50 percent of female offenders in state prisons had been using alcohol, drugs, or both at the time of their offense (BJS, 1999). Nearly one in three women serving time in state prisons reports having committed her offense in order to obtain money to support a drug habit. About half of the incarcerated women describe themselves as daily drug users.

PROGRAM ELEMENTS

Creating effective gender-responsive treatment and services must include creating an environment through site selection, staff selection, program development, content, and material that reflects an understanding of the realities of the lives of women in criminal justice settings and addresses their specific challenges and strengths (Covington & Bloom, 2002).

The specific elements listed below can be used in developing gender-responsive treatment and services. These elements are organized into the following categories: (1) structure and (2) content and context/environment.

Structural Elements

Contemporary theoretical perspectives on women's particular pathways into the criminal justice system are used to create the foundation for women's services. For example, relational theory and trauma theory fit the psychological and social needs of women and reflect the realities of their lives. See earlier discussion of the fundamental theoretical approaches.

Services for mental health and substance abuse are integrated. The concept of integrated treatment for women with co-occurring disorders (CODs), as originally articulated by Minkoff (1989, 2001), emphasizes the need for correspondence between the treatment models for mental illness and addiction. The model stresses the importance of well-coordinated treatment of both disorders. Dual recovery treatment goals are emphasized, as well as the need to employ effective treatment strategies from both the mental health and the substance abuse treatment fields. In the literature of the field of co-occurring disorders, integrated treatment is used to imply an approach to treatment that recognizes the need for a unified treatment approach to meet the needs of a client with multiple disorders.

Treatment and services are based on women's competencies and strengths and promote self-reliance. In a traditional treatment model, the therapist typically approaches assessment with a problem focus: What is missing in the client? or What is wrong with the client? Many women already are struggling with a poor sense of self because of the stigma attached to their addictions, their parenting histories, their trauma, or their prison records, for example. It may be non-therapeutic to add another problem to the woman's list of perceived failures.

A strength-based (asset) model of treatment shifts the focus from targeting problems to identifying the multiple issues a woman must contend with and the strategies she has adopted to cope. This has been referred to as assessing a woman's "level of burden" (Brown, Melchior & Huba, 1999). The focus is on support, rather than on confrontation to break her defenses (Fedele & Miller, 1988).

In using an asset model, the therapist helps the client see the strengths and skills she already has that will aid her healing. The clinician looks for the seeds of health and strength, even in the woman's symptoms. For example, the clinician portrays a woman's relational difficulties as efforts to connect, rather than as failures to separate or disconnect. The counselor repeatedly affirms the woman's abilities to care, empathize, use her intuition, and build relationships. "As a woman feels more valued, her need for alcohol, tobacco, and other drugs might diminish and her resilience increase" (Finkelstein, Kennedy, Thomas & Kearns, 1997, p. 6).

Women-only groups are used, especially for primary treatment (e.g., trauma, substance abuse). Early pioneering research (Aries, 1976; Bernardez, 1978, 1983; Graham & Linehan, 1987) indicated that group dynamics differ between all-female groups and mixed female-male groups. Fedele and Harrington (1990) conclude that single and mixed-sex groups are appropriate for women at different stages of their lives and at different stages of their treatment. Women-only groups are the modality of choice for women in the early stage of addiction recovery and for sexual abuse survivors. When a woman needs to share and integrate her experiences, ideas, and feelings and to create a sense of self (as in early recovery), a single-sex group is preferable. When the woman's experience has been validated, when she has more empathy for herself and is more empowered (as in later recovery), a mixed group may take her to the next stage of development. Although mixed groups may have their place in later recovery, it is important that primary treatment for addiction and trauma use all-female groups (with a female facilitator).

Gender-responsive screening and assessment tools are utilized, with appropriate treatment matched to the identified needs and assets of each client. For example, in order to provide appropriate care to substance abusing women, screening and assessment must identify the severity of the client's substance abuse problems and the extent of her other needs that can be addressed in the treatment program. For some screening and assessment tools, norms exist for women that can help standardize gender-specific responses; for others, this analysis has not yet occurred.

Screening is a brief, standardized process for identifying whether certain conditions possibly exist. In contrast to assessment, screening usually involves simple yes or no questions. Counselors can use many screening instruments with little or no special training. There is a need for screening processes and instruments that are designed considering women's unique needs and that are tested to ensure they are reliable and valid with this population.

Assessment is a process of examining a client's life in more detail so that diagnoses can be made for substance use disorders and possible co-occurring mental illness. Usually, a clinical assessment will delve into a variety of aspects of a woman's history and current life to form a picture of what her specific needs are.

The following important principles of assessment have been identified for women:

• Wherever possible, instruments used should be normed for women.

- A strengths perspective should be used throughout the assessment process (i.e., what strengths does the woman have that can be used in her treatment?).
- The assessment process should be appropriate for the client's language, culture, literacy level, and cognitive functioning.
- Effective means of engaging women in the topics covered to get the best possible responses include a nonjudgmental attitude with gentle and accepting approaches.
- In order to identify the complex needs associated with substance abuse in women, the assessment must be comprehensive.
- Assessments should be repeated during the course of treatment. Clients may become more open as their trust in therapeutic relationships grows; also, as people become clean and sober, their cognitive functioning changes. As treatment continues and the therapeutic relationship deepens, the client may be more inclined to disclose information that she earlier found embarrassing or painful (CSAT, 1994).

Treatment planning needs to be individualized. Just as women's lives are different from men's, women's lives are not all the same. Although there are common threads because of gender, it is important to be sensitive to differences and to acknowledge both similarities and differences. For example, there are differences in the lives of African-American women, Hispanic women, and Asian women. There are differences between heterosexual women, bisexual women, and lesbian women. There are differences between older women and younger women. There are differences resulting from privilege and oppression (Covington, 2002).

The following are additional elements to consider when structuring a program for women:

- Staff members reflect the client population in terms of gender, race/ethnicity, sexual orientation, language (bilingual), and ex-offender and recovery status.
- Female role models and mentors are provided who reflect the racial/ethnic/cultural backgrounds of the clients.
- Cultural awareness and sensitivity are promoted using the resources and strengths available in various communities.
- Transitional programs are included as part of gender-responsive practices, with a particular focus on building long-term community support networks for women.

Content and Contextual/Environmental Elements

Services need to be comprehensive and address the realities of women's lives. The Center for Substance Abuse Treatment (CSAT), a federal agency, identifies seventeen critical areas of focus for women's treatment. These issues underscore the complexity of women's treatment, the need for a comprehensive perspective, and the importance of theoretical integration and collaboration in clinical practice.

- The causes of addiction, especially related gender-specific issues (for example, factors related to onset of addiction, and the social, physiological, and psychological consequences of addiction)
- Low self-esteem
- Race, ethnicity, and cultural issues
- Gender discrimination and harassment
- Disability-related issues
- Relationships with family members and significant others
- Attachments to unhealthy interpersonal relationships
- Interpersonal violence, including incest, rape, battering, and other abuse
- Eating disorders
- Sexuality, including sexual functioning and sexual orientation
- Parenting
- Grief related to the loss of children, family members, partners, and alcohol and other drugs
- Work
- Appearance and overall health and hygiene
- Isolation related to a lack of support systems (which may or may not include family members and partners) and other resources
- Development of life plans
- Child care and child custody (CSAT, 1994, 1997)

The development of effective gender-responsive services needs to include the creation of a therapeutic environment. The primary characteristic of a therapeutic environment for women is safety. To promote behavioral change and healing, the therapeutic environment must also be inviting, noninstitutional, homelike, and welcoming, with culturally appropriate decorations and pictures. Sensitivity to trauma-related issues is critical.

The term "therapeutic milieu" refers to a carefully arranged environment that is designed to reverse the effects of exposure to situations characterized by interpersonal violence. The therapeutic culture contains the following five elements, all of them fundamental in both institutional settings and in the community:

- *Attachment:* a culture of belonging
- *Containment:* a culture of safety
- *Communication:* a culture of openness
- *Involvement:* a culture of participation and citizenship
- *Agency:* a culture of empowerment

(Haigh, 1999)

The best word to describe the environment required for women's treatment settings is sanctuary (Bloom, 1997). It is essential for women to have a physically and psychologically safe, welcoming, and healing space for their recovery process.

In order to fully address the needs of women, programs need to use a variety of interventions with behavioral, cognitive, affective/dynamic, and systems perspectives. Examples of some of the effective interventions:

Relational Model: In the 1970s, a number of theorists began to examine the importance of gender differences in understanding women's psychological development. Jean Baker Miller's Toward a New Psychology of Women (Miller, 1976) offered a new perspective on the psychology of women that challenged the basic assumptions of traditional theories. At the same time, Carol Gilligan, a developmental psychologist, was gathering empirical data that reflected fundamental gender differences in the psychological and moral development of women and men (Gilligan, 1982).

Drawing on Miller's and Gilligan's work, a number of theorists over the past 20 years have been developing a relational model of women's psychology. The three major concepts in relational theory are:

- *Cultural context.* This theme recognizes the powerful impact of the cultural context on women's lives.
- *Relationships.* This theme stresses the importance of relationships as the central, organizing feature in women's development. Traditional developmental models of growth emphasize independence

and autonomy. This theory focuses on women's connection with others.

- *Pathways to growth.* The third theme acknowledges women's relational qualities and activities as potential strengths that provide pathways to healthy growth and development. In traditional theory, women's ability to more freely express emotions, and women's attention to relationships, often led to pathologizing them. (Kaplan, 1984)

The relational model affirms the power of connection and the pain of disconnection for women. As a result, the approach requires a paradigm shift that has led to a reframing of key concepts in psychological development, theory, and practice. For example, instead of the "self" as a primary focus, there is a focus on relational development. The experience of connection and disconnection are the central issues in personality development, with repeated disconnections having psychological consequences.

Family Therapy: Family therapy is a theory and technique that approaches people within their social context. Its goal is to change the organization of the family with the assumption that when the structure of the family as a group is altered, the individual experiences within that group will also be altered (Minuchin, 1976). It assumes that individual behavior can best be understood within the context of the family and it helps family members discover how their own system operates, improve communication and problem-solving skills, and increase the exchange of positive reinforcement (CSAT, 1999a). This process supports the relational model for women in that the primary assumption in family therapy is that people continually interact with each other and that these interactions have an impact on one's identity and behavior.

Group Therapy: Women tend to engage in group therapy more often than men (Fiorentine & Anglin, 1997). This phenomenon may be linked to gender norms that support the suppositions of the relational model (i.e., women develop their sense of self in relation to others). Groups encourage the development of a sense of belonging or connectedness to others, which helps motivate women to stay in the process. This connection to others helps mitigate the pain associated with therapeutic exploration. A cohesive group offers women unconditional acceptance, no matter what their history or behaviors prior to coming to the treatment experience. Support and emotional warmth provide the psychological glue that encourages risk-taking for self-disclosure (Yalom, 1995).

The group process provides insight and understanding, and attributes meaning to life's circumstances, thereby defining a consensual reality for each person. This process allows each person to risk powerful feelings; women can experience long denied feelings with acceptance from others. Group members begin to realize that feelings are not always overwhelming and that the imagined negative consequences of releasing these feelings do not occur (Yalom, 1995).

Finally, groups afford women an opportunity to compare their attitudes toward parents, spouses, and children, and their feelings about things that have happened to them. The group can then offer the suggestion of new possibilities for feeling, perceiving, and behaving (Yalom, 1995).

Women with substance use disorders have treatment needs that are best met in women-only groups (Kauffman, Dore & Nelson-Zlupko, 1995). Women's complex histories of sexual and physical abuse, the greater tendency toward social isolation, and the stronger stigma attached to women's substance abuse all call for treatment that could not take place in mixed-gender groups. In addition, the likelihood of having a partner with substance use disorders who is exploitive or abusive makes women in these relationships more vulnerable in mixed-gender groups.

Expressive Therapy: Creative arts therapies based on art, dance and movement, drama, music, poetry and bibliotherapy can often be useful when working with women. Psychodrama is the oldest and one of the most widely used of the expressive therapies. These therapies offer methods to access and express emotionally charged material that often can not be communicated in a linear way. Some clients are able to express themselves more articulately in physical movement or in pictures rather than in words (Johnson, 2000). Expressive therapy is particularly useful when working with women who have histories of abuse and trauma.

Cognitive-Behavioral Therapy: Cognitive therapy works on the principle that the thoughts that produce and maintain feelings can be recognized objectively and altered, thereby changing the response and changing the emotional reaction. Cognitive-behavioral therapy (CBT) can help people to learn to change distorted thought patterns and negative behaviors. The goal is to recognize distorted/negative thoughts or mind-sets and replace them with positive thoughts, which will lead to more appropriate and beneficial behavior (Beck, Rush, Shaw & Emery, 1979; CSAT, 1999).

With respect to substance abuse, cognitive-behavioral therapy suggests that "substance abuse disorders reflect habitual, automatic, negative thoughts and beliefs" that must be identified and replaced with more positive beliefs and actions. Thus, strategies for relapse prevention help identify triggering events or emotional states (e.g., boredom, depression, anxiety, or the presence of drug paraphernalia) (CSAT, 1999a, p. 42). Cognitive-behavioral therapy also creates opportunities where women can learn new coping skills. This increases their self-esteem and self-efficacy, and undermines addictive behaviors by replacing them with a sense of confidence.

Other elements to consider when developing the content and context/environment in women's services:

- Services/treatment address women's practical needs such as housing, transportation, child care, and vocational training and job placement.
- Participants receive opportunities to develop skills in a range of educational and vocational (including nontraditional) areas.
- There is an emphasis on parenting education, child development, and relationship/reunification with children.
- The environment is child friendly, with age-appropriate activities designed for children.

PROGRAM MATERIALS

The following materials have been specifically designed for women and are based on the theories and principles previously discussed. (For additional materials, go to http://www.centerforgenderandjustice.org.)

Helping Women Recover: A Program for Treating Substance Abuse (special edition for the criminal justice system) is an integrated, manualized curriculum for treating women with histories of addiction and trauma. It is designed to be used in jails, prisons, and community correctional programs. Helping Women Recover is grounded in research, theory, and clinical practice. The foundation of the treatment model is the integration of three theories: a theory of addiction, a theory of women's psychological development, and a theory of trauma. The therapeutic strategies include psycho-educational, cognitive-behavioral, expressive arts, and relational approaches.

The facilitator's manual for the 17-session program is a step-by-step guide containing the theory, structure, and content needed for running groups. A Woman's Journey, the participant's workbook, allows women to process and record the therapeutic experience. The program model is organized into four modules: self, relationships, sexuality, and spirituality. These are the four areas that recovering women have identified as triggers for relapse and as necessary for growth and healing. (There is also a community version of Helping Women Recover and an adolescent version of this curriculum entitled Voices: A Program of Self Discovery and Empowerment for Girls.)

Beyond Trauma: A Healing Journey for Women is also a manualized curriculum based on research, theory, and clinical practice. While the materials are trauma-specific, the connection between trauma and substance abuse is recognized and integrated throughout the curriculum. Beyond Trauma has a psycho-educational component that teaches women what trauma is, its process, and its impact on both the inner self (thoughts, feelings, beliefs, values) and the outer self (behavior and relationships, including parenting). The major emphasis is on coping skills with specific exercises for developing emotional wellness. The curriculum includes a facilitator manual, participant workbook, and three instructional videos (two for facilitators, one for clients).

The facilitator's manual has two parts. The first part gives group leaders background information about trauma. Having a basic understanding of the depth and complexity of the issues helps the facilitator work more effectively with the group. The second part of the manual includes session outlines that are like lesson plans. There are 11 sessions total in the 3 modules: (a) Violence, Abuse, and Trauma; (b) Impact of Trauma; and (c) Healing from Trauma.

STAFFING

Programming designed for women can only be as good as its staff. A consistent theme in correctional settings is "I have received no training in how to work with female offenders." It is extremely important that all staff training include a process that identifies, acknowledges, and brings to conscious awareness, biases, judgments, and anger toward women in correctional settings. Those in a position to help must be able to interact in a manner that assists and, of course, causes no harm. Without values clarification about women who commit crimes, abuse substances, etc., service providers risk violating the "do no harm" premise. Training will also help practitioners avoid creating barriers to treatment when clients are from cultures, ethnicities, or sexual orientations different from their own (Hughes & Wilsnack, 1997). Training interdisciplinary groups is recommended, as well as cross-training among systems. The training style should be both experiential and didactic.

In order for staff to provide effective services to women, the following qualities are recommended:

- Remain consistent in caring and availability
- Be an appropriate role model for women
- Develop a treatment alliance with women clients that is mutual and collaborative, individualized, and continually negotiated.
- Maintain confidentiality
- Be a visible advocate for women who abuse substances, for stigma reduction, and for treatment (within treatment teams, the community, and the system)
- Ensure self-care, ask for and participate in supervision
- Stay current on training

PROGRAM EVALUATION

Program evaluation is another step in building gender-responsiveness. Evaluation research examines the outcomes associated with different types of services or whether matching women's needs with particular types of interventions or services produce better outcomes. What is needed is a systematic examination of the theoretical and programmatic implications of our knowledge of criminal justice-involved women.

Historically, the effectiveness of correctional treatment programs has been measured by their ability to affect recidivism. The research on correctional program effectiveness in terms of reduction of female recidivism has been insufficient. Much of the research on recidivism has focused on male offenders and little empirical evidence exists to suggest what contributes to women's recidivism or to successful transition after release from prison. Furthermore, there are problems with the use of recidivism as the only measure of program success, in general.

Evaluation Design

Process and outcome evaluations are important in terms of making adaptations in program quality and in determining the characteristics of effective interventions. Process evaluations are useful in that they describe attributes of programs and provide feedback to practitioners about the quality and integrity of program components and service delivery. Process evaluations often examine the relationship between the program's mission and its goals and objectives for program activities and services.

Outcome evaluations are valuable because they describe measures of program success or failure. They examine the short- and long-term impact of the intervention on program participants. Ideally, outcome measures used in evaluations should be tied to program mission, goals, and objectives. They should go beyond the traditional recidivism measures to assess the import of specific program attributes. Short-term and long-term outcome measures for women-specific programs could include:

- Program participation/completion/discharge
- Alcohol/drug recovery
- Trauma recovery
- Educational attainment
- Employment
- Housing
- Improved family relationships
- Parenting and reunification with children
- Physical and mental health (Bloom, 2000)

CONCLUSION

As highlighted in this article, there are a number of considerations for the development of gender-responsive treatment and services. For women who are in the criminal justice system, a gender-responsive approach would include comprehensive services that take into account the content and context of women's lives. Programs need to take into consideration the larger social issues of poverty, abuse, and race and gender inequalities, as well as individual factors that impact women in the criminal justice system (Bloom, 1996). Services also need to be responsive to women's cultural backgrounds (Bloom & Covington, 1998).

Programming that is responsive in terms of both gender and culture emphasizes support. Service providers need to focus on women's strengths, and they need to recognize that a woman cannot be treated successfully in isolation from her social support network. Coordinating systems that link a broad range of services will promote a continuity-of-care model and, equally important, help to establish a continuity of relationship. Such a comprehensive approach would provide a sustained continuum of treatment, recovery, and support services.

REFERENCES

Aries, E. (1976). Interaction patterns and themes of male, female, and mixed groups. *Small Group Behavior, 7*(1): 7-18.

Beck, A.T., Rush, A.J., Shaw, B.F., & Emery, G. (1979). *Cognitive therapy of depression.* New York: The Guilford Press.

Belknap, J. (2001). *The invisible woman: Gender, crime and justice.* Belmont, CA: Wadsworth.

Bernardez, T. (1978). Women's groups: A feminist perspective on the treatment of women. In H. H. Grayson & C. Loew (Eds.), *Changing approaches to the psychotherapies.* New York: Spectrum.

Bernardez, T. (1983). Women's groups. In M. Rosenbaum (Ed.), *Handbook of short-term therapy groups.* New York: McGraw-Hill.

Bloom, B. (1996). *Triple jeopardy: Race, class and gender as factors in women's imprisonment.* Riverside, CA: UC Riverside.

Bloom, B. (2000). Beyond recidivism: Perspectives on evaluation of programs for female offenders in community corrections. In Maeve McMahon (Ed.), *Assessment to assistance: Programs for women in community corrections* (pp. 107-138). Lanham, MD: American Correctional Association.

Bloom, S. (1997). *Creating sanctuary: Toward the evolution of sane societies.* New York, NY: Routledge.

Bloom, B. & Covington, S. (1998 November). *Gender-specific programming for female offenders: What is it and why is it important?* Paper presented to the American Society of Criminology, Washington, DC.

Bloom, B., Owen, B., & Covington, S. (2003). *Gender-responsive strategies: Research, practice, and guiding principles for women offenders.* Washington, DC: National Institute of Corrections.

Brown, V.B., Melchior, L.A., and Huba, G.J. (1999) Level of burden among women diagnosed with severe mental illness and substance abuse. *Journal of Psychoactive Drugs, 31*(1): 31-41.

Bureau of Justice Statistics (1999). *Special report: Women offenders.* Washington, DC: U.S. Department of Justice.

Center for Substance Abuse Treatment. (1994). *Practical approaches in the treatment of women who abuse alcohol and other drugs.* Rockville, MD: U.S. Department of Health and Human Services.

Center for Substance Abuse Treatment. (1997). *Substance abuse treatment for incarcerated women offenders: Guide to promising practices.* Rockville, MD: U.S. Department of Health and Human Services.

Center for Substance Abuse Treatment. (1999) *Cultural issues in substance abuse treatment.* DHHS Publication No. (SMA) 99-3278. Rockville, MD: Substance Abuse and Mental Health Services Administration.

Center for Substance Abuse Treatment. (1999a). *Brief interventions and brief therapies for substance abuse.* Treatment Improvement Protocol (TIP) Series 34. DHHS

Publication No. (SMA) 99-3353. Rockville, MD: U.S. Department of Health and Human Services.

Chesney-Lind, M. (1997). *The female offender: Girls, women and crime.* Thousand Oaks, CA: Sage Publications.

Covington, S. (1999). *Helping women recover: A program for treating substance abuse* (special edition for the criminal justice system). San Francisco, CA: Jossey-Bass.

Covington, S. (2002). Helping women recover: Creating gender-responsive treatment. In S.L.A. Straussner & S. Brown (Eds.), *The handbook of addiction treatment for women* (pp. 52-72). San Francisco, CA: Jossey-Bass.

Covington, S. (2003). *Beyond trauma: A healing journey for women.* Center City, MN: Hazelden.

Covington, S. & Bloom, B. (2002). Center for Gender and Justice, website: centerforgenderandjustice.org. La Jolla, CA.

Fedele, N., & Harrington, E. (1990). *Women's groups: How connections heal.* (Work in Progress Working Paper Series no. 47). Wellesley, MA: Stone Center, Wellesley College.

Fedele, N. & Miller, J. (1988). *Putting theory into practice: Creating mental health programs for women.* (Work in Progress Working Paper Series no. 32). Wellesley, MA: Stone Center, Wellesley College.

Finkelstein, N., Kennedy, C., Thomas, K., & Kearns, M. (1997, March). *Gender-specific substance abuse treatment.* Washington, DC: U.S. Department of Health and Human Services, Substance Abuse and Mental Health Services Administration, Center for Substance Abuse Prevention.

Fiorentine, R., & Anglin, M.D. (1997). Does increasing the opportunity for counseling increase the effectiveness of outpatient drug treatment? *American Journal of Drug and Alcohol Abuse, 23*(3): 369-382.

Gilligan, C. (1982). *In a different voice: Psychological theory and women's development.* Cambridge, MA: Harvard University Press.

Graham, B., & Linehan, N. (1987). Group treatment for the homeless and chronic alcoholic woman. In C. Brody (Ed.), *Women's therapy groups: Paradigms of feminist treatment.* New York: Springer.

Grella, C. (1999). Women in residential drug treatment: Differences by program type and pregnancy. *Journal of Health Care for the Poor and Underserved, 10*(2): 216-29.

Grella, C. E., Scott, C. K., Foss, M. A., Joshi, V., & Hser, Y. I. (2003). Gender differences in drug treatment outcomes among participants in the Chicago Target Cities Study. *Evaluation and Program Planing, 26*(3): 297-310.

Haigh, R. (1999). The quintessence of a therapeutic environment: Five universal qualities. In P. Campling, R. Haigh, & Netlibrary, Inc. (Eds.), *Therapeutic communities: Past, present, and future* (pp. 246-257). London: Jessica Kingsley Publishers.

Harris, M., & Fallot, R.D. (2001). *Using trauma theory to design service systems.* San Francisco, CA: Jossey-Bass.

Hughes, T.L. & Wilsnack, S.C. (1997). Use of alcohol among lesbians: Research and clinical implications. *American Journal of Orthopsychiatry, 67*(1): 20-36.

Johnson, D.R. (2000). Creative therapies. In. E.B. Foa, and T.M. Keane (Eds.), *Effective Treatments for PTSD: Practice guidelines from the International Society for Traumatic Stress Studies* (pp. 302-314). New York: Guilford Press.

Kaplan, A. (1984). *Female or male psychotherapists for women: New formulations.* (Work in Progress Working Paper Series no. 83-02). Wellesley, MA: Stone Center, Wellesley College.

Kauffman, E., Dore, M.M., and Nelson-Zlupko, L. (1995). The role of women's therapy groups in the treatment of chemical dependence. *American Journal of Orthopsychiatry, 65*(3): 355-363.

Merlo, A., & Pollock, J. (1995). *Women, law, and social control.* Boston, MA: Allyn & Bacon.

Miller, J. B. (1976). *Toward a new psychology of women.* Boston, MA: Beacon Press.

Minkoff, K. (1989). An integrated treatment model for dual diagnosis of psychosis and addiction. *Hospital and Community Psychiatry, 40*(10): 1031-1036.

Minkoff, K. (2001). Developing standards of care for individuals with co-occurring psychiatric and substance use disorders. *Psychiatric Services* May 2001, (pp. 597-599) Vol.52, No.5.

Minuchin, S. (1976). *Families and family therapy.* London: Tavistock.

National Institute on Drug Abuse. (1998). What we know: Drug addiction is a brain disease. In *Principles of addiction medicine* (2nd ed.). Chevy Chase, MD: American Society of Addiction Medicine, Inc.

Nelson-Zlupko, L., Dore, M., Kauffman, E. & Kaltenback, K. (1996). Women in recovery: Their perceptions of treatment effectiveness. *Journal of Substance Abuse Treatment, 13*(1): 51-59.

Owen, B., & Bloom, B. (1995). Profiling women prisoners: Findings from national survey and California sample. *The Prison Journal, 75*(2), 165-185.

Pollock, J. (1998). *Counseling women in prison.* Thousand Oaks, CA: Sage Publications.

Steffensmeier, D., & Allan, E. (1998). The nature of female offending: Patterns and explanations. In R. T. Zaplin (Ed.), *Female offenders: Critical perspectives and effective interventions* (pp. 5-29). Gaithersburg, MD: Aspen Publishers.

Straussner, S.L.A., & Brown, S. (2002). *The handbook of addiction treatment for women: Theory and practice.* San Francisco, CA: Jossey-Bass.

White, W., Boyle, M., and Loveland, D. (2002). Alcoholism/Addiction as a chronic disease: From rhetoric to clinical reality. *Alcoholism Treatment Quarterly, 20*(3/4): 107-130.

Yalom, I.D. (1995). *The theory and practice of group psychotherapy* (4th ed.). New York: Basic Books.

doi:10.1300/J015v29n03_02

"We're Not All That Criminal": Getting Beyond the Pathologizing and Individualizing of Women's Crime

MaDonna R. Maidment

SUMMARY. The theoretical and empirical traditions of those of us in academia toward the study of "women offenders" has led to a myopic approach to research based on the implicit assumption that criminalized women are markedly different from the rest of mainstream "law-abiding citizens." This treatment-based approach individualizes criminalized women and increasingly places the blame on cognitive deficiencies to account for one's wrongdoing. Such approaches are devoid of any contextual analysis as to why certain groups of marginalized women are criminalized in the first place. Canada has taken a lead role in developing therapeutic measures to correct and normalize those women (and men) it deems to be failures in our society. To counter the notion of Canada as the benevolent jailer, this essay interrogates the discourse surrounding women's involvement in crime by deconstructing the language which dominates in Canadian prisons; counteract the cognitive-based model of "corrections" which portrays criminalized women as psycho-

MaDonna R. Maidment is Assistant Professor in the Department of Sociology and Anthropology at the University of Guelph.

Address correspondence to: MaDonna R. Maidment, Department of Sociology and Anthropology, University of Guelph, Guelph, ON N1G 2W1, Canada (E-mail: mmaidmen@uoguelph.ca).

[Haworth co-indexing entry note]: "'We're Not All That Criminal': Getting Beyond the Pathologizing and Individualizing of Women's Crime." Maidment, MaDonna R. Co-published simultaneously in *Women & Therapy* (The Haworth Press, Inc.) Vol. 29, No. 3/4, 2006, pp. 35-56; and: *Inside and Out: Women, Prison, and Therapy* (ed: Elaine Leeder) The Haworth Press, Inc., 2006, pp. 35-56. Single or multiple copies of this article are available for a fee from The Haworth Document Delivery Service [1-800-HAWORTH, 9:00 a.m. - 5:00 p.m. (EST). E-mail address: docdelivery@haworthpress.com].

35

logically deficient; and elucidate the inherent contradictions in official definitions of "reintegrative success" for criminalized women. This article challenges the preoccupation of chronicling the lives of women ex/prisoners solely through a focus on individual criminal wrongdoings. Rather, the central aim is to critique the androcentric, culturally exclusive knowledge-making processes which exclude marginalized groups in the first place, most notably the voices of disenfranchised women. doi:10.1300/J015v29n03_03 *[Article copies available for a fee from The Haworth Document Delivery Service: 1-800-HAWORTH. E-mail address: <docdelivery@haworthpress.com> Website: <http://www.HaworthPress.com> © 2006 by The Haworth Press, Inc. All rights reserved.]*

KEYWORDS. Criminalized women, knowledge deconstruction, feminist epistemologies

Focussing on the world from the perspective of the margins allows us to see the world differently and, in many ways, more authentically. (Kirby & McKenna, 1989, p. 33)

The problems of recidivism and post-release mortality have less to do with the character and actions of individual women than with the intolerance and neglect shown toward women prisoners, their particular circumstances, and their needs. (Davies & Cook, 1999, p. 272)

The theoretical and empirical traditions of those of us in academia toward the study of "women offenders" has led to a myopic approach to research based on the implicit assumption that criminalized women are markedly different from the rest of mainstream "law-abiding citizens." We accept the baseline assumption that one's criminal transgressions constitute one's master status which, in turn, needs to be studied, explained, and corrected. This treatment-based approach individualizes criminalized women and increasingly places the blame on cognitive deficiencies to account for one's wrongdoing. Such approaches are devoid of any contextual analysis as to why certain groups of marginalized women are criminalized in the first place. Conventional "correctional logic" therefore dictates that if we can find a pro-social fix for the anti-social thinking of criminalized populations then we can set "these people" back on the path to conformity.

As a Canadian researcher, I am all too familiar with the erroneous label lauded on this country as a progressive leader among industrialized nations for both its ideological and material approaches to criminalized women. Undoubtedly, Canada has taken the lead in therapeutic measures to responsibilize, correct, and normalize those women (and men) it deems to be failures in our society (Pollack & Kendall, 2005) and has done an exceptional job marketing its corrections formulae internationally. To counter the notion of Canada as the benevolent jailer and to deconstruct the treatment-based model, of "corrections" which individualizes and pathologizes criminalized women, this essay aims to interrogate the discourse surrounding women's involvement in crime by deconstructing the language which dominates the control of women in Canadian prisons; counteract the cognitive-based model of "corrections" which portrays criminalized women as psychologically deficient; and elucidate the inherent contradictions in official definitions of "reintegrative success" for criminalized women. This article challenges the preoccupation of chronicling the lives of women ex/prisoners solely through a focus on individual criminal wrongdoings. Rather, the central aim is to critique the androcentric, culturally exclusive knowledge-making processes which exclude marginalized groups in the first place, most notably the voices of disenfranchised women.

RESISTING LANGUAGE USED TO INDIVIDUALIZE AND PATHOLOGIZE WOMEN'S CRIME

The neo-liberal climate is ever-increasingly more punitive, individualizing, and pathologizing of women (Neve & Pate, 2005; Pollack & Kendall, 2005; Comack & Balfour, 2004) and language is a central diversionary tactic in promulgating such ideologies. Therefore, it is imperative that the language used to describe women's involvement with the criminal (in)justice system be critically assessed. The deconstruction of language is much more than an exercise in semantics. It is precisely our use of language which contributes to the defining of certain behaviors and actions by women as a violation of their prescribed social order. It sets the most disenfranchised women in opposition to the very systems (e.g., criminal justice, social welfare, mental health) that are oppressing them economically, socially, culturally, politically, and ever-increasing, medically. To concur with Gayle Horii (2000, p. 107), "[t]o name is to know; to know is to control."

As a researcher, I continually struggle with making sense of (and keeping up with) the myriad of terminologies (e.g., women in conflict with the law, female offender, clients, inmates, facilities) and "control talk" (e.g., corrections, re-integration, rehabilitation, cognitive behavioral therapies, assertive case management) used to describe women's encounters with their oppressors. Several leading feminist authors have begun this process of deconstructing the language used to camouflage women's entanglement with the criminal justice system (Comack & Balfour, 2004; Horii, 2000; Comack, 1996; Faith, 1993). Labels such as "female offender" and "women in conflict with the law" are used to individualize women's criminality. However, as Faith (1993, p. 58) points out, a term such as "women in conflict with the law" "denies the fundamental inequality of the relationship [as] one cannot simply be in conflict with power to which one is subordinate." Likewise, the term "female offender" fails to account for the fact that only a small portion of those who offend get caught or whose offending behavior has been criminalized. It is accepted that we have all offended at various times throughout our lives. A systemic understanding of which groups get singled out and punished (or conversely which ones escape apprehension and penalization) for their offenses lends itself to characterizing the axes of social exclusion and power brokering within the criminal justice system.

Elizabeth Comack (1996) has grappled with the need to use language that sensitizes the reader to the personal and legal troubles women encounter. She postulates the phrase "women in trouble" to capture the idea that women's troubles "emanate from women's particular locations within a society that is capitalist, racist and patriarchal." Gayle Horii (2000, p. 107) takes the analysis even further in arguing that, despite the best intentions of reformers, "a prison is a prison is a prison" and the "structure of authority that produces the oppressed and the oppressors alike is the *key* to understanding the problem." Horii (2000, p. 107) takes aim at the disguising of punishment under sanitized euphemisms which fail to tackle the power structures underlying "corrections."

> [T]he language of the oppressor, those reams of rhetoric and countless nice-nellyisms that effectively mask the barbarity of imprisonment behind policies fronted by cardboard people and programs are tools of this structure which must be disabled. Overlooking the covert power of euphemisms becomes blind acceptance.

Despite the foregoing critical attention to oppressive "corrections" language, it is recognized that language deconstruction by feminist academics and activists requires more sustained attention in order to uncover the real agendas behind the systematic labeling of women as deviants and offenders in the first place (Schur, 1984). Myths and stereotypes surrounding women's criminal involvement need to be dispelled so that the capitalist, patriarchal, and racist foundations of the penal system's treatment of women are exposed. Gendered power structures are recognizably one axis of exclusion.

> Given that labels are culturally invested with ideological significances, and applied with prejudice, it is best to avoid them. Certain women are criminalized, through social processes, and these women are then labeled female offender, delinquent, woman in conflict with the law, criminal or, most courteously, lawbreaker. When we recognize the contextual bases of illegal actions and the discriminatory nature of criminalization processes as applied to either men or women, and when we demystify labeled women by showing their diversities as well as the commonalities they share as women in a gendered power structure, we lose the need for labels, or for gendered stereotypes. (Faith, 1993, p. 59)

Even a pedestrian analysis of women's encounters with the criminal (in)justice system makes clear that laws (and, by default, the entire repute of the criminal justice system) are more precisely *in conflict with women*. The overwhelming bulk of women's crime is directly linked to social, cultural, economic, sexual, and political oppression in a society which devalues women's work in the private sphere, undervalues their work in the public sphere, and continues to restrict women's full civic engagement through misogynous institutions. The criminal (in)justice system is just one more system blocking women's equality by criminalizing poverty, mental illness, past abuses, and race/ethnicity (Neve & Pate, 2005; Kaiser, 2004; Canadian Feminist Alliance for International Action, 2003; Monture-Angus, 2000). Moreover, particular groups of women based on race/ethnicity, poverty, mental illness, and age (youth and elderly) suffer disproportionate discrimination in a society which privileges an Anglo, middle-class, heterosexual, male value system.

Language is an essential management tool of neoliberalism used to regulate compliance and shift the onus onto the individual to account for

their "wrongdoing." It is through language that the powerful dehuman-
ize and demoralize the powerless. While discussions on the retooling of
language used to camouflage "relations of ruling" and power imbalances is still in its infancy, it should be a core area of concern to any serious feminist investigation. In light of these discussions, the term
"criminalized women" is invoked to emphasize the social, economic,
political, "psy-entific," and cultural *processes* which underpin the labeling of women as "offenders." It is a broader understanding of these
processes that requires our undiverted attention.

PECULIARITES AND SUBJECTIVITIES
OF RECIDIVISM SCALES

Emanating from the euphemistic language which fails to tackle the
power struggles between the keepers and the kept, one of the key
power/control strategies being masked by "corrections" is the explosive business of predicting future criminal behavior. A cornerstone
concept of "corrections" is predicated on the theory of risk management. Actuarial attempts to predict the likelihood of an individual
re-offending have gained enormous currency in the Canadian penal en-
terprise (Ross & Gendreau, 1980; Gendreau & Ross, 1987; Andrews,
1989; Bonta et al., 1995; Blanchette, 1997; Andrews & Bonta, 1998;
Motiuk & Blanchette, 1998). Underlying the "logic" of risk management is the theory of "cognitive behavioralism" which "assumes that a
person's thinking or cognition affects his or her emotions and behaviour
. . . [therefore] behaviour can be altered by changing one's thinking"
(Kendall, 2004, p 54). Cognitive behavioralism in the penal context:

> works on the assumption that offenders have faulty or deficient
> thinking which causes them to engage in immoral or criminal be-
> haviour. Programmes, therefore, aim to 'remoralise' or 'ethically
> reconstruct' offenders by teaching them to think 'pro-socially.'
> (Kendall, 2004, p. 56)

Rooted in the work of Canadian psychologists (Don Andrews &
James Bonta) at the "Ottawa School," risk prediction scales such as the
Level of Service Inventory–Revised (LSI-R) have gained international
success as "part of an escalating focus on managerialism, efficiency,
and accountability in correctional systems and a movement away from
concern with individual cases" (Shaw & Hannah-Moffat, 2004). Actu-

arial assessments satisfy a neo-liberal agenda of responsibilizing individuals as well as providing a heightened measure of accountability for prison staff (Kendall 2004). Andrews and Bonta (1998) claim to have developed a "psychology of criminal conduct" (PCC) characterized by cognitive deficiencies. With cognitive behavioralism as its rooting, this "discovery" brought renewed promise to the fledgling rehabilitative ideal of the 1970s and introduced a marketable individualizing formula which allowed for ex/prisoners to be governed in accordance with neo-liberalism. Under the broad banner of "cognitive skills," the "psy" disciplines have reinvigorated the notion of individual responsibility for criminal conduct and provided neatly prepackaged modules which can be delivered by prison staff to replace or reprogram an individual's faulty criminogenic thinking (Kendall, 2004). These cognitive behavioral therapies designed to "fix" anti-social thinking and divert individuals away from their criminal lifestyles are practically translated, for example, into recidivism scales which serve as tools of state control and coercion both within and outside prison walls.

Despite the well-documented biases of these checklist prediction scales (Shaw & Hannah-Moffat, 2004; Kendall, 2004; Kendall, 2000; Pollack & Kendall, 2005) they continue to gain enormous currency in the penal industrial complex (Davis, 2003) and ever-increasingly attract a new wave of meta-analytic designers vying for the next big breakthrough in correcting the faulty thinking of "criminals." For the purposes of this discussion, attention is drawn to the very vested and powerful groups in our society who converge to formulate (and re-formulate) these tools. Women (and by default men) who are the objects of these actuarial assessments are altogether excluded from the knowledge production/legitimation processes which define the parameters and outcomes of risk/need assessments and therefore the validity of recidivism prediction tools. To remedy the exclusion of criminalized women from the knowledge-making process, feminists advocate in favor of researching "from the margins" as the modus operandi for researching by, for, and with women, thereby privileging women's own accounts of managing their risks and needs. The margins, as best described by Kirby and McKenna (1989, p. 33) refers to:

> [t]he context in which those who suffer injustice, inequality and exploitation live their lives. People find themselves on the margins not only in terms of the inequality in the distribution of material resources, but also knowledge production is organized so that the views of a small group of people are presented as objective, as

"The Truth." The majority of people are excluded from participating as either producers or subjects of knowledge.

A radical departure from some of the well-entrenched and taken as "truth" knowledge claims about criminalized women, such as the sweeping and subjective claims of recidivism predictions, is urgently needed. The most frequently used indicator of individual successes/failures and, by default, the overall repute of rehabilitative ideologies is the use of these recidivism rates. Bonta, Rugge, and Dauvergne (2003, p. 1) claim that "knowledge of the recidivism rate of released inmates is important because it is one of many indicators of success of a prison system's attempt to reintegrate offenders safely back into the community." According to their measurements, the recidivism rate for imprisoned women is approximately 20%, only half of which represents the commission of new crimes while the remainder is related to technical violations (administrative breaches of one's conditional release). It is widely understood that most women who are imprisoned are not high risk and do not pose a threat to public safety (Hannah-Moffat & Shaw, 2003; Neve & Pate, 2005). They do, however, present a high degree of need based on histories of physical and sexual abuse; sole responsibilities for child care; and emotional/financial dependencies on abusive male partners.

The subject of risk-need classification has been well-canvassed by policymakers and academics alike (Feeley & Simon, 1992; O'Malley, 2000; Chan & Rigakos, 2002; Hannah-Moffat & Shaw, 2003). In the case of criminalized women, the "hybridization of risk and need factors" has resulted in "a substantial slippage between the concepts of risk and need." As Hannah-Moffat and Shaw (2003, p. 60) point out,

> [t]he resulting hybridization of risks and needs can lead to the identification of a "multitude of unrelated risk factors that in and of themselves provide no foundation for systemic rehabilitative interventions" (O'Malley 1999:18). The term need then is both vacuous and enabling. It is a category that can be deployed to either extend the arm of the state or to reinstate welfare-based techniques of rehabilitation, which have an extensive history of medicalizing and pathologizing women's deviance. (Hannah-Moffat & Shaw, 2003, p. 61)

Suffice it to say that the conflation of women's needs as risk markers has led to the over-classification of women prisoners and the undermining of women's attempts to break free of the transcarceral web of state and localized controls. The provision of services designed to assist women in dealing with their needs is hinged on androcentric and culturally insensitive risk-management schemes which are wholly deficient in responding to the needs of criminalized women (Hannah-Moffat & Shaw, 2003), both inside and outside the prison.

Recidivism scales as a tool for accurately measuring program outcomes are quite problematic, and there is no single measure of recidivism that does not carry with it certain disadvantages. The various measures that have been used all have serious shortcomings in terms of what they are purporting to measure and what they actually measure. Most outcome measures rely on re-arrest or re-incarceration data, both of which are problematic in that they count someone as having committed another crime when in fact they have not. An overwhelming majority of parole revocations result from technical violations of the conditions of one's release. In 2003-04, between 1-2% of federally sentenced women were returned to prison for the commission of a new offense (Canadian Association of Elizabeth Fry Societies, 2005). Therefore, failing to report monthly to a parole officer or violation of a curfew is counted in the same category as someone who commits a break and entry. Furthermore, recidivism rates do not distinguish between the types of crime which cause one to be returned to custody. Breach of probation falls into the same category as armed robbery in terms of counting success or failure. Another problem with recidivism scales is the cut-off period used to determine success. Most recidivism calculations use two years from the date of release as the typical marker of success. Therefore, if an individual makes it past two years without a return to custody they show up in official statistics as a non-recidivist. This arbitrary time period is problematic for obvious reasons, most notably its subjectivity.

The frustrations I alluded to earlier as a researcher doing work in the area of penology are rooted in having to continuously grapple with the deconstruction of "scientific" knowledge claims which fail to speak for criminalized women. From the very start, researchers have to be constantly vigilant in their attempts to dissect the motives, agendas, and subjective interpretations of correctional policies and practices. For example, if we accept the definition of recidivism as advocated by Bonta, Rugge, and Dauvergne (2003) that recidivism rates are "indicators of success of a prison system's attempt to reintegrate offenders safely back into the community," then we are faced with the troublesome acceptance of language which essentializes women, excludes them from the knowledge-making processes, and then claims to speak for their lived experiences. Core questions based on this one definition alone need to be asked. For example, who defines "success" and according to what criteria? Are we still upholding the fallacy that prisons are sites of reintegration? Who is defining the community? Is the community conceived of in the vernacular sense? When we speak of safe reintegration, whose safety are we really concerned with?

To put some of these queries about language and knowledge exclusion into context, my most recent methodological experiences in doing research with women ex-prisoners are instructive. Before I even began to conceive of a research project to investigate the lives of women ex-prisoners after their community release, it was first necessary to grapple with a conceptual understanding of how success is defined. It was recognized at the outset of this research that perceptions of success are highly subjective and vary widely depending on who is doing the defining. It was expected then that women would have quite a different definition of success than state officials. For instance, a woman involved in the criminal justice system for most of her adult life would undoubtedly have a radically different view of success than the official two-year barometer. It was critical, therefore, that women be given the opportunity at the outset to locate and name their own success and/or failure in navigating their way through the criminal justice system.

This "official versus marginal knowledge" conundrum became quite evident during the pre-testing of the research instrument. The "corrections" knowledge legitimation processes and outcomes are unilaterally imposed on women who lack input and consensus on the factors which are used to predict recidivism. One woman interviewed, for example, clearly defined herself in successful terms based on the fact that she had remained out of the system for one month. Given her extremely high level of institutionalization (25 years spent cycling between prisons and psychiatric hospitals), she proudly proclaimed accomplishment during her most recent release by setting herself up in her own apartment. Her reasons for going back inside had nothing to do with the official risk characteristics (dynamic and legal factors) lauded by psychology-based scales of recidivism. Rather, she felt that prison was her "community" and life on the outside had become "too scary." This is a quite different interpretation from the "success" indicators of recidivism proffered by criminal justice policy makers.

Notwithstanding the problematics of defining recidivism, adhering to feminist methodologies of researching from the margins (Kirby & McKenna, 1989) allowed the women in this research sample to define their own risk/need indices and therefore to name and characterize their own successes and/or failures. The balance of the research then centered around "researching from the margins" where the central concern is "enabl[ing] people to create knowledge that will describe, explain and help change the world in which [women] live" (Kirby & McKenna, 1989, p. 33). By "reclaim[ing], nam[ing], and re-nam[ing] our experience and thus our knowledge of this social world we live in and daily help to construct, [only then] will it become truly ours, ours to use and do with as we will" (Stanley & Wise, 1983, p. 205).

NEO-LIBERAL AND NEO-CONSERVATIVE STRATEGIES OF CRIMINALIZATION

In counteracting and moving beyond the psychological stranglehold of Canadian corrections, it is also imperative to understand the constrained structural and economic parameters within which certain groups of women in our society are forced to operate. In terms of a purported interest on "rehabilitation," this level of analysis is crucial as we know that the very conditions which propel women into prison in the first place are often amplified once they exit the prison. Therefore, broader structural forces surrounding women's criminality are presented which include an examination of neo-conservative and neo-liberal strategies of governance which have resulted in a dismantling of the welfare state; the offloading of collective responsibilities onto the shoulders of individuals and families; and the social constructions of disorderly populations.

Critical criminologists (e.g., DeKeseredy et al., 2003; Renzetti et al., 2001; Raphael, 2000; Young, 1999; Parent, 1998) and legal theorists, (e.g., Daly, 1994; Comack & Balfour, 2004) provide a compelling analysis of the power of the state to reproduce a particular kind of order based on race, gender, and class inequalities. Critical criminology, a term which has been in use since the 1970s, is defined as "a perspective that views the major sources of crime as the class, ethnic, and patriarchal relations that control our society . . . [and] regards major structural and cultural changes within society as steps to reducing criminality" (DeKeseredy & Schwartz, 1996, p. 239). Critical criminology, based both in its origins and contemporary writings, draws heavily from the notion of exclusivity (Young, 1999). An "exclusive society" in late modernity has been created and functions on three levels: economic exclusion from labor markets; social exclusion between people in civil society; and exclusion by the criminal justice system (Young, 1999, p. vi). Beckett and Western (2001, p. 36) point to an inherent feature of the exclusionary society wherein "welfare and penal institutions comprise a single policy regime aimed at the governance of social marginality." They point to the variations of these regimes according to their inclusionary or exclusionary agendas:

> Inclusive regimes emphasize the need to improve and integrate the socially marginal and tend to place more emphasis on the social causes of marginality. These regimes are therefore characterized by more generous welfare programs and less punitive anti-crime policies. By contrast, exclusionary regimes emphasize the undeserving and unreformable nature of deviants, tend to stigmatize and separate the socially marginal, and hence are more likely to feature less generous welfare benefits and more punitive anti-crime policies. (Beckett & Western, 2001, p. 36)

Underlying both policy regimes are neo-liberal and neo-conservative political ideologies. Neo-liberalism is "premised on the values of individualism, freedom of choice, market security and minimal state involvement in the economy. [It] marks a dramatic shift in emphasis from collective or social values towards notions of family and individual responsibility" (Comack & Balfour, 2004, p. 40). The outcome of neo-liberal strategies of governance have been a:

> [r]etreat from any professed commitment to social welfare. Instead of formulating policies and targeting spending on programs that would meet the social needs of the members of society (education, health care, pensions, social assistance), governments now focus on enhancing economic efficiency and international competitiveness. With the 'privatization' of responsibility, individuals and families are left to look after themselves. (Comack & Balfour, 2004, p. 40)

The political ideology behind a neo-liberal agenda, referred to as "social Darwinism,"

> [a]rgues for a survival-of-the-fittest reliance on market forces. The state should get out of the way of the forces that decide which regions, and which people, prosper and which don't. The only assistance the state should provide are 'incentives' to work. The policy

results of these views is a dramatic shrinking of the social safety
net. (Martin, 2002, p. 92)

Neo-conservative policies, on the other hand, shift the focus towards
a "law and order" agenda. Therefore, policies targeting the underclass
in Ontario, for example, have become the central governing tool. As
Hermer and Mosher (2002, p. 16) describe:

> [s]queegee kids, welfare cheats, coddled prisoners, violent youth,
> aggressive beggars are part of a modern rogues gallery that has
> been used by the Ontario government to justify sweeping changes
> in the public character of government. Disorder and the people
> embodying disorder have become a central resource of political
> power in Ontario, one that is produced and managed as an essential
> feature of neo-conservativism across a wide range of government
> activities.

Neo-conservatives also argue that the family (and the church) should
be the source of charity and support for the unfortunate (Martin, 2002,
p. 92). This shift toward singling out the poor and disenfranchised
groups is not a new state strategy, however. As Hermer and Mosher
(2002, pp. 16-17) make clear:

> [w]hat is new and radical about the type of disorder manufactured
> by the . . . government is that it is intentionally designed to disman-
> tle the welfare state. In other words, making up a disorderly set of
> people has come with an erosion of some of the central principles
> that have underpinned the democratic and equitable character of
> our institutions, diminishing the ways in which we are made to feel
> responsible for each other. And what is most disconcerting about
> this shift, . . . is that it has taken place at the very sites in which the
> government is responsible for some of the most vulnerable and
> marginalized in our society–those with mental-health issues, the
> young, the poor and disabled, and a disproportionate number who
> are in correctional facilities.

Social and criminal justice policy outcomes under both these regimes
result in a weakening of social service provisions for the most vulnerable in our society and a social Darwinist approach to governing. The fiscal fallout of both agendas increases the social and economic divide

between the upper and lower classes. Martin (2002, p. 97) cogently sums up the divisive qualities of each regime:

> Under a neo-liberal fiscal agenda, for example, private security, policing and correctional services expand, and treatment and social services are privatized, while public institutions face cuts and private charities remain the preferred means to deliver services to offenders and victims. On the other hand, in aid of a neo-conservative moral agenda, a law-and-order retributive approach to social disorder and dysfunction is offered to reinforce hierarchical/patriarchal social disorganization. The former claims to celebrate the autonomous individual and thus argues for all the elimination of all but the most essential intrusions by the state onto freedom of choice and action, while the latter insists on a combination of punishment and the charitable "rescue-and-reform" model for the few social services that survive.

This unrelenting target of disenfranchised and powerless groups in our society under a neo-conservative banner is perhaps most acutely evidenced in this country by recent provincial legislation which criminalizes "squeegee kids" who otherwise would be trumpeted under an entrepreneurial banner for their efforts to eke out a living on street corners and intersections offering a marketable customer service (Ontario Safe Streets Act, 1999; O'Grady & Blight, 2002). Neo-conservative and neo-liberal strategies have contributed to the off-loading and dismantling of the welfare state which, in turn, lays the blame squarely on the shoulders of individuals for their "wrongdoings."

> Taken as a whole, the legislative framework, the policies, the practices and the accompanying discourse operate to construct the poor as persons who don't deserve to be in control of anything; rather they are persons who need to be controlled, disciplined and reformed by others. Single mothers in particular represent disorder, since they stand outside the structure of both the hegemonic nuclear family and often, the labour market. Welfare recipients, and especially single mothers, are constructed as persons who ought not to possess any expectation of privacy; they are in effect, cast as objects, to be reformed by the "public" for the betterment of the "public." Thus privacy is preserved for others, for the economically privileged. (Mosher, 2002, p. 49)

Such a consciousness of individual responsibility has fuelled the explosive market for "psy-entific" fixes capable of re-forming the criminal mind. It also conveniently deflects attention away from the regressive socio-economic policies encased in neo-liberalism and the political rally for tougher law enforcement to crack down on these wayward criminals.

THE POWER OF KNOWING

To move beyond the trappings of criminology to deconstruct the power relations which pervert the manifest meanings of language and political ideologies of control, it is necessary to turn our attention to a discussion of how knowledge is constructed and legitimated according to the "relations of ruling." One attempt to value knowledge at the margins that lacks official knowledge status (i.e., legitimation) has been proffered by proponents of standpoint perspectives (Haraway, 1996; Collins, 1991; Smith, 1987). Dorothy Smith (1987, p. 108) draws the connection between power and the legitimation of knowledge and the exclusionary nature of these processes:

> A standpoint in the everyday world is a fundamental grounding of modes of knowing developed in a ruling apparatus. The ruling apparatus is that familiar complex of management, government administration, professions, and intelligentsia, as well as the textually mediated discourses that coordinate and interpenetrate it.

Standpoint feminism allows for the privileging of marginalized voices as a way to resist entrenched value-laden, androcentric knowledge claims and relies on the notion that previous feminist attempts to account for the intersectionality of race, class, and gender have been deficient. The predominantly white and middle-class women's movement ("Chardonnay feminism") had, in its focus on gender alone, essentially ignored the diversity of women's lives. The epistemological basis of feminist knowledge is experience which is "achieved through a struggle against oppression; it is, therefore, argued to be more complete and less distorted than the perspective of the ruling group of men. A feminist standpoint then is not just the experience of women, but of women reflexively engaged in struggle" (intellectual and political) (Smart, 1990, p. 80).

A standpoint perspective privileges positionality in gaining knowledge and understanding (Wolf, 1996). One's position in the social hierarchy potentially broadens or limits one's understanding of others. Members of the dominant group have viewpoints that are partial in contrast to those from subordinated groups who have greater potential for fuller knowledge. Therefore, the only way we can know a socially constructed world is to know it from within. But since our knowledge and perceptions about reality are shaped by our own unique experiences and how we interpret them, there is little or no possibility for value-free and objective knowledge. Standpoint feminism relies on the notion that previous feminist attempts to integrate the varied interactions of race, class, and gender have been deficient. "The field has particularly focussed attention on the fact that the predominantly white and middle-class women's movement had, in its focus on gender alone, essentially ignored the diversity of women's experiences, lives, and communities" (Chesney-Lind & Faith, 2001, p. 297). Smart (1990, p. 80), in her analysis of standpoint feminism states that:

> [t]he epistemological basis of this form of feminist knowledge is experience. Feminist experience is achieved through a struggle against oppression; it is, therefore, argued to be more complete and less distorted than the perspective of the ruling group of men. A feminist standpoint then is not just the experience of women, but of women reflexively engaged in struggle (intellectual and political).

Standpoint feminism challenges the modernist assumption that once we have the theory (master narrative) which will explain all forms of social behavior, we will also know what to do and that the "rightness" of this doing will be verifiable and transparent (Smart, 1990, p. 72).

A large body of feminist empiricist literature which explores claims to objectivity, grand theory, and the deconstruction of knowledge now exists (see, e.g., Keller, 1996; Smith, 1987; Haraway, 1996; Hartsock, 1998). Feminist empiricists criticize the claims to objectivity made by mainstream social science by pointing out that what has passed for science is in fact the world perceived from the perspective of men, what looks like objectivity is really sexism, and that the kinds of questions social science has traditionally asked have systematically excluded women and the interests of women. Feminist empiricism claims that a truly objective science would not be androcentric but would take account of both genders. As Dorothy Smith points out, "to direct research at women without revising traditional assumptions about methodology and epistemology can result in making women a mere addendum to the main project of studying men. It also leaves unchallenged the way men are studied" (cited in Smith, 1987).

It is important to recognize that knowledge in the everyday world is socially constructed and that the political, economic, social, and cultural contexts of knowledge generation, acquisition, and transmission have to be taken into account. Whose knowledge comes to be accepted as the "truth," who has a voice in the creation of knowledge, and what the intervening factors are that play into the legitimation process of knowledge are important tenets of feminist methodology. Dorothy Smith (1987, pp. 107-109) eloquently points out that women's lives have been outside and therefore subordinate to the relations of ruling. However, she points out that it is not only women that are excluded. The ruling apparatus is "an organization of class and as such implicates dominant classes. It also excludes the many voices of women and men of color, native peoples, and homosexual women and men. From different standpoints different aspects of the ruling apparatus and of class come into view." In this regard, issues surrounding who decides what becomes acceptable as knowledge in a particular spatial, temporal, and cultural context are paramount.

Before knowledge gets to be accepted in the everyday world it has to undergo a "legitimation process" which results in an official decision being made as to an explanation's legitimacy or lack thereof. If the decision-makers (white, patriarchal capitalists) perceive some knowledge to challenge the status quo, an approving assessment of this threatening type of knowledge might be withheld as a consequence and the finding will not be recognized as (legitimate) knowledge. Consequently, this leads to the marginalization of knowledge and many creators of subsequently marginalized knowledge have come from oppressed groups, such as women and non-white, including Aboriginal people. Conversely, much of legitimate/legitimized knowledge has come from members of the dominant group(s)–primarily white, heterosexual and male–who had (have) some affiliation with the ruling class.

Feminist writings on the value-laden and androcentric bases of scientific knowledge, such as those of Evelyn Fox Keller (1996), have pioneered the deconstruction of knowledge claims and have argued for the inclusion of feminist ways of knowing in the experimental design of (social) scientific research. Keller (1996) discusses the relationship between knowledge and power and notes that both are intermeshed–knowledge is about legitimacy and legitimacy is about power. Recently, feminists critiques of the objectivity and legitimation of science (Keller, 1996; Haraway, 1991) have entered the criminological discourse as well (e.g., Naffine, 1996; Smart, 1990; Scraton, 1990).

Epistemological contributions that attempt to deconstruct and expose the value-laden assumptions of scientific knowledge have also sparked feminist writings in the area of research methodologies. Issues grappling with power relations inherent during the research process have been an integral part of the discussions and debates. While this may be the case, there is still a lot of work to be done in this area. On this point, Ristock and Pennell (1996, p. 68) argue that "feminist discussions of research have yet to describe fully the complexity of power and struggles with subjectivity in research."

Feminist methodologies and epistemologies are inextricably linked to subsequent theory construction. Before we can theorize from data, we must understand the knowledge construction/legitimation processes that guide our research. We need to recognize the subjectivities of the researcher and take account of the power that is institutionalized in a masculinist form throughout all aspects of the criminal justice system. As Scraton (1990, p. 15) points out, "If academic discourse and its patriarchal context is to be challenged it needs to be considered within a broader framework of how ideas gain currency, become transmitted and eventually become institutionalized or consolidated as knowledge." In examining the myriad of factors that propel women into crime, we need to move beyond the boundaries of criminology in many ways and look toward the broader social, economic, political, and cultural issues that contribute to the construction of gender in society. We need to critique the knowledge-making and legitimation processes as being androcentric and similarly critique criminological theories that exclude women from their research and analyses and then argue objectivity and scientific rigor.

CONCLUDING REMARKS

This essay has taken aim at the privileged accounts of those of us in academia and other positions of authority and influence who claim to speak for the experiences of marginalized populations based on erroneous constructs of criminal and non-criminal. By accepting the language of difference and the neo-liberal rhetoric of the worthy and the worthless, we falsely dichotomize the most marginalized groups in society against the rest of law-abiding individuals and have conveniently carved a lucrative niche market for a group of professionals to then set about correcting the cognitively deficient who have failed to make it in society. We need to reverse our preoccupation with privileged accounts of knowledge which guide our research and policy agendas and focus our attention to seeing the world from the perspective of those with first-person knowledge of the racist, classist, heterosexist, and gendered ways in which our societal institutions operate. It is the thinking of those with a vested interest in promulgating an individualistic and pathological approach to treating those on the margins which is most urgently in need of correction.

REFERENCES

Andrews, D. (1989). Recidivism is predictable and can be influenced: using risk assessments to reduce recidivism. *Forum on Corrections Research, 1*(2), 11-18.

Andrews, D., & Bonta, J. (1998*). The psychology of criminal conduct*. Cincinnati, OH: Anderson.

Beckett, K., & Western, B. (2001). Governing social marginality: Welfare, incarceration, and the transformation of state policy. In D. Garland (Ed.), *Mass imprisonment: Social causes and consequences*. London: Sage.

Blanchette, K. 1997. *Risk and need among federally-sentenced female offenders: A comparison of minimum, medium, and maximum security inmates*. Research Report R-58. Ottawa: Correctional Service Canada.

Bonta, J., Rugg, T., & Dauvergne, M. (2003). *The Reconviction Rate of Female Offenders*. (User Report 2003-02). Ottawa: Solicitor General Canada.

Bonta, J., Pang, B., & Wallace-Capretta, S. (1985). Predictors of recidivism among incarcerated female offenders. *The Prison Journal, 75*(3): 277-294.

Canadian Association of Elizabeth Fry Societies. (2005). *Facts sheets*. Ottawa: CAEFS.

Canadian Feminist Alliance for International Action. (2003*). Canada's failure to act: Women's inequality deepens*. Submission to United Nations Committee on the Elimination of Discrimination Against Women on the Occasion of the Committee's Review of Canada's 5th Report. Ottawa, ON.

Chan, W., & Rigakos, G. (2002). Risk, crime and gender. *British Journal of Criminology*, 42: 743-761.

Chesney-Lind, M., & Faith, K. (2001). What about feminism? Engendering theory-making in criminology. In R. Paternoster and R. Bauchnan (Eds.), *Exploring criminals and crime* (pp. 287-302). Los Angeles: Roxbury.

Collins, P.H. (1991). *Black feminist thought: Knowledge, consciousness and the politics of empowerment*. London: Routledge.

Comack, E. (1996). *Women in trouble: Connecting women's law violations to their tistories of abuse*. Halifax: Fernwood Publishing.

Comack, E., & Balfour, G. (2004). *The power to criminalize: violence, inequality and the law*. Halifax: Fernwood Publishing.

Daly, K. (1994). Criminal law and justice system practices as racist, white and racialized. *Washington and Lee Law Review, 51*(2): 431-64.

Davies, S., & Cook, S. (1999). Neglect or punishment? Failing to meet the needs of women post-release. In S. Cook & S. Davies (Eds.), *Harsh punishment: International experiences of women's imprisonment* (pp. 272-290). Boston: Northeastern University Press.

Davis, A. (2003). *Are prisons obsolete?* New York: Seven Stories Press.

DeKeseredy, W., Alvi, S., Schwartz, M., & Tomaszewski, A. (2003). *Under siege: Poverty and crime in a canadian public housing community*. Lanham, MD: Lexington Press.

DeKeseredy, W., & Schwartz, M. (1996). *Contemporary criminology*. Belmont, CA: Wadsworth.

Faith, K. (1993). *Unruly women: The politics of confinement and resistance*. Vancouver: Press Gang Publishers.

Feeley, M., & Simon, J. (1992). The new penology: Notes on the emerging strategy of corrections and its implications *Criminology, 30*(4), 449-75.

Gendreau, P., & Ross, R. (1987). Revivification of rehabilitation: Evidence from the 1980s. *Justice Quarterly*, 4, 349-408.

Hannah-Moffat, K., & Shaw, M. (2003). The meaning of "risk" in women's prisons: A critique. In B. Bloom (Ed.), *Gendered justice: Addressing female offenders* (pp. 45-68). Carolina Academic Press.

Haraway, D. (1996). Situated knowledges: The science question in feminism and the privilege of partial perspective. *Feminism and Science*, 249-263.

Haraway, D. (1991). *Simians, cyborgs and women: The reinvention of nature*. New York: Routledge and Kegan Paul.

Hartsock, N. (1998). *The feminist standpoint revisited, and other essays*. Boulder, CO: Westview.

Hermer, J., & Mosher, J. (Eds.). (2002). *Disorderly people: Law and the politics of exclusion in Ontario*. Halifax: Fernwood Publishing.

Horii, G. (2000). Processing humans. In K. Hannah-Moffat & M. Shaw (Eds.), *An ideal prison: Critical essays on women's imprisonment in Canada* (pp. 104-116). Halifax: Fernwood Publishing.

Kaiser, A. (2004). *The criminalization of people with mental health problems: Joining together to find a way forward*. NAACJ/Justice Canada/Public Safety and Emergency Preparedness Joint Policy Forum: Human Rights of People with Mental Disabilities and the Criminal Justice System. Ottawa: ON.

Keller, E. (1996). Feminism and science. In E. Keller & H. Longino (Eds.), *Feminism and science*. New York: Oxford.

Kendall, K. (2004). Dangerous thinking: A critical history of correctional cognitive behaviouralism. In G. Mair (Ed.), *What matters in probation* (pp. 53-89). Devon, UK: Willian Publishing.

Kendall, K. (2000). Psy-ence fiction: Governing female prisons through the psychological services. In M. Hannah-Moffat & M. Shaw (Eds.), *An ideal prison: Critical essays on women's imprisonment in Canada* (pp. 82-93). Halifax: Fernwood Publishing.

Kirby, S., & McKenna, K. (1989). *Methods from the margins: Experience, research, social change*. Toronto: Garamond Press.

Martin, D. (2002). Demonizing youth, marketing fear: The new politics of crime. In J. Hermer & J. Mosher (Eds.), *Disorderly people: Law and the politics of exclusion in Ontario* (pp. 91-104). Halifax: Fernwood Publishing.

Monture-Angus, P. (2000). Aboriginal women and correctional practice: Reflections on the task force on federally sentenced women. In Hannah-Moffat, K., & Shaw, M. (Eds.), *An ideal prison: Critical essays on women's imprisonment in Canada* (pp. 52-60). Halifax: Fernwood Publishing.

Mosher, J. (2002). The shrinking of the public and private spaces of the poor. In J. Hermer, J., & J. Mosher (Eds.), *Disorderly people: Law and the politics of exclusion in Ontario* (pp. 41-53) Halifax: Fernwood Publishing.

Motiuk, L., & Blanchette, K. (1998). *Assessing female offenders: What works?* Paper presented to the International Community Corrections Association, Annual Conference. Arlington, Virginia.

Naffine, N. (1996). *Feminism & criminology*. Temple University Press: Philadelphia.

Neve, L., & Pate, K. (2005). Challenging the criminalization of women who resist. In J. Sudbury (Ed.), *Global lockdown: Race, gender and the prison industrial complex*. New York, NY: Routledge.

O'Grady, B., & Blight, R. (2002). Squeezed to the point of exclusion: The case of Toronto squeegee cleaners. In J. Hermer & J. Mosher (Eds.), *Disorderly people: Law and the politics of exclusion in Ontario* (pp. 23-39). Halifax: Fernwood Publishing.

O'Malley, P. (2000). Risk societies and the government of crime. In M. Brown & J. Pratt (Eds.), *Dangerousness, risk and modern society*. London: Routledge.

Parent, C. (1998). *Féminismes & criminologie*. Paris, Bruxelles: De Boeck Université.

Pollack, S., & Kendall, K. (2005). Taming the shrew: Regulating prisoners through women-centered mental health programming. *Critical Criminology*, 13, 71-87.

Raphael, J. (2000). *Saving Bernice: Battered women, welfare, and poverty*. Boston: Northeastern University Press.

Renzetti, C., Edleson, J., & Bergen, R. (Eds.). (2001). *Sourcebook on violence against women*. Thousand Oaks, CA: Sage.

Ristock, J., & Pennell, J. (1996). *Community research as empowerment: Feminist links, postmodern interruptions*. New York: Oxford University Press.

Ross, R., & Gendreau, P. (1980). *Effective correctional treatment*. Toronto: Butterworths.

Safe Streets Act. (1999). S. O. 1999. c.8

Schur, E. (1984). *Labeling women deviant: Gender, stigma, and social control*. New York: Random House.

Scraton, P. (1990). Scientific knowledge or masculine discourses? Challenging patriarchy in criminology. In Gelsthorpe, L., & Morris, A. (Eds.), *Feminist perspectives in criminology*. Open University Press.

Shaw, M., & Hannah-Moffat, K. (2004). How cognitive skills forgot about gender and diversity. In G. Mair (Ed.), *What matters in probation* (pp. 90-121). Devon, UK: Willian Publishing.

Smart, C. (1990). Feminist approaches to criminology or postmodern woman meets atavistic man. In L. Gelsthorpe & Morris (Eds.), *Feminist perspectives in criminology* (pp. 70-84). Philadelphia: Open University Press.

Smith, D. (1987). *The everyday world as problematic: A feminist methodology.* Boston: Open University Press.

Stanley, L., & Wise, S. (1983). *Breaking out: Feminist consciousness and feminist research.* London: Routledge & Kegan Paul.

Wolf, D. (1996). Situating feminist dilemmas in fieldwork. In D.L. Wolf (Ed.), *Feminist dilemmas in fieldwork.* Boulder, Colorado: Westview.

Young, J. (1999). *The exclusive society.* London: Sage.

doi:10.1300/J015v29n03_03

Human Rights and U.S. Female Prisoners

Zoë Sodja

SUMMARY. In December 1948, the United Nations adopted the Universal Declaration of Human Rights. The concept of universal human rights is that every person, simply by being human, has the right to be treated with dignity and equality. After a brief overview of international human rights declarations and treaties since that time, this article looks at the mistreatment of women prisoners in the U.S. today in the areas of health care, mental health, and sexual abuse, and determines that it is a violation of their human rights on a number of levels. Despite lip service by the government and the belief of many citizens that the U.S. is a country that honors human rights, when we look at what really goes on, we find that the U.S. falls behind other democratic countries in its treatment of domestic prisoners, particularly women prisoners. doi:10.1300/J015v29n03_04 *[Article copies available for a fee from The Haworth Document Delivery Service: 1-800-HAWORTH. E-mail address: <docdelivery@haworthpress.com> Website: <http://www. HaworthPress.com> © 2006 by The Haworth Press, Inc. All rights reserved.]*

KEYWORDS. Human rights, international law, prison health care, rape of women prisoners

---

Zoë Sodja, JD, is a recent law school graduate who is planning to practice law in the area of prison conditions.

Address correspondence to: Zoë Sodja, 3025 Ellis Street, Berkeley, CA 94703 (E-mail: zoe@ucsc.edu).

[Haworth co-indexing entry note]: "Human Rights and U.S. Female Prisoners." Sodja, Zoë. Co-published simultaneously in *Women & Therapy* (The Haworth Press, Inc.) Vol. 29, No. 3/4, 2006, pp. 57-73; and: *Inside and Out: Women, Prison, and Therapy* (ed: Elaine Leeder) The Haworth Press, Inc., 2006, pp. 57-73. Single or multiple copies of this article are available for a fee from The Haworth Document Delivery Service [1-800-HAWORTH, 9:00 a.m. - 5:00 p.m. (EST). E-mail address: docdelivery@haworthpress.com].

January 27, 2000. As I approached the Central California Women's Facility (CCWF) after the three-hour drive from San Francisco, I could see the demonstration outside the prison gates, about 150 people with signs. As I drew closer, I could see that this was not the usual demonstration: everyone was in black and most of the signs were replicas of tombstones, inscribed with the names of women who had recently died inside the prison, twelve in that year, including nine in the last two months. There were also pictures of the women, objects that the women had treasured, an altar with flowers. These women had been the mothers, sisters, daughters, wives of many of the demonstrators, and the anger and sorrow was palpable. Family members spoke, remembering their loved ones with sorrow and speaking of their bitterness toward prison staff.

Sorrow at the death of a loved one is something we all share when someone we love dies. But the anger and despair that these families felt was a direct result of this particular situation. Anger because these deaths were preventable, they were unnecessary. Because some women would have been released in a matter of weeks. Because whatever their illness or symptoms, these women died from medical neglect.

On December 2, 1999, 46-year-old Pamela Coffey had complained of terrible abdominal pain, numbness in her legs, and a swollen tongue which made it difficult to speak. According to eyewitnesses, a Medical Technical Assistant (MTA–a guard with low-level medical training) came out of Coffey's cell laughing as he said to a prisoner, "I can't understand a word she's saying–you can do more for her than I can." Pamela's condition grew increasingly worse within the next three hours, and the MTA was called again. He finally arrived 30 minutes after being summoned, but by then Pamela Coffey was dead. Outside investigators reviewing her death concluded that "there were significant problems with Ms. Coffey's medical care that might have contributed to her death." At the demonstration, her daughter tearfully said, "My mother was sentenced to a prison term, she wasn't sentenced to death."

Eva Vallario, 33, had a history of asthma that was poorly managed by prison medical staff. On December 15, 1999, she died in a holding cell. The report by outside investigators stated that Ms. Vallario died after choking on her vomit, and that "there is a substantial likelihood that she could have been resuscitated if she had been ventilated earlier."

Jodie Fitzgerald, Stephanie Hardie, Leila Peyton, Carolina Paredes, Michelle Wilson, Kathy Kelly: All women incarcerated in U.S. prisons. All cases with serious questions surrounding the adequacy of their health care. All dead.

Human Rights Watch, Amnesty International, and the United Nations have all issued reports on U.S. treatment of prisoners, citing violations of international standards of human rights in the areas of health care, supermax prisons, sexual abuse in prisons, the death penalty, and more. This article examines the question "what are human rights?" and explores the violations of human rights that women in U.S. prisons experience every day.

INTERNATIONAL HUMAN RIGHTS

After the horrors of World War II, a number of countries formed the United Nations to establish a foundation for peace and human rights. The concept of universal human rights is that every person, simply by virtue of being human, has the right to be treated with dignity and equality, and that this is not dependent on one's identity or status.

To this end, the U.N. adopted and proclaimed the Universal Declaration of Human Rights in December of 1948 and, in 1977, it adopted the Standard Minimum Rules for the Treatment of Prisoners. These two documents are not treaties and therefore they are not binding on any government. However, they do carry some moral authority and establish a standard for human rights and humane treatment of all persons. The Universal Declaration of Human Rights, written by Eleanor Roosevelt among others, outlines basic human rights as they pertain to civil, political, economic, social, and cultural rights. This document served as the foundation for the two legally binding U.N. human rights covenants–the International Covenant on Civil and Political Rights (ICCPR) and the International Covenant on Economic, Social, and Cultural Rights (ECOSOC).

The U.S. Constitution states that international treaties are the highest law in the land; therefore, international treaties that the United States has ratified are legally binding upon all courts in the land. The U.S. has ratified: ICCPR, 1992; International Convention on the Elimination of All Forms of Racial Discrimination (CERD, 1994); and Convention Against Torture and Other Cruel, Inhuman or Degrading Treatment or Punishment (Torture Convention, 1994). Although the U.S. ratified the ICCPR, it placed a reservation on Article 7, stating that the U.S. considers itself bound only "to the extent that 'cruel, inhuman or degrading treatment or punishment' means the cruel and unusual treatment or punishment prohibited by the Fifth, Eighth, and/or Fourteenth Amendments to the Constitution of the United States."[1]

The U.S. has *not* ratified the Convention on the Elimination of All Forms of Discrimination Against Women (CEDAW, 1980). Nor has it ratified the International Covenant on Economic, Social and Cultural Rights (ECOSOC, 1994) because it commits countries to work toward the granting of economic, social, and cultural rights to individuals.

U.S. courts of law are not obligated to follow non-ratified treaties or declarations. However, even when not ratified, these treaties and declarations can nevertheless be a tool in the struggle for the human worth and dignity of every person. They can be referred to as moral authority and international community standards. Protections under international human rights law are frequently greater than those under U.S. law. For instance, the international definition of cruel, inhuman, and degrading treatment is much broader than the definition under U.S. law, which is undoubtedly why the U.S. government placed a reservation on this section of the ICCPR.

In May 2000, the U.N. Committee against Torture spoke out about the U.S. government's insistence on adopting its own definitions of torture and cruelty, rather than those of the treaty, specifically regarding many of the conditions inside our prisons: electric shock, pepper spray, supermax prison conditions, rape of women prisoners by male guards, and racial discrimination (Peet, 2000). Amnesty International (AI) has made similar charges (Peet, 2000). The U.S. government denied the charges, and in 2002 aligned itself with some of the most oppressive and least democratic countries in the world to oppose a proposal (known as a protocol) for a new addition to the Convention Against Torture that would include international prison inspections. Washington not only opposed the inspections but lobbied hard for other nations to oppose them as well (Ford, 2002; Mungoven, 2002).

The U.S. government continues to pay lip service to human rights, putting itself forth as a humane society, but it often condones behavior that is considered torture or inhumane by the international community or that contravenes even treaties that the U.S. has ratified. The world heard about U.S. maltreatment of prisoners at Abu Ghraib and at Guantanamo, but mistreatment of prisoners here at home is also commonplace, although much less visible. In fact, some of the leaders of the Abu Ghraib situation received their training in U.S. prisons. Some were former guards, and one was a former director of prisons in Texas.

This article will discuss three areas in which U.S. disregard of international standards particularly impacts women in U.S. prisons: health care, mental health care, and sexual abuse by guards.

WOMEN PRISONERS IN THE U.S.

Women in U.S. prisons undergo violations of their human rights every day. Some of the main human rights violations that women are subjected to are in the areas of adequate health care and bodily integrity, i.e., freedom from physical and sexual abuse. Adequate, decent health care and the right to privacy of one's person[2] are recognized by the international community as basic human rights, yet the U.S. lags behind. Most U.S. citizens are unaware of the abuses that go on in our prisons unless they have been incarcerated themselves or have a family member who has been in prison.

Health Care in Prison

Rosemary Willeby suffered from Hepatitis C and liver disease. Although she had no symptoms of tuberculosis, she was placed in a TB program by prison staff and was prescribed anti-TB meds that were contraindicated for anyone with liver problems. The prison ignored her many requests to see a specialist until ten days before she died. Eventually her family received a $225,000 settlement after she died on 10/22/99.

Lack of adequate health care is a huge problem for both men and women in our prisons. Women, however, are especially vulnerable for a number of reasons: Women prisoners need and seek medical care more frequently than men partly because of their unique health care needs around pregnancy, childbirth, and other gynecological needs; women have a higher rate of drug addiction, with resulting medical issues; and women often have histories of being abused prior to incarceration.

Incarcerated women are at greater risk for serious health problems than women on the outside because of their greater likelihood of living in poverty, having poor nutrition, being substance abusers, and having limited access to preventive medical care and limited education on health issues. The majority of imprisoned women have significant health-care problems, and very few of these needs are met in prison.

Many women enter the correctional system as survivors of abuse. Many have multiple illnesses and drug problems. Often their drug problems or illnesses have gone untreated for years on the outside, so they arrive in prison already in need of medical attention. Some women are dealing with menopause. Others grow old in prison. Illnesses such as HIV and Hepatitis have higher rates among prisoners than in the general population. HIV, Hepatitis C, and breast cancer diagnoses continue to rise among women prisoners.

Prison health care is the story of medical neglect: missed medications, denial or delay of treatment, inadequate screening, huge obstacles to treatment, and callous treatment are a few of the problems incarcerated women must deal with. Health care is one of the most serious problems for prisoners. There is a pattern of neglect, sometimes even abuse, of women prisoners in need of medical care.

Health care in California's women's prisons has been condemned by the United Nations and two international human rights agencies, Amnesty International and Human Rights Watch. Amnesty International's 1998 report, called "Rights for All," condemned human rights abuses in the U.S., including serious violations inside our prisons, specifically citing problems with obtaining health care, especially prenatal care, and with sexual assault by guards inside women's prisons. Amnesty International has called on the U.S. to apply international standards of medical care to the treatment of prisoners (AI, 1998).

The ECOSOC states that nations must "recognize the right of everyone to the enjoyment of the highest attainable standard of physical and mental health" (United Nations, 1994, Art. 12(1)). In addition, "[s]tates are under the obligation to *respect* the right to health by . . . refraining from denying or limiting equal access for all persons, including prisoners" (United Nations, 1994: Committee on Economic, Social and Cultural rights, General Comment 14, para. 34). And Rule 22 of the *Standard Minimum Rules for the Treatment of Prisoners* states that prisoners shall have access to specialists, dentists, appropriate medical treatment, medications, and pharmaceutical supplies. In addition, the U.S. Supreme Court has said that the state is required to provide adequate health care to all prisoners. In fact, prisoners are the only U.S. citizens who are entitled to free health care, because they are dependent on the state for all their needs and unable to seek out health care for themselves.

One big problem in prison health care is the fact that non-medical staff (MTAs) act as gatekeepers for medical care. MTAs make the decision about whether a prisoner needs medical attention. As guards they tend to see the women as complainers and their symptoms as psychosomatic and fabricated. This is a view of women's health complaints that we also find outside of the prison setting, but in prison it becomes much more problematic because of the power the MTAs wield as to whether a woman can see a physician or even receive any treatment at all.

Compounding the MTA problem is the high incidence of complex and serious diseases among women prisoners. For example, the incidence of HIV among prisoners is at epidemic levels, ten times that of the general population, and it is even higher among women prisoners. Co-infection with Hepatitis C is also high. Hepatitis C is common: 40% of male prisoners, even higher for women. Women in prison are also at risk for other infectious diseases, including tuberculosis, STDs, and Hepatitis B. Both risky behavior prior to arrest and inadequate prison health care contribute to this problem.

In 1995, women at the Central California Women's Facility (CCWF) filed a federal class action suit, *Shumate et al v. Wilson.* This lawsuit charged that the prison's deficient medical care for chronically and terminally ill women caused needless pain and suffering in their lives. It alleged that the California Department of Corrections (CDC) lacked basic standardized systems for the delivery of health care so that women with chronic health problems experienced disruptions in their treatment and chaotic follow-up, if any.

The lawsuit describes case after case of shocking treatment or non-treatment: A seizure patient, paralyzed on her left side, was never given occupational or physical therapy. A woman who had suffered burns over 54% of her body gradually lost mobility because she was denied the special bandages that would have prevented her burned skin from tightening. A woman died of untreated pancreatitis that went undiagnosed until she was terminally ill. Many women with serious high-risk factors for breast and cervical cancer were denied necessary mammograms and pap smears. HIV-positive women have been denied necessary specialized treatment, pain medications, and hospice care.

The lawsuit was settled in favor of the women plaintiffs in August 1997, but medical care problems still exist. Here are some examples:

- MTAs: There have been numerous reports of critically ill women being refused treatment by MTAs and several women have died within hours of that refusal.
- Sick Call: Sick call hours are often cancelled so sick women cannot access a doctor or nurse when needed. Women are often forced to stand outside for long periods of time, regardless of the weather or their medical condition, to access sick call.
- Preventive Care: There is still no systematic plan for regular pap smears or mammograms.
- Medication Delays: Women seeking medical assistance for tumors or chronic pain experience delays at every step of the pro-

cess. Women whose medical conditions require that they receive regular medications for HIV, seizures, diabetes, MS, arthritis, or high blood pressure frequently have their medications disrupted for days at a time because it takes so long to refill prescriptions. This can cause a manageable condition to become critical–creating unnecessary suffering as well as unnecessary expenses for the CDC as women must be transported to an outside emergency room. With HIV, interruptions in protease inhibitors can render the medication ineffective.

- Med Line: Women must wait in line outside two or three times a day, regardless of weather or their medical condition, to obtain medications. It can be very hot or very cold, and the wait can be as long as two or three hours.
- Post-Surgical Follow-Up: Follow-up is extremely limited. Bandages are frequently not changed because MTAs insist that must be done by outside hospital staff but then do not authorize outside appointments.
- Pre-Natal Care: Pregnant women rarely receive prenatal care. In some cases, prison staff have ignored obvious danger signs (high blood pressure, no fetal heartbeat, vaginal bleeding). This has led to late-term miscarriages, premature deliveries, still births, sick infants. Also, pregnant women are shackled for transport to outside hospital and are sometimes shackled during the birthing process itself.

The situation is similar in other states. Amnesty International reports that a pregnant woman in an Arizona jail asked for help when she began bleeding, but received no help. Eventually she lost consciousness and was then rushed to the hospital, but her baby died (AI, 1998). According to AI, deficiencies in medical care in jails and prisons around the country include: "lack of screening for tuberculosis and other communicable diseases in overcrowded and unsanitary jails; too few medical and psychiatric staff; failure to refer seriously ill inmates for treatment; delays in treatment or failure to deliver life-saving drugs; inadequate conditions for prisoners with HIV/AIDS; lack of access to gynecological and obstetric services; and grossly deficient treatment for the mentally ill" (AI, 1998). AI also states that many states have begun to charge prisoners for medical treatment, which is in direct violation of international standards that medical care for prisoners should be free.

In addition to the conflict of interest when guards also serve as gatekeepers to medical care, there are grave concerns about the competency of many prison doctors. In California, reports found that in one prison, half of the doctors either have a criminal record, mental health problems, or have lost the right to practice medicine in a hospital (Martin, 2004a). Other findings in two reports from three independent medical experts state that the system is "rife with unqualified doctors working in poor conditions." Examples include: an obstetrician treating HIV patients; no examining tables; doctors who examine prisoners in their cells, touching them only through a food port in the door which measures 1/4 inch by 12 inch; prisoners' requests to see a doctor going unreviewed for months; and a neurosurgeon treating patients for internal medicine problems, even though he has no experience in the field (Martin, 2004a).

Generally, in the outside world, health services are guaranteed to meet a certain minimum standard through accreditation. But none of California's prisons is accredited by a national body with expertise in prison health care (Stoller, 2001, p. 9). In the wake of a prisoner who starved himself to death and died at only 80 pounds, California lawmakers called for more oversight of the CDC's health care system. One lawmaker stated, "right now we have a system with extraordinary costs, extraordinary liability, and very poor care" (Martin, 2004b).

In May 2005, federal judge Thelton Henderson threatened to put California's prison health care system into federal receivership, noting that the system was in a "blatant state of crisis" (Chris, 2005b). After weeks of hearings, Judge Henderson did put the health care system into federal receivership, stating that this measure was necessary to prevent unnecessary prisoner deaths. A "federal injunction has been in place for three years requiring phased-in medical improvements at each state prison, but the corrections department has met none of the goals" (Sterngold, 2005; Chris, 2005a). Judge Henderson also declared that medical care in California's prisons violated every American's constitutional right against cruel and unusual punishment. He called the conditions "barbaric."

According to the *San Francisco Chronicle*, "[Judge Henderson] estimated that a prisoner needlessly dies an average of roughly once a week," as a result of incompetence and outright depravity in the rendering of medical care' to them. He said the prison system had no 'effective management structure' to deliver adequate health care to prisoners. Henderson wasn't describing conditions in Abu Ghraib or Guantanamo Bay, but in prisons right here in California" (*SF Chronicle*, 2005).

The appointment of a receiver in the context of prison litigation is extremely rare, and is unprecedented in a system as large as California's prison health care system. The system serves more than 163,000 prisoners, employs 6,000 workers, and its budget is $1.1 billion (*Science Daily*, 2005). A receivership creates a relationship roughly comparable to one between a bankruptcy judge and a billion-dollar corporation drowning in debt (Cooper, 2005).

Mental Health Care in Prison

According to Human Rights Watch, one in six U.S. prisoners is mentally ill. Their illnesses include schizophrenia, bipolar disorder, and severe depression. The number of mentally ill people in prisons is three times as many as in mental hospitals. In fact, according to Jamie Fellner, director of Human Rights Watch's U.S. Program, "Prisons have become the nation's primary mental health facilities." This is the result of government closures of mental hospitals across the country combined with a failure to provide any other place for the mentally ill to obtain services (Fellner, 2003; HRW, 2003). Many of our mentally ill are left untreated on the streets and might not have committed crimes if they had had help.

As sentences become longer and laws often mandate incarceration even for relatively minor crimes, men and women with severe mental problems end up in prison. Once in prison, they are under-treated or not treated at all, and are frequently punished for acting out. Prison is a toxic environment for the mentally ill who find it difficult, often impossible, to comply with many prison rules and are disciplined for their inability to comply. Generally prison guards are not trained to recognize mental illness and often do not recognize it when an incident occurs.

Prisoners who break rules are punished, mentally ill or not. When mentally ill prisoners mutilate themselves or attempt suicide, they are punished. If they continue to break the rules, they are locked up for long periods of time in special units of high-security solitary confinement, such as administrative segregation (solitary confinement) or supermax prisons. Prisoners in these units live in isolation, with nothing to do and little exercise. Many prisoners in these units are already mentally ill, and lengthy terms of solitary confinement cause many to worsen and deteriorate into psychosis.

When professor and psychologist Craig Haney described his visits to supermax prisons in Texas, his reports resembled the horrific descriptions of madhouses from centuries past. Probably this country's leading expert on the psychology of incarceration, Dr. Haney testified in a 1999 Texas courtroom:

There were many people who were incoherent when I attempted to talk to them, babbling, sometimes shrieking, other people who appeared to be full of fury and anger and rage and were, in some instances, banging their hands on the side of the wall and yelling and screaming, other people who appeared to be simply disheveled, withdrawn and out of contact with the circumstances or surroundings. Some of them would be huddled in the back corner of the cell and appeared incommunicative when I attempted to speak with them . . . these were people who appeared to be in profound states of distress and pain. (*Ruiz v. Johnson*)

According to Dr. Haney, the guards said this was not unusual.

As the number of women in prison has been steadily rising, so too has the number of mentally ill women who are entering the prison system. According to the Bureau of Justice Statistics, among women prisoners nationwide, 22% of Hispanics, 20% of blacks, and 29% of whites were identified as mentally ill (BJS, 1999). At the state level, the percentage varies from 26% in New York to 49% in Oregon (BJS, 1999, p. 3).

Mental illness rates are particularly high for women prisoners because a large percentage of women prisoners have a history of physical, emotional, and/or sexual abuse. Anther factor in the disproportionately high rate of mental illness in female prisoners is their higher rate of substance abuse and addiction.

Women live with the difficulties and stresses of prison life that all prisoners face, and separation from their children is a factor especially stressful to women in prison. The majority of women prisoners have dependent children; some estimates place the number as high as 80%. Since the vast majority of prisons are in rural areas, far from prisoners' families, the separation from their children is extremely difficult for women in prison.

Another prison stressor which particularly affects women's mental health is sexual abuse by the guards. This is not an uncommon occurrence. Also, women's prisons often do not have as many programs (educational, vocational, etc.) as men's prisons.

Medication is the primary form of mental health treatment in prison, yet prisoners report having to wait long periods of time to see a psychiatrist and having great trouble getting their medications refilled. Prisoners also report such things as "putting in a slip" for suicidal thoughts and then not being seen for three weeks after that (HRW, 2003, p. 4). In one incident, after a woman had mutilated herself with a sharp pencil, the guard's response was "that's dumb"; she did not receive any help or therapy (HRW, 2003, p. 4).

Sexual Abuse in Prison

> That was not part of my sentence . . . to perform oral sex with the officer.

> –NY prisoner Tanya Ross, 1998 (AI, 1999, p. 1)

From a report by Professor Nancy Stoller, Improving Access to Health Care for California Women Prisoners:

> Summary of File 1194: Leia Prince's file contains a letter describing a pap smear and pelvic exam performed by Dr. _____ during which he inflicted undue pain and made sexual comments. Her letter suggests that the doctor continued to insert his fingers even while she complained and finally screamed. She reports bleeding for 18 hours after the exam. Having recently undergone surgery for cervical cancer, Ms. Prince had begun the healing process. The exam completely undid this healing. This letter is clear, concise, and convincing. (Stoller, 2001, p. 64)

From HRW interview with Uma M: a guard who had been harassing her entered her cell while she was alone:

> I felt fear real quick. I knew something was wrong and I didn't want to look. [Officer G] pulled the blanket. I sat up and tugged at the blanket. The other guard had the garbage can in the door and then the whole blanket came off. . . . He just tore my whole shirt. That's when he assaulted me sexually. . . . I was screaming, yelling and crying. Martha across the hall was banging on her window. While he was still in the room, I went into the shower. I felt dirty. (HRW, 1996, p. 73)

The U.S. Justice Department sued Michigan and Arizona in 1997 for failing to protect women prisoners from sexual assaults and "prurient viewing during dressing, showering, and use of toilet facilities" by male guards (AI, 1998, p. 2). In 1998, three women who reached a settlement with the Federal Bureau of Prisons were paid $500,000 for having been beaten, raped, and sold for sex with male prisoners at another prison. AI continues to report cases of sexual abuse of women prisoners by male guards. Their chronicle of abuses is shocking and extensive.

The U.S. practice of male staff having unsupervised access to incarcerated women violates international standards, such as the U.N. Standard Minimum Rules for the Treatment of Prisoners. Rule 53 states that no male staff member "shall enter the part of the institution set aside for women unless accompanied by a female officer" and "women prisoners shall be attended and supervised only by female officers."

According to international human rights standards regarding prisoners, the one exception to equal employment requirements is hiring male staff in women's prisons. Male officers should be prohibited from working in the housing units of women's prisons.

In the U.S., the majority of guards are male, according to AI (AI, 2000). Those working in the women's housing unit have plenty of temptation and opportunity not only to rape women, but also to humiliate them by watching as they shower or use toilet facilities. Degrading sexual comments by male guards are common. Women are frequently called bitches, sluts, and whores. Some guards treat them all as if they were prostitutes. A male officer was heard telling a young woman that he would "take care of her" and asked her whether "she likes a big chorizo [sausage]" (HRW, 1996, p. 73).

In some prisons, tampons, sanitary pads, and toilet paper are doled out only upon request. This practice is clearly both humiliating to the women and unnecessary for security. Sometimes male guards will refuse to dispense feminine hygiene products, laughingly saying things like, "Use toilet paper" or "Use your shirt."

Male officers guarding women's housing units, along with ineffectual grievance procedures, create a prison environment that tolerates and fosters sexually abusive behavior. Sometimes guards lure women prisoners into sexual relations in exchange for certain privileges or goods otherwise not available to the women. When such "barter-type" relationships are discovered, the male officer often claims that the sex was consensual, but because of the power imbalance, such a relationship cannot be consensual in any way. Although many states now have laws defining such sex as statutory, where consent is irrelevant, some states still do not. Some women are so accustomed to unequal and abusive relationships in their lives, as well as bartering for sex, that the situation seems normal to them, and they accept it as a condition of their imprisonment (HRW, 1996, p. 76).

Rape of prisoners by guards is considered torture according to the Torture Convention. International standards also prohibit "cruel, inhuman or degrading treatment" (United Nations, 1976, ICCPR), including sexual assault and the use of sex for barter. Verbal harassment can also constitute degrading treatment because it causes humiliation and suffering.

The lack of privacy also violates international standards. Article 17 of the ICCPR states, "No one shall be subjected to arbitrary or unlawful interference with his privacy" (United Nations, 1976). A major problem in addressing such concerns is that prisoners are often afraid to complain because they are frequently retaliated against for complaining. Sometimes a woman does not even know that there is a procedure for complaints or how to access it.

International law requires governments to ensure that abuses can be reported and investigated without fear of retaliation. Although there are procedures in place for such reporting and investigation, in practice they are ineffective. First of all, the procedure is difficult for prisoners to access because many women do not know there is a procedure or how to utilize it. In addition, the officers themselves are frequently disrespectful of the procedure, sometimes even throwing the complaint away and taunting the prisoners. (The officer may or may not be the officer about whom the prisoner is complaining.)

Some states, such as California and Michigan, require that the prisoner speak with the perpetrator informally before filing a formal complaint. Such a requirement has an intimidating effect on prisoners. And there is frequently a bias against the women prisoners, whereby prison officials do not believe them and tell them so at the investigation, often taunting them (HRW, 1996, p. 91).

There is also a lack of confidentiality, adding to the intimidation and fear of reprisal. After its investigation of prisons in Michigan, the U.S. Justice Department stated, "Many sexual relations appear to be unreported due to the widespread fear of retaliation and vulnerability felt by these women" (AI, 1998, p. 2).

What can be done about such abuses? Some states do not currently have legislation that calls for the punishment of guards for such sexual misconduct, and citizens in those states must urge their legislatures to pass such laws. Citizens should also call for the U.S. Department of Justice to maintain a secure, confidential, free hotline where prisoners can report such abuses. And it would be helpful to establish a national database of all guards and former guards who have records of such sexual misconduct, so they could no longer merely go to another prison to work.

CONCLUSION

Although the United States was one of the primary founders of international human rights in 1948, we have a long way to go in applying these standards domestically. We call on other countries to follow international law and treaties, but we fail to do so ourselves.

It is clear that the United States has failed to live up to its promise in this regard, particularly with regard to prisoners. Women prisoners lack adequate health care, including mental health care, and are often victims of sexual abuse by the guards. Since the U.S. wants to hold other countries to certain standards, we would do well to look to our own house.

American therapists, lawyers, and people of conscience must educate themselves and others about what really goes on in domestic prisons and advocate for justice, for humane and respectful treatment. Therapists, in particular, may want to work in jails and prisons and advocate for better mental health care. At the very least, therapists would do well to gain a better understanding of clients who have been incarcerated or who have incarcerated family members.

Whidney Brown of Human Rights Watch said, "A true measure of a country's commitment to human rights is its willingness to defend the human rights of its most disempowered people" (Pollard, 1998).

Abbreviations

AI: Amnesty International
CCWF: Central California Women's Facility
CDC: California Department of Correctionis
CEDAW: Convention on the Elimination of All Forms of Discrimination Against Women, 1980
CERD: International Convention on the Elimination of All Forms of Racial Discrimination, 1994
ECOSOC: International Covenant on Economic, Social and Cultural Rights, 1994
HRW: Human Rights Watch
ICCPR: International Covenant on Civil and Political Rights, 1992
MTA: Medical Technical Assistant
Torture Convention: Convention Against Torture and Other Cruel, Inhuman or Degrading Treatment or Punishment, 1994

NOTES

1. Article 7: No one shall be subjected to torture or to cruel, inhuman or degrading treatment or punishment. In particular, no one shall be subjected without his free consent to medical or scientific experimentation.

2. Article 17: 1. No one shall be subjected to arbitrary or unlawful interference with his privacy, family, home or correspondence, nor to unlawful attacks on his honour and reputation.

2. Everyone has the right to the protection of the law against such interference or attacks.

REFERENCES

AI (Amnesty International). (1998). Rights for all. Chapter 4.

AI. (1999). *"Not part of my sentence": Violations of the human rights of women in custody*. Amnesty International U.S. Report.

AI. (2000). *Amnesty International calls for restriction of the role of male guards in female facilities*. Amnesty International Report, August 9, 2000. http://web.amnesty. org/library/index/ENGAMR511242000

BJS (Bureau of Justice Statistics). (1999). *Mental health and treatment of inmates and probationers*. Bureau of Justice.

Chris, T. (2005a). CA prison health care system will be placed in receivership. *Talk Left*, 7/1/05. http://talkleft.com/new_archives/011299.html

Chris, T. (2005b). "Judge may put CA Health Care system will be placed in receivership." *Talk Left*, 5/22/05. http://talkleft.com/new_archives/010795.html#010795

Cooper, C. (2005). Prison health care seized. *Sacramento Bee*, July 1, 2005. http:// www.psych-health.com/cdc13.htm

Fellner, J. (2003). *United States: Mentally ill mistreated in prison*. Human Rights Watch, http://www.hrw.org

Ford, P. (2002). US finds strange bedfellows in UN vote on torture. *Christian Science Monitor*, April 19, 2002

HRW (Human Rights Watch). (1996). *All too familiar: Sexual abuse of women in U.S. prisons*. Human Rights Watch, http://www.hrw.org

HRW. (2003). *Ill-Equipped: U.S. Prisons and Offenders with Mental Illness*. New York: Human Rights Watch.

Martin, M. (2004a). Reports show poor medical care in state's prisons: Incompetent doctors called systemwide problem. *San Francisco Chronicle*, August 11, 2004.

Martin, M. (2004b). Scathing report on health care still not out: Agency suggests negligence in deaths at Corcoran facility. *San Francisco Chronicle*, February 26, 2004.

Mungoven, R. (2002). US loses battle against UN anti-torture treaty. *November 8, 2002, Agence France Presse*. http://www.commondreams.org/ headlines02/1108-01.htm

Peet, P. (2000). US torture. *Disinformatioon*, October 18, 2000. http://www. disinfo.com/archive/pages/dossier/id363/pg1/

Pollard, C. (1998). Watchdogs set their sights on the United States. *Slant: The Magazine of Columbia University's School of International and Public Affairs*, Fall 1998. http://www.columbia.edu/cu/sipa/PUBS/SLANT/FALL98/p6.html

Ruiz v. Johnson, 37 F.Supp.2d 855.

San Francisco Chronicle. (2005). Editorial: Death in state prisons. July 4, 2005. http://www.sfgate.com/cgi-bin/article.cgi?f=/c/a/2005/07/04/EDGD4DHTVG1.DTL& hw=thelton+henderson&sn=003&sc=392

Science Daily. (2005). US takes over California prison health care. July 1, 2005. http://www.sfgate.com/cgi-bin/article.cgi?f=/c/a/2005/07/04/EDGD4DHTVG1. DTL&hw=thelton+henderson&sn=003&sc=392

Sterngold, J. (2005). Judge orders takeover of state's prison health care system. *San Francisco Chronicle*, June 30, 2005. http://www.sfgate.com/cgi-bin/article.cgi?f=/ c/a/2005/07/01/MNGOCDHPP71.DTL&hw=thelton+henderson&sn=001&sc=1000

Stoller, N. (2001). *Improving access to health care for California women prisoners.* Submitted to California Policy Research Center, University of California, January 2001.

United Nations (1994). *International Covenant on Economic, Social and Cultural Rights* (ECOSOC). http://www.hrweb.org/legal/escr.html

United Nations. (1977) *Standard Minimum Rules for the Treatment of Prisoners.* http://www.unhchr.ch/html/menu3/b/h_comp34.htm

United Nations. (1976) International Covenant on Civil and Political Rights. http:// www.unhchr.ch/html/menu3/b/a_ccpr.htm

doi:10.1300/J015v29n03_04

Un-Domesticating Violence:
Criminalizing Survivors
and U.S. Mass Incarceration

Kolleen Duley

SUMMARY. This paper attempts to look at the ways in which women's struggles against domestic violence are criminalized and also how this type of racialized, classed, and gendered violence is connected to processes that fuel prison expansion–including the U.S-led war on drugs, the criminalization of immigration, the rampant policing in communities of color, and the reliance on the police and the criminal legal system to address domestic violence. It is my intent to place domestic violence and its connection to criminalization in a politicized context for two reasons: the first is to repudiate the tendency to look at women's response to abuse as individualized or unconnected to other types of marginalization and the second is to provide a more complex analysis of how women's differing social identities or positionalities, as women of color or immigrant women for example, may affect their experiences of both state and interpersonal violence. doi:10.1300/J015v29n03_05 *[Article copies available for a fee from The Haworth Document Delivery Service: 1-800-HAWORTH.*

Kolleen Duley is a Women's Studies PhD candidate, University of California, Los Angeles and a Steering Committee Member of Free Battered Women.

Address correspondence to: Kolleen Duley, UCLA Women's Studies Programs, 2225 Rolfe Hall, Box 951504, Los Angeles, CA 90095-1504 (E-mail: kduley@ucla.edu).

[Haworth co-indexing entry note]: "Un-Domesticating Violence: Criminalizing Survivors and U.S. Mass Incarceration." Duley, Kolleen. Co-published simultaneously in *Women & Therapy* (The Haworth Press, Inc.) Vol. 29, No. 3/4, 2006, pp. 75-96; and: *Inside and Out: Women, Prison, and Therapy* (ed: Elaine Leeder) The Haworth Press, Inc., 2006, pp. 75-96. Single or multiple copies of this article are available for a fee from The Haworth Document Delivery Service [1-800-HAWORTH, 9:00 a.m. - 5:00 p.m. (EST). E-mail address: docdelivery@haworthpress.com].

KEYWORDS. Prison industrial complex, prison, prison system, criminal legal system, policing, law enforcement, state violence, criminalization, board of prison terms, board of parole hearings, sentencing, crime, justice, incarceration, domestic violence, incarcerated survivors, incarcerated survivors of domestic violence, survivors of domestic violence, violence against women, self-defense, the war on drugs, trafficking, communities of color, Latina, African American women, Black women, women of color, white privilege, white supremacy, race, immigration, globalization, capitalism, race, gender, class, women's studies, social justice, social change, free battered women, habeas project, transnational feminism

A woman is forced to have sex with an abusive partner's friend. A woman is forced to commit sexual acts in front of her children. A woman begs for mercy while being beaten with the scorching metal face of a hot iron. These women were once considered to be victims, but many of them are now criminalized and in state prison, victimized once again by the U.S. criminal legal system. But what outrages me even more than this unjust incarceration is the fact that the social disorders that contribute to their victimization are being largely ignored. There is a great need to articulate the way in which interpersonal violence in the home urges victims to desperately attempt relief, including breaking laws for survival, but it is also important to look at how this type of violence is connected to other geopolitical processes such as those contributing to mass incarceration and neoliberal globalization.

This paper attempts to look at the ways in which women's struggles against domestic violence are criminalized and also how this type of racialized, classed, and gendered violence is connected to processes that fuel prison expansion–including the U.S.-led war on drugs, the criminalization of immigration, the rampant policing in communities of color, and the reliance on the police and the criminal legal system to address domestic violence. It is my intent to place domestic violence and its connection to criminalization in a politicized context for two reasons: the first is to repudiate the tendency to look at women's responses to abuse as individualized or unconnected to other types of marginalization and the second is to provide a more complex analysis of how women's differing social identities or positionalities, as women of color or immigrant women, for example, may affect their experiences of both state and interpersonal violence.[1]

VIOLENCE AGAINST WOMEN
IN A TRANSNATIONAL FEMINIST CONTEXT

Labeling women's history of being abused as the "root" cause of their imprisonment individualizes and pathologizes their experiences while it also obscures the more complex "roots" of their incarceration. Situating domestic violence in a political context encourages the de-individualization of women's experiences and allows us to see how this type of violence is connected to other systems of disadvantage and marginalization. For example, women's experiences with abuse are not isolated incidents of gender violence but can be seen as related to other social maladies, such as institutionalized racism, that contribute to cultural and systematic violence against women in the U.S. This expanded definition of violence against women includes the physical, emotional, and sexual abuse that the first anti-violence against women movement worked to make public. Yet, this expanded definition brings these horrific realities of systematic violence against women–where a woman is battered every 15 seconds and one in four women is raped by someone she knows–into conversation with the violence inflicted by living in a culture wrought with deeply entrenched class hierarchy, institutionalized racism, white supremacy, and mass incarceration. Thus, the systematic locking up of those labeled surplus to the global economy (Goldberg & Evans, 1999-2000, pp. 44-48)–women of color, youth, queer, transgender, and gender variant people and/or those from low-income communities–is brought into the forefront of movements that strive to end violence against women. Alternatively, by hiding the political conditions and socioeconomic processes under which marginalized people are accused of committing crimes, "offending" behavior is portrayed as unconnected to these processes and caused merely by individual failure. Equally as detrimental, this pathologizing and individualizing also hides the fact that the state ineffectually uses and posits policing and incarceration as the "solution" to domestic violence and to other types of physical and sexual abuse against women. Julia Sudbury, in the introduction to her groundbreaking edited volume, *Global Lockdown: Race, Gender and the Prison Industrial Complex*, comments on how the individualizing of domestic abuse obscures the "social disorder of mass imprisonment":

> Even where survival strategies—whether sex work, drug couriering, or welfare fraud—are recognized, they are stigmatized and homogenized by the label "offending behavior." Women's personal histories are then mined as rich sources for understanding this aberrant behavior, and childhood abuse, domestic violence, or familial dysfunction are presented as the root cause. Presenting women's experiences of abuse as the cause of incarceration individualizes and personalizes their treatment at the hands of the criminal justice system. It obscures the broader social disorder signified by mass incarceration, and it sidesteps the question of why the state responds to abused women with punishment. (Sudbury, 2005, p. xv)

To further situate domestic violence and its connection to criminalization in a larger political framework, it is important to provide a more complex analysis of the multiplicity and difference in women's experiences with interpersonal violence. Most of the earlier and much of the contemporary work on violence against women has focused solely on gender violence and has neglected to discuss how other factors in women's lives may change their experiences with violence. For instance, very little research has been done on violence against women involved in illegal activity, and until recently, there has been little research on how violence affects women of color, immigrant women, or poor women (Richie, 2003, p. 9). While discussing different analyses used in antiprison work, Beth Richie explains the impact of such "race-neutral" analysis in the article, "Queering Antiprison Work: African American Lesbians in the Juvenile Justice System":

> Feminist researchers and activists who subscribe to mainstream "race-neutral" analysis have firmly established the problems of gender violence as a problem of the abuse of power and patriarchal control of women by men. The advocacy and policy reform that result from this analysis rely heavily on the ability to establish a set of universal vulnerabilities that all women experience similarly. The rigor with which this perspective is argued leaves very little room for the consideration of difference based on race, class, age, sexuality identity, or involvement with illegal activity. (2005, p. 81)

In a different article published by Richie, she notes that although Bureau of Justice statistics (1996) conclude that the overall rate of domestic abuse against women of all races and ethnicities is the same, the way that abuse affects women may differ with compounding social positionalities.

> While the overall rates may be similar, emerging research suggests that variables such as socioeconomic status, cultural background, and age may influence the impact of domestic violence on different groups of women. Women who are black, young, divorced, earn low incomes, rent and live in urban areas are more likely to be victimized by intimates. Factors such as the limited availability of crisis intervention programs, differential use of weapons during an assault, and lack of trust of law enforcement agencies may heighten some women's vulnerability to intimate violence. (Richie, 2003, p. 8)

Further analysis into the complexities of women's race identity, community relations with police, interpersonal and state violence against women, and the community loyalties confronting battered Black women can be found in Compelled to Crime: the Entrapment of Battered Black Women (Richie, 1996).

While Richie's article in Global Lockdown invites scholars and antiprison activists to utilize a queer antiprison framework, this paper attempts to utilize a transnational feminist framework which is employed here as a perspective that sees the transnational flow of goods, capital, and bodies, as well as the hegemony of Western countries via neoliberal globalization and the U.S. incarceration and policing of poor communities of color, as "feminist issues." Using this approach, I hope to both make clear how the state criminalizes abused women and their resistance to violence and also connect interpersonal violence with the global processes that fuel prison expansion. This includes the U.S.-led war on drugs, the criminalization of immigration, rampant policing in poor communities of color, and the reliance on the criminal legal system as a solution for domestic violence.

INCARCERATING SURVIVORS OF VIOLENCE AND THE GLOBAL PROCESSES OF PRISON EXPANSION

This section focuses on how the state criminalizes women's resistance to abuse and how women's experiences with domestic violence have contributed to their incarceration. The first part of this section discusses some ways in which the circumstances of abuse or the threat of violence leads survivors into behavior criminalized by the state, including using violence to resist violence or to protect their children. The second part discusses the less publicized ways in which abuse leads women into criminalized actions, including the use of drugs and alcohol to self-medicate, while both sections attempt to connect these crimes to neoliberal globalization and the U.S. project of mass incarceration.

"Abuse," also known as battering, involves a "systematic pattern of using violence, the threat of violence, and other coercive behaviors to exert power, induce fear, and control others" (Bible, Das Dasgupta, & Osthoff, 2002, p. 1268). Battering is part of a web of social disorders, including poverty, racism, and gendered inequalities, that create cultural violence against women. Under this type of control and violence, survivors are sometimes forced by an abusive partner to commit a crime or are forced by circumstances related to abuse to commit or be involved in the commission of a crime.

> A number of scholars in the field [studying domestic violence] have identified fear induction as the primary mechanism through which violent partners achieve control. That is, victims are fearful of injury, death, or some other untoward consequence of the violence and strive to bring their behavior into compliance with the abuser's demands. (Hamberger & Guse, 2002, 1301)

This fear has also led women to be charged for "failure to protect" their children by the child welfare system or civil legal system. There have been countless incidents of women in abusive situations who have been convicted of crimes and sentenced to prison because of an abusive partner's violence against their children. One example, recently highlighted in *USA Today*, involves Linda Lee Smith, who is an incarcerated advocate for women prisoners through her work with the organization I also work with, Free Battered Women, a California-based group fighting to end the re-victimization of incarcerated survivors of domestic violence. Linda Lee Smith has served 24 years on a sentence of 15-years-to-life for not stopping her abusive partner from fatally beating her daughter, Amy. The prosecution argued that by not aggressively intervening, she condoned the violence. Although Linda's other daughter, Bethany McDermott, testified that at the time Linda had been battered and sexually tortured for months by her boyfriend, still Governor Arnold Schwarzenegger reversed the Board of Prison Terms[2] decision to grant her a release date. The governor justified his decision by saying that Linda still poses "an unreasonable threat to public safety" (Sharpe, 2005, B8). Although Linda has served 11 years more than her minimum 15-to-life sentence, with no prior convictions, this is the sixth consecutive year that Linda was denied freedom. Both the parole board and the governor's office are major barriers to release for those with life sentences. It is uncommon for someone serving a life sentence to be granted parole by the board, even if they do not have prior convictions, as can be seen in Linda's case. In California in 2004, for example, only 199 people with life sentences were granted parole out of the 2,713 who had parole suitability hearings ("The Longest Wait: A Second Chance for Lifers," 2005). Even for those who are granted parole under these formidable odds, their dates are often reversed by the Governor and it is an extremely painful process of both hope and despair. In a poem written for Free Battered Women's annual event, "Our Voices Within," planned with and for survivors inside, imprisoned survivor Brenda Clubine wrote about her distrust of the Board of Prison Terms (now the Board of Parole Hearings):

> The Board of Prison Terms,
> they say is impartial,
> this must be a joke,
> they are ex-police, D.A.'s,
> Sheriffs and Marshals. (2003)

Brenda has been denied parole by the Board of Prison Terms six times since serving more than 20 years on a sentence of 15-to-life (Clubine, 2003). It is through meeting with survivors like Brenda and reading the testimony of other women that it becomes clear how often abused women are re-victimized by the violence of state imprisonment. Why are there so few options for survivors that the only end to violence is a decades-long prison sentence? Karen Narita, who also works with Free Battered Women, is another example of a survivor sentenced for a crime related to domestic violence that she did not commit. Karen has served 20 years on a 15-to-life sentence for being present at the time her abusive husband killed a drug associate (Bible, 2005). Karen was "present" at the time of this horrific incident because her abusive partner ordered her to be there. Similarly, after receiving a brutal beating and witnessing the near fatal beating of her son, another incarcerated survivor, who wishes to remain anonymous, was told by her abuser that she was only allowed to bring her unconscious two-year-old to the hospital if she took the blame for committing the abuse. In exchange for saving her son's life, she was handed a prison sentence of 20 years-to-life for her partner's violence. If she had not saved her son's life, she may have been held responsible for his death as well as charged with neglect and had her remaining children taken by the child welfare system. Increasingly, it is women of color who are more likely than white women under the same circumstances to have their children taken away. An example of this is found in Patricia Eng's summary of Shamita Das Dasgupta's meeting report for Ms. Foundation for Women, where she notes that in New York City, African American children are twice as likely as white children to be taken away from their parents following a confirmed report of abuse or neglect, ultimately putting poor children and children of color on the "fast track" of institutional life (2003, p. 14).

Survivors are also incarcerated for using violence to defend themselves against their abusers in what many women describe as "their final attempt to save their own lives."

> When my husband impregnated our 12-year-old daughter, the children and I could stand no more. I was frantic, and this atrocity, after years of unrelenting torment, drove me to make a terrible mistake. I offer no excuses for that mistake, and I live with the guilt every day. I do believe, however, that I have paid for it, not only with 24 years in prison, but with blood, broken bones, and the pain and fear that never leave me. What my children suffered and still endure is far beyond evaluation. (Anonymous, 2005)

Often as a last resort and after being doused with gasoline and set on fire, beaten with baseball bats, shot with rifles, stabbed, locked in closets, and/or anally raped with household objects, some women defend themselves and their children from the violence that has plagued their lives for years. Almost every survivor we work with at Free Battered Women feared for her life during her marriage or partnership and believed that the only way out was going to be her own murder at the hands of her abuser. Maria Marquez explains, "One day the abuse escalated to the point that I believed in my heart that there was no way out and I could be killed" (Marquez, in Free Battered Women). When women take the life of their intimate partners, it is usually in self-defense. "Of 223 reviewed appellate opinions of battered women's homicide cases, 75% involved confrontations, [meaning the woman was being assaulted or abused at the time of the killing]" (Maguigan, 1991,

p. 397). Many of these women see this resistance as their last grasp for survival.

There are also countless women charged with conspiracy when they finally broke the silence about their abuse and a friend or family member took it upon him or herself to save her life. Caroline Anderson, who is now 62 years old and served 22 years on a 25-years-to-life sentence before being released on parole in January 2005, confided to Free Battered Women about what happened to her:

> During the 23-year marriage, I alternated between fear for my life, my children's, our various pets, my family, and even my husband's due to his temper and demonstrations of violence and threats. It was a daily struggle of just surviving, sometimes wishing I could just die or disappear, and yes, even wishing he would so the torment would be over. I made the horrible mistake of expressing these emotions to his nephew, who ended up taking his life. The only people allowed to "come around" were his friends and family, so I had no one else to talk to or turn to. (Anderson)

Caroline's story is not just one individual story of misfortune–there are hundreds more. The story of Maria Suarez, a survivor also convicted of conspiracy, helps draw the connections between systemic violence against women, U.S. incarceration, immigration, and practices of Western neoliberal globalization. Maria was forced to leave her home in Mexico in search of financial security. Although Western news media and multinational corporations promote ideologies that label the poverty of the global South as each country's own isolated failure or inability to participate in the "global market," many of these countries' economic crises are connected to Western economic foreign policies and practices of "democratization" and "redevelopment." Maria's migration and the migration of thousands of others from Mexico and Central and South America in to the U.S. each year are also connected to these policies. Julia Sudbury elaborates with one example:

> Neoliberal globalization has been a major driving force in instigating the mass migration of poor women and men from the global South. As the North American Free Trade Agreement (NAFTA) [initiated by the U.S.] and the European Union eliminated tariffs for importation of foreign products, domestic markets in the global South collapsed, throwing workers into destitution and desperation. For example, in Mexico, agricultural produce is now imported

from [subsidized] U.S. farmers, leading to mass unemployment and migration from agricultural areas such as Chiapas and Oaxaca. (Sudbury, 2005, p. xviii)

This type of necessary migration is then countered by increased policing on the U.S.-Mexico border, where military-type enforcement strategies are used and thousands of immigrants are detained in U.S. prisons and detention centers after their attempts to cross the border.[3] It was under these desperate and globalization-imposed financial circumstances that Maria Suarez legally crossed into the U.S. at the age of 16. Maria took the first "job" offered to her where she was ultimately sold for $200 into sexual bondage to a 68-year-old man.[4] Maria was raped and beaten for five years, unable to call the police or go to a shelter due to language barriers, until a neighbor finally took the life of her abuser. After 22 years in a U.S. state prison for 1st degree conspiracy for a crime she did not commit, Maria was held in an immigration detention facility before finally securing a temporary visa that allows her to remain in the U.S. while she challenges her unjust conviction and her pending deportation to Mexico. Maria's two-decades long incarceration–costing U.S. tax payers over half a million dollars–followed by her detention and pending deportation further demonstrates how her social location as a non-U.S. citizen, and her forced migration and experience with illegal economies, interpersonal violence, and incarceration connect to the projects of neoliberal globalization. The bodies of immigrants are used for labor when it is profitable for the expansion of globalized capitalism. When these bodies are considered "expendable," like Maria's after her "involvement" in the death of her abuser, billions of dollars are spent in detainment–money that could be directed towards social services and basic human rights for disadvantaged communities and that may help people like Maria avoid dangerous situations.

This type of Western globalization allows for the transnational flow of goods and capital as it interests multinational corporations, military, or wealthy elites, but keeps people, especially non-economically privileged people, women of color, and people of the global South, under tight surveillance. Kamala Kempadoo's article, "Victims and Agents of Crime: The New Crusade Against Trafficking," adds critical insight to the relations between the migration of women from the global South and underground economies of survival, including those that utilize sexualized energies (2005). This transnational feminist perspective "takes up trafficking as both a discourse and practice that emerges from the intersections of state, capitalist, patriarchal, and racialized relations of power with the operation of women's agency and desire to shape their own lives and strategies for survival and livelihood" (Kempadoo, 2005, p. 37). Kempadoo's work demonstrates how Maria's positionality quickly changed from being a self-identified agent making a decision under the constraints of the global economy to migrate in search of financial security, into a victim of abuse and forced sexual labor after migration, until finally she was determined to be an "illegal immigrant offender" by persistent racist ideology and U.S. immigration policy. Kempadoo argues that discourses on trafficking, including U.S. legislation and U.N. frameworks, are embedded in the control of migrant labor and linked to both the "criminalization of migrant women from the global South and greater policing and control of their mobility, bodies, and sexuality" (2005, p. 35). Since Maria Suarez was labeled as an offender instead of a victim, she, like most migrant people who move in search of social and financial security, was expected to immediately return–or be deported–to her country of origin. Knowing that they will face the same remnants of globalized capitalism and economic hardship upon return, many opt to stay "illegally," adding to the number of women of color detained within the confines of the criminal legal system. Further deepening the cycle, men from the global South are criminalized as agents assisting in the transportation of workers, while the corporations who employ undocumented labor and the militaries, business men, and elite who are the consumers of sexualized labor remain hidden in the shadows (Kempadoo, 2005, p. 43). Instead, it is the "illegals" of the global South, men characterized as "immoral" and "greedy" and women like Maria who are said to "drain resources and have babies" who are labeled as the "[immigrant] problem" and engulfed by the revolving door of forced migration, increased policing, detention, incarceration, deportation, and then back into migration for survival.

In keeping with the above transnational feminist practice of exposing the connections between political processes, such as globalization, immigration, and violence against women, this section will discuss less publicized connections between domestic violence and incarceration. Although women's use of violence and the violence that leads to the death of an abusive partner are more frequently discussed in the mainstream media and the general public, there are many other ways that domestic violence, as part of systemic violence against women, is connected to the U.S. web of policing, law enforcement, and incarceration. Survivors of battering are incarcerated for a range of crimes, beyond defending themselves against abusive partners, including crimes for which low-income communities of color and immigrants are targeted.

> Many battered women are in prison after being coerced into committing crimes by their abusive partners (i.e., homicides, robberies, forging checks, drug-related crimes). Others are incarcerated after using illegal means to survive or cope with the experience of battering (i.e., property/economic crimes, and using alcohol or drugs to self-medicate). Battered women may also be convicted of failing to protect their children from the abuser's violence or parental kidnapping. (Gilfus, 2002, pp. 4-5)

People in communities targeted by police violence and hit by high rates of incarceration, unemployment, and drug abuse are sometimes forced to commit crimes under the threat of violence, coercion, and out of desperation. Often born out of similarly desperate situations, survivors are sometimes incarcerated for drug-related crimes where they either use drugs to cope with the constant sexual, physical, and emotional abuse, or they may be forced to use, sell, or transport drugs by an abusive partner. Since physical and sexual abuse have been shown to be significantly correlated with substance abuse, it is not surprising how often survivors, including girls and young teenagers, turn to drugs and alcohol to deal with their pain (as cited in McCampbell, 2005, pp. 3-4). Survivors of battering may also be a part of communities where drug use and sales are common ways to cope with the loss of other basic human rights, like access to employment, health care, job security, free time, and adequately funded schools (where schools have books, healthy lunches, sanitary bathrooms, safe playgrounds, and after school programs). These economic and drug related non-violent crimes make up the convictions of most women prisoners (as cited in McCampbell, 2005, p. 3). Beth Richie also draws these connections while talking to women at the Cook County Jail in Chicago who live at the crux of multiple systems of disadvantage:

> The findings from the interviews showed a clear pattern of the women facing a life every day that was characterized by emotional, social, and economic crises and very limited material support. They described how "out of control" they felt, how much their trust of social institutions had deteriorated and how limited their network of family and friends were; a classic portrayal of socially disorganized communities where poverty has eroded indi-

viduals' opportunity and neighborhood structure
showed how approximately half of the women into
study engaged in illegal activity as a response to these
as ways to secure resources, to avoid further deterioration,
maintain their families. (Richie, 2003, p. 33)

If a survivor is not an agent at an intersection of disadvantage, that is, she has white privilege, U.S. citizenship, or is wealthy, etc., it is important to note how these privileges connect to the systems of disadvantage that locate her as a survivor of domestic violence and also place others as "more likely to go to jail than to college." The "War on Drugs" has been a powerful weapon that ensures gross disparity in the distribution of wealth and also fills prisons as part of the U.S. mass incarceration agenda. This "war," which is bolstered by heavy police presence in communities of color, especially in Black and low-income communities, has led to the skyrocketing growth in incarceration rates for people of color, especially women and youth (men of color make up the largest population of those incarcerated, as there are many more men incarcerated in the U.S. than women, and their incarceration also stems from related processes of disadvantage). Women and youth of color are convicted of using drugs or for low-level dealing and are penalized under harsh laws that provide the legal framework for increased policing and incarceration. California's "Three Strikes Law" and federal minimum sentencing guidelines were ostensibly written for high-level drug dealers or "king pins," but instead most severely affect the low-level dealers and users who don't have any information or names to "trade" in exchange for a reduced sentence. If survivors are involved with drug sales, because they were expected, forced, or chose to, they are likely to be only low-level participants and thus are trapped under these draconian drug laws. Sometimes, survivors don't even know about their partner's involvement in the drug trade, and in many cases, survivors have very little information to share with prosecutors either because they were not allowed access by their abusive partners to the ins-and-outs of the trade or they do not divulge information out of fear of retribution by their abusive partner or other drug associates.

Under the auspices of keeping children and streets "safe," this war criminalizes and labels young, dark-skinned women and poor people of color as deviant and keeps communities impoverished by keeping many of its members entrenched in the revolving doors of the prison system. This repression ultimately serves people in positions of wealth and power (whose children, of course, will remain "safe") by ensuring unemployment and a desperate workforce for low-paying service work and maintaining the hierarchies that allow little opportunity for the advancement of people of color and solidifying the positions of power for wealthy whites. Richie describes the prison as "a project that relies on the production of a criminal class who play a key role in feeding the economic and political interests of the conservative state" (2005, p. 82). She notes that in order to fill prisons, criminals need to be produced via a "vicious and elaborate web of new laws that require increased sanctions, aggressive policing strategies, and harsh sentencing policies" (2005, p. 82). The web of corporations that service the policing and prison infrastructure–contractors to build prisons, food service corporations, medical suppliers, clothing and bed linen manufacturers, high tech weaponry companies and many more–also fuels prison expansion and helps to make the prison into a true conglomeration of both product production (in this case, a criminalized disenfranchised class of people) and corporate investment, making it a true capitalist machine or "prison industrial complex."[5]

RELIANCE ON THE CRIMINAL LEGAL SYSTEM AND POLICING FOR VIOLENCE AGAINST WOMEN

While certain people and processes are being targeted for mass incarceration, commitments to finding sane, healthy, and compassionate solutions to social inequalities, like poverty and domestic violence, are masked by the appearance of an effective and rehabilitative prison and criminal legal system. The first part of this section discusses how the reliance on the state to address domestic violence fuels prison expansion and also how it perpetuates a culture of systemic violence against women by not addressing the structural inequalities upon which this type of violence relies. The second section discusses how this reliance on the state affects survivors who are accused of committing crimes and also how their experiences in the U.S. court systems can be used as evidence of the need to envision community-based solutions to violence that demand basic human rights for all its members.

The legislation meant to protect battered women has reaffirmed the reliance on policing and the criminal legal system to address domestic violence. For example, when the Violence Against Women Act (VAWA) was introduced in 1994, it was part of the "Violent Crime Control and Law Enforcement Act of 1994" which further deepened ties that both literally and ideologically connect violence against women to the use of law enforcement for both the survivors and the perpetrators of domestic violence.[6] Pro and mandatory arrest laws arose from this movement and instituted regulations for domestic violence arrests and further tightened the states' hold over women and their communities. The aforementioned report for the Ms. Foundation for Women (2003), which examines the relationship between violence against women and the criminal legal system, noted that these "mandatory processes do not allow women to make their own decisions about how to address the violence in their lives, contributing to a feeling of powerlessness for battered women." It is further noted that some feel that the system exerts control over women's lives comparable to the batterer (Eng & Das Dasgupta, 2003, p. 6). Almost as if in response to those calling for less state intervention, the California Attorney General recently released a report that further solidifies state reliance, calling for further collaboration between law enforcement, prosecutors, and judges as well as enforcing the issuing of Criminal Protective Orders in conjunction with orders of Probation (2005). Although the remedies offered in this report appear to be in defense of survivors, visualizing punishment and incarceration as just methods to ending violence against women does not address the structural barriers that contribute to systemic violence against women. Alternatives to the criminal legal system that confront these structural inequalities might include a reframing of violence against women as a public health crisis and one that needs more effective long-term responses, such as supportive, community-based infrastructures for recovery from drug and alcohol addictions or for developmental and psychological disabilities, education and job-training courses, increased federal funding for affordable housing, or the revocation of laws that prohibit former felons from access to state housing.

Increased reliance on the police and legal remedies for violence against women not only dissuades the exploration of more community-based long-term solutions, but it also deters many survivors from seeking help. The National Institute of Justice found that "increased legal advocacy resources are associated with fewer white women being killed by their husbands and more black women being killed by their boyfriends" (Eng & Das Dasgupta, 2003, p. 9). It is clear that state intervention makes some women more unsafe and if, as in this case, it is only helping white women, then it is not helping to solve the problem. For those living in low-income communities of color, there is often a hesitancy to rely on the criminal legal system because police do not represent protection, but invoke instead images of police-instigated violence, shootings, rape, unnecessary provocations and questioning, and also memories of the police brutality and "investigation" used to stifle political movements for self-determination by people of color.[7] Abused women from these policed communities may also be hesitant to call the police because, as for most abused women, this often leads to more violent vengeful beatings after the police leave. Many survivors also know that orders of protection are merely "pieces of paper," and that putting an abuser in jail for six months will only make him angrier when he gets out (Baushard & Kimbrough, 1986, p. 107). Many women say that the courts and the police don't offer any protection at all. This distrust is clear in that "a striking four-fifths of all rapes, three-quarters of all physical assaults, and one-half of all stalking perpetrated against women are not reported to the police" (Eng & Das Dasgupta, 2003, p. 15). These findings suggest that many victims of intimate partner violence do not consider the justice system an appropriate intervention.

Instead of re-victimizing and immobilizing survivors, the criminal legal system's ineffectiveness can be used to break down the ideologies that posit policing, incarceration, and the criminal legal system as effective solutions to domestic violence. Recent efforts of the Habeas Project, a collaborative volunteer organization that "seeks to free domestic violence survivors in prison who qualify for post-conviction habeas corpus relief under [California] state law," have been successful in challenging women's convictions for killing their abusive partners when evidence of battery was not presented in court.[8] The majority of survivors serving life sentences under these circumstances in California were arrested in the early to mid 1980s, but survivors are still convicted of crimes related to domestic violence without evidence of battery or expert testimony of "battering and its effects" (formerly "Battered Women's Syndrome") presented in support of their legal defense.[9] This is the case even though Evidence Code 1107, introduced in 1992 and revised most recently in 2004, specifies that in a criminal action, expert testimony related to "battering and its affects" is admissible where relevant (People vs. Romero, 2nd Cir., 1992). Prior to the enactment of this Evidence Code section, judges had the discretion to admit or exclude such evidence, resulting in the high numbers of survivors convicted in the 1980s. Yet, although the law is now "on the books," there are many reasons why such evidence might not be brought into court. These reasons also stem from and contribute to the systemic issues and structural inequalities that perpetuate violence against women and contribute to mass incarceration.

The need for evidence of domestic violence may undermine the case of battered women because, since they have been under such tight control, they often do not confide in anyone about the violence, leaving few witnesses to testify to the abuse. Elizabeth Ward confides to Free Battered Women about how this happened to her:

> I didn't have any friends because he always had a problem with whoever she was. He was able to lead me to believe that no one in my family loved me and the only time my family talked to me was when they wanted something. I stayed home because if I left anywhere and stayed gone too long I would have to suffer the consequences. (Ward)

This type of control also prevents women from going to shelters (when space is available), hospitals, and, for some, calling the police, leaving no documented "evidence" of abuse to bring to court. The abuser also often hides the violence until they are behind closed doors, leaving even fewer witnesses to testify. Eileen Row and Robbie Kina, respectively, confirm this:

> The batterer is always Mr. Nice Guy when others are around but as soon as you are alone, he or she is a monster. Like my case, I looked like the asshole in public, but behind closed doors he was the monster. (Row)

> He was always good to my family which made my claims of his violence seem like nothing at all. (Kina, 2005, p. 68)

Evidence is further excluded from court if a survivor cannot tell her legal representative about the abuse. If she is not a citizen, she may not bring attention to the violence she has faced because she fears deportation. She may also not speak the language of those who might help her or she may be too ashamed or fearful to rehash any of the horrific stories.

> I just couldn't talk about it. So traumatized was I by the memory of my unbearable suffering and by the thought of disclosing my shameful secret that I preferred to face a murder charge knowing that the sentence was life imprisonment. (Kina, 2005, p. 69)

The impact that sustained trauma has on women is complex and many do not even identify as abused women (McCampbell, 2005, p. 6). Survivors may have internalized some of the verbal assaults and degradation constantly impressed upon them by their abusers and may see themselves as incapable of healing or as deserving of punishment. Beth

Richie notes how the survivors inside Cook County Jail "recounted even extreme events as almost routine, and they rationalized their misfortune as unimportant and "part of life" (Richie, 2003, p. 30).

Robbie Kina also didn't have evidence of abuse brought into trial although her niece made a statement to police testifying to Robbie's abusive partner's attempts to kill her and his constant "bashing her up" (Kina, 2005, p. 69). Although in this case the statement was available to the defense and still no witnesses were called to testify, some legal teams purposely do not offer evidence of abuse in court in fear that it may be used against them. The existence of such a legal strategy exposes the ways in which survival strategies are criminalized while it also exposes the ineffectiveness of the criminal legal system as a solution to domestic violence. That a legal team would be forced to omit evidence clearly pertinent to the case in fear that it may show "motive" exposes the system's need to hide the complexities and conditions under which crimes are committed in order to rationalize such punishment. Instead of providing room for contextual analysis, the courts focus on specific incidents, individualizing particular cases, including those involving domestic violence, instead of addressing the complexities of any given situation. Exposing the conditions that contribute to the commission of crimes, especially crimes of survival, breaks down the ideology that criminalization and incarceration is an effective solution to domestic violence. The criminal legal system's masking of the contexts under which crime is committed exposes the short-sightedness of simply prosecuting those who commit acts of violence and brings to light the importance of addressing the "root" causes of violence as part of more effective long-term strategies. Exposing the ways in which a woman's social location and experiences with domestic violence have led her to commit a "crime" demands that the structural inequalities that contribute to this violence be addressed. Ms. Foundation for Women envisions what this might look like: "Where might we be if government accountability did not aim its efforts at criminal legal punishment, but instead centralized responsibility for basic needs and human dignity, and affirmed the human rights of all?" (Eng & Das Dasgupta, 2003, p. 16).

MAKING CONNECTIONS AND ENVISIONING A WORLD WITHOUT PRISONS

Many of the survivors working with Free Battered Women speak constantly of their search for atonement for the "crimes" they have committed, but are also keenly aware of how their situations are connected to political processes, like the U.S.-led "War on Drugs," immigrant detention, and the ineffectiveness of the policing and legal systems. They know that their story is not just one isolated story of misfortune where a man beats his wife. After having little or no access to resources for battered women and after being mistreated by police, discarded by the criminal justice system, and sent to prison for life, these women tend to distrust the web of policing, law enforcement, and legal systems that are posited as a solution to social disorders. Many are aware of how their lives are intertwined with global systems of control. They scoff at how corporations that "embezzle" millions of dollars from off-shore oil investments, break U.S. labor and environmental laws in culpability-free export processing zones in Mexico, and over-work and exploit people for billion-dollar profits receive merely a slap on the wrist for their crimes, while they, and other survivors of mass incarceration, will live every day in prison for the next 25 years. The interconnections of global systems of privilege and disadvantage are clear.

There is not one simple solution to the complex systems of state and interpersonal violence that these women have faced in their lives. Their stories serve as a site from which to resist violence and to publicize the ways that the criminal legal system has failed to protect survivors and failed to "solve" systemic domestic violence. Their painful and heroic stories also demonstrate how the patterns of abuse and systems of disadvantage converge in certain people's lives and disempower entire classes of people. We must use their stories to ask why the state responds to abused women with punishment and incarceration. Why is it that these women, after years of abuse, escape the horrors of violent homes only to be re-victimized by the violence of prison? Are they truly "dangerous to society" or has society been dangerous to them? What processes allow for such harsh punishment of women and people of color and whose interests are served with two and half million people locked up in U.S. prisons? The connections between systematic violence against women, a reliance on policing and prisons, the U.S. "War on Drugs," immigrant detention, and the projects of neoliberal globalization are very real, and it is imperative that community members, activists, and scholars attempt to look at the complexities of these interconnections. Incarcerated people are not just individual cases to be pitied, but are on the front line with other marginalized peoples at the cross-roads of the complex systems that keep certain communities impoverished, others wealthy, and fuel the fear to fund wars, imperialism, and the building of super prisons. Let us look at how those living inside the prison, those who live every day without the freedom to leave, in the heart of the beast that smashes families and communities, provide a starting point. The unique situation of incarcerated survivors isn't a place to idealize, but it is a place to appeal to those who fight violence against women, to those who fight against prisons or for labor rights, and to those who fight to reclaim the human rights torn by globalization. Our fights are intertwined in many of the same systems of domination and we must work to envision sustainable and accountable strategies. We, especially the most privileged among us, will have to make great personal and collective sacrifices and be compassionate when privileges must be acknowledged and redirected and instead our bareness surfaced. The connections are painful. But we must imagine a world that does not give advantage to those most powerful by locking down those most vulnerable.

NOTES

1. I wrote this paper as a response to Julia Sudbury's call for work that connects the criminalization of domestic violence survivors to the violence of mass incarceration. Thank you Julia for putting together the desperately needed *Global Lockdown* and thank you to all who contributed to the anthology, for your courage, critical thinking, and commitment.

2. The Board of Prison Terms is now known as the Board of Parole Hearings.

3. For further analysis, see Anannya Bhattacharjee, Jael Silliman, ed. *Policing the National Body, Vol. 1.* and also Bhattacharjee's *Whose Safety? Women of Color and the Violence of Law Enforcement* (http://www.afsc.org/community/WhoseSafety.pdf)

4. Although influenced by the dire economic circumstances, women do *choose* to cross borders in search of sex work, domestic work and agricultural work. Please see Kamala Kempadoo's article cited on Reference Page.

5. For more information on the Prison Industrial Complex, see Joel Dyer's *The Perpetual Prisoner Machine* (2000) and Angela Davis' *Are Prison's Obsolete?* (2003).

6. See http://www.ojp.usdoj.gov/vawo/regulations.htm for more information on VAWA.

7. For further information see Angela Davis's *An Autobiography (1974 or 1988)* or a *New Political Science: A Journal of Politics and Culture Special Issue: Liberation, Imagination, and the Black Panther Party* (June 1999, Volume 21, Number 2), or Assata Shakur's *Assata (1987).*

8. See www.habeasproject.org for more information and how to get involved. Pro-bono attorneys needed!

9. The term "battering and its effects" now replaces the term "battered women's syndrome" coined by Dr. Lenore Walker. Because it has been routinely critiqued since its introduction (see Mary Ann Dutton, Critique of the "Battered Woman Syndrome" Model, Revised January, 1996, available at http://www.freebatteredwomen.org/SB1385. htm.), Senate Bill 1385, lobbied by organizers of the legal/activist organization, the Habeas Project, replaces all references to "battered women's syndrome" in section 1107 of the California Evidence Code with the term "Battering and its Effects."

REFERENCES

Anderson, C. Free battered women: Survivor's speak http://www.freebatteredwomen.org/andersontestimony.htm

Anonymous. (2005, July 1). *The longest wait: A second chance for "lifers."* San Francisco Chronicle pp. B8

Anonymous, *"How would you feel if this were your sister?"* http://www.freebatteredwomen.org/anon1.htm

Bible, A. (20 May 2005). *Governor denies parole to Linda Lee Smith and Karen Narita!* http://www.freebatteredwomen.org/FreeKarenNaritaAndLindaLee.htm

Bible, A., Dasgupta, S.D., & Osthoff, S. (2002). Guest Editors Introduction. *Violence Against Women: An International and Interdisciplinary Journal,* 1268.

Baushard, L. & Kimbrough, M. (1986) *Voices set free: Battered women speak from prison.* St. Louis Missouri: Women's Self Help Center.

[CA] Attorney General's Task Force on Local Criminal Justice Response to Domestic Violence (2005). *Keeping the promise–Victim safety and batterer accountability.* http://www.safestate.org/index.cfm?navID=9

Clubine, B. (2003 July 10). *But, does it matter? Our voices within.* Healing from the Inside Out Event Publication

Eng, P. & Das Dasgupta, S. Ms Foundation for Women. (2003). Summary prepared by Patricia Eng, based on the meeting report by Shamita Das Dasgupta, *Safety and justice for all: Examining the relationship between the women's anti-violence movement and the criminal legal system,* 14 (http://www.ms.foundation.org/userassets/PDF/Program/safety_justice.pdf)

Free Battered Women. *Free battered women survivors speak: Brenda Clubine.* Retrieved July 2005, from http://www.freebatteredwomen.org/clubinestory.htm

Free Battered Women. *Free battered women survivors speak: Maria Marquez.* http://www.freebatteredwomen.org/MarquezPressRelease.htm

Gilfus, M. (2002 December). *Women's experiences of abuse as a risk factor for incarceration.* National Resource Center on Domestic Violence: Violence Against Women Network. http://www.vawnet.org/DomesticViolence/Research/VAWnetDocs/AR_Incarceration.

Goldberg, E. & Evans, L. (Fall 1999/Winter 2000). *The prison industrial complex and the global economy.* Political Environments: A Publication of the Committee on Women, Population and the Environment.

Hamberger, K.L., & Guse, C.E. (2002). Men's and women's use of intimate partner violence in clinical samples. *Violence Against Women: An International and Interdisciplinary Journal,* 1301.

Kempadoo, K. (2005). Victims and agents of crime: The new crusade against trafficking. In J. Sudbury (Ed.), *Global lockdown: Race, gender, and the prison industrial complex* (p. 37). New York: Routledge.

Kina, R. (2005). Through the eyes of a strong black woman survivor of domestic violence: An Australian story. In J. Sudbury (Ed.), *Global lockdown: Race, gender, and the prison industrial complex* (p. 68). New York: Routledge.

Maguigan, H. (1991). Myths and misconceptions in current reform proposals. *University of Pennsylvania Law Review,* 140, 397.

McCampbell, S.W. (April 2005). *Gender responsive strategies for women offenders: The Gender responsive strategies project: jail applications.* U.S Department of Justice, National Institute of Corrections. 3-4. Includes original research: Browne, A., Miller, B., & Maguin, E. Prevalence and severity of lifetime physical and sexual victimization among incarcerated women, *International Journal of Law and Psychiatry 22* (1999): 301-322. Also: Greenfeld, L.A., & Snell, T.L. (1999). *Special report: Women offenders.* Washington, DC: U.S. Department of Justice, Office of Justice Programs, Bureau of Justice Statistics. http://www.ojp.usdoj.gov/bjs/pub/pdf/wo.pdf

People vs. Romero, 2nd Cir. (1992).

Richie, B.E. (1996). *Compelled to crime: The gender entrapment of battered black women.* New York: Routledge

Richie, B.E. (2003). *Understanding the links between violence against women and women's participation in illegal activity*: Final Report. The National Institute of Justice. 29.

Richie, B.E. (2005). Queering antiprison work: African American lesbians in the juvenile justice system. In J. Sudbury (Ed.), *Global lockdown: Race, gender, and the prison industrial complex* (p. 81). New York: Routledge.

Row, E. http://freebatteredwomen.org/eileentestimony.htm

Sharpe, R. (2005, May 26). Mothers prosecuted, punished for what they didn't do. *USA TODAY,* pp. A-4.

Sudbury, J. (Ed). (2005). Introduction. *Global lockdown: Race, gender, and the prison industrial complex* (p. xv). New York: Routledge.

Ward, E. http://freebatteredwomen.org/wardtestimony.htm

doi:10.1300/J015v29n03_05

An Ecological Approach
to Understanding Incarcerated Women's
Responses to Abuse

Melanie J. Bliss
Sarah L. Cook
Nadine J. Kaslow

SUMMARY. Although women are often criticized for not leaving abusive relationships, most abused women actively attempt to protect themselves. This study proposed an ecological model to explain strategic responses to abuse, evaluating factors at four levels: Childhood, Relationship, Individual Impact of Abuse, and Community. Data was retrospectively collected from 85 incarcerated women, a population that is

Melanie J. Bliss, PhD, is a licensed clinical psychologist and a senior researcher for EMSTAR Research, Inc., an evaluation and organizational services firm; Postdoctoral Fellow, Emory University School of Medicine, 954 Wandering Vine Drive, Mableton, GA 30126 (E-mail: drmbliss@yahoo.com).

Sarah L. Cook, PhD, is Associate Professor of Community Psychology and Director of Undergraduate Studies in the Department of Psychology at Georgia State University, Georgia State University, Department of Psychology, P.O. Box 5010, Atlanta, GA 30302-5010 (E-mail: scook@gsu.edu).

Nadine J. Kaslow, PhD, is ABPP Professor and Chief Psychologist at Emory School of Medicine, Department of Psychiatry and Behavioral Sciences, Emory University, Grady Health System, 80 Jesse Hill Dr., SE, Atlanta, GA 30303 (E-mail: nkaslow@emory.edu).

[Haworth co-indexing entry note]: "An Ecological Approach to Understanding Incarcerated Women's Responses to Abuse." Bliss, Melanie J., Sarah L. Cook, and Nadine J. Kaslow. Co-published simultaneously in *Women & Therapy* (The Haworth Press, Inc.) Vol. 29, No. 3/4, 2006, pp. 97-115; and: *Inside and Out: Women, Prison, and Therapy* (ed: Elaine Leeder) The Haworth Press, Inc., 2006, pp. 97-115. Single or multiple copies of this article are available for a fee from The Haworth Document Delivery Service [1-800-HAWORTH, 9:00 a.m. - 5:00 p.m. (EST). E-mail address: docdelivery@haworthpress.com].

disproportionately affected by trauma and has unique intervention needs. A series of hierarchical multiple regression analyses confirmed that the proposed ecological model accounts for variance in six strategic response categories: placating, resisting, safety, legal, formal, and informal. Findings are discussed in terms of intervention implications.

doi:10.1300/J015v29n03_06 *[Article copies available for a fee from The Haworth Document Delivery Service: 1-800-HAWORTH. E-mail address: <docdelivery@haworthpress.com> Website: <http://www.HaworthPress.com> © 2006 by The Haworth Press, Inc. All rights reserved.]*

KEYWORDS. Incarcerated women, intimate partner violence, abuse, strategic response, help-seeking, ecological

Although social science has identified reasons why it is difficult for women to leave abusive relationships (Barnett, 2000, 2001), society still criticizes women who experience intimate partner violence (IPV) for failing to extricate themselves from violent relationships or to take steps to achieve safety. Most abused women, however, actively strategize and use help-seeking behavior and resources to prevent abuse and protect themselves (Dutton, Goodman, & Bennett, 1999; Goodman, Dutton, Weinhurt, & Cook, 2003; Wuest & Merritt-Gray, 1999). We used a nested ecological model to examine women's strategic responses to IPV.

This study uses a random sample of incarcerated women, most of whom have committed non-violent crimes. This sample is appropriate for exploring strategic response to IPV for several reasons, including ensured safety from partners at the time of the study and high prevalence rates of child and adult abuse and other trauma (Browne, Miller, & Maguin, 1999; Cook, Smith, Tusher, & Raiford, 2005; Green, Miranda, Darowalla, & Siddique, 2005). Further, these women were not accessing care or seeking help at the time of recruitment. This sample is comparable with regards to demographics of other samples of non-violent, minority women of low socioeconomic status (Cook et al., 2003). However, high prevalence of substance abuse (Staton, Leukefeld, & Logan, 2001) and borderline personality disorder symptoms (Jordan, Shelenger, Fairbank, & Caddell, 1996) suggest that incarcerated women may be more willing to take risks or manipulate others than non-incarcerated women, both of which may affect their response to violence. Using an incarcerated sample provides a unique opportunity to increase understanding of responses to IPV and generate intervention recommendations in an understudied population.

Given the scope of IPV and its consequences, many ask, "Why don't abused women leave?" Several assumptions are implicit in this question. First, the question assumes that victims should leave and that women do not leave. In actuality, most women leave but return to relationships multiple times (Barnett, 2000; Dutton et al., 1999). Abusive relationships often are characterized by perpetrators' attempts to maintain power and control and survivors' efforts to stay safe (Barnett, 2000; Fleury, Sullivan, & Bybee, 2000). A second assumption is that leaving is easy. However, women often believe that it is beneficial to stay, many are economically dependent on their partner, and partners often deny women access to social support, community agencies, or telephones (Anderson et al., 2003; Barnett, 2000; Hendy, Eggen, Freeman, Gustitus, & Ng, 2003). Inadequate criminal justice systems further complicate leaving; some women fear mutual arrest, separation from their children, and physical examinations (Fischer & Rose, 1995; Fleury, Sullivan, Bybee, & Davidson II, 1998; Wolf, Uyen, Hobart, & Kernic, 2003). Leaving is emotionally difficult, and chronic stress, anxiety, and depression reduce motivation and energy (Anderson et al., 2003; Barnett, 2001). The final assumption is that leaving guarantees safety. Many women fear retaliation or additional abuse, and leaving is often more dangerous than staying (Fleury et al., 2000; Foa, Cascardi, Zoellner, & Feeny, 2000). Women struggle with moral conflicts that pit conflicting needs and desires against each other: the need to protect themselves and their children, the need to resist their partner, the desire to preserve family relationships, and feelings of sympathy and love for their partner (Belknap, 1999). These conflicts make it difficult for them to have violence-free relationships or leave an abusive partner. Thus, a more informative question is, "How can societal systems [health care, mental health, criminal justice] support women who want safety?" To answer this question, the current study focuses on the question, "What strategies do women use in response to IPV?"

Survivor theory (Gondolf & Fisher, 1988) suggests that women protect themselves and cope with violence, and active help-seeking is the reigning hypothesis for survivors. Although women may continue a relationship with the abuser, they also seek help and/or attempt to change their abuser. National data reveal that 80% of abused women take some self-protective action; 40% use physical action; 40% use a passive or verbal response; 34% confront the offender by struggling, shouting, or chasing; and 43% try to escape, call police, or use other non-confrontational means of self-defense (Bureau of Justice Statistics, 1994, 1998).

The strategic response literature has focused on formal resources. Many studies are qualitative with limited samples from shelters or courtrooms. However, national data revealed that women not only used formal and legal resources, but responded to IPV by accessing social support, attempting to talk partners out of IPV, trying to understand their abuser, and using faith-based strategies (Arias, 1999). Findings from a community sample of abused mothers classified help-seeking behaviors into placating, active resistance, formal, informal, and emergency escape plan strategies; strategy choice depended on context (Goodkind & Sullivan, 2004).

Ecological models have been useful in understanding women's decision-making regarding IPV (Dutton, 1996; Rothery, Tutty, & Weaver, 1999). Bronfenbrenner (1977) described a person's ecology as a nested arrangement of four systemic structures: microsystem, mesosystem, exosystem, and macrosystem. Abused women are often conceptualized in terms of their abuse and responses, and their experiences and responses must be considered in the context of their lives and relationships (Dutton, 1996). Dutton offered an ecological model consisting of five overlapping systems: (1) the battered woman, her personal history, and the meaning she makes of it (ontogenetic); (2) personal networks in which the woman interacts, their history, and the meaning she makes of them (microsystem); (3) linkages between networks or systems (mesosystem); (4) larger community networks that influence the woman indirectly (exosystem); and (5) society and cultural blueprints (macrosystem). These systems influence women's strategic responses.

The current study evaluates a broad range of strategic responses beyond those typically examined and highlights ways incarcerated women responded to IPV. Strategic responses fall into six categories: placating, resisting, safety, legal, formal, and informal strategies (Goodman et al., 2003). We evaluate an ontogenetic system (Childhood), two microsystems (Relationship and Individual Impact of Abuse), and one exosystem (Community Social Support) (see Figure 1): (1) Childhood level-severity of abuse, witnessing IPV, and environment to age 16 (urban or rural); (2) Relationship level-presence of children and severity of IPV; (3) Individual level-PTSD, injury, and acknowledgement of abuse; and (4) Community level-social support. The primary hypothesis is that the overall model offers a valid explanation of women's strategic responses to IPV. This hypothesis will be confirmed if (1) at least one of the four levels (Childhood, Individual, Relationship, Community) sta-

FIGURE 1. Ecological Model of Factors Explaining Women's Strategic Responses to IPV

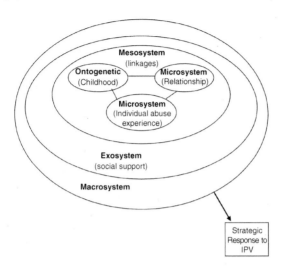

tistically explains variability in each strategic response, and (2) each of the four levels explains variability in at least one strategic response. These predictions suggest that women's overall ecology contributes to their choices.

METHODS

Sample

Participants were recruited from a maximum security state women's prison in the Southeastern United States that serves as the central receiving and diagnostic unit for the state and that houses women with serious mental illness and special health care needs. Inmates spend two to four weeks in the prison's diagnostic unit. The sample consisted of 85 participants drawn from a larger sample ($N = 403$) who had completed all of the study measures ($n = 200$) and who reported IPV from their most recent male partner. Women were included if they endorsed at least one physical or sexual abuse item or enough psychological abuse items (usually at least 2 items) to answer the strategic response measure. There was a 57% participation rate in the larger study.

Approximately 62% of the participants were African American and 38% were Caucasian. They ranged in age from 19 to 58 ($M = 33$ years).

Approximately 79% of women were single, separated, divorced, or widowed, 57% were in an intimate relationship with a man, 82% had lived with their most recent partner at some point, 81% had at least one child, and over 35% had children with their abusive partner. Almost 40% of women did not complete high school, 32% graduated from high school or obtained a GED, and 27% completed some college, trade, or technical school. Their monthly income ranged from zero to $28,000 ($M$ = $2,311); illegal income significantly skewed this variable. Most women (74%) did not have any prior incarcerations in the state. Approximately 55% were incarcerated for probation violations or parole revocation and 45% for first offenses. The average sentence (excluding Life and Death) was about seven years. Twenty-six percent were serving time for substance related offenses and forgery, and fraud and theft accounted for 42.4% of convictions. Only one woman was serving time for murder.

Procedure

Approximately 20 women from the diagnostic unit were selected randomly weekly for one year. Via institutional mail, they were invited to participate in an informational meeting. At this meeting, women who elected to sign an informed consent agreement were given an interview date to occur within two weeks. The 1 1/2-2 hour interviews were conducted in small, private, soundproof, windowed rooms located close to a security station. Prior to beginning interviews, research assistants reviewed the informed consent agreement and verified willingness to participate. Response cards for each measure were used to visually aid participants. Not all study measures were used for the current study. Upon the interview's completion, researchers debriefed participants, offered the option of receiving a study results summary, and then sent a thank-you letter that included information about community resources related to IPV.

Measures

Descriptive data. Descriptive information [age, marital status, environment (rural or urban) prior to age 16, race/ethnicity, educational status, income, children, relationship with abuser] was obtained from inmate diagnostic files and direct questions with the inmate.
Strategic responses. The Intimate Partner Violence Strategies Index (IPVS) (Goodman et al., 2003) assessed 38 methods of responding to

physical, sexual, and psychological IPV. Coding was binary for each item (0 = no, 1 = yes). Six sub-indices were placating, resisting, safety planning, legal, formal, and informal. Some items were not applicable to all women; thus, a proportional score was derived for each sub-index by summing all of the items each participant endorsed and dividing it by all applicable items. Because the measure was based on an induced variable model, factor analysis and reliability are not applicable. The measure has strong convergent validity and moderate discriminant validity.

Child abuse. The four-item Child Abuse Questionnaire (CAQ) (Goodman, 2000) assessed physical abuse experiences prior to age 16 perpetrated by a caregiver. Items inquired if participants had been (1) hit on body part other than the buttocks with a hard object; (2) thrown or knocked down, hit with a fist, kicked, beaten up, or choked; (3) burned or scalded; or (4) threatened with a knife or a gun. The ten-item *Sexual Abuse Exposure Questionnaire* (SAEQ), which inquired about invasive sexual experiences ranging from being flashed to being forced to have intercourse prior to age 16, has adequate test-retest reliability (Ryan, 1993). Items on the CAQ and SAEQ were binary and responses were summed; totals scores ranged from 0-14. The correlation between summed physical abuse and sexual abuse items was .61.

Witnessing family violence. The Traumatic Life Events Question-naire (Kubany & Haynes, 2000), which measured lifetime occurrence of 17 potentially traumatic events, has good test-retest reliability and convergent validity (Kubany & Haynes, 2000). The following ques-tion was used, "While growing up: Did you see or hear family vio-lence, such as your father hitting your mother, or any other family member beating up or inflicting bruises, burns or cuts on another family member?" Responses were binary.

Adult psychological, physical, and sexual IPV. The Conflict Tactics Scale-2 (CTS2) (Straus, Hamby, Boney-McCoy, & Sugarman, 1996) assessed the prevalence and frequency of 26 psychological and physical IPV experiences perpetrated by her most recent partner. The CTS2 is a widely used and well-validated measure of IPV, with high internal consistency reliability and well-established construct validity (Straus et al., 1996). Sexual IPV experiences were assessed using a modified Sexual Experiences Survey (SES) (Testa, VanZile-Tamsen, Livingston, & Koss, 2004). The original SES demonstrated high internal consistency reliability and test-retest reliability (Koss & Gidycz, 1985). We further modified the SES by asking questions regarding coercion, authority, in-capacitation, threat, and force for five sexual acts (touching, attempted vaginal sex, vaginal sex, oral sex, and anal sex), resulting in 25 items.

All IPV items were binary. The total IPV variable is a sum of all endorsed abuse items (range of 0-51). In the current study, IPV is highly correlated with PTSD and injury, suggesting high construct validity, and there are high correlations across forms of abuse (physical, sexual, and psychological).

Posttraumatic stress symptoms. Posttraumatic stress was measured with the Posttraumatic Stress Disorder Symptom Scale (PSS) (Foa, Riggs, Dancu, & Rothbaum, 1993). This 17-item scale taps frequency of PTSD symptoms corresponding with the DSM-IV PTSD diagnosis (American Psychiatric Association, 1994) within the past two weeks. A four point Likert-type scale ranged from zero (not at all) to three (five or more times per week), and a total score summing all responses ranged from 0-51. Women were asked to consider IPV experiences as their frame of reference. The PSS has previously demonstrated high reliability and validity (Foa et al., 1993). Reliability coefficients for the current study were .92 (overall), .86 (re-experiencing), .80 (avoidance), and .83 (hyperarousal).

Injury. Women were asked if they had experienced eight types of injuries (cut; bruised; burned; broken bone(s); knocked or choked unconscious; teeth knocked out, loosened, or broken; arm, leg, neck, or back sprained; organs damaged or injured). Each item was coded in a binary manner, and a total injury score (0-8) was created by summing responses. Created for this study, this measure was advantageous due to its brevity; however, no established psychometric properties exist. IPV and injury was highly correlated, suggesting high construct validity ($r = .54$).

Acknowledgement of abuse. After identifying their most recent partner and prior to questions about IPV, women were asked, "Do you or did you consider this relationship abusive?" Responses were coded as binary.

Social support. Participants' perceived social support immediately before incarceration was examined with 14 items derived from Cohen's Interpersonal Support Evaluation List (ISEL) (Cohen, 1985). Participants were asked to indicate whether statements were true or false. High total scores indicate more social support. This measure has adequate internal consistency reliability and validity (Cohen, 1985); the reliability coefficient for the current study was .85.

RESULTS

Descriptive Data

Strategic responses were widely used. Almost 100% of women reported that they used at least one placating response and at least one resisting response, over 90% used at least one formal response, over 75% used at least one safety response, 70% used at least one informal response, and 50% used at least one legal response. They reported using multiple responses in each category: 70% of placating responses, 65% of resisting responses, 41% of formal responses, 41% of informal responses, 33% of safety responses, and 20% of legal responses.

Prevalence of total child abuse was high; 48% experienced physical abuse and 65% experienced sexual abuse. The mean number of child abuse acts experienced was 3.04 (SD = 3.45, range = 0-13). Sixty-five percent of women witnessed IPV as a child, and 56% grew up in an urban environment. Although 81% had at least one child, just over 50% reported that a child lived with them prior to incarceration (M = 1.26, SD = 1.43, range = 0-5). The mean number of IPV acts experienced was 16.56 (SD = 11.57, range = 1-46). Women experienced a fair number of PTSD symptoms (M = 15.94, SD = 13.77, range = 0-49) and types of injuries (M = 2.16, SD = 1.89, range = 0-7). Approximately 75% of women had been injured at least once during their last relationship. Sixty percent believed their relationship was abusive. Women perceived their social support prior to incarceration to be high (M = 8.77, SD = 3.58, range = 1-13). Table 1 illustrates that many of the study variables are related in expected and theoretically consistent ways.

Study Hypotheses

Hierarchical multiple regression analyses were conducted with each of the strategic response categories serving as dependent variables. Each regression analysis had four blocks of independent variables: (1) Childhood: total child abuse, witnessing family violence, and environment to age 16 (rural or urban); (2) Relationship: number of children in the home and total IPV severity; (3) Individual Impact of Abuse: PTSD, injury, and acknowledging the relationship as abusive; and (4) Community: perceived social support. Variables were entered in terms of women's development and to control for historical factors.

A sample of 50 with eight independent variables provides sufficient power to detect large effect sizes when alpha = .05 (Cohen, 1992). Thus, with N = 85 and nine independent variables, power is sufficient to detect large effects. Distributions of independent variables were examined for normalcy. Although several variables were skewed, transformations resulted in comparable correlations with the dependent variables. Thus, non-transformed variables are presented.

TABLE 1. Intercorrelations Among Variables in Regression Model (N = 85)

	1	2	3	4	5	6	7	8	9	10	11	12	13	14
1. Child abuse														
2. Witness IPV	40*													
3. Environment	-.06	.14												
4. Children home	-.21	-.05	-.16											
5. IPV severity	44*	.31*	-.05	-.20										
6. PTSD	.38*	.27*	.07	-.13	.60*									
7. Injury	.28*	.27*	.12	-.00	.54*	.36*								
8. Acknowl. IPV	.09	.25*	.06	.15	.53*	.38*	.43*							
9. Social support	-.29*	-.30*	.00	-.00	-.18	-.43*	-.15	-.02						
10. Placating	.22*	.30*	-.18	.15	.58*	.51*	.37*	.45*	-.10					
11. Resisting	.27*	.34*	-.04	.12	.49*	.37*	.41*	.48*	-.12	.45*				
12. Safety	.20	.15	-.07	.07	.54*	.43*	.35*	.52*	-.00	.57*	.48*			
13. Legal	-.07	.06	-.06	.21*	.28*	.16	.41*	.33*	.07	.17	.31*	.29*		
14. Formal	.03	.10	-.14	.24*	.36*	.40*	.41*	.44*	.08	.53*	.46*	.49*	.47*	
15. Informal	.04	.06	-.20	.15	.33*	.31*	.52*	.38*	.10	.61*	.31*	.58*	.24*	.73*

* $p < .05$

We focus on effect size as the parameter of interest. Table 2 depicts the significant effect sizes (change in adjusted R^2) for each level of the ecological model and effects of individual variables in predicting strategic response (standardized regression coefficients). Overall, findings indicate that the ecological model offers a valid explanation of strategic responses. In support of the hypotheses, each strategic response category has significant variance accounted for by at least one ecological level, and each ecological level accounts for variance in at least two strategic response categories.

The total model predicted 40% of the variance in placating responses, 31% in resisting responses, 39% in safety responses, 14% in legal responses, 34% in formal responses, and 26% in informal responses.

TABLE 2. Summary of Effect Sizes (Change in Adjusted R^2) and Standardized Regression Coefficients (β) Predicting Strategic Responses Across All Regression Analyses (N = 85)

Variable	Placate	Resist	Safety	Legal	Formal	Informal
Childhood						
Total child abuse β	−.07	.07	.02	−.19	−.11	−.08
Witnessing IPV β	.18	.15	−.06	−.01	.03	−.01
Environment β	−.20*	−.02	−.02	.02	−.12	−.17
Adjusted R^2	.12*	.11*	.02	−.02	.00	.01
Relationship						
Children in home β	.05	.20*	.13	.26*	.23*	.13
IPV severity β	.29*	.24	.22	.23	.04	.01
Adjusted R^2	.23*	.17*	.26*	.12*	.20*	.12*
Individual						
PTSD β	.31*	.03	.19	−.01	.38*	.28*
Injury β	.05	.12	.27*	.27*	.19	.29*
Acknowl. IPV β	.14	.24*	.24*	.13	.21	.17
Adjusted R^2	.05*	.04	.11*	.05	.11*	.11*
Community						
Social Support β	.12	−.01	.13	.05	.23*	.22*
Adjusted R^2	.00	−.01	.00	−.01	.03*	.02*
Total *Adjusted R^2*	.40	.31	.39	.14	.34	.26

*$p < .05$

Based on the size and change of R^2, the Relationship level (children in the home, abuse severity) accounted for the most variance and had a medium or large effect in explaining every strategy. The Individual impact of abuse level had a small or medium effect on placating, safety, formal, and informal strategies, and it approached a small effect in explaining legal strategies. The Childhood level had a medium effect on placating and resisting strategies, and the Community level had small effects in explaining formal and informal strategies.

DISCUSSION

Findings from this study converge with others (Dutton et al., 1999; Goodkind & Sullivan, 2004; Goodman et al., 2003; Hutchison & Hirschel, 1998) to support the theory that women, including incarcerated women, respond to abuse in multiple ways. This sample was similar to a general population sample of women in use of the six response categories, with a stark exception: incarcerated women used far fewer legal responses (20% versus 58% of legal responses used in the general population) (Goodman et al., 2003). Little research has previously investigated IPV from a systemic perspective, perhaps due to a general perception that IPV is an interpersonal experience and is not influenced externally (Miles-Doan, 1998). Furthermore, an inherent assumption by society, although inaccurate, is that if women do not leave a relationship or seek help publicly, they are not working to protect themselves and their children. This study negates this belief and underscores the importance of how a woman's ecology contributes to IPV response. The following discussion highlights relations between ecological factors and strategic responses in a sample of women who eventually experienced incarceration. Future research is needed to determine whether these factors operate similarly for women who are not involved with the criminal justice system.

Relationship factors relating to children and severity of abuse had the largest effects on strategic responses. Conjointly, these factors contributed toward women's engagement in all strategic response types. Abusive partners' threats against or regarding children may prompt women to create change, particularly when mothers intend to retain custody (Rothery et al., 1999), and motherhood is related to use of public safety or legal strategies (Fischer & Rose, 1995). Indeed, current findings indicate that as the number of children increases, women use more types of resisting, legal, and formal strategies. Increasing severity of IPV positively predicts more placating strategies but does not predict other strategic response categories. One explanation for this surprising finding is that abuse severity predicts other strategic response types but is mediated by the impact of abuse factors: PTSD, injury, and acknowledgment of abuse.

The Childhood level had small, but significant, effects on strategic responses. Women may use strategies that they previously engaged in, witnessed, or perceive as effective. They may deliberately choose not to engage in behaviors that previously had poor outcomes. For example, negative experiences with law enforcement may hinder future desire to obtain protective orders or legal assistance (Fischer & Rose, 1995). Childhood environment was the sole childhood variable that significantly predicted a strategic response. Women who lived in rural communities as children were more likely to placate, the most frequently used strategy. As children, these women may not have benefited or witnessed others benefit from formal, public resources that are typically located in urban areas, such as battered women's shelters (Barnett, 2001; Krishnan, Hilbert, & VanLeeuwen, 2001). Many participants still reside in rural areas characterized by patriarchal family structures and views, strong religious beliefs, and lack of resources. Rural women often maintain privacy due to community dynamics, such as stigma and gossip (Staton et al., 2001). Many women report being afraid to call police in small communities because they (and their partner) know the officers (Barnett, 2001). Moreover, the current sample likely had vested interests in not using law enforcement. A large number reported family members with incarceration experiences, and involvement of law enforcement may lead to parole violations or parole revocations.

The Impact of Abuse microsystem had an interesting effect on responses. Acknowledging the relationship as abusive is related to resisting and safety strategies, but not to public strategies more easily associated with women who are willing to acknowledge abuse. Injury predicts safety, legal, and informal strategies, but fails to predict formal strategies, including talking to a doctor or nurse. However, the average number of injuries women experienced was two, with bruises and cuts being common, and many women attempted to conceal injuries due to shame. The degree to which PTSD affects women's help-seeking efforts is somewhat clearer. Women who reported PTSD were more likely to use placating, formal and informal resources. Data on cognitions related to PTSD in a community sample of assault victims suggested that fear motivated victims to avoid perceived danger situations and seek safety (Dunmore, Clark, & Ehlers, 1999). In a sample of battered women, a strong predictor of PTSD was coping with IPV by disengagement (Kemp & Green, 1995). Therefore, women with PTSD may strategically avoid additional IPV by avoiding their partners and arguments (placating), and by staying with others or ensuring that others are nearby (informal strategies). Increased use of formal strategies, including accessing treatment, may represent efforts to attend to psychiatric symptoms.

Social support, an exosystemic factor that explains formal and informal strategy use, is conceptualized as women's perception of available help related to a variety of life situations; this concept is different from informal strategic responses that represent women's actual utilization of friends and family in response to IPV. Women seek help from others (e.g., clergy, doctors, shelter staff, friends, family) if they are comfortable accessing support. If they do not perceive that they have support, they are less likely to try to obtain support from others, which may affect their strategy use. However, to whom the woman talks may affect the actual outcome of this action, as family members may be more likely to convince the woman to stay in the relationship than friends and helping professionals (Yoshioka, Gilbert, El-Bassel, & Baig-Amin, 2003).

In addition to the ontogenetic and microsystemic variables that affect women's response to IPV, macrosystemic factors that supersede these ecological levels are likely to be direct determinants of women's responses. Societal discrimination and oppression against women; belonging to a disenfranchised population; political, legal, and economic systems; poverty; and the drug culture may all influence women's attempts to achieve safety. Women may choose not to leave a relationship or use formal resources to avoid discrimination, involvement with the law, or exacerbation of oppression. Minority women in particular are more likely to have difficulty receiving fair treatment and cost effective access to services (Belle & Doucet, 2003; Coiro, 2001), and those without transportation or child care face additional challenges. In rural communities, it is difficult to seek help without disclosing abuse, and mental health services or IPV resources may be miles away (Mulder & Chang, 1997). Stigmatization of IPV exacerbates the victimization experience, often retraumatizing the victim. Furthermore, these factors influence some women to engage in illegal behavior. Many women in this study and others report that their partners demanded that they participate in criminal activity, such as buying and selling drugs, and they were threatened with IPV if they did not cooperate (Adamo, Holditch, & Cook, 2001; Richie, 1996). In addition, incarcerated women report that experiencing IPV increased their desire to use substances as a coping strategy, yet their substance use then served as a barrier to seeking treatment or contacting law enforcement (Staton et al., 2001).

Study limitations exist, particularly regarding methodology. The retrospective self-report nature of data collection may limit validity, as the participants were in an environment that may cause or exacerbate feelings of vulnerability, depression, or PTSD. Participants may have experienced memory failure or recall bias. The interviews occurred at a stressful time as the women adjusted to prison and many experienced distress over separation from loved ones. Research on the context of abuse and subsequent response frequently assesses mental health variables such as depression. Although data on emotional state was collected, due to participants' incarceration and the cross-sectional nature of data collection, it was difficult to link current emotional disturbance to past abuse or response.

Despite these limitations, findings help refute the notion that women do not attempt to change abusive relationships, and this study contributes to the growing body of help-seeking and coping literature regarding women's responses to IPV. Understanding how ecological factors affect strategy use may benefit interventionists and advocates who encourage help-seeking behaviors. Mental health professionals may empower women to learn intrinsic and extrinsic strategies and to seek resources to protect themselves and cope with abuse. Policy makers and community planners may benefit from study findings as they consider additional ways to build upon abused women's resources, competence, and capacity to create change.

This study offers perspectives from a rarely studied, disenfranchised group with extensive and unique needs. Compared to imprisoned men, at the time of their arrest, women are more likely to have been the primary caretaker of young children, have significant and often unaddressed health and mental health needs, and have extensive histories of abuse (Bloom, Owen, & Covington, 2003). Women were considered safe from their abusive partners, due to their own incarceration. Perceived safety may have provided more disclosure than in community-based studies. Qualitative reports from this sample and others indicate that some women believe that they have been "imprisoned" their whole life due to abuse, and they view prison as a place of safety (Bradley & Davino, 2002; Henriques & Rupert-Manatu, 2001).

Providing mental health and psychoeducation services to women both while incarcerated and as they transition out of prison is critical, particularly because many women return to their partners. Results from a sample of women in jail indicated that, if offered, 76-91% of women would be interested in interventions focusing on anger or stress management, relationships, problem-solving, and individual mental health counseling (Green et al., 2005). Interventions such as these may empower women to more effectively negotiate conflict, manage stress, and achieve safety. Incarceration may be a valuable time to address experiences of IPV (Bradley & Davino, 2002) and to process trauma, which may reduce PTSD and other psychiatric symptoms. In addition, collaboration of correctional facilities with community-based organizations can enhance women's reintegration into society, yet this coordination of services is missing from most communities (Freudenberg, 2002). Transitional planning should focus on strategic responses, correcting myths women may hold regarding various community systems and increasing their knowledge of agencies that can serve their needs. Further, social scientists, advocates, and the criminal justice system must work to de-stigmatize women with criminal records as not all domestic violence and sexual assault shelters and services assist convicted felons.

In sum, women often cannot or will not leave a violent relationship for valid reasons, yet these data suggest they make efforts toward safety. Women's choices are influenced by multiple factors occurring over their lives. As interventionists work with incarcerated, abused women, they may draw upon these findings to reduce women's guilt or shame regarding accusations that they "did not do enough"; reduce the social stigma and societal confusion regarding women "not leaving"; and better conceptualize women's experiences overall.

REFERENCES

Adamo, A. M., Holditch, P. T., & Cook, S. L. (2001). *Investigating the relation between women's incarceration and their experiences of male intimate partner abuse.* Paper presented at the American Society of Criminology Conference, Atlanta, GA.

American Psychiatric Association. (1994). *Diagnostic and Statistical Manual of Mental Disorders* (4th ed.). Washington D.C.: American Psychiatric Association.

Anderson, M. A., Gillig, P. M., Sitaker, M., McCloskey, K., Malloy, K., & Grigsby, N. (2003). "Why doesn't she just leave?": A descriptive study of victim reported impediments to her safety. *Journal of Family Violence, 18,* 151-155.

Arias, I. (1999). Women's response to physical and psychological abuse. In X. B. Arriaga & S. Oskamp (Eds.), *Violence in Intimate Relationships* (pp. 139-161). Thousand Oaks, CA: Sage Publications, Inc.

Barnett, O. W. (2000). Why battered women do not leave, Part 1: External inhibiting factors within society. *Trauma, Violence, and Abuse, 1,* 343-372.

Barnett, O. W. (2001). Why battered women do not leave, Part 2: External inhibiting factors, social support, and internal inhibiting factors. *Trauma, Violence, and Abuse, 2,* 3-35.

Belknap, R. A. (1999). "Why did she do that?" Issues of moral conflict in battered women's decision making. *Issues in Mental Health Nursing, 20,* 387-404.

Belle, D., & Doucet, J. (2003). Poverty, inequality, and discrimination as sources of depression among U.S. women. *Psychology of Women Quarterly, 27,* 101-113.

Bloom, B., Owen, B., & Covington, S. G. (2003). *Gender-responsive strategies: Research, Practice, and Guiding Principles for Women Offenders.* Washington, D.C.: National Institute of Corrections.

Bradley, R. G., & Davino, K. M. (2002). Women's perceptions of the prison environment: When prison is The safest place I've ever been. *Psychology of Women Quarterly, 26,* 351-359.

Bronfenbrenner, U. (1977). Toward an experimental ecology of human development. *American Psychologist, 32,* 513-531.

Browne, A., Miller, B., & Maguin, E. (1999). Prevalence and severity of lifetime physical and sexual victimization among incarcerated women. *International Journal of Law and Psychiatry, 22,* 301-322.

Bureau of Justice Statistics. (1994). *Violence between intimates* (No. NCJ-149259). Washington D.C.: U.S. Department of Justice.

Bureau of Justice Statistics. (1998). *Violence by intimates: Analysis of data on crimes by current or former spouses, boyfriends, and girlfriends.* Washington D.C.: Office of Justice Programs, U.S. Department of Justice.

Cohen, J. (1992). A power primer. *Psychological Bulletin, 112,* 155-159.

Cohen, S. (1985). Measuring the functional components of social support. In I. G. Sarason & B. R. Sarason (Eds.), *Social support: Theory, research, and applications.* Seattle: Martinus Nijhoff Publishers.

Coiro, M. J. (2001). Depressive symptoms among women receiving welfare. *Women & Health, 32,* 1-23.

Cook, S. L., Bliss, M. J., Dickens, T., Niolon, P. H., Lassiter, S., Poister, C., et al. (2003). *Final report: Context, meaning, and method of measuring violence against women.* Atlanta: National Institute of Justice.

Cook, S. L., Smith, S. G., Tusher, C. P., & Raiford, J. (2005). Self-reports of traumatic events in a random sample of incarcerated women. *Women and Criminal Justice, 16,* 107-126.

Dunmore, E., Clark, D. M., & Ehlers, A. (1999). Cognitive factors involved in the onset and maintenance of posttraumatic stress disorder (PTSD) after physical or sexual assault. *Behaviour Research and Therapy, 37,* 809-829.

Dutton, M. A. (1996). Battered women's strategic response to violence: The role of context. In J. L. Edelson & Z. C. Eisikovits (Eds.), *Future interventions with battered women and their families* (pp. 105-124). Thousand Oaks, CA: Sage.

Dutton, M. A., Goodman, L. A., & Bennett, L. (1999). Court-involved battered women's responses to violence: *The role of psychological, physical, and sexual abuse. Violence and Victims, 14,* 89-104.

Fischer, K., & Rose, M. (1995). When "enough is enough": Battered women's decision making around court orders of protection. *Crime and Delinquency, 41,* 414-429.

Fleury, R. E., Sullivan, C. M., & Bybee, D. I. (2000). When ending the relationship does not end the violence. *Violence Against Women, 6,* 1363-1383.

Fleury, R. E., Sullivan, C. M., Bybee, D. I., & Davidson II, W. S. (1998). "Why don't they just call the cops?" Reason for differential police contact among women with abusive partners. *Violence and Victims, 13,* 333-346.

Foa, E. B., Cascardi, M., Zoellner, L. A., & Feeny, N. C. (2000). Psychological and environmental factors associated with partner violence. *Trauma, Violence, and Abuse, 1,* 67-91.

Foa, E. B., Riggs, D. S., Dancu, C. V., & Rothbaum, B. O. (1993). Reliability and validity of a brief instrument for assessing post-traumatic stress disorder. *Journal of Traumatic Stress, 6,* 459-473.

Freudenberg, N. (2002). Adverse effects of US jail and prison policies on the health and well-being of women of color. *American Journal of Public Health, 92,* 1895-1899.

Gondolf, E. W., & Fisher, E. R. (1988). *Battered women as survivors: An alternative to treating learned helplessness.* Lexington, MA: Lexington Books.

Goodkind, J., & Sullivan, C. M. (2004). A contextual analysis of battered women's safety planning. *Violence Against Women, 10,* 514-534.

Goodman, L. M. (2000). Unpublished manuscript.

Goodman, L. M., Dutton, M. A., Weinhurt, K., & Cook, S. L. (2003). The intimate partner violence strategies index: Development and application. *Violence Against Women, 9,* 163-186.

Green, B. L., Miranda, J., Darowalla, A., & Siddique, J. (2005). Trauma exposure, mental health functioning, and program needs of women in jail. *Crime and Delinquency, 51,* 133-152.

Hendy, H. M., Eggen, D., Freeman, K., Gustitus, C., & Ng, P. (2003). Decision to leave scale: Perceived reasons to stay or leave violent relationships. *Psychology of Women Quarterly, 27,* 162-173.

Henriques, Z. W., & Rupert-Manatu, N. (2001). Living on the outside: African American women before, during, and after imprisonment. *The Prison Journal, 82,* 6-19.

Hutchison, I. W., & Hirschel, J. D. (1998). Abused women: Help-seeking strategies and police utilization. *Violence Against Women, 4,* 436-456.

Jordan, B. K., Shelenger, W. E., Fairbank, J., & Caddell, J. (1996). Prevalence of psychiatric disorders among incarcerated women: Convicted felons entering prison. *Archives of General Psychiatry, 53,* 513-519.

Kemp, A., & Green, B. L. (1995). Incidence and correlates of posttraumatic stress disorder in battered women. *Journal of Interpersonal Violence, 10,* 43-57.

Koss, M. P., & Gidycz, C. A. (1985). Sexual experiences survey: Reliability and validity. *Journal of Consulting and Clinical Psychology, 53,* 422-423.

Krishnan, S. P., Hilbert, J. C., & VanLeeuwen, D. (2001). Domestic violence and help-seeking behaviors among rural women: Results from a shelter-based study. *Family and Community Health, 24,* 28-38.

Kubany, E. S., & Haynes, S. N. (2000). Development and preliminary validation of a brief broad-spectrum measure of trauma exposure: The traumatic life events questionnaire. *Psychological Assessment, 12,* 210-225.

Miles-Doan, R. (1998). Violence between spouses and intimates: Does neighborhood context matter? *Social Forces, 77,* 623-630.

Mulder, P., & Chang, A. F. (1997). Domestic violence in rural communities: A literature review and discussion. *The Journal of Rural Community Psychology,* E1, (electronic).

Richie, B. E. (1996). *Compelled to crime: The gender entrapment of battered black women.* New York: Routledge.

Rothery, M., Tutty, L., & Weaver, G. (1999). Tough choices: Women, abusive partners, and the ecology of decision making. *Canadian Journal of Community Mental Health, 18,* 5-18.

Ryan, S. W. (1993). Psychometric analysis of the sexual abuse exposure questionnaire. *Dissertation Abstracts International, 53,* 3709A.

Staton, M., Leukefeld, C., & Logan, T. K. (2001). Health service utilization and victimization among incarcerated female substance abusers. *Substance Use and Misuse, 36,* 701-716.

Straus, M. A., Hamby, S. L., Boney-McCoy, S., & Sugarman, D. B. (1996). *The revised conflict tactics scales: Development and preliminary psychometric data. Journal of Family Issues, 17,* 283-316.

Testa, M., VanZile-Tamsen, C., Livingston, J. A., & Koss, M. P. (2004). Assessing women's experiences of sexual aggression using the Sexual Experiences Survey: Evidence for validity and implications for research. *Psychology of Women Quarterly, 28,* 256-265.

Wolf, M. E., Uyen, L., Hobart, M. A., & Kernic, M. A. (2003). Barriers to seeking police help for intimate partner violence. *Journal of Family Violence, 8,* 121-129.

Wuest, J., & Merritt-Gray, M. (1999). Not going back: Sustaining the separation in the process of leaving abusive relationships. *Violence Against Women, 5,* 110-133.

Yoshioka, M. R., Gilbert, L., El-Bassel, N., & Baig-Amin, M. (2003). Social support and disclosure of abuse: Comparing South Asian, African American, and Hispanic Black women. *Journal of Family Violence, 18,* 171-180.

doi:10.1300/J015v29n03_06

Negotiating Contradictions: Sexual Abuse Counseling with Imprisoned Women

Shoshana Pollack

Kerry Brezina

SUMMARY. Front-line workers, advocates, researchers and correctional officials in Canada, the U.S. and the U.K. have recognized the high proportion of imprisoned women who have experienced childhood sexual abuse and have called for the development of appropriate prison counseling services that take into account women's histories of trauma (Battle et al., 2003; Covington, 1998; Covington & Bloom, 2003; Scott, 2004; Task Force on Federally Sentenced Women, 1990; Van Wormer, 2001). Although researchers have pointed out the contradictions in providing treatment within an institution whose mandate is to punish (Girshick, 2003; Heney & Kristianen, 1998; Kendall, 1994; McCorkel, 2003; Scott, 2004; Marcus-Mendoza & Wright, 2004), very few mental

---

Shoshana Pollack, MSW, PhD, is Associate Professor in the Faculty of Social Work, Wilfrid Laurier University, Kitchener, Ontario, Canada.

Kerry Brezina, MSW, is currently employed as a senior therapist with Odyssey House, a therapeutic community for those striving to overcome severe addictions to drugs, alcohol, and gambling, in Auckland, New Zealand.

Address correspondence to: Shoshana Pollack, MSW, PhD, Faculty of Social Work, Wilfrid Laurier University, 120 Duke Street, Kitchener, Ontario, Canada N2H 3W8 (E-mail: spollack@wlu.ca).

[Haworth co-indexing entry note]: "Negotiating Contradictions: Sexual Abuse Counseling with Imprisoned Women." Pollack, Shoshana, and Kerry Brezina. Co-published simultaneously in *Women & Therapy* (The Haworth Press, Inc.) Vol. 29, No. 3/4, 2006, pp. 117-133; and: *Inside and Out: Women, Prison, and Therapy* (ed: Elaine Leeder) The Haworth Press, Inc., 2006, pp. 117-133. Single or multiple copies of this article are available for a fee from The Haworth Document Delivery Service [1-800-HAWORTH, 9:00 a.m. - 5:00 p.m. (EST). E-mail address: docdelivery@haworthpress.com].

Available online at http://wt.haworthpress.com
doi:10.1300/J015v29n03_07

health researchers, with the exception of those who point to the re-traumatizing nature of imprisonment on survivors of childhood abuse, incorporate this understanding of the prison environment into their recommendations of therapeutic approaches. In particular, little attention is paid to issues of power within the therapeutic relationship or the social control function of therapeutic services within the prison setting. In this paper we center the contradictions inherent in providing therapeutic services within an institution whose mandate is to punish and control. We follow this examination with a discussion of strategies for dealing with some of these power issues in order to minimize the potential for therapeutic services to replicate and reproduce dominant constructions of women prisoners as disordered and of being part of the correctional mandate of control, surveillance, and punishment.

doi:10.1300/J015v29n03_07 *[Article copies available for a fee from The Haworth Document Delivery Service: 1-800-HAWORTH. E-mail address: <docdelivery@haworthpress.com> Website: <http://www.HaworthPress.com>* © 2006 *by The Haworth Press, Inc. All rights reserved.]*

KEYWORDS. Women's imprisonment, female offenders, sexual abuse counselling, imprisoned women

Front line workers, advocates, researchers and correctional officials in Canada, the U.S. and the U.K. have recognized the high proportion of imprisoned women who have experienced childhood sexual abuse and have called for the development of appropriate prison counseling services that take into account women's histories of trauma (Battle et al., 2003; Covington, 1998; Covington & Bloom, 2003; Scott, 2004; Task Force on Federally Sentenced Women, 1990; Van Wormer, 2001). Several approaches to mental health programming have been advocated, such as those based on relational psychology (Covington, 1998; Covington & Bloom, 2003; Fortin, 2004), cognitive behavior therapy (McDonagh, Taylor & Blanchette, 2002), the strengths-perspective (Van Wormer, 2001), and feminist therapy (Dirks, 2004; Marcus-Mendoza & Wright, 2004) all of which attempt to take into account women's experiences of trauma. Although researchers have pointed out the contradictions in providing treatment within an institution whose mandate is to punish (Girshick, 2003; Heney & Kristianen, 1998; Kendall, 1994; McCorkel, 2003; Scott, 2004; Marcus-Mendoza & Wright, 2004), very few mental health researchers, with the exception of those who point to the re-traumatizing nature of imprisonment on survivors of childhood abuse, incorporate this understanding of the prison environment into their recommendations of therapeutic approaches. In particular, little attention is paid to issues of power within the therapeutic relationship or the social control function of therapeutic services within the prison setting. Rossiter et al. (1998) argue that "[t]herapeutic relationships unavoidably inherit the micropolitics of power" (1998: 28) and thus feminist mental health practice must confront the contradictions and tensions of working within contexts in which inequalities and power differentials are replicated and reproduced. In this paper we center the contradictions inherent in providing therapeutic services within an institution whose mandate is to punish and control. We follow this examination with a discussion of strategies for dealing with some of these power issues in order to minimize the potential for therapeutic services to replicate and reproduce dominant constructions of women prisoners as disordered and of being part of the correctional mandate of control, surveillance, and punishment.

CRIMINALIZED WOMEN
AND CHILDHOOD VICTIMIZATION

Research studies have shown that an exceedingly high percentage (between 77% and 90%) of incarcerated women in the U.S. have experienced traumatic experiences such as childhood sexual and physical abuse, domestic violence, and rape (Battle et al., 2003). Similar findings come from Canada (Arbour, 1996; Hannah-Moffat and Shaw, 2000; Task Force on Federally Sentenced Women, 1990). Women in prison suffer cumulative trauma as in addition to childhood abuse experiences they are often revictimized in their intimate relationships with men. (Girshick, 2003; Pimlott & Sarri, 2002; Dirks, 2004). Research has also shown that a high percentage of incarcerated women experience the psychological impacts of trauma characterized by Post Traumatic Stress Disorder (Battle et al., 2003; Girshick, 2003; Henderson, Schaeffer, & Brown, 1998).

The literature on women's pathways to crime suggests that strategies for coping with abuse, such as running away from home and drug and alcohol use (Comack, 1996; Faith, 1993; Owen, 1998; Pimlott & Sarri, 2002), increase a woman's chances of coming into conflict with the law, as do adult revictimization experiences such as violence against women

(Battle et al., 2003). Dougherty (1998) cautions, though, against assuming a direct causal link between childhood maltreatment and subsequent criminal offending since, of course, many survivors of childhood trauma do not come into conflict with the law. This is an important distinction as criminological theory and correctional risk assessments tend to utilize theories of causality in explaining criminal offending. Constructing childhood abuse experiences as the reason for women's crime, turns psychological and emotional needs into risk factors for breaking the law (Hannah-Moffat, 2004).

In addition, studies that link childhood abuse to criminalization may not capture intervening factors (Battle et al., 2003), such as those due to socio-economic marginalization and racial and cultural discrimination. A Canadian study found, for example, that racialized gender oppression and socio-economic disadvantage restricted the available opportunities for Afro-Canadian imprisoned women (Pollack, 2003). Thus, while the impact of experiences of trauma on women's lawbreaking is significant, socio-economic marginalization and other forms of social disadvantage often intersect with these experiences.

One of the unintended implications of exposing the frequency and severity of childhood abuse and intimate violence experienced by criminalized women is that correctional approaches tend to depoliticize these experiences and focus instead upon the psychological effects of gender victimization. This in turn leads to a focus upon psychological factors in explanations for women's crime. Researchers and activists have critiqued the criminological literature and correctional programming for its assumption that women's lawbreaking is caused by their psychological problems (Fox, 1999; Kemshall, 2002; Kendall, 2000; McCorkel, 2003; Pollack, 2000a) and the tendency to pathologize criminalized women. Critiques of this approach have highlighted the obscuration of structural factors, such as racism, sexism, and poverty, in the criminalization process and the denial of any rational basis for women's actions (Kendall, 2000; Pollack, 2000a; Pollack & Kendall, 2005). It has also been noted that individualizing social problems is a hallmark of neo-liberalism, as welfare states are being dismantled, employment benefits are reduced, a precarious labor market develops, and the privatization of services (including prisons) increases. Notions of individual responsibility (and blame) have gained ascendancy, and within the correctional and criminal justice context this is often manifested through therapeutic programming designed to discipline, regulate, and reform the prisoner. As prisons are mandated to reduce an individual's risk of committing further criminal acts, therapeutic programming then becomes part of regulating, controlling, and reforming "criminals" (Foucault, 1989; Fox, 1999; Kemshall, 2002; Kendall & Pollack, 2003; McCorkel, 2003).

In terms of mental health treatment models, this can be seen in the privileging of cognitive behavioral programming in prisons (Fox, 1999; Kemshall, 2002; Kendall & Pollack, 2003; McCorkel, 2003; Pollack & Kendall, 2005). At the core of this approach is the notion of a criminal mind/personality which leads women to engage in criminal activities. These programs focus on restructuring the way women think about themselves in order to prevent them from re-offending. Such approaches pathologize women's law-breaking by implying that criminal activity is the result of impairments in cognitive processes (Kendall & Pollack, 2003; Pollack & Kendall, 2005). Factors such as trauma history, race, class, gender, etc., and their impact on women's lives are deemed irrelevant and disconnected from criminal behavior. Women's attempts to discuss their experiences of trauma and marginalization are often viewed as denial or rationalizations of their offence (Fox, 1999; McCorkel, 2003). Instead, women are encouraged to internalize this criminal personality discourse in order to change their behavior–a method of self-regulation that Foucault calls *technologies of the self* (Rose, 1989). For survivors of sexual abuse, these technologies of self-governance serve to confirm what many have felt about themselves since they were children–that they are bad, worthless, and are responsible for the abuse that they have experienced (Girshick, 1999; Williams et al., 2001). Furthermore, after extensive reviews in Canada both the Auditor General of Canada (2003) and the Canadian Human Rights Commission (2003) have concluded that current cognitive behavioral mental health treatment (i.e., Dialectical Behavior Therapy) as implemented by the Correctional Service of Canada does not reflect the women-centered principles that ostensibly guide federal women's corrections in Canada.

Feminist criminologists, mental health professionals, and incarcerated women themselves agree that women in prison should be offered counseling services to deal with the impact of childhood abuse, traumatic experiences such as rape and domestic violence (Carlen, 2002; Girshick, 2003; Dirks, 2004), and the relationship between trauma and substance abuse (Battle et al., 2003; Covington, 1998; Girshick, 2003). For many women, sexual and physical abuse is not only related to psychological distress but is also linked to substance abuse problems, eating disorders, self-harm, suicidal ideation, and difficulties with anger. Although the need for providing these types of counseling services is generally undisputed, the assumptions and methods of service delivery are contested. This contestation largely results from a clash between the agenda, presuppositions, and discourse of correctional services and those of feminist therapeutic models, which emphasize collaboration, support, healing, and the impact of oppression. For example, there is often a general feeling in correctional facilities that by addressing prisoners' histories of childhood trauma, therapists will be opening 'a can of worms' that will upset the women and jeopardize the security of the institution (Scott, 2004). Further, some Canadian federal women's prisons have moved to a brief therapy model whereby prisoners are permitted only 8-10 counseling sessions per year (Canadian Human Rights Commission, 2003), clearly an inappropriate amount of support to address childhood abuse experiences. The following is a discussion of some of the systemic barriers to trauma counseling in the prison context that therapists need to acknowledge and confront if they are to offer effective trauma counseling services.

THERAPEUTIC SERVICES IN THE PRISON CONTEXT

Many have argued that given the fact that most criminalized women are convicted of non-violent crimes and the challenges of offering adequate in-prison trauma counseling, alternatives to custody should be developed in the community (Girshick, 2003; Kendall & Pollack, 2003; Battle et al., 2003). Ideally, sexual abuse therapy should be independent from the correctional system (Scott 2004), so that the service is not tied to a mandate to punish and control. Further, independent services help separate intimacy (support, counseling) from intimidation (punishment, control), a key dynamic of childhood abuse experiences (Dirks, 2004). Unfortunately, community corrections are not generally accorded much priority, and in many cases social and mental health services are no longer available (Pimlott & Sarri, 2002) as resources are being diverted into the prison business (Richie, 2002). As a result, prisons are often being used as a means of providing addiction and trauma treatment to women who would otherwise be supported in the community (Canadian Association of Elizabeth Fry Societies, 2003), a trend that may be contributing to the increase in women prisoners.

The philosophy and mandate of corrections, however, are generally opposed to those of sexual abuse counseling. Many of the power dynamics operating within the prison context replicate the oppression and marginalization women have experienced both as victims of sexual abuse and as members of the broader society. This has clear implications for feminist service providers who must deal with "a paradox where they attempt to empower women while also helping them survive in, and conform to, the oppressive prison environment" (Marcus-Mendoza & Wright, 2004: 252). The most obvious obstacle to sexual abuse counseling in prison is the prison mandate to provide punishment, control, and surveillance (Easteal, 2001; Girshick, 1999; Kendall, 1994; McCorkel, 2003; Pollack, 2004). Prisoners are monitored 24 hours a day, whether by the direct observation of guards or by electronic means such as cameras and locked doors and wards. Almost every activity in a prison is governed by rules; unfortunately not all of the rules make sense nor are they consistently enforced (Easteal, 2001; Faith, 1993; Pollock, 1998). For many women who have survived abuse, the lack of control, unequal power dynamics, and arbitrary rules they experience during incarceration replicate the dynamics of past abuse and the feelings of powerlessness these experiences evoked (Covington, 1998; Girshick, 2003; Heney & Kristiansen, 1998). Responses to these triggers might include cognitive or sensory memories, flashbacks, or sudden outbursts of emotion. While some women may recognize the connection between their past and present circumstances, others may have considerable difficulty understanding why they are suddenly overwhelmed with painful and distressing memories, thoughts, and feelings. As a result, the prison environment can send women into crisis with past memories and feelings associated with childhood abuse being reactivated and familiar coping strategies, such as self-harm, substance use, and aggression being adopted. Crisis intervention strategies often involve helping women manage and minimize the emotional and psychological distress of incarceration and the memories and feelings of past abuse that may arise.

It is not surprising that many coping mechanisms used in childhood, such as self-injury, depression, dissociation, and suicidality, may be reactivated during incarceration in order to help women manage feelings of distress and powerlessness (Girshick, 2003; Heney & Kristiansen, 1998). Prison personnel often respond to these coping strategies from a security rather than a mental health perspective and misinterpret a woman's attempts to cope with these feelings as a security risk. This is often the case with women who engage in self-harming behavior. Security staff may interpret the behavior as attention-seeking or acting out and the woman may be placed in a segregation cell without her own clothing or any of her own belongings, as punishment for her behavior (Easteal, 2001; Faith, 1993). The inability to recognize strategies for coping with the effects of sexual abuse often leads to mislabeling these behaviors as intentional disregard for institutional rules. The punishments which result from such misinterpretations only serve to compound the distress and trauma with which the women are already trying to cope and lead to increased feelings of vulnerability and powerlessness (Faith, 1993).

Informal "rules" for surviving the penal system also exist (Easteal, 2001; Pollock, 1998; Kilroy, 2005). As summarized by Easteal (2001), these rules include: don't talk, don't trust, don't feel. The underlying message is that vulnerability and weakness will be exploited by other prisoners or by staff. Both the threat of, and actual occurrences of, abuse by staff can be used as a means of punishing and controling women. Furthermore, as Kilroy (2005) states, "sexual assault by the state," such as strip searches after family visits and camera surveillance of women showering in segregation, are experienced as invasive and degrading. In an atmosphere of extreme power inequities, distrust, humiliation, and secrecy (factors which underlie most sexually abusive experiences) engaging in therapeutic work is very challenging.

In addition to ensuring the security and stability of the prison, the correctional mandate is to assess, manage, and reduce risk that prisoners pose to the institution, themselves, and the community. The primary purpose of prison programs is to reduce the likelihood that an individual will commit an offense once released from prison. Therefore programming targets those factors considered criminogenic—characteristics that are viewed as 'causing' crime and that are amenable to change. Thus discourses about risk reduction and risk management proliferate throughout the correctional system and form the foundation upon which all programming is built. Increasingly, childhood abuse is being viewed as a risk factor in women's offending (Hannah-Moffat, 2004). Consequently, therapy may be mandated and progress in treatment may be used to determine women's risk classification and/or release options. Therapeutic services, whatever the intention of the individual therapist, become part of the risk reduction apparatus; assessment, treatment, and documentation use correctional categories to evaluate such things as risk of violence and psychological and behavioral functioning. As Rose states, in relation to risk management discourses as strategies of governance in a variety of settings, ". . . the very gaze of the control professional and the nature of their encounter with their client, patient or suspect, is liable to be formatted by the demands and objectives of risk management" (Rose, 2000: 321). Trauma counseling is 'at risk' of becoming part of the overall correctional regime of punishment, surveillance, and control. This directive clearly limits the subjects that a woman may feel comfortable discussing in the therapeutic context. It may also seriously impede the ability of women to openly identify issues central to their healing such as self-harm or suicidal ideation, drug use and availability, or the abusive actions of other prisoners or staff, etc., for fear that such disclosures may be used against them.

Conscious awareness of elements such as the security focus, power-over dynamics, and the potential that therapeutic services may be co-opted into the correctional agenda should be incorporated into the philosophy, design, and treatment methods of trauma counseling services. Such consciousness is necessary in order to generate a process which is responsive to both women's long-term needs as well as those needs which result from incarceration.

ACKNOWLEDGING AND TRANSFORMING POWER IN THE THERAPEUTIC RELATIONSHIP

The following is a discussion of strategies for providing abuse counseling for women in prison that attempt to avoid perpetuating and replicating both the power imbalances of the correctional institution and those inherent in abusive relationships.

Normalizing the Impact of Trauma

Feminist-informed researchers and practitioners working with women in prisons, psychiatric facilities, and in the community have challenged the tendency to construct women survivors of abuse as personality disordered (Girshick, 2003; Kendall & Pollack, 2003; Pollack & Kendall, 2005; Rivera, 2002; Warner, 2001; Williams, Scott & Waterhouse, 2001). The literature argues that common responses to childhood abuse are functional, creative, and reasonable attempts to cope with trauma, and although they may no longer be helpful (and indeed may actually be harmful), they are not symptoms of a sick, diseased, or disordered personality structure. Furthermore, viewing women's coping strategies, such as dissociation, self-harm, and drug and alcohol abuse, as symptoms of a disorder serves to reinforce rather than alleviate women's need to utilize such strategies. The more mental health professionals attempt to constrain women's choices, the greater the need to activate coping strategies developed to deal with these types of constraints (Warner, 2001). Given that the prison environment replicates the dy-

namics of childhood abuse, it is not surprising that women prisoners often respond to feelings of powerlessness with anger, drug use,
self-injury and dissociation (Heney & Kristiansen, 1998). Unfortunately these responses are often met with punitive sanctions, such as
segregation, fines, write ups, denial of privileges, and further patholo-
gization. Anger, substance abuse, self-injury and dissociation are often
normal self-protective measures cultivated in response to traumatic
events. These self-protective strategies are often reactivated within the
prison when events and/or relationships replicate abusive dynamics or
when women have flashbacks or memories of past abuse. Responding
to women's coping strategies punitively only reinforces the need for
them to self-protect, thereby perpetuating, rather than alleviating,
women's distress and difficult behavior.

Correctional programming favors the medical discourse of pathology which underpins many mental health policies and much prison programming for women (McDonagh et al., 2002; Scott, 2004). Treatment
approaches that evolve out of this discourse employ a decontextualized
notion of women's 'disordered thinking' and dysfunctional behavior
and the ways in which women's personality 'deficits' are responsible
for their coming into conflict with the law (Kendall & Pollack, 2003;
Pollack & Kendall, 2005). Not only do these approaches define
women's post-traumatic responses as symptoms of a disorder, but an
illness-based approach to trauma survivors can be counter-productive
in treatment. Rivera (2002) found that patients in her hospital-based
program greatly benefited from having the "illness frame" inherent in
the personality disorder diagnoses challenged. Furthermore, the over-
use of psychiatric jargon often reinforces power differentials between
clients and service providers (Rivera, 2002). This language can be
alienating and perpetuates the notion that prisoners are deficient and
disordered, premises that underlie many correctional practices with
women. In addition, psychiatric discourse disempowers women by labeling behavior as incomprehensible symptoms of illness or simply bad
behavior, rather than as "meaningful coping strategies" that have
evolved from experiences of abuse (Warner, 2001:103).

Collaboration, Knowledge Sharing, and Advocacy

It is also possible to share power with prisoners by engaging in a collaborative therapeutic process. Establishing trusting relationships with
women in a context that both implicitly and explicitly warns them
against trusting anyone can be very challenging. It is important for the

therapist to be open and honest about all aspects of the therapeutic process including his/her reporting responsibilities. It is important that women have a clear understanding about what kind of information the therapist is required to share with security and other prison staff so that they are able to make informed decisions about whether or not to disclose the information in the first place (Pollock, 1998). Because of the serious limitations on confidentiality in the prison setting (Canadian Human Rights Commission, 2003), many incarcerated women are fearful of what is written about them. There is also a concern that their words and/or actions in certain situations will be misinterpreted or altered when they reappear in official correctional documents. One strategy for acknowledging the imbalance of power in the therapeutic relationship is to encourage women to participate in the documentation process, for example by co-writing session summaries and treatment progress reports. Such co-creation allows women to ensure that the therapeutic work in which they have engaged is accurately represented in official records.

Warner (2001) suggests that for survivors of abuse, the therapeutic relationship itself, regardless of where it is taking place, carries with it the potential for the re-enactment of abusive dynamics. In particular, client vulnerability and trust in the expertise of the therapist pose some risk to clients. In order to mediate this power imbalance, Warner (2001) advocates "visible therapy" in which the therapist makes explicit the "tactics of therapy" by explaining not only what the therapist is asking but also why s/he is asking it. This demystifies the therapeutic process and forces therapists to be clear about their own purposes (e.g., diagnostic, therapeutic, investigative, risk assessment, etc.), thus providing clients with the knowledge necessary to make informed decisions about how to engage in therapy. Warner's approach is also useful as a means of confronting the issue of emotional safety within the prison context. The concern of "visible therapy" is to understand how experiences of childhood abuse give rise to particular forms of gendered identity, rather than a focus on the specific details of the abuse. Thus the "focus in visible therapy is on the tactics of abuse, rather than on the physical act itself" (Warner, 2001: 122). Warner is concerned with how women survivors of childhood abuse are constructed through cultural narratives and how they come to define themselves. Her framework lends itself to a narrative therapeutic process in which women prisoners can challenge dominant constructions of themselves as pathological, criminal, bad, and sick (the internalization of which can impact behavior which perpetuates these constructions), and begin to 're-story' their experiences and self-concept. "Visible therapy" provides possibilities for client collaboration in the therapeutic process as well as for transparency in the therapist's methods and agenda. Within the prison context this approach would encourage therapists to be transparent about their role and obligations to the institution and to actively resist pathological constructions of female prisoners and their responses to abuse. Such approaches necessitate that the mental health professional be comfortable with loosening her/his grip on expert discourses and acknowledging the skills and awareness possessed by women in prison. Given that the prison context is a heightened example of the ways in which expert discourses frame and define women's experiences, their lawbreaking, and their program needs (Pollack, 2000a), allowing women to articulate and define their own needs and experiences can be particularly transformative (Pollack, 1994).

In addition to individual counseling, prison programs can also address issues of power and attempt to devise formats, procedures, and practices that provide actual opportunities for women to exercise some degree of control over their treatment and healing. This involves flexibility and creativity on the part of mental health professionals, rather than the importation of correctional programs implemented in male prisons. For example, programs that support and build positive relationships with other women have been found to increase women prisoners' sense of self-worth (Pollack, 1994; Pollack, 2000b) and positive interpersonal skills (Burke, 2002). Peer support programming allows women to learn from each other, breaks isolation, acknowledges individual skills, and builds trust (Boudin, 1998; Delgado, 2001; Pollack, 1994; Pollack, 2004). The theoretical premises of these programs acknowledge that the experiences of women in prison have been greatly shaped by systemic and structural oppressions, such as those resulting from violence, racism, poverty, sexism, and homophobia. The peer support model allows space for this discussion and provides an opportunity for women's own actions to be reflected upon, challenged, and supported. Peer support programming also helps to counter the notion that women in prison have few skills, are unable to assume responsibilities, cannot be trusted, and are emotionally unstable. The development of peer support models is often challenging in the prison context since supportive relationships among prisoners may be discouraged and perceived as a potential threat to prison security. There are many rules and regulations that discourage sharing, co-operation, and support among prisoners (McCorkel, 2003; Pollack, 2000b), so service providers may have to work with prison administration to help foster supportive and positive prisoner relationships.

Advocacy is often an essential component of therapeutic work within a prison, both in terms of supporting women as they advocate for themselves and, at times, taking a more active role and advocating on their behalf. The latter is particularly important when a woman's trauma-related behavior has been misconstrued as a security risk. It may be necessary for the therapist to educate prison staff about the impact of particular prison practices and advocate for these practices to be altered. Some examples of correctional practices that may be triggering for women who are survivors of sexual abuse include: The use of handcuffs during gynecological exams, requiring women to submit to strip searches in order to gain certain privileges and avoid certain punishments, nighttime bed checks when women are locked in rooms/cells, and being touched by someone in authority (e.g., doctor, therapist, guard, religious/spiritual leader). In order to moderate the potentially distressing impact of these routine practices on incarcerated women, it is vital that correctional staff be educated about the power of these actions to trigger past trauma as well as about the reactions women may have to the feelings of fear and powerlessness they experience. A respectful relationship with institutional staff allows the therapist to verify the connections that exist between the woman's past trauma and her current behavior and to encourage a process of cooperative problem-solving between the individual survivor and security staff (Girshick, 1999).

There are various methods of advocating for and with women within the system. Therapists may attend multi-disciplinary meetings, case conferences, and parole hearings in order to advocate on behalf of a woman. Mental health reports and assessments can be used to advocate and educate about the impacts of trauma and the relationship between these experiences and women's behavior. It is also important to help women navigate the prison system itself by explaining who is in charge of her case and paperwork, how to contact them, how the complaint process works, and whom it is best to approach to discuss a specific issue. Connecting women with outside resources, such as support workers, lawyers, prison advocates and professional governing bodies, is also a common method of helping women advocate on their own behalf.

CONCLUSION

Women's experiences of abuse in their lives more generally and in the correctional context specifically require that the therapist maintain an awareness of the historical and current impacts of lack of control in their lives. This includes maintaining an awareness of the therapist's own power in the therapeutic context. Explicit recognition that incarcerated women's behavior is not necessarily symptomatic of a personality disorder, but may be a perfectly normal reaction to the powerlessness they have experienced can be a vital part of the healing process. While such a framing does not permit women to avoid taking responsibility for their actions, it does allow for validating women's feelings, finding meaning in their behavior, and acknowledging the impact of trauma (including child sexual abuse and incarceration) on their lives (Pollack, 2004).

Moreover, effective trauma counseling in prison often means challenging one's conventional therapeutic boundaries and taking a more active role in supporting the client's needs. Due to the extreme power imbalances within the prison setting, the therapist must be creative and flexible around how to support women prisoners, both in the context of their therapeutic work and in their living environment. This may mean becoming involved in many aspects of the woman's prison life in order to help her navigate and cope with the prison system itself.

Rossiter et al. argue (1998) that it is imperative that feminist mental health professionals must not only address ethical issues such as power imbalances within the therapeutic relationship but must also extend our analysis to the organizations and institutions (i.e., the context) in which service delivery occurs. In terms of working with criminalized women, this means developing alternative practices that do not replicate and are not complicit with strategies of control, punishment, and surveillance.

REFERENCES

Arbour, Madame Justice L. (1996). *Report of the Commission of Inquiry into certain events at the prison for women in Kingston*. Ottawa: Public Works and Government Services.

Auditor General of Canada (2003). April 2003 Report. Correctional Service Canada Reintegration of Women Offenders. Ottawa: Office of the Auditor General of Canada. http://www.oag-bvg.gc.ca/domino/reports.nsf/html.20030404ce.html 09/04/2003

Battle, C., Zlotnick, C., Najavits, Gutierrez, M., & Winsor, C. (2003). Posttraumatic stress disorder and substance abuse disorder among incarcerated women. In P. Ouimette & P. Brown (Eds.), *Trauma and substance abuse: Causes, consequences and treatment of comorbid disorders* (pp. 209-225). Washington, DC: American Psychological Association.

Boudin, K. (1998). Lessons from a mother's program in prison: A psychosocial approach supports women and their children. In J. Harden & M. Hill (Eds.), *Breaking the rules: Women in prison and feminist therapy* (pp. 103-125). New York: Harrington Park Press.

Burke, A.C. (2002). Triple jeopardy: Women marginalized by substance abuse, poverty, and incarceration. In J. Fiqueira-McDonough & R. Sarri (Eds.), *Women at the margins: Neglect, punishment, and resistance* (pp. 175-201). New York: The Haworth Press, Inc.

Canadian Association of Elizabeth Fry Societies. (2003). *Submission of the Canadian Association of Elizabeth Fry Societies (CAEFS) to the Canadian Human Rights Commission for the Special Report on Discrimination on the Basis of Sex, Race and Disability Faced by Federally Sentenced Women.* May 2003.

Canadian Human Rights Commission. (2003). *Protecting their rights: A systemic review of human rights in correctional services for federally sentenced women.*

Carlen, P. (2002). Introduction: Women and punishment. In P. Carlen (Ed.), *Women and punishment: The struggle for justice* (pp. 3-21). United Kingdom: Willan Publications.

Comack, E. (1996). *Women in trouble.* Halifax: Fernwood Press.

Covington, S. (1998). Women in prison: Approaches in the treatment of our most invisible population. In J. Harden, & M. Hill (Eds.), *Breaking the rules: Women in prison and feminist therapy* (pp: 141-155). New York: Harrington Park Press.

Covington, S., & Bloom, B. (2003). Gendered justice: Women in the criminal justice system. In B. Bloom (Ed). *Gendered justice: Addressing female offenders.* Durham: Carolina Academic Press.

Delgado, M. (2001). *Where are all the young men and women of color?: Capacity enhancement practice and the criminal justice system.* New York: Columbia Press.

Dirks, D. (2004). Sexual revictimization and retraumatization of women in prison. *Women's Studies Quarterly, 32*(3/4), 102-115.

Dougherty, J. (1998). Female offenders and childhood maltreatment: Understanding the connections. In R. Zaplin (Ed.), *Female offenders: Critical perspectives and effective interventions* (pp. 227-244). Gaithersburg: Aspen Publishers.

Easteal, P. (2001). Women in Australian prisons: The cycle of abuse and dysfunctional environments. *The Prison Journal, 81*(1), 87-112.

Faith, K. (1993). *Unruly women: The politics of confinement and resistance.* Vancouver: Press Gang Publishers.

Fortin, D. (2004). "A Correctional Programming Strategy for Women." *Forum on Corrections Research.* Ottawa: Correctional Service of Canada. Available at http://www.csc-scc.gc.ca/ (Accessed 02/05/05).

Fox, K. (1999). Changing violent minds: Discursive correction and resistance in the cognitive treatment of violent offenders in prison *Social Problems 46*(1), 88-103.

Foucault, M. (1979). *Discipline and punish.* New York: Vintage Books.

Girshick, L. (1999). *No safe haven: Stories of women in prison.* Boston: North Eastern University Press.

Girshick, L. (2003). Abused women and incarceration. In B. Zaitzow & J. Thomas (Eds.), *Women in prison: Gender and social control* (pp. 95-117). London: Lynne Riener Publishers.

Hannah-Moffat, K. (2004). Gendering risk at what cost? Negotiations of gender and risk in Canadian women's prisons. *Feminism & Psychology 14*(2), 241-247.

Hannah-Moffat, K., & Shaw, M. (2000). Introduction. In K. Hannah-Moffat & M. Shaw (Eds.), *An ideal prison? Critical essays on women's imprisonment in Canada* (pp. 11-27). Halifax: Fernwood.

Henderson, D., Schaeffer, J., & Brown, L. (1998). Gender-appropriate mental health services for incarcerated women: Issues and challenges. *Family Community Health, 21*(3), 42-53.

Heney, J., & Kristiansen, C. (1998). An analysis of the impact of prison on women survivors of childhood sexual abuse. In J. Harden & M. Hill (Eds.), *Breaking the rules: Women in prison and feminist therapy* (pp: 29-44). New York: Harrington Park Press.

Kemshall, H. (2002) Effective practice in probation: An example of "advanced liberal" responsibilisation. *The Howard Journal, 41*(1), 41-58.

Kendall, K. (1994). Therapy behind prison walls: A contradiction in terms? *Prison Service Journal* (96), 2-11.

Kendall, K. (2000) Psy-ence fiction: Inventing the mentally disordered female prisoner. In K. Hannah-Moffat and M. Shaw (Eds.), *An ideal prison? Critical essays on women's imprisonment in Canada* (pp. 82-93). Halifax: Fernwood:

Kendall, K., & Pollack, S. (2003). Cognitive behavioralism in women's prisons: A critical analysis of therapeutic assumptions and practices. In B. Bloom (Ed.), *Gendered justice: Addressing female offenders* (pp. 69-96). Durham, NC: Carolina Academic Press.

Kilroy, D. (2005). Sisters inside: Speaking out against criminal justice. In J. Sudbury (Ed.), *Global lockdown: Race, gender, and the prison industrial complex.* New York: Routledge.

Marcus-Mendoza, S., & Wright, E. (2004). Decontextualizng female criminality: Treating abused women in prison in the United States. *Feminism & Psychology, 14*(2), 250-255.

McCorkel, J. (2003). Embodied surveillance and the gendering of punishment. *Journal of Contemporary Ethnography, 32*(1), 41-76.

McDonagh, D., Taylor, K., & Blanchette, K. (2002). Correctional adaptation of Dialectical Behavior Therapy (DBT) for federally sentenced women. *Forum on Corrections Research, 14*(2), 36-39.

Owen, B. (1998). "In the mix": Struggle and survival in a women's prison. Albany: State University of New York Press.

Pimlott, S., & Sarri, R. (2002). The forgotten group: Women in prisons and jails. In J. Figueira-McDonough & R. Sarri (Eds.), *Women at the margins: Neglect, punishment, and resistance* (pp. 55-85). New York: The Haworth Press, Inc.

Pollack. S. (2004). Anti-oppressive practice with women in prison: Discursive reconstructions and alternative practices. *British Journal of Social Work, 34,* 696-707.

Pollack, S. (2003). Focus group methodology in research with incarcerated women: Race, power and collective experience. *Affilia: Journal of Women and Social Work, 18*(4), 461-472.

Pollack, S. (2000a). Reconceptualizing women's agency and empowerment: Challenges to self-esteem discourse and women's lawbreaking. *Women & Criminal Justice, 12*(1), 75-89.

Pollack, S. (2000b). *Outsiders inside: The social context of women's lawbreaking and imprisonment.* Unpublished Ph.D Dissertation, Faculty of Social Work, University of Toronto.

Pollack, S. (1994). "Opening the window on a very dark day": A program evaluation of the peer support team at the Kingston Prison for Women. *Forum for Correctional Research,* 6(1), January. Correctional Service of Canada.

Pollack. S., & Kendall, K. (2005). "Taming the shrew: Regulating prisoners through "women-centered" mental health programming. *Critical Criminology: An International Journal,* 13, 1.

Pollock, J. (1998). *Counseling women in prison.* Thousand Oak, California: Sage.

Richie, B. (2002). The social impact of mass incarceration on women. In M. Mauer & M. Chesney-Lind (Eds.), *Invisible punishment: The collateral consequences of mass imprisonment* (pp. 136-149). New York: The New York Press.

Rivera, M. (2002). The Chrysalis Program: Feminist treatment community for individuals diagnosed as personality disordered (pp: 231-261). In M. Ballow & L.S. Brown (Eds.), *Rethinking mental health and disorder: Feminist perspectives.* NY: Guilford Press.

Rose, N. (1989). *Governing the soul: The shaping of the private self* (2nd Ed.). London: Free Association Books.

Rose, N. (2000) Government and control. *British Journal of Criminology, 40,* 32-339.

Rossiter, A., de Boer, C., Narayan, J, Razack, N, Scollary, V, & Willette, C. (1998). Toward an alternative account of feminist practice ethics in mental health. *Affilia: Journal of Women & Social Work, 13*(1), 9-30.

Scott, S. (2004) Opening a can of worms? Counseling for survivors in UK women's prisons. *Feminism and Psychology, 14*(2), 256-261.

Task Force on Federally Sentenced Women. (1990). *Report of the Task Force on Federally Sentenced Women: Creating choices.* Ottawa: Ministry of the Solicitor General.

Van Wormer, K. (2001). *Counseling female offenders and victims: A strengths-restorative approach.* New York: Springer Publishing Company.

Warner, S. (2001). Disrupting identity through visible therapy: A feminist post-structuralist approach to working with women who have experienced child sexual abuse. *Feminist Review, 68*(Summer), 115-139.

Williams, J., Scott, S., & Waterhouse, S. (2001). Mental health services for "difficult" women: Reflections on some recent developments. *Feminist Review,* 68, 89-104.

doi:10.1300/J015v29n03_07

Criminalized Mothers:
The Value and Devaluation
of Parenthood from Behind Bars

Angela M. Moe
Kathleen J. Ferraro

SUMMARY. With the number of incarcerated women rising in the United States, scholarship and activism has focused more explicitly on the backgrounds, criminal contexts, and programming needs of the imprisoned population. This article focuses on motherhood and relies on qualitative life-history interviews with thirty women in a southwestern detention center. The women's narratives are used to further our under-

Dr. Angela M. Moe is Assistant Professor of Sociology at Western Michigan University.

Dr. Kathleen J. Ferraro is Professor of Sociology at Northern Arizona University.

Address correspondence to: Angela M. Moe, Western Michigan University, Department of Sociology, 1903 W. Michigan Ave., Kalamazoo, MI 49008-5257 (E-mail: angie.moe@wmich.edu) or Kathleen J. Ferraro, Northern Arizona University, Department of Sociology and Social Work, P.O. Box 15300-5300, Flagstaff, AZ 86011 (E-mail: kathleen.ferraro@nau.edu).

The authors are indebted to the women who candidly shared their experiences with them. The authors also thank the administrators and staff of the detention center in which they met these women, as without their cooperation this research would not have been feasible.

The authors were grateful to receive monetary support for this research through the Center for Urban Inquiry at Arizona State University.

[Haworth co-indexing entry note]: "Criminalized Mothers: The Value and Devaluation of Parenthood from Behind Bars." Moe, Angela M., and Kathleen J. Ferraro. Co-published simultaneously in *Women & Therapy* (The Haworth Press, Inc.) Vol. 29, No. 3/4, 2006, pp. 135-164; and: *Inside and Out: Women, Prison, and Therapy* (ed: Elaine Leeder) The Haworth Press, Inc., 2006, pp. 135-164. Single or multiple copies of this article are available for a fee from The Haworth Document Delivery Service [1-800-HAWORTH, 9:00 a.m. - 5:00 p.m. (EST). E-mail address: docdelivery@haworthpress.com].

standing of the ways in which motherhood (1) resonates with incarcerated women's self-perceptions, (2) relates to their motivations for crime, and (3) informs therapeutic programming within the carceral[1] environment. In order to address the needs of a critical, yet often ignored, correctional population, we specifically examine the ways in which gender-specific therapeutic approaches may be applied to a jail facility where continuous, in-depth programming may be challenging due to inmate turn-around and unrest. doi:10.1300/J015v29n03_08 *[Article copies available for a fee from The Haworth Document Delivery Service: 1-800-HAWORTH. E-mail address: <docdelivery@haworthpress.com> Website: <http://www. HaworthPress.com>* © *2006 by The Haworth Press, Inc. All rights reserved.]*

KEYWORDS. Parenthood and prisons, criminal mothers, self-perception

THE CRIMINALIZATION OF WOMEN IN THE U.S.

Twenty-five years after the beginning of the *get tough on crime* era, the effects of our ideology on crime and punishment have been felt across the criminal processing system. Over 7.7 million arrests were made in 2003 (Federal Bureau of Investigation [FBI], 2004), a consistent increase from 7.5 million in 1995 and 7.3 million in 1991 (FBI, 1996). Over 2.1 million people are incarcerated at any given time in the U.S. (Bureau of Justice Statistics [BJS], 2005b), nearly a two-fold increase from 1994, when this number was just over 1.1 million (BJS, 1995).

While staggering, these numbers mask the enormous toll of *get tough* practices on women. While women make up a minority of those in the system, increases in their incarceration rate have exceeded those of men every year since 1981, tripling in the 1980s alone, whereas men's doubled (Kline, 1993). Over the last ten years, arrest rates for males declined 6.7% while arrest rates for females increased 12.3% (FBI, 2004). Women currently make up 7% of the U.S. prison population (BJS, 2004) and 12% of the jail population (BJS, 2005a), while in 1990 they made up 6% (BJS, 1992) and 9% (BJS, 2005a) respectively.

The rising rates of women in the criminal processing system stem from two areas of policy reform. The first is the *war on drugs,* which has resulted in greater enforcement efforts and enhanced penalties for drug related offenses (Belknap, 2001). The second involves the *feminization of poverty,* which suggests that the rise in poverty rates, along with fewer public subsidies for the poor, has contributed to women's increasing involvement in economically based crimes such as forgery, counterfeiting, fraud, and embezzlement (Belknap, 2001; Campbell, Muncer, & Bibel, 1998; Casey & Wiatrowski, 1996). The connection between the *war on drugs* and the *feminization of poverty* is well illustrated in the case of drug dealing. Selling drugs when few options for sustainable income are available puts poor women at even greater risk once arrested under our current crime policies, which ensure drug-related offenses are punished more severely than ever before. The felony record such a woman is likely to obtain because of such *get-tough* practices will effectively stunt any sustainable and legitimate employment she might find in the future (Diaz-Cotto, 1996). As further evidence of the gendered *war on drugs*, between 1986 and 1995, drug related offenses accounted for one-third of the increase of men in prison. However, they accounted for one-half of the increase of women in prison (Mauer, Potler & Wolf, 1999). Another common crime for women, prostitution, is highly correlated with drug related offenses. Both may be economically driven and are quite gendered in context within the illegitimate street market. Moreover, women may come to rely on drugs in order to numb their emotions for sex work or prostitute in order to support their addictions (Inciardi, Lockwood, & Pottieger, 1993; Maher, 1997).

In short, the crimes for which women are most likely to be arrested and incarcerated are also those that are best explained by worsening economic and social conditions. The majority of women in the criminal processing system are poor, single mothers. African American, Latina, and American Indian women are over-represented among them (Bush-Baskette, 1998; Davis, 1998; Donziger, 1996; Greenfeld & Snell, 1999). Within this context, the interconnected nature of oppression based on gender, single-parenting, poverty, and race/ethnicity is most apparent. However, this is only part of the picture. Official statistics estimate that 30-50% of imprisoned women have been abused by intimate partners (American Correctional Association [ACA], 1990; Greenfeld & Snell, 1999), although qualitative studies have found much higher rates of 80-85% (Gilfus, 1992; Moe Wan, 2001). A substantial line of research has connected the most common crimes for women to various survival mechanisms employed under coercion, battery, poverty, and substance abuse (Arnold, 1990; Chesney-Lind, 1997; Comack, 1996; Ferraro, 1997; Gilfus, 1992; Lake, 1993; Moe, 2004; Sargent, Marcus-Mendoza & Yu, 1993). The small number of women who do commit violent offenses are more likely than men to do so out of self-defense or duress. More often than not, an abusive intimate partner is the subject of self-defense as well as the source of duress (Johnson, Li & Websdale, 1998; Jurik & Winn, 1990). The criminal processing system too often ignores, downplays and blames women for the circumstances surrounding their criminalization.

PENALIZATION VS. REHABILITATION

Rehabilitative programming has suffered great blows through delegitimization and funding cuts over recent years. The treatment philosophy of the 1960s and '70s has been markedly replaced with retributive and incapacitative penal practices, resulting in the warehousing of convicted offenders (Austin & Irwin, 2001; Donziger, 1996; Bloom, Chesney-Lind & Owen, 1994). A 2004 special report published by the Department of Justice on state prisons does not even mention rehabilitative programming as an expenditure. The majority of state prison expenses come in the form of staff salaries, wages, and benefits (65%), whereas 26% is devoted to operating costs such as medical care, food, utilities, and contract housing, and 4% is spent on construction, repairs, and renovation. One is left to assume that funding earmarked for rehabilitative services is somewhere under 5% of total expenditures (Stephan, 2004).

This predicament is made even more precarious by long-standing, and often misguided, carceral practices for women. As a legacy of discriminatory treatment, women and girls in our adult and juvenile correctional systems have long suffered from either negligent treatment, aimed at resocialization into stereotypical gender roles (e.g., sewing, cosmetology, child-rearing) or non-existent rehabilitative efforts (Dobash, Dobash & Gutteridge, 1986; Rafter, 1985). Since their numbers in the criminal processing system are so minute compared to men and boys, and because they are seen as less dangerous or serious criminals, their actual needs have neither been recognized nor legitimized (Mann, 1984).

However, with increasing arrests and prosecutions of women and girls over recent decades, greater attention has been given to the needs of females in the system. Morash, Bynum and Koons (1998) were funded by the National Institute of Justice to conduct an assessment of needs and a survey of successful programs and published their conclusions in 1998. Unfortunately, most of their recommendations have not been implemented. The specific needs of female offenders have been neglected due to gender discrimination. Based on sexist misunderstandings of calls for gender equality, equal treatment of females has been translated into a *one size fits all* approach (Belknap, 2001; Chesney-Lind, 1991). Rather than investing in research on what women and girls actually need as far as programming, existing rehabilitative practices, which were developed for and by males, were made available in a blanket approach to all females. This phenomenon, aptly termed *equality with a vengeance* (Chesney-Lind, 1997, p. 152), has contributed to the continued invisibility of women and girls in the correctional realm.

GENDER-SPECIFIC NEEDS AND PROGRAMMING

While the political and social debate over gender equality is an ongoing one, there is general consensus among criminologists and criminological practitioners that criminalized women do indeed have experiences and needs distinct from those of men. Due to their high risk of violent victimization, drug addiction and involvement in prostitution, women may enter a carceral setting with very emergent needs for medical care, counseling, and support (Moe & Ferraro, 2003; Shaw, 1992). Given cuts in public subsidies, it is less likely that these women would have received adequate physical or mental health care prior to incarceration. Unfortunately, the type of services available to incarcerated women are woefully inadequate and often inaccessible (Moe & Ferraro, 2003; Teplin, Abram & McClelland, 1997; Young, 2000).

The distinct needs of women become even more obvious in the area of motherhood. Specific medical care is necessitated by the estimated 5-6% of women who enter jail or prison pregnant (ACA, 1990; Greenfeld & Snell, 1999). Beyond physical health care for expectant women, all mothers have a myriad of needs in terms of emotional and social support. Sixty-five percent of women entering prisons are parents, as compared to 55% of men (Mumola, 2000). Additionally, 65% of all incarcerated mothers with minor children had custody of them prior to incarceration, as compared to 47% of incarcerated fathers. Most report that they intend on regaining custody of their children upon release. However this may be contingent on the placement of their children during incarceration. Twenty-three percent of women report that their minor children are in the custody of their non-incarcerated parent during their confinement, compared to 90% of men (Schafer & Dellinger, 1999). Women's children are much more likely to be in the custody of their maternal grandparents or with other willing relatives. If relative placement is unavailable, women may face involvement by state child protective services [CPS] (Belknap, 2000; Owen, 1998; Ross, 1998; Schafer & Dellinger, 1999). The placement of their children often affects the type of contact women may have with them. According to a Bureau of Justice Statistics report, 54% of incarcerated mothers never have a visit from their children. Distance is also a factor here, as 60% are imprisoned more than 100 miles away from their homes (Mumola, 2000). Even telephone contact is difficult due to costs and institutional constraints on the privilege of telephone use (Sharp & Eriksen, 2003). Lack of contact between incarcerated mothers and their children creates problems for children and their mothers, during confinement and upon release.

Given these types of concerns, attention has focused on *gender-specific* programming. Gender specific programming refers to services developed for and targeted explicitly toward either males or females (Juvenile Justice Evaluation Center [JJEC], 2004). Since most traditional programs were initially developed from research on men and boys, they may already be deemed gender-specific *for males* (Rafter, 1985). When it comes to women and girls, new approaches are needed that do not duplicate historical efforts at resocialization into stereotypical feminine roles. Contemporary gender-specific programming is focused on addressing the lived experiences of females (Bloom & Covington, 1998; Zaplin, 1998). It is recognized that while women share some experiences and programming needs as men (e.g., support for parenting), these experiences and needs may be qualitatively different (e.g., women being the primary parent) and must be addressed in distinct ways. Likewise, gender-specific programming addresses women's experiences that are quite different from those of men (e.g., higher rates of sexual assault victimization), thus programming of this nature is aimed at being more holistic and comprehensive in its approach (Koons, Burrow, Morash & Bynum, 1997; Task Force on Federally Sentenced Women, 1990). Finally, gender-specific programming recognizes that female offenders have lived experiences distinct from those of males, and that the various aspects of these experiences, and the larger social context in which they occur, are often interrelated (Austin, Bloom & Donahue, 1992; Bloom & Covington, 1998).

Gender-specific programming has gained most notoriety in the arena of juvenile delinquency (see Belknap, Dunn & Holsinger, 1997; Pepi, 1998). Beginning in the early 1990s, practitioners began experimenting with new treatment programs aimed at the rising numbers of girls in the juvenile justice system (JJEC, 2004). Today, such programming is becoming more popular among adult populations as well, being targeted at both women in community corrections and prison (Austin et al., 1992; Bloom & Covington, 1998; Kendall, 1994). We argue that jail is another correctional setting that ought to be examined in terms of the utility of gender-specific programming, particularly with regard to motherhood. As discussed earlier, women entering confinement often have very immediate needs. In this context, fear, concern, and angst are quite salient. Women may enter (or re-enter) the criminal processing system with pending charges or probation revocation, while others await trial or a transfer to prison. This is a time of crisis on many levels for women, beyond the uncertainty of their criminal cases. For some women, the "temporary" pre-trial incarceration in jail can turn to years, particularly when there are male co-defendants whose cases must be re-solved prior to the woman's case. While the jail setting is often ignored as a site for therapy and gender-specific programming, we argue that it is a necessity, given the very immediate needs and often crisis-laden states of the women detained there.

METHODS AND SAMPLE DEMOGRAPHICS

Our findings are based on qualitative life-history interviews with thirty women in a southwestern detention center. The second author of this article negotiated access to the detention center. We traveled to the facility over a series of weekends in the spring of 2000 to conduct inter-views with women who indicated ahead of time that they were inter-ested in talking to us. Of the approximately 200 women incarcerated at the facility, 65 volunteered to participate. We interviewed 30 of them. None of these women were screened by us, or to our knowledge by the detention center administration, for their involvement in the project. We had no pre-conceived requirements for participation, other than that the women be willing volunteers. Our sample was limited to 30 due to scheduling conflicts (some women were working, sleeping, visiting guests, or at court during the hours we were on site) and budget con-straints (for our travel and the $10-20 stipends provided for each partici-pant). Informed consent was obtained from the participants, all of whom allowed us to audio-record the interviews for later transcription. All provided their own, or were assigned, pseudonyms in order to main-tain confidentiality. The interviews were conducted in private rooms at the facility, out of earshot of staff. They lasted anywhere between 30 minutes and three and a half hours.

Our sample was fairly diverse, yet representative of the population of women detained at the facility as well as the female carceral population in the U.S. On average, the women were 34 years old, the youngest being 21 and the oldest being 50. Fifteen women were white (50%), seven were African American (23%), three were Latina (10%), two were American Indian (7%), and three identified as biracial (10%). Nearly all of the women had little to no legitimate income prior to their incarceration. Twenty-five of the women had already been convicted and sentenced; the majority were being detained on probation violations. Three women had been convicted but were awaiting sentencing and two were awaiting trial. These two women were by far facing the most serious of ramifications, both having been charged with murder. All of the rest of the women were convicted of drug offenses, prostitution, or property offenses.

The interviews were conducted as part of a larger project on the link between women's victimization and offending. However, as our interviewing approach was semi-structured, the interviews often flowed into other topics. We utilized this interviewing approach based on our understanding of standpoint epistemology, wherein the contributions to research by members of socially, historically, or economically marginalized groups are privileged above the contributions of members of more privileged groups (Bar On, 1993; Hartsock, 1987). Rather than predetermine a structured list of topics, our aim was to allow issues to arise as the women saw fit. Among the most common of issues raised in this format was motherhood.

Motherhood stood out as an important theme in several respects. Ninety percent (n = 27) of the women were mothers. They averaged three children each and the vast majority (92%) had children under the age of 18. Two of the women were also pregnant, and one had given birth just one day prior to her incarceration. The women discussed the ways in which they viewed themselves as mothers, the role of parenting in their criminal offenses, and their need for social support within the carceral setting.

FINDINGS

When the women began talking about their lives prior to incarceration, what we first noticed was the way in which they viewed themselves as parents and, in particular, the social significance placed on their motherhood. After hearing about their views on motherhood and listening to the contexts in which they explained their criminality, it became clear to us that motherhood and criminality were inexplicitly linked.

Motherhood and Self-Perception

The women viewed motherhood from two primary vantage points. The first was as a valuable social status, one that required that women uphold, or at least try to uphold, hegemonic standards of motherhood (Kline, 1995). In this vein, the women viewed motherhood as a highly coveted status. By speaking of themselves as good mothers, they seemed to be struggling to think less about their current negative status and instead concentrate on a more positive social status. In so doing, they were able to think of themselves as something other than *criminal*–an asset and a valuable member of society.

A couple of observations illustrate the importance of the women's identity in this regard. Several women reminisced about their children, recalling births, birthdays, accomplishments at school, and the like. A few had photos or sketches of their children and where possible, they returned to the interview rooms in order to show them to us. However, one woman went a step further. During the interview with India, a 31-year-old American Indian woman, the conversation turned to her visible tattoos. As she began describing them, it became clear that they were tattoos with the names of her six children–one tattoo per child. Each contained colors and designs that reminded her of that child. Her most recent tattoo was of a heart with flowers surrounding a blank space on her right breast. This one was reserved for her youngest child whose name she had not yet had tattooed. All of her kids were staying with their father's sister and she planned to reunite with them upon release.

Thus, in their own ways, the women viewed themselves in a positive light, as mothers devoted to their children above all else. Regardless of whether the law or public opinion would agree with such assessments, the power of this self-perception was undeniable. More than providing a buttress against negative connotations of their criminalized state, seeing themselves as good and worthy mothers provided the women with a kind of strength and resilience they may not have derived from anywhere else.

However, the women still struggled to reconcile their past. Several expressed great remorse about their situation, and simultaneous to seeing themselves as mothers, they internalized the social stigma attached to their crimes. As Lisa, a 27-year-old Latina, explained about her use of crack cocaine during pregnancy:

> It's awful [crying] . . . just seeing her. She's a little angel from God. For me to just imagine one hit, you know, what it does to me. Imagine what it did to her little brain. . . . [crying harder] Just like for me to hurt her, just horrible. . . . CPS got involved. I mean I don't blame them. The hospital called them, and you know, they treated me like a monster, and I felt like a monster. I knew I was a monster, but the remorse I feel, the hurt.

Such pain over the loss of children was prominent among women whose drug addictions were the impetus for state intervention. In the following two narratives, we hear from Julianna, who was addicted to crack, and Linda, who was addicted to both crack and heroin. Both were black, 35 years of age, and each had four children, although the oldest of Julianna's was an adult. Like Lisa, both of these women were likely deemed the least deserving of the *mother* label, and both used their religious beliefs as a basis for redemption and the belief that they would be seen as good mothers again and reunited with their children. Their persistence in this regard was so strong that it seemed almost vital to their survival.

> I believe in my heart of hearts, once you birth a child, they can take your child from you for so long but that child will come back. Listen to a lot of these talk shows on how families are starting to reunite. Just look at the awesome power of God to bring families back together that haven't been together for 14, 20, 30 years. I have a dream that one day my two children that is within the state, I will see them [sic]. We will reunite and be together. With my other children in Nebraska, I have no doubt that I will see them. They'll be family. God will show me the way for us to reunite and be together again. That's my strong belief. . . . He [God] spoke to me. . . . "I'm gonna' pick you up and I will turn your life around and I will make you want success and great things. Most of all, I will make you a great woman of God. . . . I'm gonna bring you back to your children again." That, right there, is enough for me to hold on, to walk through the storm and the rain, and move on with my life.

> –Julianna

I ask God to give me my life back, give me my children back. I'm okay with where I'm at because I know when I leave here it won't be long before I can reunite with my children. Not right away, but eventually it's goin' to come together. I know God is gonna' give them back to me. I know I'm goin' to see them real soon. Without them, I'm nothin'. I just thank God.

–Linda

Similar to the way in which Juliana and Linda talked about the children they had lost, so too did Buckwheat, a 44-year-old black woman whose son had been killed in a drive-by shooting:

These Christian women come out here for a Valentine's thing. . . . They gave out these little heart shaped doilies and they had a little prayer on them and they said to all of us, "These are special gifts that we're goin' to give you and hopefully the right one is goin' to reach you." Well, it surprised me about the one that they gave me because it said, "I gave my son to the Lord. . ." and he would live forever. I said, "Oh my God." And He told me to let it go. To let him go.

Such religious conviction was common among the African American women. As we discuss elsewhere (Ferraro & Moe, 2003a), the use of religion, particularly Christianity, was a popular coping strategy as the women were able to attend church and prayer groups several times a week. Moreover, the majority of volunteers inside the detention center were from area churches. Thus, due to their religious beliefs prior to incarceration and/or the religiously guided social support inside the facility, women turned to their faith for comfort, empowerment, and cultural pride. As found elsewhere (Ross, 1998), however, religion served as both a mechanism of survival as well as social control in that while providing comfort, it also conveniently reinforced an ideology wherein women turned inward or toward God for an explanation of their circumstances, rather than toward the structural conditions that reinforce violence against women, racism, and poverty.

The second way in which the women viewed motherhood was as a pragmatic obligation to provide for their children, which in most instances was made difficult due to poverty, abuse, and drug use. As we will discuss in the next section, the women's obligations to provide for their children were often connected to their motivations for committing crimes. In terms of their self-perceptions, however, they also spoke about their practical role as a *mom*, and in doing so, they expressed a great deal of guilt about being absent. During her interview, Lonna, a 31-year-old Latina/White woman, was quite concerned about her three kids. They were staying with her mother-in-law and while she visited with them regularly, she blamed herself for not being there. She indicated that while she felt badly for missing both of her daughters' birthdays, she was particularly worried about her 14-year-old son, who was acting out and getting into trouble. While she was still married to the children's father, he showed little concern for their welfare, being gone most of the time on drinking and gambling binges:

> My son's in a lot of trouble. He'll leave in the middle of the night or he won't come home from school. I'd look for him and I could find him. I'm not there to do that anymore and he [her husband] won't do it. He's hanging out with bad little kids and stuff. I put him in counseling before I came in here. He [her husband] was supposed to take him to counseling. He took him and dropped him off at his friend's house . . . didn't go to counseling. . . . [crying] They don't have a mom or a dad. My mother-in-law asked my son, "Why are you acting this way?" He says, "Why do I have to come home? I don't have a family." I hear in the background my older daughter saying, "It's true. My mom's in jail and my dad's out partying." Damn. [long pause]

In order to cope with such guilt, Lonna did what she could to stay connected to her children: "I write to my kids and stuff and I made my daughter a little birthday card. She was all happy but I didn't want her to have nothing so my mother-in-law sent her balloons from me at school. So they know that I'm not forgetting about them."

Others also wrote to their children. Angel, a 41-year-old black woman awaiting sentencing for writing fraudulent checks, spoke about the relationship she was able to maintain with her eldest of seven children, who was also incarcerated:

> My son and I write letters every week to each other. We've been doing some wonderful communication since I've been here. I try to make each letter to him some kind of lesson. I feel like I'm still teaching him and so I use the letters as an opportunity to put that mothering in there for him and try to keep him on track and keep his spirits lifted and, you know, make sure he's growing.

Of course such strategies are dependent upon women being both literate and having familial support on the outside. Literacy is a significant problem, as only 55% of jailed women have a high school education and 12% have less than an eighth grade education (Greenfeld & Snell, 1999). Moreover, women must rely on family or friends to put money into their accounts in order for them to purchase paper, pens, envelopes, and postage. However, where it was possible, such contact somewhat buttressed the lack of institutional support for motherhood on the inside.

Similar to the ways in which women who had lost their children due to state intervention or death retained the social status of *mother*, one woman tried to emulate the notion of having contact with her son by writing him stories and poems, even though he never received them. Orca, a 31-year-old white woman being detained on a probation violation (original charge was drug-related), had lost custody of her son after over a decade of battling an addiction to crack. She felt that writing served a functional purpose in keeping her emotionally tied to her son. Even though she did not know where he was and would likely never have contact with him again, her writing helped her feel as if she was fulfilling some sort of motherly duty: "I write a lot. It's the only way I can cope. I write things for my son, children's poems and books." Soon after describing this type of communication during our interview, we heard a baby crying in the visitation room. Orca fell silent and began weeping.

Regardless of their circumstances, the women retained their motherhood status. Doing so allowed them to think about the future, to a time they might be outside the control of the criminal processing system and fully able to parent their children. Even for those who had lost their children, continuing to see themselves as mothers was an important coping mechanism. In most cases, doing so provided comfort, motivation for change, and resistance to the social stigma placed upon them.

Motherhood and Criminality

Motherhood seemed connected to the women's criminality in numerous ways. In most cases, motherhood, and the responsibilities thereof, provided the motivation for women's economically based offenses.

For example, Angel, quoted earlier, began writing fraudulent checks in order to pay for the exorbitant childcare, grocery, and housing costs she incurred as a single mother of seven children. She had been on her own since the age of 17 and had managed to get through two and a half years of college. She had been working at decent-paying jobs until her abusive husband found her. She then moved to the southwest but had trouble finding employment. It was at this point that she started writing bad checks:

> The check writing went off and on for a period, for a number of years . . . sometimes I was getting benefits [public subsidies], sometimes I wasn't. I would have to supplement my income writing the checks, buying the groceries, stealing money from the bank to pay for rent or to pay for a car repair. You know, it was always something. . . . There were a couple of times I went to the bank and wrote checks for cash and made it out for $1,000 cash that was for covering things, bills, stuff like that.

For Angel, and several others, economically based crimes, were connected to abusive partners as well as motivated by the need to provide for their families. Alicia, a 21-year-old African American/white woman, provided a similar rationale for drug dealing:

> I don't regret it because without the extra income, my kids wouldn't be fed every day. Even though I do have a good job when I work and stuff like that, it's hard raising two kids by yourself. . . . You get used to having money every day and you don't have to worry about the electric being off or the rent being paid. Your check is like your hard earned money, you're not going to spend it ridiculously like, "Oh, let's go buy a $100 pair of shoes with it." You know what I'm saying? You budget it because it's the only thing you look forward to for paying your bills . . . but that money goes so fast. As soon as you get it, the kids need new clothes or spend $20 at the Circle K for candy. . . . We may not have chosen the right paths to go along in life, but I'm not a dummy. . . . They get mad at you if you can't get a job in two weeks. Who in the hell is going to employ you? I'm not going to McDonald's. McDonald's is not going to pay my rent. That's what they want you to do. Lower your self-esteem to where you will take anything. I'm sorry, I have never worked for a $5 an hour job, not since I was a teenager. I'm not going to now. I have two kids to support. Where am I going to live with them? In a shelter, making $5 an hour? I'm not going to subject my kids to something like that. I'd rather just do my prison time if I have to do it and get rid of all of this.

Although she was the youngest of our interviewees, Alicia seemed very cognizant of some of the larger social structures that affected her situation. She was the mother of a three year old and a five year old, and she had been on her own since she was 17. She had no family support and had been involved with an abusive man. While she had completed technical training as a nurse's assistant, she found that the $10 an hour she made was not enough to provide for her family. Although she believed that selling crack was wrong, she also felt justified in doing it because of the support it provided for her kids.

Lonna's story was similar to Angel's and Alicia's. She was in jail for violating probation, but her original offense was welfare fraud. She blamed her husband for stealing the family's grocery, rent, and utility money and putting her in the predicament of having to collect extra checks:

> I don't want to make it sound like it was all his fault but it is. There came a time when there was sometimes no water in the house, no electric, no food. So while I was working I collected welfare. Not only that, sometimes he would take my money anyway no matter if he was working or not. It didn't matter. Sometimes he'd just take my money anyway, so I would go and get extra checks.

In total, 27% (n = 8) of the women were being detained on probation violations. In most instances, the violations involved relatively petty matters such as missing an appointment with their probation officers or skipping a drug test. The most serious probation violation involved Patrice, a 28-year-old Black woman serving a 120-day sentence for smoking marijuana. Patrice's original crime of welfare fraud was directly connected to her need to provide for her three kids, and began when her children's father was sent to prison and she was struggling financially: "I wanted my baby a baby bed and wanted her this and I wanted her that and he wasn't there. I didn't know where he was. Just one day he disappeared." The drug conviction was a felony, which Patrice was beginning to realize would complicate her ability to find a legitimate job, as she had just been placed on work release:

> When I went for my sentencing, I thought he was going to let me go because I paid for all of my restitution for the welfare check and everything. My lawyer's like, "We think she should be released." And the judge goes, "No, I'm going to give her about 120 days . . . you shouldn't have smoked that joint." . . . I don't think he was

very fair at all. I think that a felony is for somebody who did something really actually bad. I ain't sayin' what I did wasn't a crime. I
know it was a crime. I just can't imagine why he would give me a
felony because I broke probation and smoked a joint. I write down
"felony" on my applications and everybody goes, "Oh no, we
can't hire you.". . . A lot of us are in here for probation violations.
The judge didn't care that we had kids.

The difficulties of complying with community supervision requirements were addressed frequently. The women who did so believed that
such requirements placed additional burdens on an already strained situation and negatively impacted their kids. Alicia described the requirements of her intensive probation:

Three to four times a week, counseling, but you have to pay for it.
One girl said she was paying like $60 a week just for three counsel-
ing sessions. Every time it was $20 . . . bang. . . . They expect us to
have a full time job, which is fine, counseling four times a week,
on top of community service two hours a day, so that's ten hours a
week, so where is the time for your kids? And they know some
people have kids, but they don't care. You mess up any step of the
law and they're violating you and putting you in prison. And if you
don't go to counseling when they say to go, you're violated even if
you drop clean every day. If you mess up in any of those areas, say
the traffic is bad, or say my daughter is asthmatic. She goes into an
asthma attack in the middle of the night, I have to make sure I page
my IPS [intensive probation supervision] worker and make sure he
calls me back in time before I go to the doctor. My daughter could
be suffocating in this time while he's taking his time calling me
back and they don't care. You leave without them knowing, you're
violated. They don't care if you're dying or your kids are dying.
Good thing my daughter hasn't been in the hospital. She has a
heart murmur. Anything can happen to her and I don't feel like
that's right for them to violate if I am at the hospital with my child.
Even if I get there right away and I page them, they say, "Well, too
bad. You're prison bound." That's what IPS stands for: in prison
soon. A lot of people say that.

A final observation about probation violations is noteworthy. In
cases where women had violated their probation through a new offense,
as well as other cases where women knew they were going to be in trou-

ble with authorities (e.g., an arrest warrant being issued), the majority turned themselves in. Before doing so, however, they often negotiated placement of their children so as to lessen the chance that state authorities would intervene and place their children in foster care or other undesirable locations. They did not feel they could rely on their current partners for this.

On the whole, these narratives resonate with *pathways to crime* research, which is primarily concerned with the ways in which a person's life experiences may situate her or him in ways that make criminal offenses more attractive. Within feminist scholarship, pathways research has been connected most directly with prior victimization, the typical scenario often involving a battered woman who kills her abuser (Arnold, 1990; Belknap, 2001). It has also been used to examine avenues of criminalization outside of interpersonal victimization (e.g., drug use, prostitution), though all of these experiences are often interconnected within a woman's lived experience (Daly, 1992, 1994; Owen, 1998; Richie, 1996). Based on these narratives, motherhood, in and of itself or combined with exigent factors such as abuse, drugs, and poverty, appears to be a pathway toward criminality.

In a different vein, motherhood was sometimes connected emotionally to crimes. Women who had lost custody of their kids because of abusive partners and/or drug addictions often spoke of crimes they committed as a result of such loss. Almost all of these crimes involved substance abuse. A total of ten women (30%) had permanently lost their children due to state intervention. Gillian, a 36-year-old white woman, faced severance of her parental rights after her abusive husband molested their nine-year-old daughter. During the case, she had separated from her husband and moved in with her mother. She felt as if she had done all she could to do comply with state authorities, but she eventually lost her daughter permanently. She immediately began using crack:

> We went to court and they tried to say I had a drug and alcohol problem. I didn't even do drugs back then. I smoked pot, but since I've been here, I haven't smoked no weed. I did drink. They said I had a drug problem and I don't even know where they got that. I wasn't even doing drugs. I did start drugs after I lost her. About two to three months later, I did it. I was like, "Hell, they said I did it." I didn't have nothing to lose then. I had already lost her, so that's when I started doing drugs.

Similar experiences were shared by two women who were still struggling to maintain their parental rights. One of them, Marie, a 27-year-old white woman with a three year old and a five year old, was serving six months for prostitution. She had turned to prostitution to support a long-time drug addiction. CPS became involved with her family after her husband had gotten high and rolled her kids in a stroller onto a busy highway. Marie's addiction worsened after this, as she turned to crack, cocaine, heroin, and methadone. However, despite being intermittently homeless and abused by her husband, Marie had managed to get sober, find an apartment, and file for a divorce in order to comply with CPS. The state was still moving toward terminating her parental rights, but Marie remained hopeful. She explained how drugs related to the situation with her kids:

> I think getting them back is a real strong drive for me to stay out of drugs. It gives me something to concentrate on. I know if I touch those drugs, the kids are gone. I'll never even have a fighting chance. So, I know I can't. The only barrier I see is just the last court date. I didn't go because I was high. I knew they were takin' them and I couldn't bear to hear about severance and adoption as they planned, so I just didn't go. That didn't help. I just hope it ain't the same judge.

Need for Social Support as Mothers

There was limited recognition within the detention facility of motherhood or the powerful role it played in the survival of the inmates. The only therapy available to the women occurred in a group setting and was run primarily by one counselor. The program appeared fairly comprehensive in that it addressed topics such as domestic violence, anger management, and substance abuse. Brina, a 27-year-old white woman, commented on how she and others felt about having access to this therapy. In particular, she was struck by a movie they had watched about a woman who mistreated her baby. While Brina had not been in that same predicament, she did feel as if she had lost her two-year-old daughter because she had left her in another state in the custody of her best friend after being arrested and extradited for embezzlement:

> It hit home with me because of losing my baby . . . the consequences are still the same. It brings hope to the women in here . . . who have lost them [children] to circumstances. It gives you hope

that you can straighten yourself out. You can get everything rearranged and on the right track.

Others commented that participation in this program was a unique experience and one that they would not be able to have on the outside. Indeed, this program was unique, even within a jail setting. According to the National Institute of Justice, only about 20% of jailed women receive mental health services upon admission (Harlow, 1998). This is quite negligent given that incarcerated women report psychological counseling as being the single most important service they need (ACA, 1990). Despite the availability of this program, some women did not even acknowledge its existence and instead drew attention to the continued needs of the inmates. This indicated to us that not all the women either found the group-based program effective or had access to it:

> I see so many girls in here that don't need to be in prison. They need to be intensively in some sort of therapy. They've been so severely abused that their personality is just splintered. They don't even know who they are. They're just shells of people. They need to be put back together before they can begin to be expected to understand any kind of responsibility or consequences.
>
> –Angel

For one woman in particular, just having the opportunity to talk to us was therapeutic. Sherrie was a 40-year-old white woman with four children, three of whom were under the age of 18. She had lost them to the state due to her involvement with an abusive man. She had lived on the streets on numerous occasions in order to hide from him, but was eventually seen as an unfit mother for not doing more. She began the interview relatively reserved, but opened up as it progressed. At one point she spoke about her fragile emotional state:

> Yeah, I've got to get some of this stuff out. You know, you people are the first people I've talked to . . . I've told nobody any of this, you know? And it's hard. . . . And even right now it's just the bare surface, you know? If I start talking, I'm going to be like Humpty Dumpty. I'm going to fall and you ain't going to find all those pieces. That's what I'm afraid of, that I'll lose it completely mentally, you know? It's going to take a lot.

For another woman, opening up in this way was too painful. One of our shortest interviews was with Theresa, a 39-year-old white woman, whose parental rights to her four children had been terminated in the previous year. Similar to some of the stories in the previous section, she was serving six months for a second D.U.I. (driving under the influence). While she had long battled alcoholism, her use worsened after state authorities informed her that they were going to move toward severance. She had managed to remain sober and comply with state authorities for over two years; however, after a weekend visit from her abusive ex-husband, the state changed its position on the dependency case. Theresa appeared to be in shock throughout the 40-minute interview, which was formally ended after she became too distraught to talk.

But there were instances where the women spoke about how they were using incarceration, regardless of what they felt about it and the lack of institutional support, as a time for future planning. Lonna had survived a 14-year abusive marriage in which her husband constantly stole the family's money to support his drug and alcohol use. Initially caught for welfare fraud (described earlier) and after being arrested for violating probation, she had finally come to the realization that she needed to end the relationship for the benefit of her three minor children. While she was attending group counseling in order to learn how to break free of the relationship, her situation was illustrative of how helpful a well-staffed, comprehensive, advocacy-based program could be:

> While I'm here, I'm not going to make it a waste of time. I'm going to do what I can to get ahead. . . . I think it's a good thing that I came to jail . . . I'm not going back home. I'm getting a divorce when I leave here. I'm just going to take the kids and leave. That's my plan when I leave here. . . . It's a good thing I'm here I guess. Not for the kids but it will be better in the long run.

In most other instances, the women expressed a lack of support for their motherhood. Such opinions were not reserved for the detention center alone, but rather from the treatment the women received throughout the criminal processing system, the effects of which were only magnified in the carceral setting. As Alicia stated regarding the judge who sentenced her:

> If you really cared about me being a good parent, what is 90 days in here really going to do for my children? . . . Some of us in here do have families. It's broken up two times because the father's not

there and then the mom is not there because they have to be locked up. . . . We're not all bad people.

There was only one woman in our sample who claimed she was receiving institutional social support. However, upon considering the circumstances of her life, it became clear why she would feel this way. Boo, a 27-year-old Latina, had been in and out of jail several times prior to our meeting. In the last five years, in between incarcerations, she lived on the streets and supported herself through prostitution, drug sales, shoplifting, and burglary. She admitted being addicted to crack, heroin, and alcohol. She had three minor children and was pregnant at the time of the interview. In the following excerpt, Boo describes the kind of support she found in the detention center:

> To me this is my home away from home 'cuz I don't have nobody on the outside. So it's kind of hard for me but then at the same time I like it in here 'cuz I get that special attention that I crave. . . . I know all of the COs [correctional officers] here. They're like my uncles and aunts . . . they're real good people to me. I like them. . . . I get taken care of in here very well. They give three pregnancy bags a day which contain two cartons of milk, two orange juices, and two fruits and you get three pills three times a day during breakfast, lunch and dinner.

For Boo, having access to prenatal vitamins and nutrition, as well as knowing the staff, translated into institutional social support. Other women recognized the lack of institutional support for their motherhood. Mary, a 32-year-old white woman with a nursing degree who was arrested for D.U.I., shared her observations of how pregnant women were treated: "This girl went into labor and she was so scared and she screamed and cried and nobody came. Finally several of us started screaming until somebody responded because she was getting ready to deliver her babies, her twins, all alone." In order to help, Mary used her education to assist others manage the dismal health care services available in the facility: "I help people fill out medical slips. A lot of these people come in here and they don't know how to read and write and they can't really put it together and say what it is they want to say . . . people in here need an advocate."

Throughout these narratives, we see issues that a gender-specific program could address. In lieu of such a program, women began helping themselves by creating their own informal peer support system. As Boo described, they lifted each other's spirits and helped each other out whenever possible: "We clown a lot. We make each other laugh and stuff. Otherwise we'd be sitting in our rooms and we'd go crazy. That's why a lot of people do the things they do. I've seen a couple people hang themselves in here. I've seen people go crazy." To some extent, the counselor who worked most closely with the women during the group sessions was trying to institutionalize these efforts. As Angel attested:

> I've done a lot since I've been here. I taught a class . . . the counselor here is really, really good and she lets us do what we want to do in the group so now since I've taught the class, a couple of the other girls are putting together exercises and they're going to also get up and teach a class. You have to have something to do in here and there's not enough programs.

Such support was critical for many of the women, and the format used by the counselor fits well within the gender-specific model we discussed earlier. However, while notable, she was alone in her efforts and as previously mentioned, the program she ran did not seem to be accessible to or known by all of the women. Institutional barriers to communication with loved ones on the outside worsened the situation. As mentioned previously, the women no longer received writing utensils, paper, envelopes or postage from the facility. Such items had to be purchased from commissary with funds put on the women's accounts from outside the facility.

Even calls to the outside, since they must be collect calls, required loved ones to have disposable income. This caused quite a burden, as attested by Shakilla, a 34-year-old, black woman with a 14-year-old daughter who was in the custody of her mother. Shakilla had been trying to maintain regular contact with her daughter but was no longer able to because her mother had a $300 phone bill from the many collect calls. Phone calls from the detention center cost the receiver $1.90 for each 15 minutes. Her mother was on a fixed income and did not have the money to cover those types of bills. Shakilla feared that continuing phone contact would take money away from that which was needed to provide for her daughter.

Not surprisingly then, the stipends we provided for interviews produced a strong incentive for participation. Some women expressed concern about their friends inside the facility who for whatever reason were not able to be interviewed. While sharing funds was prohibited by administrators, they indicated that they still planned to do so. In short, without outside resources, several women lost contact with their families, particularly their children. Again, simple and relatively affordable forms of tangible support, which could be a part of a therapeutic program, could go a long way toward helping women feel connected and empowered.

DISCUSSION:
PROGRAMMING POSSIBILITIES

Women in this study both accepted and challenged hegemonic discourses on mothering by retaining and defending their motherhood status under the most dire of circumstances. We do not mean to suggest that all were the most protective and nurturing of parents. Indeed many were not. Some put their children at great risk by their decisions and behavior, while others had attempted to provide for their children through illegal means. The question of what may be best for the children of these women and whether the women ought to have contact and/or custody of them is beyond the scope of this paper. Our focus is on how women's symbolic or pragmatic status as mothers fed into their motivations for crime and the ways in which they survived incarceration. In this regard, therapeutic programming that concertedly addresses issues related to family, parenting and motherhood would be helpful. Specifically, an assets-based approach to therapy within jail settings may go a long way toward helping mothers focus on their futures, with or without their children. Given the crisis state women may be in upon incarceration, as well as the short time in which they may be incarcerated at a jail or detention facility, such a program would need to be adaptable and short-term.

A framework for such a therapeutic program is van Wormer's strengths-restorative approach (2001). Building on strengths theory (see Saleebey, 1997) within the social work discipline and restorative justice principles (see Hahn, 1998; Johnstone, 2001), this model is premised on identifying and using the strengths of an individual to build support systems around her as she works to more fully recognize and recover from negative experiences throughout her life. In the case of incarcerated women, such negative experiences are probably numerous and may include prior childhood or adult victimization, poor family relations, poverty, racism, sexism, miseducation, physical and mental health problems, substance abuse, and of course criminalization. Such experiences may be aggravated by motherhood, single-parenting, and CPS intervention.

While still relatively new in the correctional arena, strengths-restorative approaches have been utilized with juvenile offenders (Clark, 1998; Pepi, 1998) and domestic violence victims (Hoyle & Sanders, 2000). A few articles have laid a framework for adapting it to female offenders (Wilson & Anderson, 1997; van Wormer, 1999) and in van Wormer's (2001) book, the structure and method of the program is elucidated more fully. The program would begin by recognizing and legitimizing these many negative experiences, on an institutional level, so as to help women to understand that they are not alone in having them and that there is a larger social context, perhaps well beyond their control, in which they occurred. For women who are already cognizant of this, such a program may at least offer a setting for receiving and building social support as they negotiate the legal system and plan for the future. Social workers, counselors, or therapists running the program would not excuse the women's offending behavior or even justify it; the goal would be to simply provide a space for women to safely reflect on the difficulties in their lives and to see them from varying perspectives. This could be very powerful for women who blame themselves entirely for what happens to them, rather than seeing the larger social structures that support patriarchy, racism, and poverty.

The main aspect of the program, however, is to assist women in moving beyond the point of recognition and toward strategizing and action. In this respect, the program would provide a platform for women to know and appreciate their individual strengths and the ways these strengths may be used in the future. It would allow women to go beyond thinking about how they would like their lives to be to planning for their lives upon release. Grounded in realistic goals and possibilities for achieving them, administrators of the program would assist, and perhaps advocate on behalf of, women who need such things as a G.E.D., safe housing, substance abuse treatment, parenting skills, child care, legal representation, employment, and transportation. While the women's caseworkers or probation officers may address some of these needs, within the program the assistance would be couched in a therapeutic setting that would provide social support along with encouraging of women to make their own choices rather than follow another person's directives.

While presented as just a framework here, *strengths-restorative* therapy, as van Wormer (2001) conceptualizes it, may be implemented in varying contexts as a gender-specific program, encompassing a holistic perspective of the types of concerns and experiences women may have while recognizing that each woman may be distinct in her need, experiences, individual assets, and ways of coping (Austin et al., 1992). In this way, motherhood could be addressed, legitimized, and supported within the carceral context, regardless of what a woman's circumstances as a parent are on the outside. For those who need and want it, realistic plans could then begin as to how to remain safe, stay out of the legal system, and support one's family upon release. For those mothers who no longer have rights to their children, the program could be a healing process that may eventually foster a realistic plan for living independently. This type of framework could be adapted to individual or group-based therapy (van Wormer, 2001) and formatted for short-term use (Berger & Andrews, 1995, as cited in van Wormer, 2001) such that women in jail would benefit, if in no other way than from greater social support. And while we recognize that a carceral setting represents the epitomy of oppression and is among the least desirable of spaces for therapeutic progress, we also know that it may actually be the safest place for women who on the outside face violence, poverty, and rampant drugs (Bloom & Covington, 1998; Ferraro & Moe, 2003b).

CONCLUSION

Women have been disproportionately affected by the *war on drugs* as well as increased poverty and the eradication of public services. Moreover, the contexts of their crimes have yet to be fully recognized by the criminal processing system. While advocacy and social reform must target these arenas, until or unless meaningful change occurs, women will continue to be criminalized at astronomical rates. These women will continue to face a host of issues upon entering the criminal processing system. They may be recovering from the physical, sexual, and emotional abuse inflicted by intimate partners; dealing with the effects of street violence, poor nutrition, absent medical care, and/or substance abuse; and reconciling the crimes they committed. In most instances, they will also be mothers with dependent kids for whom they worry, cry, pray, and vent. Their children are also harmed in ways that may reproduce their experiences that led their mothers to jail. We have argued for greater attention to jailed women, a carceral population that has been largely ignored. We advocate for greater focus on the immediate needs of this population and the development of short-term, gender-specific

strengths-restorative based therapy. This is only a first step, and resources and support following release are essential to women's continued success as mothers and as citizens. While we focus here on women
in jail, we endorse the increased use of alternatives to incarceration and
the reversal of the trend toward harsh, punitive responses to non-violent
crimes.

The value of motherhood for the women in this study, and other
women ensnared in the crime processing system, is multifaceted. It
would behoove us to begin addressing the needs of incarcerated mothers in a more concerted and systematic way, with the hope that they may
better come to terms with the reality of their situations and, if given the
opportunity, strive to provide the best possible upbringing for their
children. Their futures are not hopeless. Many have survived circumstances worse than incarceration and will continue to survive despite
insurmountable odds. We must recognize this and choose to support
them through the process, instead of ignoring, scapegoating, and
criminalizing them.

NOTE

1. In using the term "carceral," we mean to imply all situations of confinement
within the justice system, be it a juvenile facility, adult detention center, jail, or prison.

REFERENCES

American Correctional Association. (1990). *The female offender: What does the future
hold?* Laurel, MD: Author.
Arnold, R. (1990). Processes of victimization and criminalization of black women. *So-
cial Justice, 17,* 153-166.
Austin, J., Bloom, B., & Donahue, T. (1992). *Female offenders in the community: An
analysis of innovative strategies and programs.* Washington, DC: National Institute
of Corrections.
Austin, J. & Irwin, J. (2001). *It's about time: America's imprisonment binge.* Belmont,
CA: Wadsworth.
Bar On, B.-A. (1993). Marginality and epistemic privilege. In L. Alcoff & E. Potter
(Eds.), *Feminist epistemologies* (pp. 83-100). New York: Routledge.
Belknap, J. (2000). Programming and health care responsibility for incarcerated
women. In J. James (Ed.), *States of confinement: Policing, detention, and prisons*
(pp. 109-123). New York: St. Martin's Press.
Belknap, J. (2001). The invisible woman: Gender, crime and justice (2nd ed.).
Belmont, CA: Wadsworth.

Belknap, J., Dunn, M., & Holsinger, K. (1997). *Moving toward juvenile justice and youth-serving systems that address the distinct experiences of the adolescent female.* Ohio: Gender Specific Services Work Group Report.

Bloom, B., Chesney-Lind, M., & Owen, B. (1994). *Women in California prisons: Hidden victims of the war on drugs.* San Francisco, CA: Center on Juvenile and Criminal Justice.

Bloom, B. & Covington, S. (1998). *Gender-specific programming for female offenders: What is it and why is it important?* Paper presented at the meeting of the American Society of Criminology, Washington, DC.

Bureau of Justice Statistics. (1992). *Census of state and federal correctional facilities 1990* (NCJ 137003). Washington, DC: U.S. Department of Justice, Office of Justice Programs.

Bureau of Justice Statistics. (1995). *Prison and jail inmates at midyear 1994* (NCJ 151654). Washington, DC: U.S. Department of Justice, Office of Justice Programs.

Bureau of Justice Statistics. (2004). *Prisoners in 2003* (NCJ 205335). Washington, DC: US Department of Justice, Office of Justice Programs.

Bureau of Justice Statistics. (2005a). *Jail statistics.* Washington, DC: US Department of Justice, Office of Justice Programs.

Bureau of Justice Statistics. (2005b). *Prison and jail inmates at midyear 2004* (NCJ 208801). Washington, DC: U.S. Department of Justice, Office of Justice Programs.

Bush-Baskette, S. (1998). The war on drugs as a war on Black women. In S. Miller (Ed.), *Crime control and women* (pp. 113-129). Thousand Oaks, CA: Sage.

Campbell, A., Muncer, S., & Bibel, D. (1998). Female-female criminal assault: An evolutionary perspective. *Journal of Research in Crime and Delinquency, 35,* 413-428.

Casey, K. A,. & Wiatrowski, M. D. (1996). Women offenders and "three strikes and you're out." In D. Shichor & D. K. Sechrest (Eds.), *Three strikes and you're out: Vengeance as public policy* (pp. 222-243). Thousand Oaks, CA: Sage.

Chesney-Lind, M. (1991). Patriarchy, prisons, and jails: A critical look at trends in women's incarceration. *The Prison Journal, 71,* 51-67.

Chesney-Lind, M. (1997). *The female offender: Girls, women, and crime.* Thousand Oaks, CA: Sage.

Clark, M. D. (1998). Strength-based practice: The ABC's of working with adolescents who don't want to work with you. *Federal Probation, 62*(2), 46-53.

Comack, E. (1996). *Women in trouble: Connecting women's law violations to their histories of abuse.* Halifax, Canada: Fernwood.

Daly, K. (1992). Women's pathways to felony court: Feminist theories of lawbreaking and problems of representation. *Review of Law and Women's Studies, 2,* 11-52.

Daly, K. (1994). *Gender, crime and punishment.* New Haven, CT: Yale University Press.

Davis, A. Y. (1998). Public imprisonment and private violence: Reflections on the hidden punishment of women. *Criminal and Civil Confinement, 24,* 339-351.

Diaz-Cotto, J. (1996). *Gender, ethnicity, and the state: Latina and Latino prison politics.* Albany, NY: State University of New York.

Dobash, R.P., Dobash, R.E., & Gutteridge, S. (1986). *The imprisonment of women.* Oxford: Basil Blackwell.

Donziger, S. (Ed.). (1996). *The real war on crime: The report of the National Criminal Justice Commission.* New York: Harper Perenial.

Federal Bureau of Investigation. (1996). *Uniform Crime Reports: Crime in the United States, 1995.* Washington, DC: Department of Justice, US Government Printing Office.

Federal Bureau of Investigation. (2004). *Uniform Crime Reports: Crime in the United States, 2003.* Washington, DC: Department of Justice, U.S. Government Printing Office.

Ferraro, K.J. (1997). Battered women: Strategies for survival. In A. Carderelli (Ed.), *Violence among intimate partners: Patterns, causes and effects* (pp. 124-140). New York: Macmillan.

Ferraro, K.J., & Moe, A M. (2003a). Jail culture: Women's stories of survival and resistance. In B.H. Zaitzow & J. Thomas (Eds.), *Women in prison: Gender and social control* (pp. 65-93). Boulder, CO: Lynne Reinner.

Ferraro, K.J., & Moe, A.M. (2003b). Mothering, crime, and incarceration. *Journal of Contemporary Ethnography, 32*(1), 9-40.

Gilfus, M.E. (1992). From victims to survivors to offenders: Women's routes of entry and immersion into street crime. *Women and Criminal Justice, 4*(1), 63-89.

Greenfeld, L.A., & Snell, T. L. (1999). *Bureau of Justice Statistics special report: Women offenders* (NCJ 175688). Washington, DC: US Department of Justice.

Hahn, P.H. (1998). *Emerging criminal justice: Three pillars for a proactive justice system.* Thousand Oaks, CA: Sage.

Harlow, C.W. (1998). *Profile of jail inmates, 1996* (NCJ 164620). Washington, DC: Bureau of Justice Statistics.

Hartsock, N. (1987). The feminist standpoint: Developing a ground for a specifically feminist historical materialism. In S. Harding (Ed.), *Feminism and methodology* (pp. 157-180). Milton Keynes, Great Britain: Open University Press.

Hoyle, C., & Sanders, A. (2000). Police response to domestic violence: From victim choice to victim empowerment. *British Journal of Criminology, 40*(1), 14-36.

Inciardi, J., Lockwood, D., & Pottieger, A.E. (1993). *Women and crack-cocaine.* New York: Macmillan.

Johnson, B., Li, D., & Websdale, N. (1998). Florida mortality review project: Executive summary. In American Bar Association [ABA], *Legal interventions in family violence* (pp. 40-41). Washington, DC: US Department of Justice.

Johnstone, G. (2001). *Restorative justice: Ideas, practices, debates.* Devon, UK: Willan.

Jurik, N.C., & Winn, R. (1990). Gender and homicide: A comparison of men and women who kill. *Violence and Victims, 5*, 227-242.

Juvenile Justice Evaluation Center. (2004). *Gender specific programming.* Washington, DC: Justice Research and Statistics Association.

Kendall, K. (1994). Therapy behind prison walls: A contradiction in terms? *Prison Service Journal, 96*, 2-11.

Kline, M. (1995). Complicating the ideology of motherhood: Child welfare, law, and First Nation women. In M.A. Fineman & I. Karpin (Eds.), *Mothers in law: Feminist theory and the legal regulation of motherhood* (pp. 118-141). New York: Columbia University Press.

Kline, S. (1993). A profile of female offenders in state and federal prisons. In *Female offenders: Meeting the needs of a neglected population* (pp. 1-6). Laurel, MD: American Correctional Association.

Koons, B., Burrow, J., Morash, M., & Bynum, T. (1997). Expert and offender perceptions of program elements linked to successful outcomes for incarcerated women. *Crime & Delinquency, 43*(4), 512-532.

Lake, E.S. (1993). An exploration of the violent victim experiences of female offenders. *Violence and Victims, 8*(1), 41-51.

Maher, L. (1997). *Sexed work: Gender, race and resistance in a Brooklyn drug market.* New York: Oxford University Press.

Mann, C.R. (1984). *Female crime and delinquency.* Tuscaloosa, AL: University of Alabama Press.

Mauer, M., Potler, C., & Wolf, R. (1999). *Gender and justice: Women, drugs and sentencing policy.* Washington, DC: The Sentencing Project.

Moe, A.M. (2004). Blurring the boundaries: Women's criminality in the context of abuse. *Women's Studies Quarterly, 32*(3-4), 116-138.

Moe Wan, A.M. (2001). *Strategies of survival: Studying the links between women's victimization and offending.* Unpublished doctoral dissertation, Arizona State University, Tempe.

Moe, A.M., & Ferraro, K.J. (2003). Malign neglect and benign respect: Women's health care in a carceral setting. *Women and Criminal Justice, 14*(4), 53-80.

Morash, M., Bynum, T.S., & Koons, B. (1998). *Women offenders: Programming needs and promising approaches.* Washington, DC: US Department of Justice.

Mumola, C.J. (2000). *Incarcerated parents and their children, Bureau of Justice Statistics Special Report* (NCJ 182335). Washington DC: Department of Justice.

Owen, B. (1998). *"In the mix": Struggle and survival in a women's prison.* New York: State University of New York Press.

Pepi, C. (1998). Children without childhoods: A feminist intervention strategy utilizing systems theory and restorative justice in treating female adolescent offenders. In J. Harden & M. Hill (Eds.), *Breaking the rules: Women in prison and feminist therapy* (pp. 85-101). New York: The Haworth Press, Inc.

Rafter, N.H. (1985). *Partial justice: Women in state prisons, 1800-1935.* Boston: Northeastern University Press.

Richie, B.E. (1996). *Compelled to crime: The gender entrapment of battered black women.* New York: Routledge.

Ross, L. (1998). *Inventing the savage: The social construction of Native American criminality.* Austin, TX: University of Texas Press.

Saleebey, D. (Ed.). (1997). *The strengths perspective in social work practice.* New York: Longman Press.

Sargent, E., Marcus-Mendoza, S., & Yu, C. H. (1993). Abuse and the woman prisoner: A forgotten population. In B.R. Fletcher, L.D. Shaver, & D.G. Moon (Eds.), *Women prisoners: A forgotten population* (pp. 55-64). Westport, CT: Praeger.

Schafer, N.E., & Dellinger, A.B. (1999). Jailed parents: An assessment. *Women and Criminal Justice, 10*(4), 73-91.

Sharp, S.F., & Eriksen, M.E. (2003). Imprisoned mothers and their children. In B.H. Zaitzow & J. Thomas (Eds.), *Women in prison: Gender and social control* (pp. 119-136). Boulder, CO.: Lynne Rienner.

Shaw, M. (1992). Issues of power and control: Women in prison and their defenders. *British Journal of Criminology, 32*(4), 438-452.

Stephan, J. J. (2004). *State prison expenditures, 2001. Bureau of Justice Statistics Special Report* (NCJ 202949). Washington, DC: Department of Justice.

Task Force on Federally Sentenced Women. (1990). *Creating choices.* Ottawa, Canada: Ministry of the Solicitor General.

Teplin, L.A., Abram, K.M., & McClelland, G.M. (1997). Mentally disordered women in jail: Who receives services? *American Journal of Public Health, 87*(4), 606-609.

Van Wormer, K. (1999). The strengths perspective: A paradigm for correctional counseling. *Federal Probation, 63*(1), 51-59.

Van Wormer, K. (2001). *Counseling female offenders and victims: A strengths-restorative approach.* New York: Springer.

Wilson, M., & Anderson, S. C. (1997). Empowering female offenders: Removing barriers to community-based practice. *Affilia, 12*(3), 342-358.

Young, D.S. (2000). Women's perceptions of health care in prison. *Health Care for Women International, 21*(3), 219-234.

Zaplin, R.T. (1998) *Female offenders: Critical perspectives and effective interventions.* Gaithersburg, MD: Aspen.

doi:10.1300/J015v29n03_08

Children and Families:
Mothers Who Are Incarcerated

Rivka Greenberg

SUMMARY. The incarceration of women who are mothers affects not only the women, but their children and families. The children are at high risk developmentally, psychologically, emotionally, and economically. This article identifies concerns and interventions for the children, families, and incarcerated women. Risk factors, as well as resiliency factors, are recognized, framing the intervention work needed to support optimal growth, development, and mental well-being of the children and families of incarcerated mothers. doi:10.1300/J015v29n03_09 [Article copies available for a fee from The Haworth Document Delivery Service: 1-800-HAWORTH. E-mail address: <docdelivery@haworthpress.com> Website: <http://www.HaworthPress.com> © 2006 by The Haworth Press, Inc. All rights reserved.]

KEYWORDS. Incarcerated mothers, children, families, risk, resiliency, therapeutic support, interventions

---

Rivka Greenberg, PhD, is an independent consultant working with agencies and individuals. Her work encompasses children at risk and children with special needs, and their families; family focused treatment; early childhood education and intervention; infant and child development; and families/parenting.

Address correspondence to: Rivka Greenberg, PhD, P.O. Box 7753, Berkeley, CA 94707 (E-mail: rigreenb@lanset.com).

[Haworth co-indexing entry note]: "Children and Families: Mothers Who Are Incarcerated." Greenberg, Rivka. Co-published simultaneously in *Women & Therapy* (The Haworth Press, Inc.) Vol. 29, No. 3/4, 2006, pp. 165-179; and: *Inside and Out: Women, Prison, and Therapy* (ed: Elaine Leeder) The Haworth Press, Inc., 2006, pp. 165-179. Single or multiple copies of this article are available for a fee from The Haworth Document Delivery Service [1-800-HAWORTH, 9:00 a.m. - 5:00 p.m. (EST). E-mail address: docdelivery@haworthpress.com].

Available online at http://wt.haworthpress.com
doi:10.1300/J015v29n03_09

INTRODUCTION

For many people, the words *incarceration* and *imprisonment* initially evoke reactions, including avoidance and anxiety, as well as negative images of bars, cells, and locks. The terms do not generally evoke thoughts of children and families. The history of women who have been incarcerated in the United States is long, with documentation from the 1790s. The first prison for women opened in Indiana in 1873 (Harris, 1993). Yet, until fairly recently, children of incarcerated mothers have not been identified as a group of children with particular developmental and mental health needs. As the number of incarcerated women has increased, awareness that these children are at high risk for adverse psychological outcomes is increasing.

The transactional model is a useful framework for understanding the impact of mothers' incarceration on their children. This model, as first posited by Sameroff and Chandler in 1975, and refined in later years, asserts that the interplay among multiple individual and environmental factors will affect, and even determine, the eventual outcomes (Sameroff & Fiese, 2000). Circumstances that adversely affect growth and development are identified as risk factors. Circumstances that support and strengthen growth and development are identified as resiliency or protective factors (Vance & Sanchez, 1998). Risk and protective factors may be environmental and/or biological and can occur in different spheres of life: individual, family, and community. Examples of environmental risk factors include teen pregnancy; income below the poverty level; a family where no parent has full-time, year round employment; a household head who has not completed high school; single parent households; influence of substance abuse; foster care; and parental incarceration (Annie E. Casey Foundation, 2005). Biological risk factors associated with children include premature birth; prenatal exposure to substances; substance abuse; poor health; abuse and neglect. As the number of risk factors increases, they have a cumulative effect over time, increasing the potential negative impacts on the children (Johnson & Waldfogel, 2002).

Until recently, children of incarcerated mothers have been almost invisible to the professionals concerned with children and families; they have generally not been included in discussions of children at risk (Simmons, 2000). However, these children are at very high risk for adverse developmental and mental health outcomes, due to multiple risk factors in their lives (Park & Clarke-Stewart, 2003). Utilizing the concept of cumulative risk, i.e., the accumulation of multiple risk factors over time, it can be predicted that the greater the number of risk factors that a child has, the greater the risk for adverse outcomes (Johnson & Waldfogel, 2002).

Women are more often the primary (or sole) caregivers of their children (Braithwaite, Treadwell & Arriola, 2005). When the mother is incarcerated, what happens to the children? The mothers of these children may also have substance abuse issues, and developmental and learning disabilities. Viewed this way, it becomes clear that the impact of the actual incarceration is only one element in a continuum of risk factors that may affect the children of incarcerated mothers.

Therapists working with the children and families of incarcerated mothers will benefit from an understanding of the risk factors affecting these children. This paper identifies risk factors, as well as resiliency factors, that should be taken into account in order to bring the transactional model into balance to support optimal growth, development, and mental wellbeing of the children of incarcerated mothers. While this article focuses on the children, successful intervention often depends on providing support for the entire family, the caregivers and, whenever possible, the women who are incarcerated.

HOW MANY CHILDREN AND PARENTS ARE WE TALKING ABOUT?

In 1999 there were 72 million minor children in the United States. Of those, it is estimated that 1,498,800 children, or 2.1%, had parents in prison. From 1991 to 1999, the number of minor children who had incarcerated parents increased from 936,500 to 1,498,800. During this period, the number of women in prison more than doubled, increasing by 106%. While the number of children with a father in prison grew by 58%, the number of children with a mother in prison nearly doubled, increasing by 98% (Mumola, 2000).

The impact of this increase is profound. Women are more likely to be the primary caregivers of children; when the father is imprisoned, the child's care generally continues with the mother. However, when a mother goes to prison, her children also experience major, traumatic disruption in their lives. The vast majority of these children are moved to the care of grandparents or other relatives, or they enter the foster care system. When their mother is incarcerated, children are five times more likely to enter foster placement than when their fathers are incarcerated (Krisberg & Temin, 2001).

ISSUES FOR CHILDREN OF INCARCERATED MOTHERS

Keith, age 5, was in the living room of the apartment he shared with his mother, Jessica, and 6-month-old breast-fed baby sister, Andrea, when five police officers entered. After a brief conversation, Jessica was handcuffed and taken away by four of the officers, while the children watched and cried. One officer remained to find someone to come for Keith and Andrea. The next time they saw their mother it was a year and a half later. At that time, they were living with their aunt, and calling her "Mom."

This story, which is common, can be viewed from a number of perspectives. These events, and their long-term consequences, affect the children developmentally, psychologically, emotionally, and economically. For many children, this scenario depicts an escalation in a life that may already feel like a roller coaster ride with no end. That their mother, who was their primary caregiver, was removed so abruptly, with no comforting supports, and for such a long time, was very traumatic. This raises issues for the children, such as physical and emotional loss, feelings of abandonment, and the trauma of a major interruption in the attachment process. An event such as this interrupts and profoundly affects even the simplest of everyday activities, such as a child's ability to nurse and to be weaned gradually, with major consequences for the child's emotional well-being (Travis, Cincotta & Solomon, 2003).

The topic of children at risk, and the effects of interruptions in their normal social and emotional development, is becoming more prominent in the literature (Kaufman & Henrich, 2000; Zeanah & Boris, 2000). It is well known that separation from parents can have long-term adverse effects on children's development (Egland & Erickson, 1999; Jervay-Pendergrass, Erdelyi & Mendelsohn, 2005; Landy, 2002), and these concerns are directly applicable to children whose mothers are incarcerated (Marfo, Goldman-Fraser & Fernandez, 2005; Park & Clarke-Stewart, 2003).

However, few studies have specifically addressed the effects of a mother's incarceration on her children. There have been no studies of children from the time of parental incarceration to the time of release (Travis & Waul, 2003). The scarcity of research is acutely apparent in the lack of clarity in the literature around critical caregiving issues, such as what to tell the children about their parent's absence, and whether or not it is in the best interest of children to visit their parents in prison (Hairston, 2003).

Traumatic events affect each person on an individual basis, depending on their age, developmental level, and temperament (Groves, Lieberman, Osofsky & Fenichel, 2000). Many children of incarcerated mothers are affected by chronic trauma, that is, multiple traumatic events, such as chaotic family lifestyles, violence, family anger, and abuse (Rice & Groves, 2005). Trauma is recognized as an exceptional experience that can overwhelm an individual's coping capacity.

Travis and Waul (2003) have identified five general negative effects on the children of incarcerated parents:

- Children always experience the loss of a parent as a traumatic event;
- Trauma diverts children's energy from developmental tasks;
- Children find it even more difficult to cope in situations characterized by uncertainty;
- Children's reactions to a situation will vary over time;
- Children experience the stigma of having a parent in prison (p. 16).

Children exposed to traumatic events respond by communicating their feelings in their behaviors, their words, and often in their play. Some of the outcomes that have been identified include re-living or re-experiencing the traumatic events; internalizing the events by withdrawing, or externalizing them by being disruptive; fearfulness; developmental and behavioral regression; and physical symptoms, such as headaches and stomach aches (Gurwitch, Silovsky, Schultz, Kees, & Burlingame, 2005).

For children of incarcerated parents, the "Five S's"–*stigma, shame, separation, secrecy,* and *silence*–play a big role in their lives. *Stigma* describes how teachers, classmates, and society in general perceive and behave towards children when they learn that their mothers or fathers are in jail or prison. *Separation* is the empty space in children's lives without their parent. *Shame* is what many children feel when they understand what is happening, and when people make thoughtless or unkind comments. This leads to keeping the parent's imprisonment *secret* in an attempt to avoid the pain of stigma and shame. *Silence* refers to the behavior of all concerned–the child who has no one with whom to talk who might understand, and others who do not know what to say. We can imagine how the "Five S's" play out when, for example, the child is in school and preparations for Mother's Day begin. What is the child to say when asked if her mother is coming for the party?

Children see the world differently than do adults. It can be confusing and strange. The literature indicates that often children are not told where the parent has gone, or they are told that the parent is away at school or in the military. A number of articles have commented on the importance of reassuring children that they were not the cause of the incarceration (Sazie, Ponder, & Johnson, 2001).

Children's living arrangements after the mother's incarceration are extremely significant in determining their risk and protective factors. Will the children live with another parent, grandparents, relatives, friends, or in foster placement? If the children are placed in kinship care, many families may experience financial hardship. For example, if children are placed with grandparents, the fixed retirement income on which they live will not be increased. The family's dependents increase, but the resources do not (Hairston, 2003). Very little is known clinically about the attachment of children to new caregivers in cases of parental incarceration. What is the impact of this substitute care? What happens if there is little stability and the children receive little emotional support?

Maintaining contact with the incarcerated mother and developing a relationship that will maintain any semblance of the pre-existing one is a major challenge. Incarceration imposes many barriers to maintaining and supporting the parent-child connection. Among these barriers are visits. It is estimated that of the women incarcerated in 2000, 54% of mothers had no visits with their children that year (Mumola, 2000). There are many obstacles to making visits: the distance from the home to the prison, which is often in a remote geographical area; scheduling problems; and the cost of the trips. Visiting procedures add to the difficulty. Some jails and prisons have a "no contact" rule; the children can look at the prisoner, but may not touch her (Johnston, 1995). It is difficult to imagine the pain and the confusion of a child seeing a parent after a long separation and being prevented from touching her.

From a family perspective, the criminal justice system is dysfunctional and, some would say, abusive to families. The previous scenario, depicting the arrest, shows that not only is the law enforcement system not working in concert with child welfare services or the family, but their actions cause harm. It is estimated that one out of five children is present when their parents are arrested (Park & Clarke-Stewart, 2003). A majority of law enforcement agencies identified in a paper by Nieto (2002) lacked protocols for caring for the minor children when the custodial parent is arrested.

The majority of incarcerated women are in prison due to drug-related charges. Data from 1991 indicate that 72% of women in federal prisons were there for drug-related convictions (Smith, Krisman, Stozier, & Marley, 2004). Many of these women are addicted to substances. The overlap between children prenatally exposed to substances and/or raised in substance abusing environments and children with incarcerated parents is evident. They are at risk for many of the same sequelae, developmental, behavioral, emotional, and educational, as well as for continuing the intergenerational pattern of addiction (Greenberg, 2000). Drawing upon the more robust literature relating to children raised in substance abusing environments can assist in guiding the treatment of children of incarcerated parents.

The issues facing the children of incarcerated mothers are multifaceted and complex, involving psychological, developmental, educational, and environmental, factors. Because of this, mental health interventions can be enhanced by adopting strategies that address resiliency factors; cognitive understanding and psychological insight; maintenance of family connections and support for caregivers; and mental health support for mothers and families.

ENHANCING RESILIENCY FACTORS

The transactional model, including the cumulative effect of multiple risk factors, has been identified as a way of framing the lives of children of incarcerated parents. The next step is to begin to identify resiliency factors which can work towards countering these risk factors. This requires developing new ways of approaching the needs of these children and their families. In 2000, a coalition of advocates, providers, representatives from government agencies, and others formed the San Francisco Partnership for Incarcerated Parents. They have recently developed and published *Children of Incarcerated Parents: A Bill of Rights* (2005), which states:

1. I have the right to be kept safe and informed at the time of my parent's arrest.
2. I have the right to be heard when decisions are made about me.
3. I have the right to be considered when decisions are made about my parent.
4. I have the right to be well cared for in my parent's absence.
5. I have the right to speak with, see, and touch my parent.

6. I have the right to support as I struggle with my parent's incarceration.
7. I have the right not to be judged, blamed, or labeled because I have an incarcerated parent.
8. I have the right to a lifelong relationship with my parent.

The publication of these rights begins to frame incarceration, not just as an individual concern, but as a family concern. The field of gender specific substance abuse treatment has made great strides in outcomes based treatment programming which increasingly includes addressing and implementing family focused treatment (McComish et al., 2003; Stevens & Patton, 1998). It is not only the addicted person–or the incarcerated parent–who needs intervention and support, but it is also the family, with particular emphasis on the needs of the children. We must keep in mind that it is the parent, not the child, who is incarcerated.

The next steps will include promoting these rights, creating systems to support them, and providing ongoing follow through. This will require interagency, intersystem, and interdisciplinary collaboration and planning (Bruner, Kunesh & Knuth, 1992). Criminal justice agencies, along with social services, educators, and mental health providers, as well as families and communities, will need to develop ways to work together to build new models of care. In particular, it is of vital importance to develop programs within the criminal justice system that will promote healthy family development, and support parental recovery and change. Mothers and children need positive, proactive support to assist them in developing coping skills and building resiliency during this difficult and stressful period in their lives as individuals and families.

BIBLIOTHERAPY

Children have many questions and thoughts about the separation from their mother. They often require support to express them. Some of the questions that children may have of the parent include, "Where are you?"; "Why are you there?"; "When are you coming home?"; and "Are you okay?" Questions that are not likely to be asked directly include, "Do you blame me?"; "Was it my fault?"; and "Do you still love me?" (Osborne Association, 1993). Children, who do not have all the information, or a clear understanding of the situation, may generate their own explanations that are not based in reality.

Bibliotherapy is a therapeutic technique which uses age appropriate books to address relevant life issues by means of a story. Topics may include disabilities, chronic illness, divorce, and a new baby. Children need age appropriate information about their mother's incarceration and how it affects their lives. For most adults, explaining imprisonment is difficult, and finding the words and explanations for this emotionally charged subject is challenging. Bibliotherapy is extremely useful for both children and their caregivers. The stories are designed to give children some information on the subject, and to help them understand and gain insight into their feelings. Children can identify with the situations in the story, and it eases the way into supportive communication around this difficult subject. The children can view and hear the story from the safety of a lap, or in the shelter of someone sitting next to them. They can stop the story if their feelings overwhelm them, and they can read it again and again to continue to understand their situation and process their feelings.

This approach has three stages: identification and naming of the issues, catharsis, and insight. The stories often provide practical coping strategies, and enable the children to see that this situation happens to other people and they are not alone (Abdullah, 2002). The tone of these books is positive, and they teach without lecturing. A number of books on the subject of incarcerated parents are available, including *Visiting Day*, by Jacqueline Woodson (2002), and *Mama Loves Me From Away*, by Pat Brisson (2004).

KEEPING FAMILIES CONNECTED

Despite research demonstrating the importance of visits to incarcerated mothers in maintaining the family connection, studies have found that up to 50-60% of incarcerated parents are not visited by their children (Mumola, 2000). In spite of the obstacles identified above, supporting caregivers in arranging these visits can be critical to successfully reconnecting mothers with their children after release. The Children of Prisoners Library has published a booklet called, *Visiting Mom or Dad* (Adalist-Estrin, 2003). This publication identifies ways to prepare the child for the visit. From a child development perspective, it identifies what children may do, what caregivers can do to prepare for the visit, and what parents can do to make the visit successful.

It is important that the children's caregivers be provided with support in order to enable them to support the children and ensure that family connections are maintained. Caregivers can support children by providing reassurance; listening without judging; answering questions honestly; providing consistency in the children's lives; celebrating significant events such as birthdays; acknowledging successes in school, sports, and other activities; respecting the parental bond by not voicing or showing disrespect to the incarcerated parent; understanding that children may display pain or anger through negative behaviors; and seeking the support of teachers, clergy, and therapists when needed (Reilly, & Martin, n.d.).

MENTAL HEALTH SUPPORT FOR MOTHERS

Mental health support for incarcerated mothers has a direct impact on the mental health of their children. The lives of incarcerated women include histories of sexual, physical, and/or emotional abuse and domestic violence. Using the model of gender specific substance abuse treatment, programming that rehabilitates and treats can provide the foundation for change for children and families. An important component of gender specific treatment includes assessment of needs, including mental health assessments. Studies of incarcerated women suggest that many of them have co-occurring disorders, including substance abuse, post traumatic stress disorder, depression, and other serious mental illnesses (Covington, 2003). These conditions require identification and intervention for the sake of the inmates, as well as for their children and families.

Kathy Boudin, writing from prison, identifies the important work that can be done by incarcerated women themselves, when they address their own emotional needs, and the questions that they find most difficult to ask, such as "How is it that I loved my son so much, yet I made choices that resulted in my arrest, and in my leaving him?" (Boudin, 1998, p. 105). Incarcerated mothers need help in answering practical questions as well, including, "How can I continue to parent while I am incarcerated?" and "How can I support my children while I am separated from them?" Programs are beginning to be developed to help incarcerated women to address their parenting issues, as well as issues related to mental health and substance abuse (Kubiak, Young, Siefert & Stewart, 2004; Park & Clarke-Stewart, 2003).

MENTAL HEALTH SUPPORT FOR FAMILIES

Mental health support and treatment for the families of children of incarcerated mothers enhance the environmental resiliency factors, and increase the children's chances of achieving optimal mental health outcomes. The infant mental health model, utilizing promotion, prevention, and intervention which encompass the family, can provide the necessary structure. Referrals for child therapy and/or family therapy are appropriate, both within the temporary family configuration and when the parent re-enters the home. Therapists will benefit from understanding the many permutations of family configuration that may result from incarceration in order to provide the counseling and therapeutic interventions needed by everyone concerned. When beginning to work with children whose families are involved in the criminal justice system, therapists should become familiar with the family and caregiving issues created by the incarceration.

The needs of family members at reunification, including reintegration of the parent into society, are multiple and complex. Family systems theory can help therapists to understand the strengths and barriers faced by these families, and guide them in assessing what supports are needed. The issues faced by parents who return home after being incarcerated have some similarities to those faced by military personnel who have been apart from their families for long periods of time (Thompson, 2005). In addition, the reality of recidivism–at least 50% return to prison within the first year and 70% within three years–cannot be ignored. Therapeutic intervention can help to prevent recidivism by addressing issues caused by the parent's absence, such as abandonment, separation, and inconsistency, and by promoting healthy ways of coping and growing.

NEXT STEPS

Many local and national voluntary organizations are doing important family support work. However, the children and families of incarcerated mothers are not generally viewed as a distinct group, with specific needs and requiring specific kinds of support. A beginning was made when ten demonstration sites were funded by the National Institute of Corrections to address the needs of children of incarcerated parents and evaluated by the National Council on Crime and Delinquency (Bush-Baskette & Patino, 2004). A great deal more research on the needs of these children and their families remains to be done. This should be the beginning of many ongoing projects that can build on the findings of the previous projects, and promote the development of evidence-based effective practices to support the children and families of incarcerated mothers (Erickson & Kurz-Riemer, 1999).

CONCLUSION

After a year and a half of separation, Keith, Andrea, and their aunt have been able to travel to the prison to meet with the children's mother, Jessica, on a regular basis every other month. This continued for two years until Jessica was paroled. For three years, the children and their aunt were in contact with a therapist who had expertise in the area of incarceration. They were able to work on the issues resulting from the traumatic separation from their mother, the loss of her from their daily lives, and the relocation and attachment to their aunt. The aunt was provided with guidance to help her support the children during this process and to receive support for herself. Jessica was able to participate in support groups in prison. When Jessica is paroled, the entire family will work with the therapist on the children's transition from their aunt's home to their mother's. The needs of the children will be addressed, as well as the needs of both of the sisters as they realign their lives.

It is hoped that stories like this will become the norm, so that children and families of incarcerated mothers can be supported in moving from crisis and risk to the development of supportive, healthy families, with optimum mental health for each family member.

Useful Resources

Family and Corrections Network website, http://www.fcnetwork.org, 32 Oak Grove Road, Palmyra, VA 22963, (434) 589-3036, (434) 589-6520 fax

Children of Incarcerated Parents, Sydney Gewitz Clemens, http://www.eceteacher.org

Child Welfare League of America, http://www.cwla.org/programs/incarcerated/default.htm

Center for Children of Incarcerated Parents, http://www.e-ccip.org, P.O. Box 41-286, Eagle Rock, California 90041 (626) 449-8796

Friends Outside, website, http://www.friendsoutside.org/index.html, Friends Outside, National Organization, P.O. Box 4085, Stockton, CA 95204, Phone: (209) 938-0727, Fax: (209) 938-0734

Legal Services for Prisoners with Children, website, www.prisonerswithchildren.org, 1540 Market St., Suite 490, San Francisco, CA 94102 (415) 255-7036

REFERENCES

Abdullah, M.H. (2002). *Bibliotherapy*. Eric Digest. Retrieved from http://www.indiana. edu/~reading/ieo/digests/d177.html

Adalist-Estrin, A. (2003). *Visiting mom or dad*. Retrieved from http://www.fcnetwork. org/cpl/cplindex.html

Annie E. Casey Foundation, Kids Count (2005). *Children at Risk State Trends 1990-2000*. Retrieved from http://www.aecf.org/kidscount/c2ss/index.htm

Boudin, K. (1998). Lessons from a mother's program in prison: A psychosocial approach supports women and their children. *Women and Therapy, 21*(1), 301-125.

Braithwaite, R.L., Treadwell, H.M., & Arriola, K.R. (2005). Health disparities and incarcerated women: A population ignored. *American Journal of Public Health, 95*(10), 1679-1681.

Brisson, P. (2004). *Mama loves me from away*. Honesdale, PA: Boyds Mills Press, Inc.

Bruner, C., Kunesh, L.G. & Knuth, R.A. (1992). *What does the research say about interagency collaboration?* North Central Regional Educational Laboratory. Retrieved September 18, 2005 from http://www.ncrel.org/sdrs/areas/stw_esys/8agcycol.htm

Bush-Baskette, S. & Patino, V. (2004). *The National Council on Crime and Delinquency's evaluation of the project development of National Institute of Corrections/Child Welfare League of America's planning and intervention sites funded to address the needs of children of incarcerated parents. Final report*. Oakland, CA: National Council on Crime and Delinquency. Retrieved September 11, 2005 from http://www.nccd-crc.org/nccd/n_pubs_main.html

Covington, S.S. (2003). A woman's journey home: Challenges for female offenders. In J. Travis & M. Waul (Eds.), *Prisoners once removed* (pp. 259-282). Washington, DC: The Urban Institute Press.

Egland, B. & Erickson, M.F. (1999). Findings from the parent-child project and implications for early intervention. *Zero to Three, 20*(2), 3-10.

Erickson, M.F. & Kurz-Riemer, K. (1999). Knowledge bases to inform infant/family practice. *Zero to Three, 20*(2), 23-27.

Greenberg, R. (1999/2000). Substance abuse in families: Educational issues. *Childhood Education, 76*(2), 66-69.

Groves, B.M., Lieberman, A.F., Osofsky, J.D., & Fenichel, E. (2000). Protecting young children in violent environment: A framework to build on. *Zero to Three, 20*(5), 9-13.

Gurwitch, R.H., Silovsky, J.F., Schultz, S., Kees, M., & Burlingame, S. (2005). *Reactions and guidelines for children following trauma/disaster*. Retrieved October 17, 2005, from http://www.apa.org/practice/ptguidelines.html

Hairston, C.F. (2003). Prisoners and families: Parenting issues during incarceration. In J. Travis & M. Waul (Eds.), *Prisoners once removed* (pp. 259-282). Washington, DC: The Urban Institute Press.

Harris, J. (1993). Babies in prison. *Zero to Three, 13*(3), 17-21.

Jervay-Pendergrass, D., Erdelyi, P.J. & Mendelsohn, A.L. (2005). Language delay and its relationship to separation. *Zero to Three, 25*(6), 21-26.

Johnson, E.I. & Waldfogel, J. (2002). *Children of incarcerated parents: Cumulative risk and children's living arrangements.* Northwestern University/University of Chicago Joint Center for Poverty Research. Retrieved from http://www.jcpr.org/policybriefs/vol5_num4.htm

Johnston, D. (1995). Parent-child visits in jail. *Children's Environments, 12*(1), 33-56. Retrieved from http://www.canr.uconn.edu/ces/child/newsarticles/CCC743.html

Kaufman, J., & Henrich, C. (2000). Exposure to violence and early childhood trauma. In C.H. Zeanah, Jr. (Ed.), *Handbook of infant mental health* (2nd ed., pp. 195-207). New York: Guilford Press.

Krisberg, B.A., & Temin, C.E. (2001). *The plight of children whose parents are in prison.* NCCD Focus. Retrieved from http://www.nccd-crc.org/nccd/n_pubs_main.html

Kubiak, S.P., Young, A., Siefert, K., & Stewart, A. (2004). Pregnant, substance-abusing, and incarcerated: Exploratory study of a comprehensive approach to treatment. *Families in Society, 85*(2), 177-186.

Landy, S. (2002). *Pathways to competence.* Baltimore: Paul H. Brookes.

Marfo, K., Goldman-Fraser, J., and Fernandez, M. T. (2005). Expanding our view of separation in the lives of young children. *Zero to Three, 25*(6), 56-61.

McComish, J.F., Greenberg, R., Ager, J., Essenmacher, L., Orgain, L.S., & Bacik, W.J. (2003). Family-focused substance abuse treatment: A program evaluation. *Journal of Psychoactive Drugs, 35*(3), 321-331.

Mumola, C.J. (2000). *Incarcerated parents and their children,* Bureau of Justice Statistics Special Report, US Department of Justice. Retrieved October 11, 2005 from http://www.zerotothree.org/coping/HHinfo.html

Nieto, M. (2002). *In danger of falling through the cracks: Children of arrested parents.* Sacramento, CA: California Research Bureau, California State Library.

Osborne Association. (1993). *Sustaining and enhancing family ties for children of incarcerated parents Serving special children: Volume II.* Long Island City, New York: Osborne Association.

Park, R.D., & Clarke-Stewart, A. (2003). The effects of parental incarceration on children: Perspectives, promises and policies. In J. Travis & M. Waul (Eds.), *Prisoners once removed* (pp. 189-232). Washington, DC: The Urban Institute Press.

Reilly, J., & Martin, S. (n.d.) *Children of incarcerated parents. What is the caregiver's role?* Retrieved from http://www.canr.uconn.edu/ces/child/newsarticles/ CCC743.html

Rice, K.F., & Groves, B.A. (2005). *Hope and healing: A caregiver's guide to helping young children affected by trauma.* Zero to Three Press: Retrieved from http://www.zerotothree.org/coping/HHinfo.html

Sameroff, A.J., & Chandler, M.J. (1975). Reproductive risk and the continuum of caretaking casualty. In F.D. Horowitz, M. Hetherington, S. Scarr-Salapatek, & G. Siegel (Eds.), *Review of child development research, Vol. 4* (pp. 187-244). Chicago: University of Chicago Press.

Sameroff, A.J., & Fiese, B.H. (2000). Models of development and developmental risk. In C.H. Zeanah, Jr. (Ed.). *Handbook of infant mental health* (2nd ed., pp. 3-19). New York: Guilford Press.

San Francisco Children of Incarcerated Parents Partnership (2005) *Children of incarcerated parents A bill of rights.* Retrieved from http://www.sfcipp.org/

Sazie, E., Ponder, D., & Johnson, J. (2001). How to explain jails and prisons to children: A Caregivers Guide. Salem, Oregon: Inside Oregon Enterprises.

Simmons, C.W. (2000). *Children of incarcerated parents.* Sacramento, CA: California Research Bureau, California State Library.

Smith, A., Krisman, K., Stozier, A.L., & Marley, M.A. (2004). Breaking through the bars: Exploring the experiences of addicted incarcerated parents whose children are cared for by relatives. *Families in Society, 85*(2), 187-195.

Stevens, S.J., & Patton, T. (1998). Residential treatment for drug addicted women and their children: Effective treatment strategies. In S.J. Stevens & H.K. Wexler (Eds.), *Women and substance abuse: Gender transp*arency (pp.235-250). New York: The Haworth Press, Inc.

Thompson, B.A. (2005). Life support: A system of care for military families. *Zero to Three, 25*(6), 49-55.

Travis, J., & Waul, M. (2003). Prisoners once removed: The children and families of prisoners. In J. Travis & M. Waul (Eds.), *Prisoners once removed* (pp. 1-29). Washington, DC: The Urban Institute Press

Travis, J., Cincotta, E.M., & Solomon, A.L. (2003). *Families left behind: The hidden costs of incarceration and reentry.* Urban Institute, Justice Policy Center. Retrieved September 11, 2005 from http://www.jcpr.org/wp/WPprofile.cfm?ID=364

Vance, E., & Sanchez, H. (1998). *Creating a service system that builds resiliency.* Retrieved from, http://www.dhhs.state.nc.us/mhddsas/childandfamily/technicalassistance/risk_and_resiliency.htm

Woodson, J. (2002) *Visiting day.* New York: Scholastic Press.

Zeanah, C.H., & Boris, N.W. (2000). Disturbances and disorders of attachment in early childhood. In C.H. Zeanah, Jr. (Ed.). *Handbook of infant mental health* (2nd ed., pp. 353-368). New York: Guilford Press.

doi:10.1300/J015v29n03_09

Locked Up Means Locked Out:
Women, Addiction and Incarceration

Vanessa Alleyne

SUMMARY. In one of the quietest but most significant social phenomena of our time, national statistics indicate that the number of incarcerated women has quadrupled over the last 20 years. The status of women of color in America, already precarious, is further eroded under this new world order, as 54% of the incarcerated female population is African American or Latina. Harsh drug laws, mandatory sentencing, and policing strategies which focus on smaller crimes have succeeded in netting large numbers of mothers, grandmothers, single breadwinners and other women whose primary offenses prior to arrest were being poor and often having a substance abuse problem. Once incarcerated, new difficulties are visited upon these women, including family dissolution, precipitous declines in mental health, and often loss of child custody as legal cases wend their way slowly through the system.

Vanessa Alleyne, PhD, is Assistant Professor and Coordinator of the Addiction Studies Program at Montclair State University, New Jersey. She works collaboratively with the Council on Drug and Alcohol Abuse of Bergen County, graduate students in the Department of Counseling and Human Development, and the Bergen County Sheriff's Department to bring assessment and treatment services to incarcerated women at the Bergen County Jail in Hackensack, NJ.

Address correspondence to: (E-mail: alleynev@mail.montclair.edu).

[Haworth co-indexing entry note]: "Locked Up Means Locked Out: Women, Addiction and Incarceration." Alleyne, Vanessa. Co-published simultaneously in *Women & Therapy* (The Haworth Press, Inc.) Vol. 29, No. 3/4, 2006, pp. 181-194; and: *Inside and Out: Women, Prison, and Therapy* (ed: Elaine Leeder) The Haworth Press, Inc., 2006, pp. 181-194. Single or multiple copies of this article are available for a fee from The Haworth Document Delivery Service [1-800-HAWORTH, 9:00 a.m. - 5:00 p.m. (EST). E-mail address: docdelivery@haworthpress.com].

The commonly reported statistic that 80% of all crimes committed have drug involvement holds true for women as well. Most women in prison are untreated substance abusers with high recidivism rates that correlate with greater addiction severity. Typically, each return to incarceration signifies a deeper level of addiction, with associated declines in health, employment opportunity, and social functioning. The quantum increase in incarceration for women is linked directly to drug and alcohol addiction, yet little has been done to address the issue. Many prison systems are ill equipped to handle the influx of women, from a variety of perspectives. County jails, historically designed to be shorter term holding areas for those with minor offenses or awaiting a state prison bed, are now handling many more female prisoners for much longer periods of time. Social, health, and substance abuse services for these women are grossly inadequate, if available at all.

This article will address the double bind of addiction and incarceration that women face today in unprecedented numbers. It will discuss, via case study and review, the precipitous erosion of mental health and family functioning that typically occurs when substance abusing women are incarcerated instead of treated. The paper will discuss the national silence which has surrounded this very public epidemic, particularly regarding the country's discomfort and resulting inability to confront the debilitating effects of addiction and incarceration on women and families. Finally, this paper will discuss effective strategies for change, arguing that a first step must include an appreciation for the unique perspective and experiences that addicted women have and bring to a correctional environment. doi:10.1300/J015v29n03_10 *[Article copies available for a fee from The Haworth Document Delivery Service: 1-800-HAWORTH. E-mail address: <docdelivery@haworthpress.com> Website: <http://www.HaworthPress.com> © 2006 by The Haworth Press, Inc. All rights reserved.]*

KEYWORDS. Addiction, women and incarceration, double bind, substance abuse, psychosocial effects of incarceration, trauma, cocaine treatment, zero tolerance, policing mental health of women in prison

VIVIAN

Vivian[1] is a 31-year-old African American woman who used marijuana and alcohol in slowly increasing amounts over the past several years as she became more heavily involved with a man who was an illicit drug trafficker. She lived in public housing and graduated from high school with dreams of pursuing a career in art design before becoming pregnant in her senior year of high school. She soon had two children and worked part-time as a cashier in a local store.

Vivian was arrested during a raid of the bodega in which she worked and was found with an unprescribed pill, Vicodin, in her pocket. Ironically, Vivian had occasionally used Vicodin for legitimate pain purposes, with a long-term herniated disc in her back, but would usually get them "locally" rather than through a prescription. However, this was Vivian's second arrest for drugs. The first was for being in a car with a man who had drugs. They were stopped by the police one night and both were arrested. She was given probation, which she did not complete to the probation officer's satisfaction (she continued to associate with the drug involved man). Thus, she had a violation of probation on her record at the time of her second arrest.

Vivian was arrested and sent to the county jail. Her children, a boy and a girl, were put into foster care. She had no viable extended family available to take the children. She remained in jail awaiting arraignment for one week and met her public defender for the first time during that brief court session, where she pleaded not guilty to charges of illegal possession of a controlled substance. Vivian could not post the $5000 bail (10% cash) set by the judge, so she was returned to jail to await trial or a plea offer.

As with so many others, self advocacy from inside proved to be extremely difficult for Vivian. She was horrified to learn that most of her female colleagues in jail waited anywhere from three to six months before hearing back from their attorneys for bail reduction requests, plea offers, or trials. Frustrated and angry, Vivian spent hours each week trying to establish contact with her children through Child Protective Services. She would write to the case worker and to her children weekly, and occasionally had access to a telephone via rare trips to the Law Library to contact the CPS worker about them. She was told eventually that the children were well, had been sent to two separate foster homes, and that she could write letters to them through the agency. The foster families had not agreed to bring her children to the jail for a visit. Thus, she wrote letters to her children and sent them to the case worker, but couldn't really tell whether or not her children were getting them.

Three months later, Vivian's public defender arrived with a plea offer from the prosecutor: three years in state prison, out in nine months with good behavior. Vivian felt that getting substance abuse treatment would be a better option for her though, because without it she believed she might not qualify to get her children back. She refused the offer and asked the attorney again for treatment. The public defender agreed to go back to the judge and make a case for treatment instead of incarceration.

The public defender put Vivian's name on the list for his office's investigator to seek treatment options for her. There was no counselor, case manager, or social worker at the jail to provide this critically needed function. The public defender's investigator, with hundreds of similar and worse cases, had to arrange for the jail to transport women to and from the treatment facilities for treatment interviews. The interviewing and assessment process took two and a half months for Vivian, which she later learned was actually less than usual.

During this time, Vivian was evicted from her apartment because she was not there to pay rent. All her possessions, including her children's clothing and furniture, were lost.

After several months, the judge in Vivian's case approved treatment in lieu of incarceration. However, he approved long-term intensive treatment of 12 to 18 months in an inpatient program for women.

Approximately one month later Vivian was notified that a bed had opened up for her at one of the two long-term intensive treatment programs for women in her part of the state. Now nine months into this jail experience, Vivian faced the decision of whether to spend another twelve to eighteen months in a severely restrictive "therapeutic community" for substance abusing women or nine months in state prison. By this time Vivian had heard about drug court as well, but shied away from this when she learned that she would be required to participate in its monitoring program for the next four years. Given her earlier probation violation for merely associating with her former boyfriend, Vivian knew this was an impossible task for her.

Missing her children, worried about them, without further word from her boyfriend, profoundly isolated and depressed by nearly a year already spent in jail, Vivian opted for the shortest route to freedom: via state prison. She decided that she would rather attend outpatient day treatment after prison and have her children with her at home while doing so. Thus, she pleaded guilty to a felony conviction, was sentenced to three years, and returned to jail to await the bus to state prison.

The women's state prison, operating at 138% of capacity for many years, took another six weeks to transport her from the jail. Vivian knew she would get credit for some of her time in jail, but didn't know how much or when it would be applied to reduce her sentence.

When she arrived at the state prison, it took another month for Vivian to move through the classification process, be placed and audited for time served. She learned that she would have to serve another two months in order to become eligible for release. Vivian was exhausted and frightened for much of the first two weeks at the prison. While in jail she had heard many stories about women and guards in prison, and didn't want trouble from anyone. She was concerned about being approached by gangs, about potential violence, and about how to stay out of the way of the corrections officers, who had a reputation for being particularly rigid and unforgiving.

Two months later, Vivian was given a release date and two referral slips: one to an outpatient drug treatment program in her area, the other to a shelter.

On the day of her release, Vivian was given a bus ticket to a major city near her neighborhood and five dollars.

As Vivian boarded the bus for her home area, she felt that she'd aged 20 years in a little more than one. The stresses of the past 18 months washed over her, and she sobbed out loud for the first time in years. In fact, she looked much older than her 32 years, and her hair had thinned significantly during her incarceration. She returned to her neighborhood, placed her name on the shelter waiting list for that evening, and went to the social service center to apply for reinstatement for public assistance.

Two nights later, a very shaky Vivian lay in her shelter bed, at 3:00 a.m., beside herself with anxiety, frustration, and anger at the downward spiral from which she felt unable to emerge. Aside from the inhumane and unsafe conditions she was forced to endure in the shelter, she'd just learned that day that she was now ineligible for welfare benefits because of her felony conviction. (Section 115 of the welfare reform act of 1996 provides that persons convicted of a state or federal felony drug offense for using or selling drugs are subject to a lifetime ban on receiving cash assistance and food stamps. While 34 states have since modified or eliminated this draconian legislation in recent years, she unfortunately lived in one of the 16 states that has not. Vivian was one of 35,000 African American women who were directly affected by this ban.)

Without assistance Vivian knew that she had no visible means of support, and as such could not demonstrate to Child Protective Services that she could become self sufficient and provide adequately for her children. Her children were two of over 135,000 who were also negatively and directly impacted by the ban. Thus, her greatest desire, to be reunited with her two children, now separated from her for well over a year, seemed further away than ever.

With a felony conviction on her record, Vivian was soon to learn that she was locked out of receiving public housing and food stamps as well. She was ineligible for a wide range of jobs that screen out those with criminal records or felony convictions. Even her dream to pursue art design in college was to elude her, as she was now ineligible for federal student loans or grants. She could not even vote during election time to support candidates who could overturn these so called "acts of reform."

Gradually Vivian began to realize that her prison sentence had continued on the outside. Being locked up had in effect locked Vivian out of all legitimate routes away from a drug involved lifestyle. She felt like a caged bird. Consequently, she began a slow drift back toward her former boyfriend, not because she saw a real future with him, but rather out of fiscal necessity and emotional neediness. He rescued her, but with a high price tag–involvement in exactly the lifestyle that Vivian wanted and needed so much to avoid.

Nonetheless, with no other useful options in sight, Vivian decided to move in with him. She attended a day drug treatment program in order to qualify to get her children back as soon as possible. She got her old job back at the bodega, paid mostly under the table, and began to work on creating a reasonably believable, yet clearly fictitious, presentation to the system which now threatened to permanently remove from her the only family she had left.

The criminal justice system in which Vivian became engulfed was itself immersed in failure to keep pace with its own voracious appetite for incarceration. Its inability to handle her relatively minor substance abuse transgression in a timely and effective manner was but a symptom of a system run amok. Societal costs of such a system are enormous: $20,000 to $30,000 per year for Vivian to be incarcerated; $3,600 to $14,000 (depending on the state) a year per child for placement in the foster care system; elimination of Vivian's current income and reduction of future work opportunities; the cost of her homelessness and further descent into poverty; and the eradication of Vivian's and her family's upward mobility by defunding educational access (Freudenberg, 2002; Kassebaum, 1999).

The psychosocial costs of Vivian's incarceration may be even greater. How does one begin to quantify the short, and long-term effects of trauma experienced by Vivian's small children as they were suddenly removed from their homes and placed with strangers? Of their vulnerability to a myriad of future psychological and educational difficulties related to this sudden devastation of home, family, and all things familiar? How can we measure the psychological devastation that Vivian experienced in a harsh, overcrowded, isolated prison system designed to create and enforce conditions of extreme deprivation? What value should be placed on the lost opportunity for comprehensive substance abuse treatment that could have been offered while Vivian was made to languish in jail for nine months before ever reaching state prison? (Freudenberg, 2002; Kassebaum, 1999; CASA, 2001).

Recent experience with trauma associated with terrorism, war, and natural disasters (e.g., 9/11 attacks, Hurricane Katrina and its aftermath in Louisiana) has shown how devastating the impact of trauma can be for individuals, families, and society as a whole. The traumatic events experienced by this family, sadly enough, must be understood to reverberate throughout society, as more and more women with substance abuse difficulties are drawn into a grossly underprepared, overburdened criminal justice system.

The United States of America leads all nations on earth in the rate of incarceration of its citizens (Karberg & Beck, April 16, 2004). Last year 726 of 100,000 persons in the United States were under correctional supervision, including parole, probation, or in pre-trial detention. This rate is significantly ahead of other countries next on the list–Belarus and Russia, each at 523 per 100,000.

Within this population of more than 2.1 million persons, more than 185,000 are women (8.7%). The United States ranks 15th in the world in the percentage of women in its population who are incarcerated. In this era of newer, higher, and greater levels of achievement and progress for women, another milestone has quietly been reached: never before have more women been confined in correctional facilities.

The growth of women's incarceration is nearly double the rate for men over that past two decades. These rates are disproportionately due to the American political war on drugs, given that women in prison are more likely than men (30% vs. 20%) to be serving a sentence for a drug charge (Mauer, Potler, & Wolf, 1999).

A confluence of national policies and actions have created the current crisis which disproportionately impacts poor women and women of color. Three related national phenomena occurred during the 1980s which shifted and sharply increased rates of incarceration for women, disrupting millions of families and wreaking havoc on overburdened drug treatment and criminal justice systems in the process. Those phenomena are discussed in detail here.

THE DEMOCRATIZATION OF DRUG USE

Cocaine, once a major drug of abuse for middle- and upper-middle-class whites in the 1970s, began its advance across class and racial lines when new forms of use were discovered. The introduction of co-caine in freebase and crystallized forms ("crack") lowered economic barriers posed by the powdered version of the drug, thereby democratiz-ing its use. Cocaine became available to anyone with access to three dollars and the simple chemical recipe to convert the powder to a purer, more potent smokable form. Thus, larger numbers of individuals who had heretofore been shut out of using the trendy drug were quickly drawn into its vortex. Unaware that the pace of the addictive process was highly accelerated with the use of this more potent version of the drug, thousands of women in urban and rural settings began to experi-ence the relentless intensity of the brain-produced cravings for more of the drug. The resulting increase in associated nonviolent criminality, e.g., theft, prostitution, to satisfy drug cravings led to a sharp spike in the numbers of women in detention (Alleyne, 2004; Pallone & Hennessy, 2003).

"JUST DESSERTS"

On the federal level, a shift occurred partly in response to the rise of cocaine related crimes which continues to reverberate to this day. Pallone and Hennessy (2003) describe a "just desserts" model of correc-tional practice which began to take hold in the 1970s, partly in response to cocaine's spread, but also in reaction to reports which emerged cast-ing doubt on the effectiveness of rehabilitation for prisoners. The "just desserts" model (Allen, 1981; Morris, 1974; von Hirsch, 1984) argued for prisons to be places of precise and inflexible punishment and inca-pacitation. Congress then supported this ideology through the passage of two major pieces of legislation which became the cornerstone of the Reagan Administration's War on Drugs. The first, the Criminal Sen-tencing Reform Act of 1981, focused on mandatory sentencing for many drug crimes, thereby removing judicial discretion for many types of offenses. The second, the Omnibus Crime Reduction Act of 1986, mandated incarceration for numerous drug use, possession, and sale of-fenses which heretofore had ended in probation, fines, or significantly lower sentences. A particularly onerous example of the draconian na-ture of these changes was seen in the "three strikes you're out" federal law created to send three time convicted felons to prison for life *without the possibility of parole.*

ZERO TOLERANCE POLICING

Simultaneously, a new pattern of police practice began to emerge in major U.S. cities. In New York City, for example, a new philosophy of police practice known as "zero tolerance" used computer technology and directed daily law enforcement efforts toward eliminating "quality of life" crimes (Bratton, 1998; Greene, 1999), as opposed to an earlier focus on large scale drug operation organizers. These hyperaggressive strategies were implemented by NYC Police Commissioner William Bratton, who posited that cities could once again be made more livable if smaller crimes could be prosecuted, e.g., panhandling, turnstile jumping, public vagrancy, prostitution. In the process of pursuing these daily "nuisance" crimes, thousands of new individuals (mostly poor, mostly African American and Latino) would be drawn into the police fingerprint data base. Operating on the hypothesis that larger crimes are often committed by individuals with prior records, Bratton saw this as a two-pronged victory in that petty misdeeds would decrease while the police fingerprint database was built up for easier apprehension of future criminals.

These practices had a devastating impact on poor women and people of color. Violations which earlier could have been satisfied through fines, community service, or continued without a finding were now offenses which landed women in jail. The inability to meet bail guaranteed that these women would serve time in city or county jails awaiting disposition of their cases. An overburdened criminal justice system with too few public defenders then virtually assured that poor women would languish behind bars, often for longer than what the eventual sentence would require.

FALLING CRIME, RISING INCARCERATION?

The Sentencing Project (2004) reported that crime rates have fallen for the last 14 years, yet prison incarceration rates have risen 52% during the same period. Karberg and Beck's (2004) astute analysis of Bureau of Justice statistics indicates that the *entire increase in prison incarceration rates* is due to the changes in sentencing policy and practice. While government and political figures are often quick to publicize and align themselves with the decline in crime rates in the popular media, little discussion of the continuing rise in incarceration rates typically follows (Jackson & Naureckas, 1994).

DOUBLE DISPROPORTION: WOMEN OF COLOR

It must be noted that quantum increases in women in prison have disproportionately affected Black and Latina women. They are sentenced to prison for drug offenses at rates that far outpace their numbers in the population, and their rates of arrest. Thirty-two percent of New Yorkers are African American or Hispanic women, for example, yet they constitute 91% of the people who are sentenced to prison for drugs in the state (Mauer et al., 1999). Most women receive prison sentences for non-violent drug related crimes.

Thus, disparities in arrests, hyperaggressive policing, and sentencing policy have been disproportionately felt by poor women of color and their families. Vivian's story highlights the subtle shift in resources which has taken place in many states, away from public policy which provides a modicum of education and health care support for low income women of color and their families to the subsistence standards found in correctional facilities and foster care systems.

SUBSTANCE ABUSE, MOTHERHOOD, AND INCARCERATION

For a mother, to be faced with the option of long-term treatment isolated from loved ones, versus being reconnected with children through prison bars, is tantamount to having no choice at all. The plea bargain system and judges' failure to consider fully the range of substance abusers that are now caught in the criminal justice web creates a mockery of the ideals of both justice (let the punishment fit the crime) and drug treatment (let the treatment fit the client). Contemporary substance abuse treatment has made great progress in differentiating among substance abusers. Earlier notions of "one size fits all" treatment, where early stage abusers and chronic relapsing long-term users were sent to 28-day inpatient rehabilitation, have given way to evidence based decisions supported by patient placement criteria (Mee-Lee, 2001). Yet many judges have failed to note the distinctions. Additionally, judicial decision making appears to be further constrained by what may be a politically driven need to preserve incarceration-like conditions by referring many more women to long-term intensive treatment than may actually qualify for it based on clinical evidence. This, coupled with the restricted number of slots available for mental health and substance abuse treatment, results in outcomes that are all too often detrimental to women, children, and families.

MENTAL HEALTH AND DRUG TREATMENT

The need for substance abuse treatment in the United States greatly outstrips resources directed to this serious public health concern. On any given day in this country, an estimated 22.2 million individuals would diagnostically qualify for substance abuse treatment in this country, yet fewer than 2 million receive it (SAMHSA, 2005). While acknowledging that many of the millions who need treatment may not be actively seeking it, there still remains a disparity in service provision that is unmatched in other areas of health.

In recent years social science literature has begun to report on the shift away from de-institutionalization to criminalization of mental health illnesses (Freudenberg, 2002; Navasky, 2005). Far more persons with mental health concerns are put behind bars than given treatment in hospitals. Large numbers of mentally ill, chemically addicted individuals are sent to, and remain, in jails and prisons for much longer periods of time for relatively minor offenses which are usually directly traceable to their mental illness (Butterfield, 1998). Perhaps the most stark indicator of this public policy shift can be seen in state and federal government budgets, where in recent years spending for prison expansion in some states has exceeded that for spending on police and other local budgetary items (Butterfield, 2002).

The move to "criminalize rather than medicalize" has been particularly damaging to women, who are seven times more likely to enter prisons with histories of untreated post traumatic stress, sexual abuse or assault, and depression. Often women report using drugs or alcohol as forms of self medication, in order to offset the impact of these difficult histories (CASA, 1998).

Mental illness and drug addiction are psychological and physiological phenomena, not character flaws. Yet women are caught in the triple stigmatization that comes from being female, in prison, and addicted. Women who may be psychologically fragile are often further damaged by the punitive, harsh environments found in correctional facilities.

STRATEGIES FOR CHANGE

Change for incarcerated women must emerge first from public awareness. As is the case for life behind bars, all too often those not directly impacted would rather look the other way and ignore the systematic troubles that are now visited upon hundreds of thousands of women and their families. Social and economic analysts and policy makers may be more directly aware of the injustices visited upon incarcerated addicted women, but are loathe to act, fearing political backlash. Yet with the numbers of women behind bars rising yearly, along with larger portions of state and federal budgets, in the face of falling crime rates, that posture is more and more difficult to maintain.

Ideas for change must begin with an appreciation that the perspective and experience of women is not the same as for men. "Few research studies on female inmates have been conducted, but most of those conclude that women exhibit differences in the severity and uniqueness of certain needs compared with male inmates" (Brennan & Austin, 1997). In 2003 The National Institute for Corrections issued a groundbreaking report on gender responsive strategies for women offenders (Bloom, Covington, & Raeder, 2003). The report called for acceptance of a guiding principle that gender makes a difference as a *starting point* for change. If that perspective is brought to bear in correctional facilities, it can result in structural changes that appreciate that women's pathways into prison are drug related more often than not; that relationships emerging from untreated trauma and addiction are all too often at the root of incarceration; and that family connections are often a significant motivating factor throughout the criminal injustice process.

Even a small reallocation of existing prison dollars would begin to address the huge gap between women who need treatment and those who receive it behind bars. Estimates of treatment need indicate that 25% of those in prison who need treatment, receive it (CASA, 1998). Given the overrepresentation of incarcerated women with drug related problems, it is a fair assumption that this statistic would be much higher if limited to women. From a clinical change perspective, it is clear that drug use is reduced and eliminated more effectively when treatment is obtained (Baekeland & Lundwall, 1975; Simpson, Joe, Rowan-Szal, & Greener, 1997). Thus, prisons and society as a whole would be well served to consider these issues and move to implement changes based on these ideas. Until these strategies and others are brought to the fore, we are all caged birds, trapped in a system of our own creation.

NOTE

1. Vivian's story is a composite of several clients with whom the author worked in a New Jersey jail. Her name and other identifying information has been changed.

REFERENCES

Angelou, M. (1970). *I know why the caged bird sings.* New York, NY: Random House.

Allen, F. A. (1981). The decline of the rehabilitative ideal: Penal policy and social purpose. New Haven: Yale University Press.

Alleyne, V. L. (2004). *The relationship between Black racial identity, motivation, and retention in substance abuse treatment.* Unpublished doctoral dissertation, Columbia University, New York, NY.

Baekeland, F., & Lundwall, L. (1975). Dropping out of treatment: A critical review. *Psychological Bulletin, 82,* 738-783.

Bloom, B., Covington, S., & Raeder, M. (2003). *Gender-responsive strategies: Research, practice, and guiding principles for women offenders.* Washington, DC: National Institute of Corrections.

Bratton, W. (1998). *Turnaround: How American's top cop reversed the crime epidemic.* New York, NY: Random House.

Brennan, T., & Austin, J. (1997). *Women in jail: Classification issues.* Washington, DC: National Institute of Corrections. http://nicic.org/pubs/1997/013768.pdf.

Butterfield, F. (1998, March 5, 1998). Prisons replace hospitals for the nation's mentally ill. *New York Times,* p. A1.

Butterfield, F. (2002). *Study finds increase at all levels of government in cost of criminal justice.* New York Times, p. A14.

CASA. (1998). *Behind bars: Substance abuse and America's prison population.* New York, NY: National Center on Addiction and Substance Abuse at Columbia University.

CASA. (2001). *Shoveling up: The impact of substance abuse on state budgets.* New York, NY: National Center on Addiction Studies at Columbia University.

Freudenberg, N. (2002). Adverse effects of US jail and prison policies on the health and well-being of women. *American Journal of Public Health, 92*(12), 1895-1899.

Greene, J. A. (1999). Zero tolerance: A case study of police policies and practices in New York City. *Crime & Delinquency, 45*(2), 171-187.

Jackson, J., & Naureckas, J. (1994). *Crime contradictions: U.S. News Illustrates flaws in crime coverage: Fairness & Accuracy in Reporting* (FAIR).

Karberg, J. C., & Beck, A. J. (April 16, 2004). *Trends in US correctional populations: Findings from the Bureau of Justice Statistics.* Paper presented at the National Committee on Community Corrections, Washington, D.C.

Kassebaum, P. (1999). *Substance abuse treatment for women offenders: Guide to promising practices. Technical Assistance Publication Series 23.* [DHHS Publication No. (SMA) 00-3454]. Rockville, MD: U.S. Department of Health and Human Services.

Mauer, M., Potler, C., & Wolf, R. (1999). *Gender and Justice: Women, Drugs and Sentencing Policy*. Washington, D.C.: The Sentencing Project.

Mee-Lee, D. (Ed.). (2001). *ASAM patient placement criterial for the treatment of substance-related disorders* (2nd-Revised ed.). Chevy Chase, MD: American Society of Addiction Medicine.

Morris, N. (1974). *The future of imprisonment*. Chicago: University of Chicago Press.

Navasky, M., O'Connor, K. (2005). Frontline: The new asylums. Boston, MA: WGBH Educational Foundation.

Pallone, N. J., & Hennessy, J. J. (2003). To punish or to treat: Substance abuse within the context of oscillating attitudes toward correctional rehabilitation. In N. J. Pallone (Ed.), *Treating substance abusers in correctional contexts: New understandings, new modalities*. Binghamton, NY: The Haworth Press, Inc.

SAMHSA. (2005). 2003 National survey on drug use and health: Findings. Retrieved October 30, 2005, from http://oas.samhsa.gov/nhsda/2k3nsduh/2k3Results.htm

Simpson, D., Joe, G. W., Rowan-Szal, G. A., & Greener, J. M. (1997). Drug abuse treatment process components that improve retention. *Journal of Substance Abuse Treatment, 14*(6, 1997 Nov-Dec.), 565-572.

von Hirsch, A. (1984). The ethics of selective incapacitation: Observations on the contemporary debate. *Crime & Delinquency, 30*(2), 175-194.

doi:10.1300/J015v29n03_10

Voices of Pride:
Drama Therapy with Incarcerated Women

Abigail Leeder
Colleen Wimmer

SUMMARY. This paper demonstrates how drama therapy assists incarcerated women in freeing themselves from internalized oppressive beliefs. In the context of a drug and alcohol treatment program for incarcerated[1] women, the authors assist the women in building three distinct bridges to healing: a new relationship to one's self, to other women, and to the community. Writing exercises, performance techniques, and group drama therapy empower women to express their diverse voices. As the women risk sharing their personal stories and journeys of recovery, they begin to actively envision a different future for themselves. The participants discover talents that offer them an opportunity to experience themselves in a different light, no longer bound by the stigma of being in prison. doi:10.1300/J015v29n03_11 *[Article copies available for a fee from The Haworth Document Delivery Service: 1-800-HAWORTH. E-mail address:*

Abigail Leeder, MA, is currently the Project Coordinator for the Alliance for Sexual Assault Prevention at the University of Oregon.

Colleen Wimmer, MA, MFTI, is currently a Primary Counselor and Family Program Coordinator at Project Pride in Oakland, CA.

Address correspondence to: Abigail Leeder, MA, 550 E 40th Ave., Eugene, OR 97405 (E-mail: abigirl72@hotmail.com) or Colleen Wimmer, MA, MFTI, 2551 San Pablo Avenue, Oakland, CA 94612 (E-mail: pomegranatetrail@hotmail.com).

[Haworth co-indexing entry note]: "Voices of Pride: Drama Therapy with Incarcerated Women." Leeder, Abigail, and Colleen Wimmer. Co-published simultaneously in *Women & Therapy* (The Haworth Press, Inc.) Vol. 29, No. 3/4, 2006, pp. 195-213; and: *Inside and Out: Women, Prison, and Therapy* (ed: Elaine Leeder) The Haworth Press, Inc., 2006, pp. 195-213. Single or multiple copies of this article are available for a fee from The Haworth Document Delivery Service [1-800-HAWORTH, 9:00 a.m. - 5:00 p.m. (EST). E-mail address: docdelivery@haworthpress.com].

Available online at http://wt.haworthpress.com
doi:10.1300/J015v29n03_11

KEYWORDS. Addiction, domestic violence, drama therapy, family therapy, group therapy, incarcerated women, performance, poetry, psychodrama, recovery, role-play, substance abuse

Drama liberates us from confinement, be it socially or psychologically induced. The dramatic moment is one of emancipation.

(Emunah, 1994, p. xiii)

INTRODUCTION

In the context of a drug and alcohol treatment program for incarcerated women and their children, our intention as Drama Therapists is to assist women in freeing themselves from internalized oppressive beliefs about themselves and other women. Specifically, our goal is to help the women build three distinct bridges to healing: a new relationship to one's self; a more compassionate understanding of other women facing similar struggles; and a new sense of being a valuable contributor to the greater community.

Writing exercises, performance techniques, and group drama therapy empower the women to express their diverse voices–the voices of women who are often not heard. This approach also encourages participants to experiment with new roles as successful, productive, and resourceful women. As they risk sharing their personal stories and journeys of recovery, they begin to actively envision a different future for themselves and their children. They discover new talents–as writers, artists, performers, MCs, and actors–and in doing so, they experience themselves in a different light, no longer bound by the stigma of their pasts or of being in prison. Furthermore, by taking performances into the larger community, the women are given the opportunity to bridge the gap between the ways incarcerated women are viewed by the public and the reality of their authentic struggles to overcome their addictions and traumatic pasts.

PROJECT PRIDE

Project Pride is a residential drug and alcohol and co-occurring disorder treatment facility in the heart of West Oakland, California. It is a division of the East Bay Community Recovery Project. It houses approximately 40 mothers and 40 children, from infancy to 8 years old. The ages of the women range from 18 to 45.

Project Pride is organized to serve two different populations. It contracts with the State of California to provide a mother-infant program for prisoners of the California Department of Corrections (CDC). Approximately half of the population are prisoners serving the last portion of their sentences, from three months to several years. The other half of the population is comprised of what we call "Perinatal" clients, women who are referred from the community, through Child Protection Services (CPS), or are sentenced to residential treatment as an alternative to county jail.

The residents of Project Pride are extremely diverse in age, ethnicity, race, socio-economic backgrounds, culture, and addiction history. Approximately 17% of the clients are between the ages of 18-25, 48% between 26-35, and 35% between 36-48. Approximately 33% are African American, 26% white, 11% Hispanic, 5% Asian/Pacific Islander, 3% Native American, and 4-18% other or lack of data. In addition to differences in age and ethnicity there are also great variations in mental and emotional functioning and in education and literacy levels. This diversity is compounded even further by the fact that there is a wide spectrum of experience in relation to motherhood, domestic violence, past histories of sexual abuse and trauma, and involvement with husbands and boyfriends with varying degrees of substance use and criminal behavior. There are also various differences in cultural values, including what is tolerated in relationships and beliefs about child rearing.

Many of the women with whom we work suffer from co-occuring disorders. Some have been diagnosed with or have severe symptoms of depression, PTSD, eating disorders, occasional psychosis, and learning disabilities. Many of the "Perinatal" clients are on methadone treatment for heroin addiction or are being treated for mood or other mental disorders with medication. The women who come to us through the California Department of Corrections are not diagnosed with mental disorders. Prisoners who are diagnosed do not qualify for the Mother-Infant Program. Consequently, many of the women mask their mental health issues to be admitted to our program. While perhaps not severe, these clients also exhibit symptoms of PTSD, depression, anxiety, and other mental disorders.

Within the dynamics created by these variables, the women at Project Pride are in the process of grappling with themselves and each other as they work toward making sense of their past choices and choosing a new path for their future. As with any diverse group, their motivation for and commitment to making changes vary widely. Some of these women are learning, perhaps for the first time, how to be mothers and deeply desire a new and different life for themselves and their children, while others are facing more fear and resistance about making significant changes. All of them are preparing to reenter the community. Our intention as Primary Counselors and Drama Therapists is to support their growth at various levels and to assist them in expanding the roles they play in the world.

DRAMA THERAPY

Drama therapy is a field of practice that has its roots in both psychotherapy and theater. Informed by psychoanalytic, behaviorist, and humanistic psychology, drama therapy utilizes theater processes to foster emotional and psychological growth (Emunah). Renee Emunah (1994), one of the pioneers in the field of drama therapy, describes an integrative, process-oriented framework for drama therapy with goals rooted in psychotherapy and conceptual bases in theater, dramatic play, role-play, psychodrama, and dramatic ritual. Pointing to the relationship of drama therapy to humanistic psychology, Emunah explains that a dramatic enactment can help the client to "create a bridge between human limitations and human aspirations, between who we are and whom we hope to become" (p. 27). And, like psychoanalysis, the exploration of personal history is a key component of long-term drama therapy, as is the cultivation of both personal insight and ego strength. Additionally, the action-oriented nature of drama therapy is similar to behaviorist approaches. According to Emunah, "the attention given in behavioral therapy to the breaking of maladaptive patterns and the acquisition of new coping skills is very akin to goals in drama therapy" (p. 31).

At Project Pride, drama therapy is used in a variety of different ways and we have adapted drama therapy processes to fit into much of the psychological work that is done with the women. We run a 12-week-long Domestic Violence Drama Therapy group, and we each facilitate a weekly "caseload" Drama Therapy group where we meet with the clients assigned to us to explore relevant issues they are facing in their lives. We also facilitate a Multi-family Education Group and incorporate drama therapy techniques into our curriculum. Apart from these weekly groups, we utilize drama therapy in one-on-one counseling sessions with our clients and also produce "Voices of Pride," an intensive week-long writing and performance workshop.

Through the use of various dramatic structures, improvisational games, sound and movement exercises, writing and performance, we encourage women to express their innate creativity, and to find new ways to play and new ways to build relationships with each other. Drama brings an element of playfulness and spontaneity that is sorely missing from these women's lives in prison and in treatment. It also gives them a chance to experience an alternative way of having fun that is different from experiences with drugs or making fun at each other's expense. In all of our groups, we play warm-up games that help the women to relax and interact with one another in new ways. The silly and creative nature of these games allow the women to let off steam and become more present and available to one another, leaving the stresses of daily life and enjoying authentic connections with one another.

According to Emunah, "Drama, by its very nature induces empathy and perspective" (1994, p. xv). Our experience has confirmed that drama therapy builds trust and teamwork among the women. In various groups, as the women open and share their stories with one another they begin to realize that their apparent differences are small in comparison to the similarity of their struggles. Through role-plays and role reversals, the women get the chance to step into each others' shoes and the shoes of other people in their lives: "Role-playing someone else's story gives you the opportunity to be a part of their life and for them to look at you as a part of their life as well," said one participant, "I think that actually opens us up to one another a little more. There is a certain bond, a certain trust after that." Building trust in an environment where trust is hard to come by is a very important part of their healing process. It may also be one of the few opportunities that the women have had to experience trust; it is not unusual for a new arrival to Project Pride to comment that she trusts no one in her life.

Drama therapy can also enhance self-esteem, especially the performance-oriented work that we do. When the women create a skit or write a poem and it is received with respect and admiration, the women are reminded that they have something valuable to offer. Their creativity is acknowledged and their talent as a poet, writer, or performer is recognized. The clients begin to see themselves and one another in new ways. This in turn encourages the women to take the risk to try on other roles. As described by Emunah, "The use of drama as therapy fosters liberation, expansion and perspective. Drama therapy invites us to uncover and integrate dormant aspects of ourselves, to stretch our conception of who we are" (p. xvii).

DOMESTIC VIOLENCE DRAMA THERAPY GROUP

[The DV group] made me feel stronger about myself . . . to not be afraid of this man and to stand up for myself.

–DV Group participant

The Domestic Violence Drama Therapy group is a 12-week group held weekly for 1.5 hours. The group is largely voluntary, though a few of the women have been mandated by Child Protection Services to participate in a domestic violence group, or by their primary counselor at Project Pride as a part of their treatment plan. After the second meeting the group is "closed," meaning we will take no more participants and the women commit to being there for the duration of the 12 weeks.

The group averages eight women per session. They are a mix of CDC (residents from the California Department of Corrections) and "Perinatal" clients. In each group there is racial diversity, differences in class and education, as well as a range of experiences of domestic violence. Many of the women are married or have been married; some of them are still married to abusive partners.

The intention of the group is to educate the women about domestic violence as well as to build self-esteem, to give them the opportunity to practice new ways of being, and to face and resolve past events. Many, if not all of Irvin Yalom's (1995) Therapeutic Factors in Group Psychotherapy are present and met throughout the sessions including, but not limited to: empathy for others, universality, imparting of information, imitative behavior, interpersonal learning, group cohesiveness, catharsis, and existential factors.

Drama therapy is a unique and helpful modality for the topic of domestic violence in group therapy for many reasons. As previously mentioned, it is very useful in building the necessary trust and teamwork among the women that will enable them to safely explore deeper issues. Equally important, dramatic enactments can provide the aesthetic distance needed to examine and deconstruct scenarios that are perhaps too emotionally loaded to discuss. Depending on the willingness and the ego strength of participants, the enactments can be more sociodramatic in nature, i.e., a role-play of a stereotypical controlling boyfriend, or personal, i.e., a specific scene from a participant's past. Drama therapy is very flexible and can be a container for both the deep pain of personal trauma as well as a way for the women to laugh and play together as they enact some of the absurdities of life in domestic relationships.

The intention at the beginning of the 12-week session is to build safety and trust among group members. To facilitate this, the initial session and the beginning of each subsequent session consist of improvisational warm-up games drawn from various improvisational theater or drama therapy sources. Warm-up games are an essential part of the group process. They help the group to become present in the moment, get the blood flowing, and shift the mood and energy of the group.

One example of a warm-up game is called "Greet, Argue and Make-up." In this game each woman pairs up with three different members in the group. With their first partner, the women act as if they are best friends who have just reunited. Next, they find another partner and have an argument, and finally they find a new partner and make-up with her as if she were the one with whom they had been fighting. While there are alliances and struggles among the women when they are "on the floor" in their residences, this warm-up gives them a structured opportunity to role-play other possibilities, while fostering a certain level of connection.

Often at the beginning of the 12-week series we will explore the sociodramatic make-up of the group, giving the women a chance to see who is in the group and to recognize the universality of their experiences. In the first session we often do the exercise: "Step Into The Center If." The women stand in a circle and the facilitator starts a sentence with: "Step into the center if . . ." and then completes a sentence with a statement. Everyone for whom that statement is true steps into the center of the circle. We start out quite general, yet geared toward family and personal information: "Step into the center if you were raised by your mother . . . , if you graduated from high school . . ." From there we often move into edgier questions: ". . . if you have ever hit someone . . ." (this often brings everyone in to the middle), " . . . if you have ever been hit . . ." After a little while, they are encouraged to call out their own statements. On occasion they will go very deep, very quickly: "Step into the center if you have ever been raped . . ." (often the majority of the women), " . . . if you have ever been molested . . . , if it was by someone you knew . . . , if you still love your abuser . . . , if you ever had your teeth knocked out," etc. Guidelines for voluntary participation are laid out at the beginning of the session, and the women are reminded that they have a choice in how much they disclose. For many of them, it seems as though there is a palpable sense of relief as they realize through this activity that they are not the only woman with these experiences.

In an environment where the women are interacting daily with each other, there is often fear about disclosing too much and having it used against them. At the beginning of the 12-week series, confidentiality and disclosure is of particular concern. By the end of the series, the sharing of personal stories has built a level of deepened intimacy among the group's participants, and the fears of disclosure seem small in comparison to the rewards of empathy and support.

After warming-up, most of our drama therapy groups begin with a "check-in," giving the women a chance to process and share about their week and be more present with one another. Throughout the series, the women share about past experiences as well as their current circumstances. Many of the women are at choice points in their relationships: Separated from their relationships by circumstance, they now have the opportunity to assess their previous choices and explore new ones.

The bulk of each session includes some sort of dramatic enactment or role-play. This can, again, be a more "distanced" scene where we create composite characters in "typical" abusive situations, or more personal stories that the women have actually experienced. In past sessions we have both explored the Power and Control Wheel developed by the Domestic Abuse Intervention Project. We have also enacted different scenes from the "Cycle of Violence" concept developed by Dr. Lenore Walker (1979). To illustrate the cycle of violence, participants gather in groups of two or three and find a way to play out the different phases of the cycle: The Honeymoon Phase, The Tension Building Phase, and the Violence Phase. The opportunity to see the cycle acted out as opposed to just being discussed brings a tangible understanding of the cycle to the participants–they relate to the stories because they have lived them.

Again, when the clients recognize the universality of their experiences, they feel a sense of relief and shared understanding. While the participants may have a hard time not blaming themselves for their past history of abusive relationships, they can empathize with another woman in a similar situation. They recognize in the enactments that the woman is not to blame for her victimization. With time they may be able to view their own situation in a similar way.

Another exercise that has a powerful impact on the women is the use of imaginary phone calls. A disconnected cell phone is placed on a chair in the center of the circle and, one at a time, the women make telephone calls to an imagined recipient. In past groups women have called their abuser, their children, a deceased relative, and even God. The opportunity to be witnessed in the expression of their anger or hurt gives the women a sense of support that they may never have had before. One of the participants summed up the impact of the exercise this way:

> When I pretended to call my son's father, who abused me for seven years, it felt good to say everything I wanted to say towards him, and that relieved a lot of my anger toward him. I think that once the anger came out I could forgive myself for not being educated enough on domestic violence, not blame myself like: "Why did I let this man do this?" but to actually let it out and react it [sic] and say the things I knew I wasn't going to get hit for.

As illustrated above, an exercise like this can assist a woman in reclaiming some personal power from a situation in her past in which she was powerless. Dramatic reenactments of a specific scene from a client's life can also be a way to aid in healing past trauma. By replaying the scene in a safe environment with the support of the group, the client is given the opportunity to practice a new way of being in the situation, or to use the reenactment to gain valuable perspective they may not have had in the original experience.[2] It is important when doing reenactments that the client is guided by a trained drama therapist to prevent re-traumatization. Participants are often reminded that they have choices about how far to take a scenario and when to stop the process.

In these enactments, we can utilize the group to play out different aspects of a participant. This gives the participant the opportunity to see and address her own conflicting emotions and parts of herself. The client is led through a process where she casts members of the group to play out these parts. She then either talks directly to these aspects of herself or she gives the actors lines that represent what each of these parts feel.

In one enactment in the Domestic Violence group, a woman cast someone to play her teenage self who was stuck in an abusive relationship. Jennifer, the client, was able to use the opportunity to address this younger part of her. She spoke directly to her 15-year-old-self, assuring her that she would ultimately be safe from this man, that she was not to blame for her situation, and that she forgave her for her choices. After Jennifer said what she needed to the actor in the role of her younger self, they reversed roles so that the actor could repeat the words that Jennifer had spoken, giving Jennifer the chance to receive her own words of blessing and forgiveness.

Each session and series of the Domestic Violence group is different. The group make-up, the interpersonal dynamics, and the individual stories of the women are attended to within the context of a drama therapy group, yet without a specific formula. During each meeting our intention is to use our collective creativity to respond to the individual needs of participants and the needs of the group as a whole.

While drama therapy is well-suited for topic-oriented group work such as domestic violence, it is also a powerful modality for general group therapy. In addition to the DV group we utilize drama therapy in weekly groups comprised of women on our caseload. Using similar structures we explore life topics relevant to the women. The topics are as diverse as the women and range from facing their addiction to the realities of motherhood. Coming together weekly in a safe and contained environment, the drama therapy caseload groups serve as a place to process the week's events and the struggles of life. In addition to the DV group, the caseload groups serve as another environment where powerful personal healing can take place for the women.

MULTI-FAMILY EDUCATION GROUP

The Multi-family Education Group is a voluntary group held on Saturday mornings, lasting 90 minutes. We define "family" as any supportive family member or friend. The women are encouraged to come to the group even if their friends and family cannot attend. We emphasize that the group is an opportunity where the women can educate themselves about unhealthy behaviors within families and about how they can chose new behaviors for themselves, as well as encourage them in their children, and in doing so break cycles of violence, abuse, and neglect.

One of the primary goals of the Multi-family Education Group is to educate the women, their family members, and close friends about family dynamics as they play out in the context of addiction. The first 30-40 minutes of the group is didactic, therefore cognitive in nature. This includes lectures, videos, interactive handouts, discussion, etc. The remaining 50-60 minutes is dedicated to exploring how this information can be "played out" and therefore understood and integrated in a "lived" sense. This is achieved through drama therapy warm-up exercises that lead into role-plays of typical family dynamics and occasionally into enactments that are highly personal. In some instances, the family members may be in the room, yet it is often the case that they are not physically present but rather evoked as a character in the enactment.

While the Multi-family Education Group shares many of the same approaches as the other drama therapy groups, especially in its use of warm-up exercises and role-plays of varying degrees of depth, it is in some ways an entirely different experience. One of the main differences is that–in keeping with the Project Pride philosophy that family secrets are destructive–the group encourages an open exploration among all family members, including children from the age of five or six and above. Another difference is that the group, while voluntary, is never closed. This means that at any given time a family member or an entire family, a friend, or even a resident may attend the group for the first time. These two factors alone dictate that each topic must be self-contained and accessible to a variety of ages.

It is often the case that many of the CDC residents have family members who live at quite a distance and may attend only a few of the Family groups. Since some of these family members may not have experienced any kind of therapy before, we are faced with an additional challenge: how to introduce them to therapy, and more specifically drama therapy, in a gentle and safe way that sparks their desire to seek out therapeutic resources in their local communities. It has been our experience that, over a period of time, a core group of women comes to the group on a regular basis. They not only provide continuity in the group, but they are often the most willing participants in the enactments, modeling to newcomers that "silly exercises" can be fun as well as meaningful. In this way, new family members are included in the group in the more comfortable role of "the audience."

The flexibility inherent in drama therapy lends itself to the complexities of a group like this, and this is most evident with the children. While the children often seem busy drawing or coloring, paying very little attention to the discussion, when it comes time for the enactments they are eager participants. In one instance, we began to form a "Stage Picture" of each of the family roles in a family with addiction: the hero, the enabler, the mascot, the lost child, the dependent (the addict), and the scapegoat. A "Stage Picture" is simply a moment frozen in time where the participants in the exercise strike a pose depicting the body language of each role. When the exercise began, the children spontaneously rushed to join the stage picture. As they struck poses, heroic and sad, it became clear that they had been listening all the time (something that we know is often the case in daily life).[3]

The goal of the "Stage Picture" exercise is to authentically embody the role based on one's own experience and interpretation, which has been stimulated by a previous discussion of the roles. After the participants strike their poses, each one is asked to say one line that comes spontaneously to mind. "I will save you and everyone else in this family," says the Hero, for example, while the Scapegoat may say something like: "Who are you looking at? Get off my back!" If the facilitator senses that the participants have a strong desire to explore the role further she then asks them to repeat their lines and respond spontaneously to each other in character. This moves the "Stage Picture" into an improvisational scene, where participants can further explore the behavior of any given role.

In groups that have a high degree of trust and cohesiveness, the "Stage Picture" can be intensified by asking a volunteer to "sculpt" (or position) her family members in their typical "family roles." Another possibility is to sculpt a family scene depicting a moment frozen in time, from the past or the future. Enactments of a past experience can be especially effective because the "family roles" can emerge spontaneously through the action: a client may experience an "Aha!" moment when she realizes that a usual behavior of a family member corresponds to a "family role" that we have discussed.

In addition to explorations of family roles, the Multi-family Group gives a client various opportunities to play out scenes from the past in order to gain more *insight* into her family dynamics or scenes from the future to *practice* making new decisions under the constraints and pressures that exist in her family. Sometimes we use visual arts to stimulate creativity to begin the drama therapy process. The material inherent in the artwork can reflect mythological or archetypal themes that are often collectively shared by the group. In these instances, the enactments themselves tend to become mythical, blurring the lines between the past and the future, and thereby *combining* insight into the past and practice for the future within a very short time frame.

This was particularly the case for a client named Robyn[4] when she drew a picture of a brick house. The house represented the wall that she needs to keep up to protect her family from the temptations and pain of the outside world and especially from her younger sister who still uses drugs. A member of the group referred to the wolf outside huffing and puffing, trying to blow the house down. Though no one in the room mentioned the vulnerable little pigs it seemed the group was aware that Robyn could play out any one of those roles. Among the women, Robyn had a reputation for behaving like a vulnerable little girl. The scene of meeting her sister at the door when she wanted drugs was very familiar to Robyn–it had happened many times before. But because Robyn would soon be on parole she chose to enact the scene as if it were in the future. The question that hung in the room was whether Robyn would remain in the role of the little girl and allow herself to be victimized by the needs of her sister or do something different. The mythological framework held all of these components together, and the stage was set for Robyn to confront her sister.

As the enactment began, Robyn chose someone to play her sister and then three people to play her internal resources: "survival, love, and strength." Robyn reversed roles with the other "actor" to show the group how her sister might come to the house "tweaking" to ask for money and to tempt Robyn with drugs. (This also helped the "actor" cast in the role gain further insight into how to play the role of the sister more authentically.) Throughout her stay at Project Pride, Robyn has been learning how to communicate firm boundaries without going into a rage or, as she was prone to do before prison, resolving most disputes with a physical fight. Here, as the enactment unfolded, Robyn held her ground firmly; both affirming her worries and care for her sister, but respectfully refusing to let her sister in the door. At one point in the enactment, Robyn broke the action to explain to the group that she felt tempted to leave with her sister and that was why she was fighting so hard. This time however, she was fighting with strong, firm, and compassionate words, instead of with her fists.

Role-plays in the Multi-family Education Group can also bring awareness to the importance of how, in addition to our families, our friendships impact important decisions in our lives. In one instance, Katie began by asking a friend for forgiveness for not attending to her child who inadvertently completely destroyed her friend's houseboat. Through the enactment Katie realized she felt obligated to her friend out of guilt for destroying his property. She ended the enactment by expressing this to him, confirming her love for him, but also telling him that she needed to let the friendship go for the time being because he was still using drugs. Within the space of 15 minutes, the client was able to move through a complex combination of feelings–obligation, guilt, love–to then come to the cognitive understanding that she could no longer be around her friend for the safety of her child and the sake of her own recovery. And finally, she was able to practice what she might say to her friend in real life.

Drama therapy can serve as a rehearsal for life, a chance to practice a conversation that needs to take place. As we know, in families with addiction, those conversations are crucial to the recovery of the entire family. Our hope is that the Multi-family Education Group will help clients, and their families and friends, to begin or deepen that process. But even in circumstances where the conversations are not possible due to the death, absence, or reluctance of a family member, the dramatic enactments serve a purpose that is much like the exercise of writing a letter that is never sent. The practice of enacting the conversation gives the client perspective, insight, and often a cathartic release, and *all* of this allows her to move on in her recovery and to make better choices for the family she is creating.

Ultimately, this is our deepest hope for the women: that through the various games, exercises, role-plays, and fully developed enactments they will feel empowered to create healthier families. The dramatic structures implicitly encourage an understanding that family rules–spoken and unspoken–are not hard and fast "givens" but guidelines to explore, play with, and modify to meet the needs of every person in the family. At the same time, the warm-ups and the playful games often give their families new ways of having fun together, while an exploration of family rituals honors the healthy bonds that nurture them. The arena of multi-family group drama therapy is vast. But with the courage and commitment so often shown by the women, their families, and friends, it becomes a fertile ground for exploring the diverse needs and possibilities of a healthy family.

VOICES OF PRIDE

The "Voices of Pride" week-long writing and performance workshops take place approximately every 2-3 months. The workshops are sponsored by the local Bay Area public television station KQED as part of its Community Outreach program.[5] Two writers and performers from the community and two drama therapists, as well as staff from Project Pride and KQED, collaborate to produce the workshops. The workshops consist of two-hour sessions each day for four days, with a small public performance on the fifth day.

The first day involves screening a documentary film on a topic relevant to the lives of the women. Some of the films included: "What I Want My Words to Do to You," playwright Eve Ensler's writing workshop for women in a high security prison; "Girl Trouble," adolescent girls' struggles to build their lives in the context of an organization they developed and continue to run for girls in-risk; and "Prison Lullabies," female prisoners adapting to the realities of motherhood while raising their babies in prison and then, upon their release, in their communities.

After the screening the women are given various writing exercises to assist them in responding to the film. The women are always encouraged to diverge from the exercises if they become inspired to write something else. The purpose of the workshop, as the name suggests, is to help the women find their individual voices. We encourage any expressive effort on the part of the women, including passionate voices of dissent and difficulty. The writing exercises are interspersed with dramatic exercises, improvisational games, and performance techniques. Aside from preparing the women for the performance, these dramatic techniques give the women access to metaphorical material that is often held deep within their psyches. Though the workshop is mandatory for all of the women, each woman can choose to engage in the process of writing, reading, enacting, and performing at any given point. We have found that this voluntary aspect of the workshop has been essential for the women to build trust in the facilitators and their peers, and to create a sense of safety that allows for their otherwise dormant creativity to step forth. In an atmosphere of unconditional support, each of the women finds her own way of entering into her experience, working with it, and transforming it into a work of art. Through this process the women gain some mastery over experiences that have, to a large extent, held power over them.

One woman, for example, refused to write for the first few days of the workshop. On the third day she participated in a writing exercise, but then would not read it. This continued into the second workshop months later when she then let a facilitator read her piece anonymously for her in the performance. Finally, again months later, the same woman participated in the writing exercises, was able to read her own piece, and then even performed a poem she had written while in prison about her childhood abuse and its impact on her. Obviously the trust built over time and the gentle encouragement, yet lack of force, allowed for this client's unfolding. There have been many surprising occasions where a woman does not outwardly engage the process during the week, but arrives on the morning of the performance with a piece in hand ready to perform.

Drama therapy techniques are especially adept at providing a wide range of possibilities while fostering group cohesion. Even the most resistant women can be enrolled as "audience," while another tentative woman may be willing to venture forth as a "director" to suggest ways a skit can be modified or enhanced. Likewise, some women are reluctant to "perform" in a skit, but they are eager to play the role of expert on a panel discussing prostitution, for example, or to engage in a mock news interview that also involves questions from the audience. The possibilities are as rich and as varied as the lives and imaginations of this diverse group of women.

The purpose of these performance workshops is to assist the women in finding their voices, in whatever form their voices may come–harsh, quiet, ecstatic, tired, etc.–and most important to honor whatever it is that they may have to say. Finally, we hope to encourage them to speak their voices proudly with a new found sense of self. We would like to share a few performance pieces, to let the women speak for themselves:

> When I think back on my life, in times of old
> I remember a child too frightened to hold.
> She is afraid to love, afraid to give,
> and sometimes at night she is afraid to live.
> Her body has been beaten, her heart badly broken,
> the tears of a child, not loud enough spoken.
> She remembers awaking to the touch of a man,
> touching a touch she didn't quite understand.
> So she turns to her mother, but her mother is gone.
> So she looks for a reason to carry on.
> She remembers the pain, the sorrow, the guilt.
> She prays the father and child both heal.
> She remembers praying for justice to come
> to the man who killed her without the use of a gun.
>
> > > > –B

> A life like no other
> tough, rough and all that stuff,
> raised in the projects, what a life,
> you better think twice
> before going out at night.
>
> What are girls supposed
> to be made of?
> Sugar and spice?
> That would have been nice,
> but yeah right, not my life.
>
> All I ever wanted
> was to be loved
> not a dope fiend,

pushed around and shoved.
No life, nothing
to look ahead to
that seems to be my life.
Right?

But then there goes
that big bright light
I see even in the
darkness of night
telling me that doesn't
have to be my life.

Changes I have made,
it's a miracle
I am saved.
Dope fiend, meth monster,
that's my past.
I am free, free at last.

–J

CONCLUSION

Our main goal in our work with drama therapy at Project Pride is to engage the imaginations and creativity of women who usually view themselves in confined ways, in and out of prison. We encourage them to see themselves as more than convicted felons, drug addicts, or overwhelmed single mothers. Many of the women are able to engage the process of actively claiming new roles: "competent and loving mother," "healthy woman," "student," and "professional." Through dramatic enactments and participation in the performance workshops the women are recognized, both by their peers, and by themselves, as more than just women with traumatic histories who have landed in a treatment program. They transcend their past and are able to, at least for a time, free themselves to uncover new possibilities. These possibilities are often far beyond those provided by the daily structure of their lives in prison and the past chaos of their lives in the streets. Their stories become their healing and through play and enactment they are able to give voice to their own innate creativity. One client summed it up this way:

It is really about this energy that is there. And you get the opportunity for no one to say "calm down," "that's too violent," "that's too that," "that's too this." And you get to express it, however, whatever, you want to say. No judging. That's what was really amazing for me, that your drama is your therapy.

NOTES

1. As described later, approximately half of the women in our facility are referred to us from the community, some of whom are in a "drug diversion" program, which means they enter treatment instead of serving jail time. But most, if not all, of these women have served some jail time in the past. For this reason, though technically they are not currently incarcerated, they still suffer from oppressive beliefs about themselves related to their past involvement in drugs, crime, and imprisonment.

2. Role-plays and enactments in a drama therapeutic process are similar to Psychodramatic processes. Psychodrama, a field of psychotherapy where personal issues are enacted, was founded by J.L. Moreno (1889-1974). Psychodrama is one of the sources of drama therapy and psychodramatic structures can be a component of many drama therapy groups. Psychodramatic methods can be highly useful for healing personal trauma in a group context.

3. For a more detailed explanation of these roles see Sharon Wegscheider-Cruse, "Another Chance: Hope and help for the Alcoholic Family." While a five-year-old cannot know the full implications of playing the "hero" in a family with addiction, the exercise provides the family with a common language and experience that is the beginning for understanding how addiction impacts the dynamics in the family. Our hope is that over time the older members of the family will gain a more sophisticated understanding, as well as the tools to help the younger children.

4. All names of clients have been changed to protect confidentiality.

5. This KQED Community Outreach is part of the Making Connections Media Outreach initiative. KQED Community Outreach is currently compiling curriculum produced through this workshop to create a curriculum guide that can be distributed with the films to other organizations and providers that work with offenders and ex-offenders. See resources for contact information. Information about the films used for the KQED collaboration workshops can be found at: www.reentrymediaoutreach.org.

REFERENCES

Emunah, R. (1994). *Acting for real: Drama therapy process technique and performance*. New York: Brunner/Mazel.

Power and control wheel. (n.d.). retrieved November 28, 2005 from http://www.duluth-model.org/documents/PhyVio.pdf

Walker, L. (1979). *The battered woman*. New York: Harper and Row.

Yalom, I. D. (1995). *The theory and practice of group psychotherapy* (4th ed.). New York: BasicBooks.

RESOURCES

Blatner, A. (2000). *Foundations of psychodrama: History, theory, and practice* (4th ed.). New York: Springer.

Boal, A. (1992). *Games for actors and non-actors.* London: Routledge.

Fraden, R. (2001). *Imagining Medea: Rhodessa Jones and theater for incarcerated women.* Chapel Hill: University of North Carolina.

Jennings, S. (1995). *Dramatherapy with children and adolescents.* London: Routledge.

Landy, R. (1994). *Drama therapy: Concepts, theories and practices* (2nd ed.). Springfield, IL: Charles C Thomas.

Leveton, E. (1992). *A clinician's guide to psychodrama* (2nd ed.). New York: Springer Publishing Company.

Shah, S., Project Manager, Community Outreach sshah@kqed.org, KQED, Inc., 2601 Mariposa Street, San Francisco, CA 94110-1426 (415) 864-2000 www.kqed.org

Spolin, V. (1963). *Improvisation for the theater.* Evanston, IL: Northwestern University Press.

Sternberg, P. (1998). *Theatre for conflict resolution: In the classroom and beyond.* Portsmouth, NH: Heinemann.

Sternberg, P. & Garcia, A. (1994). *Sociodrama: Who's in your shoes?.* Westport, CT: Praeger.

Thompson, J. (1999). *Drama workshops for anger management and offending behaviour.* London: Jessica Kingsley.

doi:10.1300/J015v29n03_11

Countering Correctional Discourse: Development of a Feminist Support Group for Women Prisoners in Guam

Iain K. B. Twaddle
Rita Setpaul
Venus E. Leon Guerrero
April I. Manibusan
Jo An Riddle

Iain K. B. Twaddle, PhD, is Associate Professor of Psychology at the University of Guam.

Rita Setpaul, MA, and Venus E. Leon Guerrero, MA, are doctoral candidates in clinical psychology at Alliant International University, San Diego.

April I. Manibusan, BA, and Jo An Riddle, BA, are graduates of the Psychology Program at the University of Guam.

Address correspondence to: Iain K. B. Twaddle, Division of Social and Behavioral Sciences, University of Guam, UOG Station, Mangilao, Guam, 96923 (E-mail: itwaddle@uog9.uog.edu).

The authors would like to thank Daniel Duenas, MSW, Forensic Administrator, Arlene Bownds, RSAT Counselor, and the other RSAT staff at Guam's Department of Corrections for their assistance throughout this research project. The authors also wish to thank the women who participated in this study and all of the women who participated in the RSAT Women's Group.

Previous versions of this paper were presented at the 8th European Congress of Psychology in Vienna, Austria, July 2003, and at the XXV International Congress of Applied Psychology in Singapore, July 2002.

[Haworth co-indexing entry note]: "Countering Correctional Discourse: Development of a Feminist Support Group for Women Prisoners in Guam." Twaddle, Iain K. B. et al. Co-published simultaneously in *Women & Therapy* (The Haworth Press, Inc.) Vol. 29, No. 3/4, 2006, pp. 215-237; and: *Inside and Out: Women, Prison, and Therapy* (ed: Elaine Leeder) The Haworth Press, Inc., 2006, pp. 215-237. Single or multiple copies of this article are available for a fee from The Haworth Document Delivery Service [1-800-HAWORTH, 9:00 a.m. - 5:00 p.m. (EST). E-mail address: docdelivery@haworthpress.com].

SUMMARY. This article discusses the development of a feminist support group for women prisoners enrolled in a six-month substance abuse treatment program in an adult correctional facility in Guam. After the completion of five Group cycles, a follow-up study was conducted in the community using qualitative, feminist, and participatory methods. Results indicate that the Group was successful in helping women prisoners to address trauma, addiction, and the stresses associated with incarceration. Nevertheless, participants reported having significant difficulty transitioning into the community upon release and 23% were sent back to prison for parole violations. Recommendations are outlined for gender-responsive programming, both within women's prisons and in the community, to support women offenders after release. doi:10.1300/J015v29n03_12 *[Article copies available for a fee from The Haworth Document Delivery Service: 1-800-HAWORTH. E-mail address: <docdelivery@haworthpress.com> Website: <http://www.HaworthPress.com> © 2006 by The Haworth Press, Inc. All rights reserved.]*

KEYWORDS. Women, prison, feminist, support group, gender-responsive programs, empowerment, qualitative research

U.S. PRISONS

The prison population in the United States has quadrupled since 1980, giving the U.S. the highest incarceration rate in the world, with over two million inmates currently in prison (2,019,234 at midyear 2002; Bureau of Justice Statistics, 2003a, 2003b). This dramatic rise in the number of Americans behind bars has resulted not so much from an increase in actual crime rates, but rather from the "war on drugs" and "get tough on crime" legislation of the past two decades, including mandatory sentencing and "three-strikes" laws as well as restrictions on the availability of parole (Chesney-Lind, 1991, 2003; Human Rights Watch, 2003; Morash & Schram, 2002). While the U.S. incarceration binge seems to be against the principles of freedom and democracy upon which American society is putatively grounded, the living conditions inside U.S. prisons equally violate American ideals, with pervasive human rights abuses consistently documented in recent years (Human Rights Watch, 2004). Critics of the escalating prisonization of American society have advocated for changes in criminal law, prison reform, and ultimately for decarceration and the abolition of prisons as the dominant response to crime (e.g., American Civil Liberties Union, 2004; Chesney-Lind, 1991; Critical Resistance, 2004; Davis, 2003; Prison Activist Resource Center, 2004). At the same time, prison activists have sought to provide more immediate assistance to those individuals currently serving prison sentences. But as Angela Davis (2003) explains, "a major challenge of this movement is to do the work that will create more humane, habitable environments for people in prison without bolstering the permanence of the prison system" (p. 103). The goal of this research was to meet this challenge by developing a feminist support group for women prisoners incarcerated in an adult correctional facility in the Pacific Island of Guam.

WOMEN IN U.S. PRISONS

In recent years, feminist scholars and prison reform activists have been concerned about gender disparities in incarceration rates, as the number of women in U.S. prisons has been growing at a significantly greater rate than the number of men (Phillips & Harm, 1998). For example, between 1984 and 2002, the population of female prisoners increased 355% compared to an increase of 186% for male prisoners. While women represented only 5.3% of prisoners in 1984, they now comprise 8.2% of the total prison population (Bureau of Justice Statistics, 1995, 2003a, 2003b).[1]

Incarcerated women are primarily ethnic minorities (67%), including African Americans (48%), Hispanics (15%), and other ethnicities (4%).[2] The majority of women in prison have extensive histories of psychosocial trauma including unemployment and poverty,[3] drug addiction,[4] and physical and sexual abuse.[5] Almost two-thirds of women in prison (65%) are mothers of children under 18, and the majority of these mothers are the primary caregivers. Most are non-violent offenders (72%) serving sentences for drug (34%), property (27%), and public-order offenses (11%) (Bureau of Justice Statistics, 1994, 1999).[6] From these statistics, we can see that prisons are increasingly being called upon to deal with women on the margins of society, those who are ethnic minorities, economically disadvantaged, and single mothers, with histories of physical and sexual abuse and drug addiction.

Pat Carlen (1988) suggests that women caught up in the criminal justice system have been marginalized by a combination of their class position, their gender, their race, and their refusal to submit to the exploitative social relations that accompany the ideology of "respectable working-class womanhood." Lori Girshick (1999) points to childhood trauma in the lives of women prisoners, highlighting their multiple traumatic experiences, including abuse, teen pregnancy, and school failure, as well as family instability due to factors such as poverty, alcoholism, and parental absence. According to Kathryn Watterson (1996), child abuse plays a central role in instigating many women's criminal careers:

> Abuse is what kicked off alcohol or drug addiction in many of these women; it's what made them run away from home and get into trouble with the law in the first place when they were juveniles . . . and it's what has kept them in trouble with the law as grown women who bear the label of criminal. (p. 36)

The high concurrence of trauma and drug abuse in the histories of women prisoners supports Watterson's contention, suggesting that their addictions may represent attempts to self-medicate (Belknap, 2003). Thus, women's drug use and criminality can be seen as forms of resistance to poverty, powerlessness, and victimization, as attempts "to survive within the constraints experienced by women, minorities, and lower classes" (Morash & Schram, 2002, p. 37). Through this lens, a rather disturbing, but very real picture emerges in which women of color, women in poverty, women with limited vocational opportunities, women who are single mothers, and women who have been traumatized as children, in sum, those who are most in need of social support, are the very same women that our society is sending to prison.

Inside prison, women prisoners are retraumatized through a series of carceral disciplinary tactics, including strict supervision and surveillance, arbitrary rule enforcement, monotony, lack of privacy, assaults on self-respect, and outright abuse (Pollock, 1998). In fact, women prisoners are subjected to a more stringent disciplinary regime than male prisoners, with write-ups, loss of privileges, and solitary confinement doled out for minor rule infractions that tend to be overlooked in men's prisons (Dobash, Dobash, & Gutteridge, 1986; McClellan, 1994). Of particular concern is the pervasive sexual victimization of women in U.S. prisons (Morash & Schram, 2002). Human Rights Watch (1998) has documented numerous incidents of rape and other forms of sexual assault, verbal degradation, and privacy violations by male prison guards against female prisoners. In addition, institutionally sanctioned sexual assault is imposed on all women prisoners through strip searches, including body cavity searches, which are routinely conducted in the name of security (Girshick, 1999; Heney & Kristiansen, 1998; Watterson, 1996). These tactics reveal the gendered nature of prison regimes and the indignity of patriarchal forms of social control. As Cindy Bruns and Teresa Lesko (1999) contend, "the prison system is a microcosm of the patriarchal power system that not only emulates but surpasses the insidious oppression that exists in patriarchy" (p. 72).

TREATMENT PROGRAMS FOR WOMEN PRISONERS IN THE U.S.

Despite the growing population of women prisoners, few specialized rehabilitation and treatment programs have been developed to meet their needs. This is partly because the emphasis placed on rehabilitation in the 1960s and 1970s has been replaced by an ethos of punishment and deterrence, leading to reductions in rehabilitative programming in both women's and men's prisons. However, the limited availability of women's programs is also due to the marginality of women within the prison system, their relatively smaller numbers compared to male prisoners, and the system's failure to meet the needs of the escalating female prison population (Morash & Schram, 2002; Pollock, 1998, 2002).

Regarding treatment services, women prisoners typically have limited access to mental health care, substance abuse treatment, and physical and sexual abuse recovery programs (Covington, 1998; Owen, 1999; Watterson, 1996). Those treatment programs that are available for women in prison are usually modeled after rehabilitation programs for male prisoners, which emphasize behavior control (Coll, Miller, Fields, & Mathews, 1998; Kelley, 2003). When applied to women, these programs often blame the victim by focusing on the correction of female prisoners' "dysfunctional criminal behaviors," while ignoring their difficult life experiences. According to Lori Girshick (2003), even when more progressive programs are available for women prisoners, "it is questionable whether the environment inherent in a prison setting lends itself to promoting personal growth and change" (p. 171).

On the other hand, Cindy Bruns and Teresa Lesko (1999) argue that feminist therapists have an obligation to work in patriarchal institutions such as prisons so as to "subvert the system from within" (p. 83). They warn that feminist therapists will face multiple dilemmas as they try to follow the ethical principles of feminist therapy, emphasizing "the equal worth of all people" and "a commitment to reducing the effects of oppression" (p. 71), within an institutional setting that actively promotes the oppression of women. Nevertheless, they suggest that it is "in the belly of the beast" that feminist therapy has its greatest potential to subvert patriarchy, and therefore, encourage feminist therapists to take up the challenge of subversive healing within penal institutions.

If prison support programs are to be effective in helping women prisoners to address their histories of trauma and addiction, to cope with the stresses of prison life, and to prepare for life in the community upon release, such programs will require creative strategies to ensure that they are aimed at empowering rather than oppressing women and to avoid being co-opted by the prison's disciplinary regime. Merry Morash and Pamela Schram (2002) recommend the development of gender-responsive programs that educate women prisoners to see their criminality within the context of their disadvantaged positions in society and help them to resist and overcome their victimization. They advise that these programs be exclusively for women as "mixed-gender settings tend to reproduce women's oppression and domination by men" (p. 168). In addition, follow-up care may be required to ensure that the prison's correctional structure does not undo the positive effects of empowerment strategies. In essence, when working within the punitive and oppressive environment of the prison, "moments of positive experience–or even humane treatment–must be found and negotiated by individual women and their advocates" (p. 196).

GUAM'S PRISONS

Guam is an unincorporated territory of the United States and the largest island in the western Pacific region known as Micronesia. The population of Guam is roughly 155,000 of which approximately 65,000 are Chamorro (the indigenous people of Guam), 12,000 are other Pacific Islanders, and 61,000 are Asian (U.S. Census Bureau, 2003). Guam has two adult correctional institutions run by the Government of Guam Department of Corrections (DOC), including the Guam Adult Correctional Facility, a minimum to maximum security prison, and the Hagatna Detention Facility, housing both federal and local detainees. As of May 2003, the inmate population in these two facilities was approximately 523 (Government of Guam, DOC, 2003). According to the International Centre for Prison Studies (2003), Guam has the 28th highest incarceration rate in the world (334 per 100,000).

Women in Guam's Prisons

As in the mainland U.S., Guam has recently seen a significant increase in the number of women in prison. In the last 17 years, the number of women prisoners has risen 273%, from approximately 11 in 1986 to 41 in 2003. Women prisoners, like their counterparts in the mainland U.S., make up approximately 8% of the total prison population. The majority of female prisoners in Guam are women of color (93%): 66% are Chamorro, 10% are other Pacific Islanders, and 17% are Asian. Approximately 61% of female prisoners in Guam are incarcerated for drug offenses, including both possession and distribution. In 1998, to deal with the increasing number of female prisoners, a separate women's facility was built adjacent to the main prison complex within Guam's Adult Correctional Facility. The new women's facility is a minimum to medium security unit staffed by female guards with capacity for 54 prisoners in 27 double-occupancy cells (A. Sablan, DOC Director, personal communication, March 13, 2001; Government of Guam, DOC, 2003).

Treatment Programs for Women Prisoners in Guam

Women prisoners in Guam are permitted to attend mental health treatment programs in the men's facility, including classes on substance abuse, anger management, and domestic violence. Nevertheless, this has not meant that women prisoners have reasonable access to appropriate mental health care. First, treatment programs designed for male prisoners are often inappropriate for female prisoners as they do not address women's unique needs and experiences. Second, female prisoners are placed in these mental health classes alongside male prisoners. Such co-ed programs are unsuitable for prison populations, as the women find themselves working through their histories of abuse in the company of men with extensive histories as perpetrators of abuse. Moreover, co-ed programs are particularly inappropriate in Pacific Island cultures, where it is often taboo to discuss sensitive topics in mixed-gender groups. Third, in order to attend mental health programs held in the main facility, women prisoners are sometimes strip-searched when leaving and again when returning to the women's facility. Fourth, female prisoners are denied access to mental health classes whenever there is a shortage of guards who are required to escort them to the main correctional facility. Finally, in 1999, when DOC developed a new Residential Substance Abuse Treatment Program for prisoners with drug dependencies, only male prisoners were admitted.

Development of a Support Group for Women Prisoners in Guam

To address these concerns, the first three authors developed a specialized support group exclusively for women prisoners. The Group was proposed as a component of the Residential Substance Abuse Treatment Program (RSAT), a federally funded program for the rehabilitation of prisoners with drug dependencies. Prisoners selected for the program are moved to the RSAT Unit, a minimum-security, 24-bed facility adjacent to the main prison complex providing a more comfortable living environment, with rooms instead of cells and greater freedom of movement. Over a six-month period, RSAT prisoners participate in a comprehensive mental health program addressing drug and alcohol dependency, relapse prevention, anger and stress management, psychosocial dynamics, and spirituality. After successful completion of the program, prisoners are granted early release into the community where they are required to attend a co-ed Parolee Aftercare Group one night per week for six months.

Once our proposal for the Women's Group was approved by the DOC administration, female prisoners became eligible for RSAT, and in July 2000, four women were admitted into the program. Women prisoners participated along with male prisoners in all aspects of the RSAT program, with the exception of the Women's Group, which met for one hour, twice a week in an RSAT classroom. The Group was facilitated by two female counselors (the second and third authors).

The Group model was based on a feminist theoretical orientation (see Enns, 1997; Greenspan, 1993; Hill, 1998) and thus differed from traditional prison rehabilitation models in several ways. First, participants were empowered to confront issues specific to gender that may not otherwise be discussed in co-ed settings, such as their histories of victimization and abuse. Second, we shifted the traditional power dynamics of the therapist-client relationship to a more egalitarian approach, reflecting caring cooperation rather than professional distance. This allowed Group members to take an active role in facilitating their personal growth and to participate in directing the Group's focus. Third, we employed a support group model to enable participants to work together with the other women in the Group as they learned to cope with their struggles. Fourth, we encouraged participants to express and explore their emotions including anger, regret, loneliness, fear, and frustration, to receive empathic feedback from the facilitators and Group members, and to work through their painful feelings within the Group. Fifth, we helped participants to explore the social roots of their problems and empowered them to develop new strategies for addressing their personal, socioeconomic, and political circumstances. Finally, we strived to make the Group sensitive to Pacific Island cultures by recognizing the unique roles of Pacific Island women and helping participants to develop life strategies consistent with these roles. In sum, the Group was aimed at providing a supportive environment for women prisoners to share and work through their experiences of victimization and empowering them to make positive changes in their lives.

As the pilot group proved to be effective, the Women's Group was established as a standard component of the RSAT program. For subsequent Group cycles, the sessions were increased to five times a week and RSAT counselors took over as the facilitators. After five cycles of the Women's Group were completed, we conducted a follow-up study in the community using qualitative, feminist, and participatory methods. The purpose of the study was to evaluate the effectiveness of the Women's Group in helping participants to address the traumatic experiences from their pasts, to cope with the stress of incarceration, and to prepare for life in the community after release.

RESEARCH METHODOLOGY

Women's Group Participants

A total of 24 women participated in the RSAT Women's Group (five six-month cycles; 4-6 women per cycle). Of the 24 participants, 20 (83%) were Chamorro, three (13%) were Caucasian, and one (4%) was Asian. Their ages ranged from 20 to 59, with an average age of 37. Sixteen (67%) were single, four (17%) were married, and four (17%) were separated or divorced. Twenty (83%) had children. Of the 24 women who entered RSAT, 22 successfully completed the program and were released into the community, while two were sent back to the main women's facility due to program violations. Of the 22 who were released, five returned to the prison due to parole violations (one per cycle), representing a recidivism rate of 23%.

Research Participants

Working through the RSAT Aftercare Program and the DOC Parole Office, we attempted to contact all of the women who had attended the Group. Once contacted, the women were asked to participate in an interview to evaluate the Group's effectiveness. Of the 22 women who graduated from RSAT, we were able to interview 13 (59%). Nine were interviewed in the community from 3 to 27 months after their release. Four (the members of the pilot group) were interviewed in the prison just prior to their release. One member of the pilot group was interviewed a second time when she returned to the Adult Correctional Facility as a recidivist. We were not able to interview the other nine for several reasons: one had been reincarcerated with no visitation privileges, one moved off-island, and the other seven could not be contacted. Of the 13 women interviewed, 11 (85%) were Chamorro, one (8%) was Asian, and one (8%) was Caucasian. Their ages ranged from 27 to 59, with an average age of 40. Eight (62%) were single, one (8%) was married, and four (31%) were separated or divorced. Ten (77%) had children. All had been unemployed at the time of their arrest. Six (46%) had been incarcerated for drug use or possession, four (31%) for drug distribution, and three (23%) for other offenses. All but one (92%) had a history of previous incarcerations. All had extensive histories of drug use starting from their teens or early twenties.

Interview Design

Semi-structured interviews were conducted by one of four female researchers (the second, third, fourth, and fifth authors) in sessions lasting 45 to 90 minutes. All interviews were tape-recorded and transcribed verbatim. The interviewers first obtained demographic information regarding personal history and criminal record. A series of open-ended questions followed, inviting participants to describe their experiences in the Women's Group, as well as to reflect on their life experiences prior to, during, and after incarceration. In the spirit of feminist and participatory research, the interviews were designed as interactive dialogues aimed at empowering participants to confront and overcome their marginalization. In the final segment of the interviews, participants were asked to share their thoughts on the needs of women recently released from prison and to help create practical solutions to meet those needs. Ultimately, the interviews were intended to reflect an emancipatory, advocacy-based approach to research (see Lather, 1991; Nielsen, 1990).

Qualitative Analysis

Data analysis procedures were based on the constant comparative method used in grounded theory (Charmaz, 1995; Lincoln & Guba, 1985; Strauss & Corbin, 1994). Initial coding was conducted by writing key words in the margins of the transcripts to describe each unit of information. These initial codes were compared within and across transcripts to create a more focused set of codes or themes. All transcripts were then re-coded based on these themes, adapting and revising the themes as each meaning unit was added. Finally, related themes were compared, synthesized, and refined to develop broad, yet distinct conceptual units of analysis or categories. The analysis yielded eight categories: (1) recovery from trauma, (2) recovery from drug addiction, (3) problems with co-ed groups, (4) sense of community, (5) separation from family, (6) interpersonal stress within the prison, (7) recommendations for improvement, and (8) transitioning into society. The presentation of the results includes a description of each category as well as illustrative quotations from the interviews in order to privilege the participants' voices.

RESULTS

Recovery from Trauma

The most salient category that emerged from the analysis was *recovery from trauma*. The main theme associated with this category was that the Women's Group provided a safe environment to talk about traumatic experiences from the past, such as repeated incidents of victimization and abuse. In particular, participants described sexual abuse from childhood and physical abuse from their adult relationships with men. For many of the participants, the Women's Group was one of the few times in their lives that they had been able to share these traumas with others:

> I thought the Women's Group was very useful because we addressed abuse issues from relationships that we wouldn't have felt comfortable addressing in the main co-ed group. There was sexual abuse issues that came up . . . very early childhood stuff and relationships with men that were causing trouble in our lives.

I thought it was very personal for the women to be together alone. We got to share our personal issues from our whole entire life . . . what traumatized us when we were young. We got to talk about our sexual experiences with men . . . what we went through and a lot of really deep, deep issues that we didn't even realize were holding us back. And that's what traumatized us and made us turn to drugs. A lot of women need this Group because there's a lot of women that went through molestation when they were young and a lot sold themselves for drugs. So it gave them a chance to let that all out. And as long as you hold that in you'll never break through your recovery.

The secrets of my life . . . I cannot tell anybody, not even my own family, my own children, my sister, my brother . . . nobody knows. It's just very personal and when I open up it's very difficult to talk about. In the Women's Group, it took me 3 or 4 weeks until I started talking about stuff. Emotions . . . they come out . . . just like the feelings of the past . . . my childhood . . . what my family used to do . . . you know . . . abuse. I'm very ashamed about it. My father made me marry with a man, and they tie me up and my new husband raped me. It's a bad thing in my life. The Women's Group is the first time I opened my thoughts . . . my secrets of my life.

Recovery from Drug Addiction

A related category pertained to participants' *recovery from drug addiction*. The main theme expressed was that the Women's Group helped members to discover the roots of their addictions. Participants said that as they shared their histories of victimization in the Group, they began to see that physical and sexual abuse were the underlying causes of their drug use. This insight motivated them to "stay clean" and to seek new ways of coping with the stresses in their lives. Group therapy was seen as a good alternative to drugs:

Instead of picking up drugs again, or bad habits, it's good to find a good form of group, like the Women's Group, so you don't have to fall back on those things.

Problems with Co-Ed Groups

The third category focused on *problems associated with co-ed groups*. In the interviews, participants discussed in detail the difficulties they encountered in the co-ed groups. The primary theme was that the men tended to be insensitive and judgmental, particularly when the women talked about their histories of abuse and victimization. This feedback demonstrates the cultural inappropriateness of certain topics in mixed-gender settings and clearly underscores the importance of having a group exclusively for women. In general, participants reported feeling more comfortable sharing personal issues in the Women's Group:

> There are many issues I won't speak about in the co-ed group because the men are very insensitive. I believe that part of my addiction had a lot to do with being abused by my other half, but when I talk about the abuse, the men become very judgmental. So I feel more confident speaking in the Women's Group without having to get judged from the men. The men think it's your fault, or I deserve it, and I felt that that's how the Group here helped me out.

> It was very difficult for me talking about women's issues when you're in a group with men. . . . You express something or you share your experience of what happened and they give you the look like it's your fault. Issues like incest, even issues about rape . . . I wasn't able to talk about that in the co-ed group . . . because when you leave the group you could feel the tension and you can see how the guys look at you.

> One girl in the co-ed group shared a very sensitive thing that happened in her life . . . and then the men outside after group would make small sarcastic remarks to tease her . . . they belittled or made fun of what she shared in class. That's why I'm glad that there were two groups, the Women's Group and the co-ed group.

Sense of Community

The fourth category reflected participants' appreciation for the *sense of community* that developed among the members of the Group. There were three closely related themes in this category: (1) the Group helped participants' to feel less isolated, (2) it gave them a sense of belonging, and (3) it provided a valuable source of social support. Overall, participants said that the acknowledgement and support they received from the other women in the Group played a vital role in their recovery:

> Being here in the Women's Group, I realized that I'm not the only one with a problem. Before in the past, I used to always think I've got it worse . . . you know, my past is worse than anyone else's. Coming here to this Group and hearing other people's problems, and knowing that they've been through what I've been through, makes me feel that I'm not alone in this . . . and for that reason we can support each other here.

> The Women's Group was very empowering . . . it created a camaraderie. The bonding that we had empowered me . . . so that when I got out and went back to that abusive relationship, it was always in the back of my head that I didn't have to do that any more. . . . I could make it on my own. And I didn't need to be in any relationship with any man to be a whole person.

Separation from Family

The fifth category addressed the *separation from family* that inevitably accompanies incarceration. In Pacific Island cultures, women's roles within the immediate and extended family are central to their identity. In the interviews, participants talked about the emotional pain they felt as a result of the separation, as well as the sense of shame associated with not fulfilling their roles as daughters, wives, and mothers. They said that the Group helped them to cope with the separation by providing a supportive environment to talk about their families. They also reported that the Group helped them to prepare to resume their roles in the family after release:

> The support from the Women's Group really helped each of us share our loss, like separation from our kids, families, and those things. After I started using drugs, my ex-mother-in-law had my kids, so I feel like I'm not a mother. When I was in prison for nine months, I kept telling myself enough is enough, I'm ready to be a mother. So here I am, I'm a mother.

Interpersonal Stress Within the Prison

The sixth category focused on *interpersonal stress within the prison*. Within the confines of penal institutions, where personal freedom is severely restricted, interpersonal interactions are deeply infused with tension. In the interviews, participants talked about feelings of frustration and humiliation arising from interpersonal conflicts with guards, staff, and fellow prisoners. At the same time, they stressed the importance of learning to negotiate these conflicts in order to "survive." Participants felt that the Group helped in this process by providing a safe place to vent about the interpersonal conflicts they encountered:

> I feel that when I can't deal with the people out there, I come into the Women's Group stressed. And after I'm done releasing it in here, it helped me to accept the people out there, because I already let it out and I'm not carrying that burden with me anymore.

Recommendations for Improvement

The seventh category incorporated a number of *recommendations for improvement.* A primary concern among the participants was that the Group facilitator role rotated among the RSAT staff. In a few sessions, male staff and even prison guards served as facilitators due to staffing shortages. Participants said that these inconsistencies made it difficult to develop trust. One reported fears that what she said in Group would be told to RSAT staff and guards leading to adverse consequences. Another complained that some facilitators were judgmental when Group members shared their personal experiences. A third felt that some facilitators could not relate to her because they had not experienced abuse or addiction. Nevertheless, all participants viewed the Women's Group as a vital component of the RSAT program. One recommended that the Group be expanded to include more women. Another suggested that a similar group be offered in the main women's facility:

> Well what they need in the main women's facility is a women's meeting like this, you know, cause some people come in traumatized and leave out traumatized, not fixing the problem. A lot of women that I know down there are going through some big, heavy stuff that needs to be let out . . . they need a group like this.

Transitioning into Society

The eighth category centered on *transitioning into society.* The main theme here was that participants encountered significant difficulties after their release from prison due to the lack of support programs for women parolees. The concern we heard repeatedly was, "I had nowhere to go." Participants recommended the development of community after-care programs, such as a women's transitional shelter:

> After I came out of prison, it was very hard for me. As a person I didn't have anything. I'm not from Guam. . . . I didn't have a family. . . . I didn't have no place to live. I was so nervous. . . . I didn't know where I was going to live . . . I was gonna be homeless! I lost everything. I had no home, no clothes to wear, no money, no car . . . no friends.

> I think we need to have a women's place . . . because for a lot of women that are coming out . . . their families have either abandoned them or had enough of them. And they don't have anywhere to go except back to another drug house or back to the streets . . . back to their same life. If women had a place, something like the Lighthouse Recovery Center [men's transitional shelter], then I think women would have a better chance to make it out there. There's no safe environment, they have no money, no food, no nothing. What else are they gonna do? They're either gonna go back to dealing drugs, back to prostitution, or just back to the same. A lot of women want to change their life. They're tired of that dead end life, but they have nowhere else to go.

> I was thinking about the relapse rate of the people that went through RSAT. The ones that relapse are people who basically went either back to their home or back to their relationship. But the men that came straight from RSAT to the Lighthouse, they're clean today. It's not fair that the men have a place to go and the women don't.

DISCUSSION

According to Cindy Bruns and Teresa Lesko (1999), "groups can be a particularly effective way of working with issues of power and oppression, providing a powerful antidote, through connection with others, for the shame engendered by . . . patriarchy and racism" (p. 80). The results of this study support this contention. Research interviews indicate that the RSAT Women's Group was highly successful in helping women prisoners to recover from past traumas, to address the underlying causes of drug addiction, to develop a sense of community within the Group, to cope with the separation from their families, and to manage interpersonal stress within the prison. Participants said that they particularly valued the opportunity to address their problems in a gender-segregated setting, and that the support they received from women in the Group played a significant role in their recovery. However, interview data also suggest that to ensure its effectiveness, the Group should have consistent facilitators throughout each six-month cycle, and sessions should not be led by untrained staff such as prison guards. Moreover, facilitators must maintain confidentiality in the Group and should encourage Group members to talk freely, being careful not to judge them. Finally, facilitators should either have personal experience in dealing with trauma, addictions, and recovery or should have training in addressing these issues.

Despite the success of the Women's Group, participants encountered significant problems after their release from prison. Most had difficulty finding new living arrangements, and thus, returned to the homes and communities they had lived in prior to their arrest. Unfortunately, this usually meant returning to environments that had fostered and supported their drug use and other criminal activities. The women interviewed suggested that a women's transitional shelter would provide a safe and structured environment to support them as they reintegrate into the community. However, no such program was available in Guam at the time of this study.[7] The lack of transitional programs for women parolees in Guam reflects similar needs across the United States (see Girshick, 1999; O'Brien, 2001).

CONCLUSION

The Need for Gender-Responsive Programs in Women's Prisons

There is currently a critical shortage of gender-responsive rehabilitation and treatment programs in women's prisons in Guam and throughout the United States. Those programs that are available for women prisoners often fall prey to a corrections logic which teaches that the source of "criminality" lies within the prisoners themselves–their attitudes, their beliefs, and their behaviors–rather than their difficult life experiences. To be effective, rehabilitation and treatment programs in women's prisons must be based on new models that challenge conventional notions of criminality and help women to break free of the discursive as well as institutional bonds that bind them. Feminist practitioners have led the way through programs emphasizing equality, caring, consciousness raising, and empowerment. The results of this study suggest that a women's support group based on these principles can be highly effective in helping women prisoners to address trauma, addiction, and the stresses associated with incarceration. We recommend that similar programs be developed to serve the growing population of women's prisons throughout the United States. In addition, we recommend that comprehensive gender-responsive programming be developed to assist women prisoners in their multiple spheres of need, including education, job training, life skills, drug and alcohol recovery, abuse recovery, and family visitation.

The Need for Community Aftercare Programs for Women Parolees

In this study, feedback from women parolees coupled with a recidivism rate of 23% indicates that therapeutic interventions provided inside prison are inadequate for addressing the socioeconomic barriers women face after release. This is consistent with other research evaluating the needs of women on parole who participated in prison drug treatment programs (e.g., Prendergast, Wellisch, & Wong, 1996). Such programs may be insufficient for a number of reasons. After release, women parolees may experience post-traumatic stress due to the trauma of incarceration (Gorski, 2001; Haney, 2002). Many are simply overwhelmed by the multiple demands of their new lives in the community (Watterson, 1996). Parolees are expected to rapidly find employment, housing, and transportation and to return to their roles within their families. Yet, their ex-convict status makes it difficult to find work that is sufficient to meet their basic needs and to obtain affordable housing in a safe environment free from drugs and violence. In addition, they may have to fight to regain the custody of their children. With these obstacles, many women parolees find themselves back in the same situations they left prior to their incarceration: the same abusive living environments, the same drug-ridden neighborhoods, the same poverty and marginality. It is not surprising that many women eventually return to drugs and other forms of law-breaking as a means to get by.

In order to effectively reduce recidivism rates for women parolees, therapeutic interventions provided in prison must be followed by comprehensive aftercare programs in the community addressing a wide range of psychological, social, and economic needs. Transitional housing programs such as halfway houses and residential treatment centers are needed to provide a safe, structured, and drug-free environment as parolees adapt to their new life situations (O'Brien, 2001). Such residential programs are particularly important for female parolees, many of whom might otherwise be forced to return to abusive living environments. Family-based residential programs that permit women to live with their children are also needed so as to give parolees the opportunity to resume their roles as mothers while re-establishing their lives in the community. In addition, aftercare programming should provide social services, such as financial aid and vocational training, as well as continued treatment services addressing addictions, mental health, and abuse recovery. We recommend that these transitional programs be gender-responsive with the dual aim of supporting and empowering women as they work towards reintegrating into society (see O'Brien, 2001).

The Need for Prison Reform and Alternative Community-Based Programs

As we work towards the development of gender-responsive programs for women prisoners and parolees, we should also recognize that the problems experienced by women offenders–from economic hardship, to abuse, to addiction–would be better addressed outside the prison, an institution poorly equipped to resolve the complex struggles of disadvantaged women in society (Owen, 1999). Many feminists argue that people should not be sent to prison for non-violent crimes (e.g., Watterson, 1996). Others have called for the abolition of prisons altogether (e.g., Davis, 2003; Howe, 1994).[8]

A national survey of community-based alternative sentencing programs for women offenders demonstrates that a "rational and compassionate justice system" for women is possible (Austin, Bloom, & Donahue, 1992, p. 33). Model programs reviewed in the survey include both residential services (e.g., residential treatment centers, therapeutic communities) as well as nonresidential interventions (e.g., home confinement, probation supervision, day treatment). According to the report, the most promising programs were those that used an empowerment model, those that coupled emotional support with practical skill development to prepare women for employment, and those employing an ethnically diverse staff, including a balance of professionals and recovering ex-offenders. We recommend that the availability of such programs be expanded to meet the needs of the growing numbers of women caught up in the criminal justice system. At the same time, we recommend a broader ideological shift towards a feminist vision of justice based on equality, compassion, and shared responsibility, replacing punishment, for both women and men, with opportunities for mediation, reconciliation, healing, and forgiveness (see O'Brien, 2001).

The Need for Social Change

If we are to truly help women within the criminal justice system, we must ultimately focus on changing the social conditions that lead to their marginality and subsequent criminal activity (Davis, 2003). Thus, we must look beyond the control of women within formal custodial institutions such as prisons, by focusing on women's oppression within the workplace, the home, the nuclear family, and throughout society (Howe, 1994). We must also interrogate social structures supporting all forms of inequality and social injustice, including poverty, racism, and sexism. Finally, we should educate the American public about the characteristics of U.S. prison populations, the indignity of prisoners' treatment, and the social forces that lead to imprisonment, so that they will be able to make informed judgments about the desirability of maintaining our current penal system (Carlen, 1988). Ultimately, we need to move away from ideologies that lay the focus of blame for social problems on "criminals" while ignoring the very real inequities that permeate our society.

NOTES

1. Based on estimated men's and women's populations of state and federal prisons and local jails.

2. Many social theorists argue that the disproportionate representation of ethnic minorities among incarcerated persons points to the inherent racism of the criminal justice system (e.g., Cole, 2000; Davis, 2003; Milovanovic & Russell, 2001; Ross, 1998).

3. Approximately 53% of women in state prisons were unemployed prior to their incarceration, compared to 32% of men (Bureau of Justice Statistics, 1994). Almost 30% of women in state prisons were receiving welfare assistance prior to their incarceration, compared to 8% of men (Bureau of Justice Statistics, 1999).

4. Approximately 50% of women in state prisons were daily drug users prior to their incarceration; 40% were under the influence of drugs when they committed their offense (Bureau of Justice Statistics, 1999).

5. Fifty-seven percent of women in state prisons reported that they had been physically or sexually abused at some time in their lives. Forty-six percent of women in state prisons reported physical abuse; 39% reported sexual abuse (Bureau of Justice Statistics, 1999).

6. Percentages are for women in state prisons.

7. Results of this study have recently been included in a grant proposal to fund a new transitional living shelter for women in Guam (The Oasis Empowerment Center, founded by Rob and Allison Zimmerman).

8. For further discussion of the prison abolitionist movement, see The Coalition for the Abolition of Prisons (2001) and the International Circle of Penal Abolitionists (2002).

REFERENCES

American Civil Liberties Union. (2004). *Prisons*. New York: Author. Available at http://www.aclu.org/Prisons/PrisonsMain.cfm

Austin, J., Bloom, B., & Donahue, T. (1992). *Female offenders in the community: An analysis of innovative strategies and programs*. San Francisco: National Council on Crime and Delinquency. Available at http://www.nicic.org/pubs/1992/010786.pdf

Belknap, J. (2003). Responding to the needs of women prisoners. In S. Sharp (Ed.), *The incarcerated women* (pp. 93-106). Upper Saddle River, NJ: Prentice Hall.

Bruns, C.M., & Lesko, T.M. (1999). In the belly of the beast: Morals, ethics, and feminist psychology with women in prison. *Women & Therapy, 22*(2), 69-85.

Bureau of Justice Statistics. (1994). *Women in prison*. Washington, DC: U.S. Department of Justice. Available at http://www.ojp.usdoj.gov/bjs/abstract/wopris.htm

Bureau of Justice Statistics. (1995). *Prisoners at midyear 1995*. Washington, DC: U.S. Department of Justice. Available at http://www.ojp.usdoj.gov/bjs/abstract/pam95.htm

Bureau of Justice Statistics. (1999). *Women offenders*. Washington, DC: U.S. Department of Justice. Available at http://www.ojp.usdoj.gov/bjs/abstract/wo.htm

Bureau of Justice Statistics. (2003a). *Correctional populations, 1980-2002*. Washington, DC: U.S. Department of Justice. Available at http://www.ojp.usdoj.gov/bjs/glance/tables/corr2tab.htm

Bureau of Justice Statistics. (2003b). *Prisoners and jail inmates at midyear 2002*. Washington, DC: U.S. Department of Justice. Available at http://www.ojp.usdoj.gov/bjs/abstract/pjim02.htm

Carlen, P. (1988). *Women, crime and poverty*. Milton Keynes, U.K.: Open University Press.

Charmaz, K. (1995). Grounded theory. In J.A. Smith, R. Harre, & L. Van Langenhove (Eds.), *Rethinking methods in psychology* (pp. 27-49). Thousand Oaks, CA: Sage.

Chesney-Lind, M. (1991). Patriarchy, prisons, and jails: A critical look at trends in women's incarceration. *The Prison Journal, 71*(1), 51-67.

Chesney-Lind, M. (2003). Reinventing women's corrections: Challenges for contemporary feminist criminologists and practitioners. In S. Sharp (Ed.), *The incarcerated women* (pp. 3-14). Upper Saddle River, NJ: Prentice Hall.

The Coalition for the Abolition of Prisons. (2001). Available at http://www.noprisons.org/

Cole, D. (2000). *No equal justice: Race and class in the American criminal justice system.* New York: New Press.

Coll, C.G., Miller, J.B., Fields, J.P., & Mathews, B. (1998). The experiences of women in prison: Implications for services and prevention. In J. Harden & M. Hill (Eds.), *Breaking the rules* (pp. 11-28). New York: The Harrington Park Press.

Covington, S.S. (1998). Women in prison: Approaches in the treatment of our most invisible population. In J. Harden & M. Hill (Eds.), *Breaking the rules* (pp. 141-155). New York: The Harrington Park Press.

Critical Resistance. (2004). Available at http://www.criticalresistance.org/

Davis, A.Y. (2003). *Are prisons obsolete?* New York: Seven Stories Press.

Dobash, R.P., Dobash, R.E., & Gutteridge, S. (1986). *The imprisonment of women.* New York: Basil Blackwell.

Enns, C.Z. (1997). *Feminist theories and feminist psychotherapies: Origins, themes, and variations.* New York: The Harrington Park Press.

Girshick, L.B. (1999). *No safe haven: Stories of women in prison.* Boston: Northeastern University Press.

Girshick, L.B. (2003). Leaving stronger: Programming for release. In S. Sharp (Ed.), *The incarcerated women* (pp. 169-183). Upper Saddle River, NJ: Prentice Hall.

Gorski, T.T. (2001, March 1). Post incarceration syndrome. *Addiction Exchange, 3*(4). Available at http://www.mid-attc.org/addex/addex3_4.htm

Government of Guam, Department of Corrections. (2003). *Corrections daily headcount verification report of May 30, 2003.* Mangilao, Guam: Author.

Greenspan, M. (1993). *A new approach to women & therapy* (2nd ed.). Blue Ridge Summit, PA: Tab Books.

Haney, C. (2002, January). *The psychological impact of incarceration: Implications for post-prison adjustment.* Paper presented at the U.S. Department of Health and Human Services National Policy Conference, Washington, DC. Available at http://aspe.hhs.gov/hsp/prison2home02/

Heney, J., & Kristiansen, C.M. (1998). An analysis of the impact of prison on women survivors of childhood sexual abuse. In J. Harden & M. Hill (Eds.), *Breaking the rules* (pp. 29-44). New York: The Harrington Park Press.

Hill, M. (Ed.). (1998). *Feminist therapy as a political act.* New York: The Harrington Park Press.

Howe, A. (1994). *Punish and critique: Towards a feminist analysis of penality.* London: Routledge.

Human Rights Watch. (1998). *Nowhere to hide: Retaliation against women in Michigan state prisons.* New York: Author. Available at http://www.hrw.org/reports98/women/

Human Rights Watch. (2003). *Incarcerated America.* New York: Author. Available at http://www.hrw.org/backgrounder/usa/incarceration/

Human Rights Watch. (2004). *U.S. prisons.* New York: Author. Available at http://www.hrw.org/prisons/united_states.html

International Centre for Prison Studies. (2003). *Prison brief for Guam (U.S.A.).* London: Author. Available at http://www.kcl.ac.uk/depsta/rel/icps/worldbrief/oceania_records.php?code=195

International Circle of Penal Abolitionists. (2002). Available at http://www. interlog. com/~ritten/icopa.html

Kelly, M.S. (2003). The state-of-the-art in substance abuse programs. In S. Sharp (Ed.), *The incarcerated women* (pp. 119-148). Upper Saddle River, NJ: Prentice Hall.

Lather, P. (1991). *Getting smart. Feminist research and pedagogy with/in the postmodern*. New York: Routledge.

Lincoln, Y.S., & Guba, E.G. (1985). *Naturalistic inquiry*. Beverly Hills, CA: Sage.

McClellan, D.S. (1994). Disparity in the discipline of male and female inmates in Texas prisons. *Women and Criminal Justice, 5*, 71-97.

Milovanovic, D., & Russell, K. (2001). *Petit apartheid in the U.S. criminal justice system: The dark figure of racism*. Durham, NC: Carolina Academic Press.

Morash, M., & Schram, P.J. (2002). *The prison experience: Special issues of women in prison*. Prospect Heights, IL: Waveland Press.

Nielsen, J.M. (1990). *Feminist research methods*. Boulder, CO: Westview Press.

O'Brien, P. (2001). *Making it in the "free world": Women in transition from prison*. Albany, NY: State University of New York Press.

Owen, B. (1999). Women and imprisonment in the United States: The gendered consequences of the U.S. imprisonment binge. In S. Cook & S. Davies (Eds.), *Harsh punishment: International experiences of women's imprisonment* (pp. 81-98). Boston: Northeastern University Press.

Phillips, S., & Harm, N.J. (1998). Women prisoners: A contextual framework. In J. Harden & M. Hill (Eds.), *Breaking the rules* (pp. 1-9). New York: The Harrington Park Press.

Pollock, J.M. (1998). *Counseling women in prison*. Thousand Oaks, CA: Sage.

Pollock, J.M. (2002). *Women, prison, and crime* (2nd ed.). Belmont, CA: Wadsworth.

Prendergast, M.L., Wellisch, J., & Wong, M.M. (1996). Residential treatment for women parolees following prison-based drug treatment: Treatment experiences, needs and services, outcomes. *Prison Journal, 76*(3), 253-274.

Prison Activist Resource Center. (2004). Available at http://prisonactivist.org/

Ross, L. (1998). *Inventing the savage: The social construction of Native American criminality*. Austin: University of Texas Press.

Strauss, A., & Corbin, J. (1994). Grounded theory methodology: An overview. In N.K. Denzin & Y.S. Lincoln (Eds.), *Handbook of qualitative research* (273-285). Thousand Oaks, CA: Sage.

U.S. Census Bureau. (2003). *2000 Census of population and housing: Guam*. Washington, DC: U.S. Department of Commerce. Available at http://www.census.gov/census2000/guam.html

Watterson, K. (1996). *Women in prison: Inside the concrete womb* (Revised ed.). Boston: Northeastern University Press.

doi:10.1300/J015v29n03_12

Recovering Selves:
Women and the Governance of Conduct
in a Residential Drug Treatment Program

Julie A. Beck

SUMMARY. This is an ethnographic study of a therapeutic-community drug treatment program comprised of mostly court-mandated clients. It explores how women interact with treatment practices and the language of recovery. I argue that deep and inherent contradictions exist between treatment practice and the needs of drug-using women. In particular I investigate the gender and race implications of drug treatment as a moral project aimed at self-reinvention. I also examine tensions between normalizing power and punishment in the therapeutic community. Treatment is analyzed in the therapeutic community as reflective of broader cultural and neoliberal values that privilege notions of family, community, and responsibility. I claim that the treatment ideal of the self-reliant, active citizen is profoundly problematic for women and mothers. doi:10.1300/J015v29n03_13 *[Article copies available for a fee from The Haworth Document Delivery Service: 1-800-HAWORTH.*

Julie A. Beck is a doctoral candidate in Sociology, University of California, Santa Cruz.

Address correspondence to: Julie Beck, Doctoral Candidate, Sociology Department, University of California, Santa Cruz, 1039 Kains Avenue, Albany, CA 94706 (E-mail: beckinovsky@sbcglobal.net).

[Haworth co-indexing entry note]: "Recovering Selves: Women and the Governance of Conduct in a Residential Drug Treatment Program." Beck, Julie A. Co-published simultaneously in *Women & Therapy* (The Haworth Press, Inc.) Vol. 29, No. 3/4, 2006, pp. 239-259; and: *Inside and Out: Women, Prison, and Therapy* (ed: Elaine Leeder) The Haworth Press, Inc., 2006, pp. 239-259. Single or multiple copies of this article are available for a fee from The Haworth Document Delivery Service [1-800-HAWORTH, 9:00 a.m. - 5:00 p.m. (EST). E-mail address: docdelivery@haworthpress.com].

KEYWORDS. Drug treatment, therapeutic community, gender, race, social control, punishment, neoliberalism

THE TREATMENT PROGRAM IN CONTEXT

I walked up the steps and through the heavy wooden doors of Your Place, a residential treatment facility. This impressive turn of the century building possesses an orderliness that coincides with the purposeful bustle of the multiracial residents and staff counselors, and watchful managers. On stairway landings and at the heads of the large meeting rooms are posted treatment program logos and hand-written recovery slogans: "Learn to Listen," "Who Am I?" "I Get What I Give," "Respect Yourself," "Today is a New Day," "Eternal Change Within." Up yet another flight of stairs is the enormous meeting room where morning and evening meetings are held as are the disciplinary "house meetings" and other important group gatherings in this self-named "family" of the therapeutic community.

This article explores how women interact with and are affected by treatment practices and recovery discourses in a therapeutic community drug treatment program. I investigate how treatment and the administering of "care" in the therapeutic community (commonly called a *TC*) become subsumed in highly regulatory technologies of discipline and reform. I also examine the gender and racial implications of therapeutic controls. In so doing, I seek to illustrate the deep discord between treatment aims and practices and drug-using women's lived experience.

Between the summer of 2000 and the spring of 2002 I conducted ethnographic field research in a nonprofit residential therapeutic community in California, which I am calling *Your Place*.[1] This program is based in the community, as opposed to in a jail or prison, and includes two main residential facilities which house nearly 200 residents, two-thirds of whom are court-referred (mostly probated or entering from California's jails and prisons). In recent decades, drug treatment programs have increasingly become linked with the correctional system, largely as a result of the drug war and California's subsequent jail and prison overcrowding crisis. The treatment program population is divided roughly evenly between African-American and white residents, with about 10% Latina, Asian, and Native American residents. Although Your Place is a co-ed program, I focus on women's experience, both because women's drug treatment is understudied, and because of the disproportionate effect of the war on drugs on women.

My analysis builds on the work of Foucault with the aim of contributing a gender and race perspective to how individual bodies are regulated and disciplined. I also analyze therapeutic controls as an aspect of modern government. Liberal government, according to Foucault, is a political order bent on "the governance of conduct," one that "attempts to construct a world of autonomous individuals and free subjects" (Dean, 1999, p. 65). I discuss the therapeutic community (fondly referred to as "the family" at the program) within today's punitive *neoliberal* environment in which the "private" sphere of the family and market is privileged.[2] Within this social context, I examine the therapeutic community as a reconstituted "family" backed by the threat of incarceration.

This exploration is a critical inquiry into the practices of all TCs and an examination of therapeutic controls more broadly. It is in no way meant as an attack on Your Place, for whose dedicated staff and residents I have great respect. The problem is not that the TC's personal-responsibility approach encourages accountability for one's actions, but that the mantra of personal responsibility masks and ignores social structural forces which play into women's lives and drug use (including institutional control in the TC). My core argument is that the treatment imperative of self-correction and self-reinvention poses gender and race-specific tensions and contradictions for women and mothers. Treatment practices also tend to reproduce patriarchal controls. Moreover, I claim that treatment ideologies seek to recover citizens by shaping drug users to fit a particular ideal of subjectivity; the recovered citizen is raced and gendered as white and male. This article is divided into two main sections: In the first, I analyze the practices and family-like infrastructure of the TC. In the second, I discuss the specific contradictory effects these have on women.

Surveillance and Punishment

Before looking inside the therapeutic community, it is important to understand the general context of residential treatment. The TC is tightly linked with the criminal justice system. Entering Your Place effectively entwines drug users in elaborate webs of surveillance backed by the state's punitive power. Through its contractual arrangements with the California Department of Corrections and with the county, the TC cooperates with the state and county parole and probation departments and the local sheriff's department over the referral of drug offenders to treatment. (Drug offenders are probated, paroled, or furloughed through early-release programs from jail or prison, to the residential treatment program.) The TC also returns to court or to custody those who fail to complete the program. Jessie Bailey, the Your Place intake director, a white woman and herself a former drug user, shakes my hand with a warm, yet matter-of-fact manner, explaining,

> [The county] came to us with this plan . . . and we all kind of worked it out, I think, together. I mean, we provided a solution to their overcrowding problem and it just really worked hand in hand–and a contract came out of it. They pay good money for immediate placement. . . . Now a client will go before the country parole board, which makes the decision, and then they refer to the [treatment] program. . . .

Being court-mandated to treatment at Your Place to some degree alleviates the force of the law upon drug users, who might otherwise remain in (or be sentenced on drug charges to) jail or prison. But it allows them no escape from social control. For, state power is filtered through therapeutic practices, intensifying discipline and surveillance.

I am claiming that the TC normalizes rather than punishes per se. Its highly structured treatment regimen of behavior modification and largely peer-based surveillance is backed by the constant threat of state punishment. In this sense, the TC dually controls women. The door is unlocked, but walking out of it for more than a sanctioned outing will lead one back to court or custody. Bailey explains, "We call probation [or] parole right away telling them which way [the client] went and what they were wearing, I mean that's the kind of relationship we have with [corrections]." Some have claimed that community-based sanctions such as Your Place create a "net widening effect" in that more types of offenders are intensely supervised outside the prison walls (Holman & Brown, 2004, p. 198). But unlike the prison, the TC employs a complex array of "therapeutic tools" that include peer pressure and sanctions for rule-breaking. Moreover, inside its walls, the therapeutic community reconstitutes notions of family, self, community, and work in order to re-socialize drug users.

THE "PRIVATE SOCIETY"
OF THE THERAPEUTIC COMMUNITY

Drug Treatment at Your Place entails an intensively disciplinary agenda of behavior modification and near total surveillance of clients. The drug user is not merely reformed but taught to be *self-reforming* through peer pressure and treatment practices aimed at promoting moral self-correction. By the 1990s, the burden of rehabilitation had shifted from society to the individual such that the offender "had to be responsibilized and rendered a rational actor" (Kruttschnitt & Gartner, 2005, p. 78). Pat O'Malley claims that "criminological practice today . . . isolates individual offenders from their social contexts . . . and renders them individually responsible for the risks and harms they create for others (O'Malley, 2004, p.187). Tracy, a white resident who is advanced in the program, illustrates the concept of "responsibilization." Reflecting on her progress at Your Place, she explained,

> I knew it was going to be hard work from the get-go, so I said, "okay": I had to strap up my boots. I knew it was going to be tough, but I was ready for it, I was ready to fight for my life. And that's what I had to do. . . . I put my trust in [the program] and whatever they asked of me I did. . . . [I had to] humble myself and realize I was broken. And as soon as I was able to do that, and fight to retain that humility, and realize that that was the foundation of how I was able to change and be teachable–I had to stay open-minded so I could be taught.

What do humility and "teachability" reveal about how social control and subjectivity operate for drug-using women in the TC? To begin with, rehabilitation at Your Place occurs within a highly structured environment ironically that maintains a familial, quasi-voluntary atmosphere in which clients are expected to be self-motivated to change.

Notions of Family

The TC employs metaphors of home to describe itself. One of the most ingratiating practices at Your Place is its ritual of welcoming incoming residents called "the Your Place welcome." When a new member of Your Place is admitted, upon being introduced at Evening Meeting by an assigned "big brother" or "big sister," the entire "family" gives a loud, hearty greeting, exuberantly chanting at the top of their voices: "*Welcome Home!*" This is followed by deafening foot stomping, cheers, and clapping. The program calls the whole of its members–residents, staff members, managers, directors, and program "alum"–"the family," and residents are asked to refer to each other as their "brothers and sisters." Additionally, the physical structure of the institution is referred to as "the house," and treatment takes place within the imagined community of the "therapeutic community." Through its physical layout with its homey kitchen and living-room/group-meeting room lined with couches and pillows, and using metaphors of home that infuse treatment discourses and terminologies, the TC offers a "safe space," as one program manager put it, to focus on personal change. This private society resonates as well with core neoliberal values, which Lisa Duggan (2003) identifies as privatization and responsibility.

"The Creed," the program's motto, mounted on the wall of the main meeting room, serves as another unifying mechanism. Chanted in unison after certain group sessions, the Creed bears messages of inner growth, self-knowledge, hard work, personal change, and spirituality to guide individuals on the path of recovery; it is the moral backbone of Your Place. Other treatment slogans such as "own your own," "get off your pity-pot!" and "eternal change within" admonish residents in self-reflection and accountability, and explicitly frame recovery as the self-controlled, active citizen who responsibly seeks self-improvement.

But being a good citizen in the TC family, "strapping up [one's] boots" as Tracy put it, who explained that in "fighting for her life" in the treatment program she had to "be a soldier" (or pulling oneself up by the bootstraps, I will add), is not necessarily a useful or productive goal for women in the program. This becomes especially apparent for women of color. Women often agree to enter residential treatment in order to get control of their drug use as well as to avoid incarceration, to regain child custody, and because they have no other way of procuring needed social services. For example, Anita, an African American resident who is on parole, asked her parole officer to place her in the TC in hopes that graduating from a well-respected treatment program would improve her chances of procuring legal, paid work; she specifically felt it would counter the stigma she carries as a female drug felon. Like most of the women at Your Place, Anita is a mother with children in foster care: she did not complete high school, has no marketable skills, has been in and out of jail and prison for drug possession, petty drug sales, and prostitution, and has been through prior drug treatment programs. In a quiet voice she explained that her history of being a "repeat offender" has made it very difficult for her to get employment once released from prison,

> What brought me here was I needed work, I have felonies, and you cannot get jobs coming up out of prison. They want to know, you know, what were you doing all this time? And you put "in prison" [on the job application] and they want to know–and especially for women, you're looked at like, "*you* were in *prison?*" And so, it makes it hard. And plus, with my history of repeat offender and felonies, you just don't get jobs that easily. . . . But one of my main issues is, once I leave here, will I be able to get work to support myself and my daughter?

Women with criminal records suffer intensive social stigma essentially for failing to live up to societal ideals of femininity and motherhood, and African American women like Anita are disproportionately represented in the criminal justice system. The spousal abuse and the employment discrimination Anita experienced as a female ex-felon, she says, ". . . took me back out to soliciting: I prostituted or sold drugs to pay off my bills." Beth Richie's (1996) notion of gender entrapment describes Anita's oppressive situation, in which she prostituted and used or sold drugs to escape dependency on a violent male partner, but whose criminalization for drug-related activity then further trapped and stigmatized her.

Anita's story also reveals the irony of becoming responsibilized in the treatment program. At Your Place, she worked hard on improving herself. She learned about reliability, interpersonal communication, and modifying her behavior. She was even promoted to Leaders, a select group of residents with special decision-making privileges, and put in charge of acting as peer role models for the "house." But learning to take responsibility in the TC does not protect against the social structural barriers such as gender violence, stigma, and job discrimination that effectively prevent women and women of color from acting as rationally-choosing free agents in society.

Mitchel Dean points out that under liberal forms of government, certain social groups historically have been deemed lacking in the attributes required to exercise rights, attributes such as autonomy and responsibility. Ironically, these groups and individuals are therefore subjected to "systems of domination," to "all sorts of disciplinary, bio-political and even sovereign interventions" intended to render them responsible enough to exercise freedom (Dean, 1999, p. 134). In the therapeutic community, women are subjected to intensive discipline and surveillance; they are taught to "work on themselves," to conform to particular constructions of self as recovering addicts. These therapeutic controls add to the layers of social and institutional domination that low-income drug-using women, and especially women of color, already experience. For example, notions of work in the TC help to reform and shape drug users into particular kinds of citizens.

Notions of Work: Self-Work

Every resident holds a job in the "house." Residents' unpaid labor doing chores such as cleaning, cooking, unloading food, laundry duty, and other daily jobs constitutes the core and sole labor force running the treatment institution. However, work has a dual meaning in the TC; more than physical labor, it primarily involves the *psychological "work"* involved in the production and reinvention of self. The treatment program employs metaphors of building and construction such as "therapeutic tools," or simply "tools," to describe this psychological labor which I am calling *self-work*. The imperative of working on oneself is the heart of treatment in the TC. "Doing the work," or "working your program" to use treatment lingo, connotes "building" in the sense of building moral character. For example, relapse prevention classes teach residents self-awareness and how to stop "the addictive cycle" by curbing their temptation to use drugs and identifying their "triggers." Similarly, Gloria, an African American program "graduate," models to the family how she learned to control her anger and follow directions,

> Life doesn't always go my way, I had to learn to live with that, or else I'll use crack again. . . . I came into [the program] with rage–acting out, not knowing how to ask for help. I was blessed in this program because I *didn't* get my way. . . . I learned to do what they asked of me even if I didn't understand at the time.

Achieving recovery in the TC means becoming a "clean," responsible, self-controlled agent and citizen. According to Foucault, government concerns not just formal politics, but "practices of the self" (Dean, 1999, p. 12). But what kinds of selves and social subjectivities is treatment practice based on?

Notions of Self: Racial Overtones of "Getting Clean" in the TC "Family"

The ideal of the recovered addict, the self-controlled citizen of the TC, is constructed in direct opposition to the indulgent addict. This is an implicitly racial construction that accords with the autonomous, "civilized" white, male subject of liberal individualism. For instance, treatment slogans found at Your Place such as "Treatment Saves Lives: The Streets Kill!" imply distinctions between the racialized urban space of the street and the safe, "clean" therapeutic family. Darin Weinberg claims that street life is degraded in the TC through "accounts of collective descent from an idealized past to a current state of general desolation 'out there'" (Weinberg, 2000, p. 612). Metaphors of dirt and cleanliness also imply the active citizen, such that "cleanliness flows from deliberate effort, dirtiness mere dissolution" (p. 613).

Moreover, in the TC, addiction is often framed (despite references to the disease model) as a dangerous self-indulgence, and recovery, as self-control. In a relapse prevention class at the TC, such distinctions are emphasized by drawing on images from popular culture that capitalize on America's long history of representing drugs and drug users as racialized threats to the social order. The following scene offers an example:

> In the multi-purpose room of Your Place, about forty residents are lounging on couches and chairs in front of a video screen. They are gathered to watch the 1931 film, *Dracula,* as part of a Relapse Prevention class at the TC. The invited guest speaker facilitating the session is a white woman who holds a Master's Degree in addiction studies, who explained that the film *Dracula* is a "symbolic portrayal of addiction." During the discussion that followed the screening, she described the protagonist, Renfield, as a weak character whose curiosity allowed him to be lured by Dracula. She explained that Renfield "consciously chose to ignore the warning signs" of addiction.

In this workshop, addiction is symbolized through a monster metaphor. Like addiction, Dracula is an insatiable, seductive, deadly force, foreign and darkly corrupting. Residents in turn internalize these notions of addiction through self-descriptions as monstrous or selfish. An African American resident in the workshop discussed her "triggers" saying, "I know I'm in trouble when the dragon inside wakes up!" Later, another female resident explained, "Addicts are selfish—we're self-possessed, that's our disease. We don't care about anyone else– even our families," and assured me that the "cure" for this "disease" is to "give back" to the community. Program staff also sometimes portray drug users as fiendish. For example, Darren, an African American program manager, opened an emergency "family meeting" by deploying a common reprimand reserved for disciplining the "house" when it gets out of control: "Tell me, is there anyone in this room who is *not* a dope fiend and a criminal?!" he angrily demanded of the residents. (The expression "dope fiends and criminals" is used interchangeably with playful sarcasm by Your Place staff, most of whom are themselves former drug users.) Like Dracula, "dope" and crime, with their implications of racial impurity, have been read more broadly as metaphors for the moral decline of Western culture.[3]

On the other hand, recovery masquerades as the antidote to dangerous addiction at Your Place. It seems that the recovered subject is one who successfully excises the addicted self, which some have referred to as the racialized Other within (Friedling, 2000). Ann Stoler (1995) understands the moral citizen subject of western democracies in general to be racially-derived. She argues that Foucault's nineteenth-century bourgeois subject was not only a biopolitical product of extracted sexual/moral discourse, but was formed in opposition to the racialized, "primitive" Other of European imperialism. I am suggesting that the TC's mission to re-form drug users and recover citizens, to produce self-governing "clean" individuals, is an implicitly racial project. "Getting clean" also resonates with neoliberal values, which are themselves ensconced in whiteness and middle-class norms.[4]

One way that identities and selves are recovered or achieved in the TC is through exercising personal volition in advocating for oneself, even in the face of state authority. Self-advocacy is in turn promoted as an avenue of empowerment. For example, Dwain, one of the facilitators of the Parenting Class, a reserved, middle-aged African American man, lectured to a class full of women about taking a personal-approach strategy with the Child Protective Services department (CPS), under the authority of which many of their children are being held. Seeking to help the female residents cope with state authority in their lives, he stressed the importance of their relationship with their CPS worker, admonishing, "We're used to seeing CPS as bad," impressing upon the women that this is the wrong attitude and urging, "Get on the phone and get CPS to work for you. . . . When we're on parole, we think that our agent [social worker] is our enemy, but CPS is not your enemy today but your best friend!" Dwain explained to me after the class that he encourages the women "to 'prove by your behavior that you can handle unsupervised visits,'" and to "work" with CPS. Here, private solutions to structural issues, such as establishing personable relationships and "friendship" with state authorities are the program's answer to patriarchal state controls. It is questionable, however, whether this strategy will in fact procure more favorable visitation terms between mothers in treatment and their children. In addition, Dwain's emphasis on redeeming one's self as a mother with CPS through demonstrating good behavior can tend to further entrench women in guilt and shame. Women and mothers in the program report feeling deep guilt over their past drug use, and are extremely sensitive to comments that challenge their status as mothers; they have strongly internalized society's estimation of them as failed women and bad mothers.

In addition to self-advocacy, recovery also requires demonstrating self-reliance. Incoming program residents are made to take responsibility by clearing up their outstanding arrest warrants. Potential clients must sign a "guilty letter" which is sent to the court, and in many cases then take a bus (paying the fare, if possible) to the county or counties where the warrants were issued and appear in court. (Often, a person can avoid re-arrest by working off the offense while remaining in treatment.) Bailey explains this moral test in terms of empowerment,

> So there's all these little things–and it is *empowering* them, basically. We really believe that. We don't want to take care of them, we don't want to take care of their legal stuff; we want to help them resolve their *own* legal stuff. They got themselves into this; they got to get themselves out of it!

The notion that rather than the TC taking care of people with substance abuse problems they should take of themselves is one that resonates with anti-welfare discourses (social help makes the poor lazy, or in treatment terminology, might "enable" bad behavior). Thus, I have described some of the ways that those deemed unworthy of rights and freedoms, drug addicts, must be rendered personally accountable and self-reliant in order to enjoy individual freedoms and liberties.

These cultural discourses and practices of responsibility and choice that resurface in the TC, however, and the treatment imperative of moral self-determination, are replete with contradictions for women and especially women of color in the program. They also reproduce patriarchal social controls.

CONTRADICTIONS OF SELF HELP

I examine below how several areas of treatment–self-focus, surrender, and choice–create specific contradictions and potential roadblocks for women in recovering subjectivity.

Self-Focus: "I Was Like a Zombie, or One of Those Cult People. . . ."

Coupled with institutional social control, drug-using women have been subjected to "domestic" controls and violence. In making its primary mission the promotion of personal responsibility and accountability for one's actions, the TC overlooks social structural factors that play directly into women's drug use. Women face gender and race-specific barriers to achieving the treatment program's ideal of self-sufficiency. And efforts to make them responsible eclipse deeper structural inequalities and issues such as sexual and physical violence, lack of education, job skills, and affordable childcare, intensive social stigma, and a diminished sense of self and self-worth.

The TC demands self-reinvention through intensive focus on oneself and one's behavior, "being selfish in a good way," to reiterate a program saying. Yet, as women's group sessions in the program illuminate, many women have either been socialized against having strong boundaries of self growing up, having been expected to be caretakers of men, parents, siblings, children, and have a diminished sense of self and self-worth from experiencing sexual and gender violence. Domestic violence and sexual abuse characterize the experience of more than 80% of the women at Your Place; this figure is also reflected in statistics on female prisoners and drug users.

Laura is a white middle-class resident whose experience of gender socialization and low self-esteem highlights the difficulty of being "selfish" in recovery, of putting oneself and self-interest first. She explains,

> I mean, I wasn't okay unless I could help someone else, I mean, I found broken boy friends all the time because I knew I could fix them and they would love me if I fixed them. . . . *So it's a big thing trying to be selfish.* But in actuality, it really isn't selfish at all, it's self-*less*. It's um you know–I don't really have an identity right now. I have a structured rule–following, uh, I'm a number, I'm a person who goes to work and I'm in a classification. I don't really feel like I'm doing what I am doing as much for myself as I am

demonstrating that I can do what needs to be done. (Emphasis
added)

Laura's feeling of being controlled and self-effaced in the program,
of being robbed of a sense of self through its strict rules and sanctions
(the "structured rule-following" as she put it) also reveals how the TC
can reproduce the effacement women experience in the patriarchal family or in prison.

Similarly, Diona, an African American Your Place resident from a
middle-class family, discusses how an abusive relationship with a male
partner diminished her sense of self,

> You don't have *anything–nothing*. Your soul, your mind, your
> thoughts–everything belongs to this person. I couldn't smoke
> without him–everything was done together, we were together 24
> hours a day 7 days a week. . . . I realized that my mind was being
> controlled by every thought. I had no friends, I wasn't encouraged
> to be around my family unless he knew it was going to beneficial
> to him and us. . . . With a person who controls . . . your every move-
> ment and your thoughts . . . the harder it is for other people to keep
> positive things in your psyche or your being. I was like a zombie,
> or one of those cult people. . . .

Diona's experience points to the contradiction between treatment's
emphasis on self-improvement and the reality of domestic violence,
which violently denies her a sense of self and agency. The diminished
sense of self with which both Diona and Laura entered the program as
survivors of sexual and gender violence, coupled with the program's ri-
gidity, makes self-building especially challenging.

Surrender: "I Surrendered . . . and I Was an Emotional Wreck. . . ."

The myriad of controls in the TC can replicate patriarchal controls in
specific ways. For example, the problem of female selflessness is reinforced by the requisite "surrender" in treatment discourse and practice.
Your Place uses the same self-help mantra of surrender found in 12-step
programs. Surrender demands "letting go" of what one "cannot change"
and focusing only on what one "can change"–*oneself.* But surrendering
is replete with tensions and contradictions for women, especially if they
are mothers. Sarita, a young, biracial white and Latina woman, is a
leader and a role model in the TC. Her enthusiastic, proactive attitude

and ability to articulate the program's principles, which she has deeply internalized, earned her respect as a "success story" in the program. She explained to me,

> I surrendered . . . and I accepted that I messed up and that there's lot of change that needed to be made in my thinking and what I need to do with my life. And I trusted, I began to trust [in the treatment process] and feel safe, that even though the baby's in CPS [Child Protective Services] and has a foster mother, he's safe. So I was able to focus on myself . . . what changed me was I felt like if I kept focusing on [the baby] and trying to fix things–because every time I tried to fix things they never work, and every time I ran my life, I ran into walls–it was either prison, or jail, or the baby in CPS. So I had to surrender and have my Higher Power jump into my life.

But, as Sarita's narrative reveals, "surrender" takes on new meaning for women in treatment who are mothers; surrendering control to a Higher Power becomes conflated with surrendering custody and control of their children to the state. That is, in order to intensely focus on herself and achieve self-transformation, Sarita had to first trust that her baby was safe in the state's hands. But asking women to "surrender" the connection with their children to "get recovery" is deeply traumatic for both mothers and children. Tears welling up, Sarita described how her baby reached for her as his foster mother carried him away from a visitation session,

> So umm, it was hard for me–you know–to see him here for a couple hours on a Saturday, and he would leave with the CPS driver, and . . . you know? I was an emotional wreck, you know? But I had to get it together. He was safe and it was time for me to focus on myself. And all I could see was that "it wasn't in my time it was in God's time." So I began working on myself and being okay with the situation. Because you have to be okay with the situation in order to move on.

Exclusively focusing and working on themselves, however, contradicts the reality of most low-income women's lives as mothers, who are often the sole financial and emotional supporters of children. Recovery is framed at Your Place as a kind of heroic, individualistic journey in direct conflict with the norms of good motherhood. Consequently, these women experience deep internal conflict over these irreconcilable values. Even middle-class white women have anxiety over how they can conform to the "professional," male, white standards and those of the self-less, caring, emotionally available "mother."

In this sense, recovery requires a masculine and racial ideal and prototype of the "clean" citizen who has mastered control over his drug use, one that emulates neoliberalism's self-interested, self-controlled individual. The quasi-religious discourse of "surrendering to a Higher Power" also eclipses state authority (Child Protective Services) in drug-using women's lives, and may even help them rationalize the loss of their children. These constructs of treatment and recovery further entrench women in systems of state control, ironically, through the very treatment processes that are intended to offer them control over their lives. Essentially, the model of subjectivity women are being socialized to conform to contradicts the interdependency inherent in childrearing. In this sense, the quasi-statal TC family ironically robs women of their own children and families. African American and Latina women report feeling particularly powerless to protect their children while they are in the program, especially if they feel those children are at risk for exposure to violence and drug activity. Treatment rhetorics of choice further create deep, often irreconcilable, tensions for women.

THE TROPE OF CHOICE

Today I will be aware of the consequences of my actions: The easier wrong or the harder right?

(A Your Place daily motto)

Beneath these daily words posted on a long sheet of butcher paper in the TC's main entryway are inscribed the signatures of approximately 50 program residents. Ironically, after removing drug users from their communities, families, neighborhoods, or prison to rehabilitate them, the TC actively promotes the concept of "choice." This rhetoric of choice surfaces, for example, in the familiar sermons delivered to the family at the reprimanding "family meeting" where program staff remind the residents that they made a *choice* to do drugs and to engage in the behaviors they did out "on the streets," and therefore that they can also choose to change. But discourses of responsibilization assume a rational and free actor (Kruttschnitt & Gartner, 2005), one who enjoys the liberty of choice and moreover, who accepts responsibility for the choices she has made in her life.

The assumption of a freely choosing agent can be deeply problematic for drug-using women, who internalize notions of choice in ways that suggest they are responsible for their social conditions. I visited Tracy one evening at her apartment for "outpatient" residents who have succeeded in the program. A white, middle-aged woman without children, Tracy had spent many years in prison for addiction-related crimes and sold her body when she was using drugs. She describes her work as a prostitute in terms of free choice, saying,

> First of all, I made a *choice* to prostitute because I wanted to do drugs, so this was just one avenue I *chose,* as well as my crimes and drug dealing, and other crimes–paper crimes. . . . I wasn't victimized as a prostitute–I chose to prostitute, because it gave me independence, it gave me quite a lot of money, and it gave me–I didn't have to depend on *anybody,* and I had control. And I had validation–sexual validation. And I don't feel any prostitute's a victim, I just don't, I'm sorry, I don't. You know, it's the *choices* they made, or I should say the choice *I* made.

If selling her body allowed Tracy a degree of autonomy and financial independence, the level of choice involved merits further examination. Tracy claims she chose both prostitution and criminality because she "wanted to do drugs," yet the links between female drug use, violent male partners, and prostitution are well documented. Discourses of choice obscure larger social structural issues such as poverty, lack of social services, and feelings of low self-worth that contribute to women's "choice" to prostitute and use drugs.

Similarly, Sarita, who like Tracy, is advanced in the program, internalizes the rhetoric of choice and personal responsibility. She described her frequent run-ins with the penal system and her record of petty theft using the program's framing of drug-related behavior, in terms of "allowing" state authority into her life.

> I've allowed so much authority in my life: I'm sick of it, but I've *allowed* it, I kept breaking the law for authority to be in my life–shame on you! So, now I need to change. . . . I will be held accountable for any mistakes I make in my life today, and I will have dignity and integrity.

These narratives reveal how women at Your Place strongly internalize rhetorics of responsibility, claiming accountability even for their criminalization.

Staff members also use the rhetoric of choice. In a class lecture about responsibility, Dwain, the parenting class leader and himself a former drug user, reminds the women, "CPS [Child Protective Services] didn't take your kids–You *gave* your kids to them–you–we–did everything we could to say, 'Come and get them'!" In trying to instill responsibility and redirect the women's anger at the system for placing their children in foster care, he overlooks the ways the state punishes those it deems "unfit" women and mothers, or the intense gendered stigma that drug-using women experience. Losing their children, in this narrative of responsibility and choice, is the logical consequence of the irresponsible "choice" they made to use drugs. Focus on choice implies blame, which compounds the deep shame these women already feel as failed women and mothers in society's eyes.

I have argued that women in the TC experience profound contradictions between the imperative of personal responsibility and the structural forces for which they are *not* responsible. Moreover, recovery is modeled after a liberal individualistic ideal of subjectivity, the white male who possesses resources, the privilege of autonomy, and the necessary freedom and resources for self-determination. One must ask whether attempts at the responsibilization of dominated and controlled populations in fact empower and engender freedom. The following story begs this question.

"Where's the Justice?!"

Sarita's situation starkly illustrates the contradictions and ironies of therapeutic practices as they clash with women's lived experience. Weeks away from graduating the program, Sarita, (who earlier spoke of surrender), though she has been told she will regain custody of her baby upon leaving the treatment program, faces a tough legal battle to get her twin daughters back from her ex-husband, who battered her during their marriage. She is currently holding the twins' father in contempt of court for violating the visitation order. However, as she had just found out, the court mediator, in his letter to the court, omitted the father's history of domestic violence, other charges, and his contempt of court. Instead, he focused on Sarita's drug-use and arrest history prior to treatment. Sarita was furious at the news. Despite her status as a "success story" in the TC, she argued in self-defense, telling me,

Today I run my life. You know, and [yet] I feel so *powerless*. And I have to get a lot of support [from program peers], because it's *such* as disappointment, it's like, where's the justice? You know, yeah, I messed up, and yeah, I do have a record, and yeah, I'm a parolee, and yeah, my baby is in CPS, and yeah, all my kids have a different father–*and,* you know, the bottom line is that *he's* not following through, and I have a court order.

Sarita has gained control of her drug habit, become a model TC citizen, and even "broke the cycle" of the domestic violence she had been "allowing," and has also landed a job as a city clerk with the help of Your Place. Yet she demanded angrily,

So, where's the justice in all this? When I am going to be seen as a productive individual of society, who's changed their life around, and who wants to be unified with her son, and is doing healthy things today. You know? When does that come in? You know, I don't know when that's going to come in–I'm powerless, I pray on it, you know . . . and I'm just fighting, I'm struggling, everyday is a struggle for me.

Sarita's narrative ironically invokes the self-help ideal of trust in a higher power simultaneously with the fact of being *robbed* of power. She sees that despite her success in the program, she is still powerless to rebuild her family. Her disillusionment with the TC and drug treatment is apparent: she told me, "Yesterday I called [the residential director] and said, 'I don't want to even be here anymore, I did what you people told me to do–I did it, and I'm still fucked, basically,' excuse my language." If Sarita is a recovery success story in the eyes of the treatment program, in society's eyes she is still a failed women and a bad mother. And if she "runs her life today" to reiterate program lingo, then why does she feel so powerless?

Ultimately, one must both question the appropriateness of efforts to responsibilize drug users as a core treatment practice, and ask how treatment methods extenuate the social control of women who have used illegal drugs, an already profoundly dominated population.

CONCLUSION

I have tried to point out the limitations of treatment approaches in achieving the autonomy and freedoms they promise, claiming that processes of responsibilization further dominate marginalized populations. Becoming a reformed drug user through successfully reinventing oneself, I have argued, is deeply problematic for women in light of social structural inequality and the weight of state authority in their lives. For it is but another manifestation of social control, albeit in the form of good citizenship. Specifically, the quasi-statal "family" of the TC both eclipses and reproduces operations of the patriarchal state in these women's lives. Additionally, I have suggested that recovered subjectivity follows a racial logic; the ideal of the self-controlled, self-actualizing individual emulates a white male, bourgeois construct of citizenship. Yet, ironically, gendered and racial social barriers are precisely what prevent even recovered women from exercising full citizenship.

Several changes are needed. First, drug treatment must be disentangled from the penal system and social-control settings. Women in treatment also need protections from male abusers; legal advocacy, especially in the struggle for reunification with children; job skills and employment; housing for their families; the ability to return to their communities; and strategies for fighting discrimination and stigma they face as drug users and felons. Immediate concrete steps should include allowing children into treatment programs on a wide scale and offering family services that include comprehensive domestic violence education. Challenging the social-control setting and personal-responsibility/personal-change imperative of drug treatment can open the way for needed social and policy changes both inside and outside of the therapeutic community.

NOTES

1. At Your Place, I engaged in ethnographic field research, where I conducted nearly forty interviews with female residents, staff members, program managers, social workers, and criminal justice personnel. I also participated in and observed the daily operations of the treatment program over an eighteen month period, observing group sessions, classes, meetings, disciplinary practices, and participating in program celebrations and events. To protect the confidentiality of my interviewees and those in the program, I changed the names of interviewees and those I observed, omitted all identifying information about people and events, and assigned a code number to interviews and notes, which I stored in a locked file cabinet.

2. The liberal redistributive state, or Keynesian state, differed from today's neoliberal state, which embraces a form of classical liberal laissez-faire economics. Keynesianism lasted from WWII until the mid 1970s. Associated with the New Deal Coalition, it promoted sustained economic industrial growth, compromise between labor and capital, and social spending to mitigate inequality, including provision of a so-

cial safety net for the poor. Neoliberals, on the other hand, favor the small state and privilege the market, individual over government responsibility, and cost-effectiveness. Lisa Duggan (2003) distinguishes neoliberalism from welfare liberalism in that while the latter redistributed wealth downward, the former redistributes wealth *upward.* Moreover, U.S. neoliberalism is influenced by the New Right, or neoconservativism that privileges marriage above other social institutions and favors law and order policies.

3. The image of Dracula, the foreigner from Transylvania, has been widely analyzed as representing drug addiction, sexual seduction, and moral corruption. In a similar vein, drug users and drugs in U.S. cultural narratives are commonly depicted as morally corrupt, dangerous, or foreign threats–narratives that reflect American racial fears. For example, historically during cyclical U.S. drug scares, illegal drugs have been routinely demonized along with the immigrants and communities of color with which they have been associated (see Reinarman, 1997). During the Reagan years, poor women in particular were racialized and gendered in specific ways through media depictions of "crack mothers" who lacked morals (Roberts, 1997). These racialized images of urban and moral decline have also helped rationalize in recent decades a neoliberal agenda of cutting social programs for the poor while funding incarceration.

4. Taken as a whole, neoliberal values include: an ethic of individual responsibility; the privileging of the family, community and the individual; cost-effectiveness; accountability; entrepreneurial spirit; the small state and the privileging of the market; individual autonomy; self-reliance; and images of the active citizen (O'Malley, 2004).

REFERENCES

Dean, M. (1999). *Governmentality: Power and rule in modern society,* London: Sage Publications.

Duggan, L. (2003). *The twilight of equality: Neoliberalism, cultural politics, and the attack on democracy.* Boston: Beacon Press.

Friedling, M. P. 2000. *Recovering Women: Feminisms and the representation of addiction.* Colorado: Westview Press.

Holman, B. R., & Brown, R. A. (2004). Beyond bricks, bars, and barbed wire: The genesis and proliferation of alternatives to incarceration in the United States. In C. Sumner (Ed.), *The Blackwell companion to criminology.* London, Blackwell Publishing.

Kruttschnitt, C., & Gartner, R. (2005). *Marking time in the golden state: Women's imprisonment in California.* Cambridge: Cambridge University Press.

O'Malley, P. (2004). Penal policies and contemporary politics. In C. Sumner (Ed.), *The Blackwell companion to criminology.* London, Blackwell Publishing.

Richie, B. (1996). *Compelled to crime: The gender entrapment of battered black women.* New York: Routledge.

Reinarman, C., & Levine, H. G. (Eds.). (1997). *Crack in America: Demon drugs and social justice.* Berkeley: University of California Press.

Roberts, D. (1997). *Killing the black body: Race, reproduction, and the meaning of liberty.* New York: Vintage Books.

Stoler, A. L. (1995). *Race and the education of desire: Foucault's History of Sexuality and the colonial order of things.* Duke University Press.
Weinberg, D. (2000). "Out there": The ecology of addiction in drug abuse treatment discourse. *Social Problems, 47,* 606-621.

doi:10.1300/J015v29n03_13

Moving from Needs to Self-Efficacy: A Holistic System for Women in Transition from Prison

Patricia O'Brien
Nancy Lee

SUMMARY. One hundred women participated in a needs assessment and goal-planning process at a community-based agency soon after release from prison. The assessment indicated some fit between women's identified needs and how they placed themselves on "contemplation" ladders that facilitated their planning for reentry. Follow-up interviews with 14 women found a high level of satisfaction with the process, though they struggled with unmet goals. Participants and social service providers made programmatic recommendations that go beyond social services to address economic and self sustainability in the transition from prison to community. doi:10.1300/J015v29n03_14 *[Article copies available for a fee from The Haworth Document Delivery Service: 1-800-HAWORTH. E-mail address: <docdelivery@haworthpress.com> Website: <http://www. HaworthPress.com> © 2006 by The Haworth Press, Inc. All rights reserved.]*

Patricia O'Brien, PhD, is Associate Professor in the Jane Addams College of Social Work at the University of Illinois at Chicago.

Nancy Lee is a graduate student at the Jane Addams College of Social Work at the University of Illinois at Chicago.

Address correspondence to: Patricia O'Brien, Associate Professor, University of Illinois at Chicago, Jane Addams College of Social Work, 1040 W. Harrison, MC 309, Chicago, IL 60607 (E-mail: pob@uic.edu).

[Haworth co-indexing entry note]: "Moving from Needs to Self-Efficacy: A Holistic System for Women in Transition from Prison." O'Brien, Patricia, and Nancy Lee. Co-published simultaneously in *Women & Therapy* (The Haworth Press, Inc.) Vol. 29, No. 3/4, 2006, pp. 261-284; and: *Inside and Out: Women, Prison, and Therapy* (ed: Elaine Leeder) The Haworth Press, Inc., 2006, pp. 261-284. Single or multiple copies of this article are available for a fee from The Haworth Document Delivery Service [1-800-HAWORTH, 9:00 a.m. - 5:00 p.m. (EST). E-mail address: docdelivery@haworthpress.com].

KEYWORDS. Prison, reentry, change processes

The Bureau of Justice Statistics reports that the rate of women's incarceration has outpaced that of men ever since 1995 (Harrison & Beck, 2005), and that the bulk of their offenses are drug possession and property crime convictions. The continued incarceration of women for behaviors that arguably could be treated in the community is a major social justice issue requiring national reform.

Until that time, the increasing numbers of impoverished women returning to often under-resourced communities, with one more strike against them, is a pressing concern for feminists of every stripe and those working in health, mental health, and family settings. Nearly one out of two women released from state or federal prison facilities is rearrested, most often for violation of parole conditions, rather than for the commission of a new crime (Langan & Levin, 2002). Clearly, for most women, the transition from prison back into home and community is complex and avoiding crime can be the least of their problems.

Researchers have identified a number of economic and social barriers for prisoners returning to communities across the country every year (Visher & Travis, 2003; Bloom, Owen & Covington, 2004). These legal and practical barriers include non-existent ties to the workforce, low levels of educational attainment, substance abuse and mental health issues, and the additional stigma related to having been convicted of a felony (Petersilia, 2003). For women, additional challenges include issues related to regaining care of their children and multiple emotional and mental disorders, often related to addiction and trauma, as well as their emotional response to the incarceration itself (Kubiak, 2004; O'Brien, 2001).

Differences between male and female convicted persons in behavior, life circumstance, and parental responsibilities have broad implications for almost every aspect of women's criminal involvement and after-prison opportunities. Gender differences have been documented in studies of prison populations, including differences in offense type, the significance of separation from family members and children, less availability of educational, vocational, and treatment programs for women prisoners due to their smaller proportion of the prison population, and approaches by correctional staff who ignore or minimize women's needs (Belknap, 2001; Pollock, 2002).

In spite of the multiple and complex problems associated with reentry, there is a percentage of women who, against the odds, successfully address the array of issues that in many cases contributed to their criminal involvement, and slowly but surely regain their sense of identity and place in reconstructed lives. As the country is beginning to come to grips with the out-of-control costs of incarcerating women and men in the continuing war on drugs, there is a greater openness to creating and funding programs that offer some promise for reducing rates of recidivism as they assist former prisoners in the transition home.

After a brief literature review that examines some of the elements associated with women's successful exit from prison, this paper describes a reentry program for women created in a large, urban community in the Midwest, with the eighth largest prison population in the country (Harrison & Beck, 2005) where an estimated 2,000 women return every year after serving prison sentences. Furthermore, we present findings from a study of the program in its first year of implementation.

LITERATURE REVIEW
ON WOMEN'S SUCCESSFUL REENTRY

A number of studies have described characteristics of incarcerated women as compared to the general population such as a high prevalence of mental illness (Teplin, Abram, & McClelland, 1996), low level of education attained (Harlow, 2003), and number of and responsibility for children (Greenfeld & Snell, 1999). Some authors have also identified a high rate of victimization by childhood sexual abuse and adult partner violence among women prisoners (Bonta, Pang, & Wallace-Capretta, 1995; Gilfus, 1992). Women in transition from prison have identified their needs for successful reentry as well as the multiple barriers they perceive and experience (O'Brien, 2001; Parsons & Warner-Robbins, 2002). These include finding housing, creating ties with family and friends, finding a job or legitimate source of income, staying "clean" (from substance use if applicable or mandated), desistence from illegal behavior, and meeting parole conditions. Most released women live with family or friends until they find a job, can accumulate some money, and then find their own residence.

Finding a job is often an initial concern among former prisoners, who have fewer job skills and a shorter work history than men (Greenfeld & Snell, 1999). Greater life satisfaction and well-being have been found among women who attained employment success (Lambert & Madden, 1976; Schulke, 1993). In one of the first experimental studies of women's recidivism, it was income support rather than employment itself that promoted success (Jurik, 1983).

Koons and associates (1997) found that program participants most often felt that staffing characteristics were important to the success of programs, followed by the acquisition of needed skills. Holtfreter and Morash's cluster analysis study of a sample of women offenders' needs found that a wide variety of programs is required and that the group at highest risk of recidivism is most likely to have substance abuse, mental health, and child-related needs. They conclude, "Programs providing wrap-around services that organize access to a great many different program elements tailored to each woman, or programs that are very holistic in providing many services at one source, would be helpful for this group" (2003, p. 152). Building on what is known about the multiple needs of women exiting prison and consistent with this charge to develop a holistic response, ReConnections was established as a community-based program on the south side of Chicago where many former prisoners return to reconstruct their lives. The remainder of the paper discusses findings from a study of the first year's implementation of the program. The purpose of the study was: (1) to describe the women who participated in the program and their needs after release from prison; (2) to "hear" the participants experience using the service; (3) to learn from staff what they believed was useful about what they were doing as well as any recommendations for change; and (4) to learn from providers in the community what they perceived about the services and their opinions about what else could address released women's needs. Finally, we were interested in learning whether there was a fit between what the women identified as their needs and how they assessed their "readiness to make changes" over time as represented on a series of ladders representing different goal areas. Based on the transtheoretical model of behavior change (Prochaska & DiClemente, 1983) and as Brown and associates (2000) adapted it to their work with HIV affected women, we theorized that as women had the opportunity to consider the different areas of their lives, they might use the ladders as timelines for establishing goals for future attention (O'Brien & Young, 2006).

RECONNECTIONS PROGRAM

With a background of ten years of experience working with incarcerated women, staff and volunteers developed ReConnections as a "one stop" approach focused on assisting women to identify and address their immediate concrete needs as well as to assess where they most want to concentrate their future efforts for managing their reentry. These future efforts included an opportunity for women to identify immediate and more distant needs that, if addressed, could promote successful reentry. In addition, the staff approached the assessment as both a process for discussing challenges as well as a product to guide the woman toward other services and support.

In the planning phase of the assessment, a "ladder" provides a visual mechanism for women to identify their location on a continuum of readiness to address a variety of needs including: basic needs, entering or continuing alcohol or drug treatment, education and career, resolving trauma and mental health, physical health care, relationships with family members, and maintaining safety (see Figure 1 for example). Each point on the ladders signifies the importance of that particular issue at the time of the assessment as represented by a point in time when she might address it (if relevant to her situation).

FIGURE 1. Ladder 1: Meeting Basic Needs

Meeting Basic Needs
Each rung on the ladder below represents where you might be in your thinking about *meeting basic needs.* Cirlce the number that indicates where you are now in terms of *being able to meet your basic needs.*

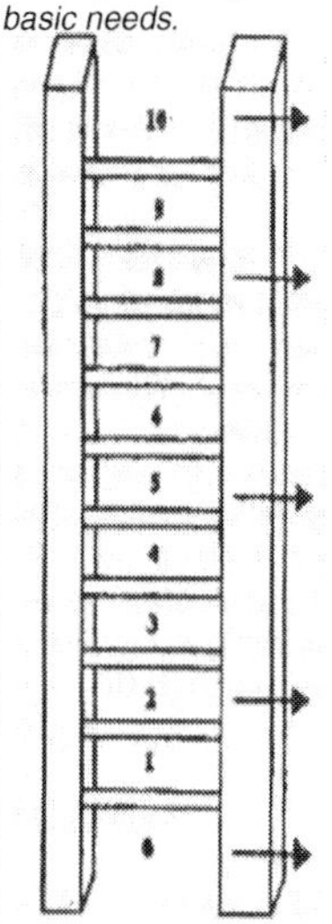

10 — I have been able to meet my basic needs of food, clothing, housing, and transportation for the last 6 months and still am able to do so.

8 — I have been able to meet my basic needs for less than the past 6 months.

5 — I am trying to find ways to meet all of my basic needs within the next 30 days.

2 — I am trying to think of ways to meet all of my basic needs within the next 6 months.

0 — I haven't thought about meeting my basic needs.

A mixed-method study of the ReConnections project after its first year of implementation (January-December 2004) focused on (1) developing a profile of the women who used the services, their expressed needs and identified levels on the assessment ladders; (2) eliciting from program participants their assessment of the services they had received and perceived impact on their progress in reentry; and (3) eliciting from staff and community partners their perceptions of service impact. Methods included an anonymous review of the first year's records of service, focus groups with program participants who volunteered to attend, and interviews with the staff and other service providers.

STUDY FINDINGS

Profile of Program Participants

The majority of women seeking services from ReConnections during 2004 were predominantly African American (92%), in their thirties (mean = 37.4 years), and single or unmarried (72.5%) with at least one minor child (66.3)%. Table 1 summarizes the women's characteristics at the time of assessment.

The income source for the participants varied. While 37.2% of the respondents indicated that they had no form of income, a majority of clients had some combination of income sources including food stamps, SSI or Social Security, Public Aid (TANF), or unemployment income. Seven of the women were employed at the time they requested services but likely were not making wages sufficient to meet their needs and support their children.

Many of the clients in the sample (46.4%) were referred to the ReConnections program by staff who went to state prison facilities to provide information or from other agencies that knew about their services (36.1%). The remaining respondents were referred by friends, family, or other individuals. Given the reduction of services within prison facilities as the population has increased as well as the importance of what Travis and Visher (2003) call the "moment of release," it becomes crucial to ensure that women exiting prison are informed of services available to assist them in their communities prior to their release. The median lapse of time between respondents' release from prison and their initial contact with ReConnections was .53 month (a little over two weeks), ranging from 1 day to 9.19 years! The long time out

TABLE 1. General Participant Characteristics

Characteristic	Percent
Race (n =100)	
African American	92.0
Caucasian	4.0
Hispanic	4.0
Age (n = 100)	
24 & under	3.0
25-34	34.0
35-44	44.0
45-54	17.0
55 & above	2.0
Mean	37.4 years
Range	19-58 years
Marital Status (n = 91)	
Single/unmarried	72.5
Married	12.1
Widowed/separated/divorced	15.4
Minor Children (n = 97)	
Yes	66.3
No	33.7
Mean	1.68 children
Range	1-7 children
Length of Incarceration (n = 85)	
6 months or less	40.0
> 6-12 months	17.6
> 12-18 months	12.9
> 18 months	29.4
Mean	19.2 months
Median	8.13 months
Range	1-150 months

of one participant is accounted for by someone who had been a client of the agency prior to the start of the ReConnections program.

Needs

A portion of the ReConnections assessment allows clients to indicate specific needs they may have in a range of categories. Almost all of the clients specified that assistance or support was needed for basic living needs. Over 90% also identified needs within the vocational/employment and income support areas. Almost three-fourths of the sample identified needs associated with their physical or mental health and the need for a support system.

Basic Needs: Women most frequently reported needs in this category. As Figure 2 presents, a majority of the women indicated that assistance was needed for transportation (78.1%), clothing (67.7%), and food (58%). A significant number (40.6%) also reported housing needs.

Vocational/Employment Needs: Nearly all of the respondents, 94.6%, reported that they needed assistance associated with vocation and employment. Overall, women indicated that job placement (64.1%), job training (52.2%), and education (30.4%) were their top vocation and employment needs (Figure 3).

Income Needs: Of those who responded, 94% reported needs associated with income. A majority of these needs were associated with desire for employment (52.4%). A smaller percentage needed assistance with public aid applications for SSI, Medicare, or TANF.

Physical/Mental Health Needs: Almost 80% of the sample specified that they had physical or mental health needs. Almost forty percent (37.8%) reported that they required assistance for dental services, a percentage not unlike Young's (1997) study of women's reported health needs at admission to a prison in Washington state. About a quarter (22.2%) of the sample indicated a need for mental health services, 18.9% with a physical exam, 15.6% with drug treatment, and 14.4% with medication needs (Figure 4).

FIGURE 2. Women's Basic Needs (n = 96)

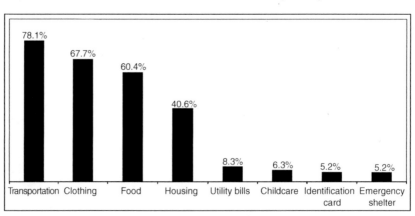

FIGURE 3. Vocational/Employment Needs (n = 92)

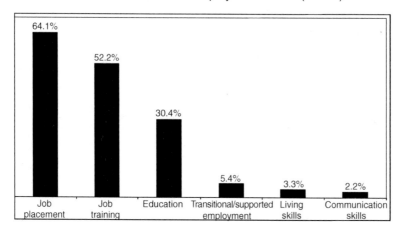

FIGURE 4. Physical/Mental Health Needs (n = 90)

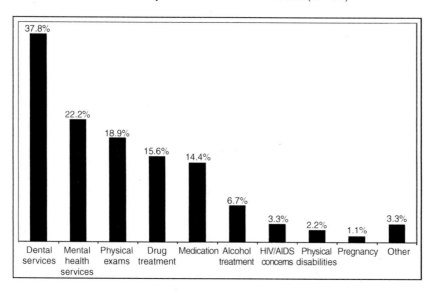

Support System Needs: Almost 70% of the women indicated a need for some type of support. Spiritual needs were most frequently reported by almost 31% of the women. Additionally, 26% of the respondents specified that assistance was needed in the area of social/support groups and 25% in relationships with children. Interestedly, 16% indicated a need for support in their relationships with service providers, higher than the percentage who indicated that need with other family members (14%), friendships with others (8%), and partners (6.8%) (Figure 5).

In addition to assessing the women's level of perceived need, ReConnections staff asked a few basic screening questions about substance use and mood.

Substance Use: At the time of the assessment, 16.7% of the respondents indicated that they had consumed alcohol in the last 30 days, 2.8% had used crack, and 5.6% had used some other drug. A total of 11% of the respondents said that they participated in 12-step meetings. Almost 60% (57.3%) indicated that they were part of some alcohol or drug treatment program at the time of the assessment (n = 82). The median age of women's first drink was age 16. Most respondents consumed alcohol either weekly (40%) or daily (37.8%). The median time sober for the sample was 7.3 months. The median age of women's first illicit drug use was 20.5 years old. A majority of those who used illicit drugs (83.5%), did so on a daily basis. The median time clean for the sample was 9.5 months.

Mental Health: Research has broadly documented the substance abuse and mental health among individuals involved with the criminal justice system–factors that are likely to contribute to difficulties upon return to the community. A series of questions focused on coping, stress, and depression were used to assess women's mental health distress that could inhibit their ability to address identified needs. On the

FIGURE 5. Support System Needs (n = 88)

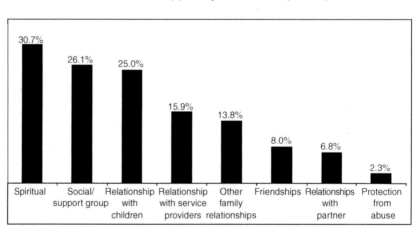

coping and stress items (Table 2), women in this sample did not express a high degree of stress.

Women self-reported the degree of depression they felt by answering an array of four items. Table 3 summarizes their mean response. The concern was to capture whether women might need to be referred for further psychological assessment and/or to discuss whether how the woman was feeling would get in the way of her making decisions or following up on linking with services that would assist her reentry. The total mean score of 8.16 (median of 8) on all items indicates that this sample of women was not extremely distressed and, in fact, might be considered within normal range for this population, considering their immediate situation of recent release from prison.

Contemplation Ladders

During their assessment process at ReConnections, clients rate themselves on a scale of 0 to 10 on a series of "contemplation ladders" (O'Brien & Young, 2006). Each of the seven ladders focuses on a different perceived need or identified change area for women who have been recently released from prison. In general, the higher the rating, the more the individual is focused on that immediate issue (see Table 4 for all scores on all dimensions). A nonparametric test was used to assess whether relationships existed between specific ladders and other variables in the assessment.

TABLE 2. Coping and Stress Items

Question	Frequency	Percent
If you were feeling stressed, how well do you think you could handle it by yourself? (n = 87)		
1 = Not at all/not very well	14	16
2 = OK	56	64
3 = Very well	17	20
In the next week, do you think you will need to use drugs to get through the day? (n = 87)		
1 = No, definitely not	78	90
2 = Probably not	6	7
4 = Probably yes	3	3
In the next week, do you think you will get so stressed out you just can't handle it? (n = 85)		
1 = No, definitely not	48	56
2 = Probably not	27	32
3 = Probably yes	10	12

TABLE 3. Depression Items (n = 82)

Statement	Frequency	Percent
I feel depressed		
Rarely/not at all	26	32
Some of the time	47	57
Most of the time	9	11
I feel lonely		
Rarely/not at all	26	32
Some of the time	49	58
Most of the time	7	9
I have crying spells		
Rarely/not at all	39	47
Some of the time	36	45
Most of the time	7	9
I feel sad		
Rarely/not at all	22	27
Some of the time	54	64
Most of the time	6	8
Total score		*Mean = 8.16, sd*, 3.01
Alpha coefficient		.80

TABLE 4. Average Scores* on Contemplation Ladders

Category	Mean	SD
Meeting basic needs (n = 86)	3.95	1.62
Entering or continuing alcohol and drug treatment (n = 80)	5.67	3.38
Education and career (n = 87)	4.56	1.97
Resolving trauma and meeting emotional needs (n = 71)	3.45	3.27
Getting and using health care (n = 86)	4.85	2.88
Building and maintaining relationship with family and children (n = 83)	5.43	2.98
Increasing physical safety and decreasing chances of physical harm (n = 51)	5.12	3.78

*Each ladder was scored 0-10.

Meeting basic needs (n = 86): The average response for the meeting basic needs ladder was 3.95. This indicates that, on average, clients were in the range of trying to find ways of meeting basic needs within the next 30 days to six months. No significant associations were found between the basic needs ladder and the clients' reported basic needs.

Entering or continuing alcohol and drug treatment (n = 80): The average response for how clients were doing in regards to entering or continuing alcohol and drug treatment was 5.67. This indicates that, on average, clients were in the range of thinking about entering drug or alcohol treatment within the next 30 days and having received treatment for substance use for the last 6 months or less. No significant associations were found between the entering or continuing alcohol and drug treatment ladder and the clients' reported substance use information and needs.

Education and career (n = 87): The average response for the client's educational or career status and situation was 4.56. This indicates that, on average, clients were in the range of thinking about getting a job or going to school with the next 30 days to six months. An association was found between this ladder and the client's need for assistance with SSI or Social Security income (Chi-square = 3.44; df = 1; p = .064).

Resolving trauma and meeting mental/emotional needs (n = 71): The average response in how clients were resolving trauma and meeting mental/emotional needs was 3.45. This indicates that, on average, clients were in the range of thinking about entering treatment for their mental or emotion needs within the next 30 days to six months.

Getting and using health care (n = 86): The average response for clients' perception of progress in regards to getting and using health care was 4.85. This indicates that, on average, clients were in the range of thinking about getting or using health care within the next 30 days or the next six months. An association was found between this ladder and drug treatment needs the client reported on the assessment (Chi-square = 3.41; df = 1, p = .065).

Building and maintaining relationships with family and children (n = 83): The average response for how the clients' perceived they were building and maintaining relationships with family and children was 5.43. This indicates that, on average, clients were in the range of thinking about taking steps to build or maintain relationship with their family or children within the next 30 days and having taken steps to build or maintain relationships with family or children within the last few months. Associations were found between this ladders and needs related to making or developing friendships (Chi-square = 8.21; df = 1; p = .004) and with one of the questions in the coping scale: "In the next week, do you think you will get so stressed out, you just can't handle it?" (Chi-square = 8.03; df = 1; p = .005).

Increasing physical safety and decreasing chances of physical harm (n = 51): The average response for how clients' indicated they were doing in terms of increasing physical safety and decreasing chances of physical harm was 5.12. This indicates that, on average, clients were in the range of thinking about taking steps to increase physical safety and reduce chances of physical harm within the next 30 days and having taken steps to increase their physical safety and reduce chances of physical harm for the last few months. No significant associations were found between this ladder and the clients' reported needs with protection from abuse or self.

From the review of self-reported data on the contemplation ladders, women at the time of the assessment at ReConnections were most ready to address issues in the area of entering or continuing alcohol or drug treatment (which may have also been associated with their parole conditions), building and maintaining relationships with family and children, and increasing physical safety and decreasing chances of physical harm. The question of whether the ladders are a useful part of the assessment for women who are just beginning reentry after release from prison is not answered by this data. Hearing from some of the program participants was the next phase of the study that helps in addressing that question.

Follow-Up with Program Partieipants

Fourteen women who had participated in services with ReConnections were interviewed in three focus groups to assess their satisfaction with services, their current self-assessed progress in reentry, and recommendations for further services. The fourteen women were very similar to the overall sample of participants: all were African-American, most (64%) were unmarried or single, and their average age was 40.2. The focus group participants had been out of prison an average of 13.5 months. Participants were recruited by a letter from the staff at ReConnections with an informational flyer about the focus groups. Anyone who received services from ReConnections during 2004 was eligible to participate in the group; a small incentive and public transportation cards were provided as well as refreshments at the time of the group.

Women who attended the focus groups (18% of the total number of 85 for whom the staff had current addresses) were very satisfied with the services they had received from ReConnections. Questions for the focus groups ranged from how the women had heard of ReConnections to how they assessed their current progress in reentry since their release from prison. The focus groups provided information on participants' perceptions of why the program was effective in meeting the needs of former inmates. Analysis concentrated on convergence of opinions among the women as well as the unique cases. A likely limitation of the focus groups is that it was the women who were most satisfied with the program who attended the groups; however, women did offer some recommendations for what they perceived could be improved that could better address their needs during reentry.

Factors concerning perceptions of program staff were integral to the perceived impact of the program. Across all 14 respondents, the level of comfort and support that participants felt with the staff seemed most relevant to their evaluation of the program. Comments such as the following were typical of every group:

> When I first met _____, my heart just relaxed. I just poured my tears out. I came back the next day to fill out the paperwork.

> The first time I came here I felt a welcoming from a stranger. More than even my family. My family gave me so much pressure. There was more stress at home than while I was in prison. Talking to _____, I got support and compassion from her. She made me feel better about coming back to society.

> To me, she's like an angel. When you first meet her, you won't be scared to talk to her at all. She just has a glow and warmth.

This sense of support was articulated even more strongly in relation to one of the staff who is also a formerly incarcerated woman.

> I could turn to her. She's someone I could talk to, someone to call, someone who's been where you've been. Sometimes when family and friends don't understand, don't want to understand, don't want to listen, I can turn to her.

An intentional strategy for ReConnections is the use of the "contemplation ladders" to assist the women in goal-setting or planning that is expected to be both comprehensive in addressing multiple dimensions and more visually meaningful to the woman. When women were asked about their perception of the ladders in the focus groups, most remembered looking at them. Some felt that they were useful. For example, one woman said:

> It gave me something to go to for the next day. The ladder gave me inspiration to try. I was just using it to go toward my goals.

> It worked for me to assess my needs. It was helpful.

> I never set goals before . . . now I've completed all of them [the ladders].

> It broke it down, where you're at and you could see it. It helps you see where you've improved. It helps you see where you're at and puts it in focus.

For several of the women however, the goal-setting approach was premature.

> That ladder was like I'm just coming home, why are you asking me these questions? It put me ahead of where I was.

> I got out last year and got in touch with and came here. I thought the assessment, it was personal. Too personal to talk about with a stranger, with someone you don't even know.

Women in the focus groups also reported that the concrete assistance they received from ReConnections including personal items, gifts for children, bus passes, and referrals for food, furniture, clothing, lawyers, emergency and transitional shelters, psychological counseling, and job placement centers was crucial to their process of reentry. Getting immediate needs addressed such as getting a state-issued ID card and finding out about other resources was "a starting point."

> They gave me a voucher. When I got out of jail I had no ID. They got me my birth certificate, my state ID, and my social security care. They were good.

> The job referrals were real basic. You would go to them and there wasn't anything, but those people would connect you with other people. Like a starting point. You just have to get information from all types of sources.

In addition to information about services, as one woman put it, "I got some love out of the services. Not too many programs out there that you can get that. Programs, resources, and love." Another woman echoed this when she said: "It's not just about the tables and chairs. Sometimes you just need someone to talk to once in awhile. We all need that."

Despite these supports, for some women, the barriers are greater. As one woman said,

> They were helpful, you know, with clothing and food. As far as the workplace, I'm 58. Training programs they sent me to said that I was too old. Well, what am I supposed to do? I'm not dead yet, am I? I haven't been back here cause I don't think they have anything they can do. I've started helping my neighbor clean her place and she's in some rich clubs so I get some work through work of mouth right now.

Finally, one woman eloquently reflected what many women murmured agreement with when she said:

> My thing with ReConnections or any other service organization is that we have to be diligent ourselves. We've got to do the footwork. I came out on March 22, 2004 and by March 24 I got my driver's license and my state ID. Once I got mobility, I came here right away. I found out who was. I talked to her. I listened to what she had to say. You know, clothing, food, shelter. But I didn't need shelter at the time. I got clothing and food referrals from here. They even had connections with the Bottomless Closet [a clothing resource]. It's hard coming out here. We got a lot of obstacles. [Points to her hand] We got this. Just our color is a problem, on top of being an ex-offender. I had doors shut in my face all the time. I cried almost every day. But you know what, you just got to be diligent. Take that energy you were using to look for drugs and try to find a job. I refused to use drugs. If you use, you'll still be jobless. They might want you to pass a drug test. I was diligent. I used ReConnections for support. Six months after I was back to living like I was like in prison. I had to live in a shelter, swallowed my pride.

As can often be true with focus groups, the women who attended used the groups to give information and support to each other. This was especially important to several women who, when asked about their progress since their release from prison, indicated they were not yet where they had hoped to be. For one woman, it's just a matter of not having sufficient income from legitimate employment.

I'm not satisfied at all. Maybe half way. The work I do, it's not set. It's when people want. So it could be once a month, once a week, or 3 times a week. It's an iffy thing, but that's my income. Except for Public Aid, I get $100 from there, but that doesn't take me far.

Another woman expressed much more intense frustration and disappointment:

I've regressed. I relapsed and I'm very disappointed with myself. To be so old, to have all the information, to know that Jesus is the way. I know about recovery. I don't know what it is against me. I just can't figure me out. Maybe I'm just evil or maybe I'm just lazy and don't want to do it. I don't even know.

Overall, the women recognized the progress they have made, even if they knew they still had some distance to go and needed to "hold on." One woman, summarized her progress by saying:

At first, I thought I was half, [meaning 50% along the way]. But just listening to everybody, I realize I'm blessed. I have housing. I have my little boy with me. That was the biggest thing, having my son with me. I did work before I got laid off. And I have family and friends who are helping. They'd pay for the electricity this month or something. They know I'm trying. I choose to get up every day and to get out of my house. As long as I have transportation. I have a 5 year old depending on me. I have to do what I can. I'm constantly doing things. I want to go to bible study tonight. I want to raise my son that way, but me too. I got to work on me. So I'm 75% good. The other 25%, my job and a couple of other areas I need to work on.

Another added:

When I got out I set a plan, number 1 get an apartment. I went through a lot, _____ helped me keep my sanity. I've been on my own since I was 16. I'm sleeping on my Daddy's couch and I wasn't happy. I've never been a bad person, just went the wrong way. Going to prison helped me. I told the judge thank you. I never got in trouble before. I got 9 months everyone else got 5, 10 years. Love of money is the root of all evil. Getting closer to God and I have a closer bond with my children. I put all this hurt and pain on my children. My son said I'm going to jump off building. I'm a better person now. I'm like a baby, I am going through a transformation. There's a better way. Find your purpose in life. God said be still, listen and obey. _____ put me on track to where I should have been. My season is over for being dead load. This is my season to bloom.

Finally, another woman proclaimed (and heads nodded in agreement around the group):

> When I first came, I was at my bottom. But now, the sky's the limit and I'm way up there. No cigarettes, no drugs, no nothing. My first job, I made $4.38 an hour, it was $35 a day. Not even minimum wage, but I did it because I had a self-esteem. Later it was $56 a day and soon to be $64 a day. I'm paying my bills. My kids can ask me for something and I can tell them, "If you're good." I clean my house. I take care of my kids. I had to have a zero balance on my utilities and I got that down. I buy food. In this place, they paved the road for that. You can do anything you want. You just can't straddle the fence. We want this future, but you got to leave the drugs behind. This is not a game. Functional addict, there's no such thing. You want and you want, but that means you have to put that stuff down. You can't let the penitentiary or an "x" to dictate your life. I'm up there and I'm loving it.

Finally women, were asked what would improve the program for them or other women transitioning from prison. Recommendations were suggested in three areas: employment, comprehensiveness, and prerelease linkage. In the employment arena, women wished that ReConnections could offer a more active start for women seeking employment by helping them with direct access to jobs, such as housekeeping or reception work, even "if only for a short probationary period." One woman also mentioned the need for a "one-stop shop":

> If this was where I could get everything, that'd be great. The loving environment here. If I didn't have to go to Safer, it would've been great. And support groups, like this here, that would be good too. Just to talk, not about just drugs, but women issues.

A third area of recommendation related to starting the program before women were released from prison: "They should have the program for women in prison who are really trying to change. Get housing for a year to help them out."

Follow-Up with Staff

A group interview with the three program staff focused on their perception of the use of the program, lessons learned, recommendations for improving it for better addressing women's needs after release from prison, and their opinions of work with other service providers. Each of the staff members have a "therapeutic" philosophy toward their work in that their emphasis is on "welcoming" the woman home and opening the conversation to enable each woman to articulate their needs. As one staff said, her focus is that ReConnections offers "some place to come without judgment" which requires active listening and support in the process. There is some tension between the time required to complete the assessment and the time spent in the support phase that each staff member believes is necessary to developing a relationship of trust. To address this tension, staff indicated a need to extend the initial assessment to two sessions that would more logically enable staff to address initial needs and then move on to the planning related to completing the ladders. Staff also recognized that there may need to be more detailed assessment of women who are psychologically distressed so that better linkages with services can be made. The staff identified the major outcomes for ReConnections as: creating an alliance, building a relationship, assessing needs, making appropriate referrals, and facilitating stability.

Follow-Up with Collaborative Service Providers

Interviews with the five service providers most often used as referrals in the ReConnections program were conducted by phone to identify their experience in working with the women referred by ReConnections to them, what improvements might be required for better linkage, and opinions about services for formerly incarcerated women generally. The services represented by these community providers included emergency shelter, a recovery home for addicts, transitional housing, social services agency (source of furniture, clothing, and food), and a *Life Skills* program established with a local community college under a contract with the State Department of Corrections. Each respondent communicated appreciation for ReConnections and a sense that their collaboration for service referrals has worked well and has been mutually beneficial. All of the respondents believed it was necessary to have a system specifically targeted to work with women exiting prison. As one provider said:

> Women leaving prison have so many issues. In addition to just re-adjusting to society, especially if they have been in prison for a while, they have other issues. Many of them need to reunite with their children, find housing and jobs, and try to stay clean, sober, and mentally intact. Case management for women who are just leaving prison is an excellent concept–a needed program.

Other service gaps that providers identified included placement in specific jobs that pay a livable wage and access to permanent housing that would include the woman's children. One provider also pointed out the need for "wrap-around services from people who are sensitive to their [formerly incarcerated women's] circumstances," though she went on to say that the staff at ReConnections are "wonderful with what they do, but it would be good if they could do more." Another provider pointed out that the need for services and support has grown at the same time that there has been shrinkage of budgets and resources. All the providers believed that the ReConnections program had been useful to their program by supporting and assisting specific clients, letting clients know about their programs, and in one case, "making us aware of the challenges facing women who have been imprisoned."

DISCUSSION

This paper has described the examination of a community-based intervention with women after their release from prison to an urban community. The review of the program included both an identification of participant characteristics, and interviews from participants, staff members, and service providers to elicit perceptions about the program's impact. This amassed data provides a case study of what can help women in the transition from prison to community. The following are some major findings or themes that can inform other efforts:

1. Inreach to the prisons where women reside is crucial. Many of the program participants knew staff members from seeing them at different prison facilities and so were predisposed to "trust" the program and seek out services once released.

2. Both concrete assistance and the availability of nonjudgmental support are necessary for women rebuilding their lives after release from prison. Participants appreciated the specific assistance they received, but they were more energized and engaged in the services because they felt listened to and supported.

3. Response to the immediate crisis and planning for next steps are different stages of assistance. Although participants and staff were somewhat favorable about using the "ladders" to develop goals, they also indicated that both time and other more crucial concerns prevented them from fully engaging them to plan for addressing multiple concerns. This was borne out by the lack of association between what women identified as needs and how they rated themselves on the ladders. Although the transtheoretical model (Prochaska & DiClemente, 1983) may have some therapeutic use with participants, it is based on a rational actor assumption of behavior related to a cognitive self-examination by the individual. It could well be that the time shortly after release is not the right time for such a self-examination and that work with women regarding next steps needs to be more "planned" based on natural processes of readiness–that is, as a woman has to address an issue, she will be more willing to plan for how much she might do so.

This paper has described what in some ways, may be a simple process of beginning the work with women exiting prison and attempting to rebuild their lives. At a recent international conference on "what works with female offenders," noted researcher on gender responsive policies Barbara Bloom asked participants to shift the focus from "what works" to what is the work we have to do, not only with female offenders but across society to bring about reconciliation, so that we can stop the run-away incarceration of our sisters, mothers, daughters, and partners.

REFERENCES

Belknap, J. (2001). *The invisible woman: Gender, crime, and justice* (2nd ed.). Belmont, CA: Wadsworth.

Bloom, B., Owen, B., & Covington, S. (2004). Women offenders and the gendered effects of public policy. *Review of Policy Research, 21*(1), 31-48.

Bonta, J., Pang, B., & Wallace-Capretta, S. (1995). Predictors of recidivism among incarcerated female offenders. *The Prison Journal 75*(1), 277-294.

Brown, V.B., Melchior, L.A., Panter, A.T., Slaughter, R., & Huba, G.J. (2000). Women's stages of change and entry into drug abuse treatment: A multidimensional stages of change model. *Journal of Substance Abuse Treatment, 18*, 231-240.

Gilfus, M.E. (1992). From victims to survivors to offenders: Women's routes of entry and immersion into street crime. *Women & Criminal Justice, 4*(1), 63-89.

Greenfeld, L.A., & Snell, T L. (1999). *Women offenders.* Washington, DC: Bureau of Justice Statistics (NCJ 175688).

Harlow, C.W. (2003). *Education and Correctional populations.* Washington, DC: Bureau of Justice Statistics (NCJ 195670).

Harrison, P., & Beck, A.J. (2005). *Prisoners in 2004.* Washington, DC: Bureau of Justice Statistics (NCJ 210677).

Holtfreter, K., & Morash, M. (2003). The needs of women offenders: Implications for correctional programming. *Women & Criminal Justice, 14*(2/3), 137-160.

Jurik, N.C. (1983). The economics of female recidivism. *Criminology 21*(4), 603-622.

Koons, B.A., Burrow, J.D., Morash, M., & Bynum, T. (1997). Expert and offender perceptions of program elements linked to successful outcomes for incarcerated women. *Crime and Delinquency, 43*(4), 512-532.

Kubiak, S.P. (2004). The effects of PTSD on treatment adherence, drug relapse, and criminal recidivism in a sample of incarcerated men and women. *Research on Social Work Practice, 14*(6), 424-433.

Lambert, L.R., & Madden, P.G.. (1976). The adult female offender: The road from institution to community life. *Canadian Journal of Criminolgy and Corrections 18*(4), 319-331.

Langan, P.A., & Levin, D.J. (2002). *Recidivism of prisoners released in 1994.* Washington, DC: Bureau of Justice Statistics (NCJ 1993427).

O'Brien, P. (2001). *Making it in the "free world": Women in transition from prison.* Albany, New York: State University of New York Press.

O'Brien, P., & Young, D.S. (2006). Challenges for formerly incarcerated women: A holistic approach to assessment. *Families in Society, 87*(3), 359-366.

Parsons, M.L., & Warner-Robbins, C. (2002). Factors that support women's successful transition to the community following jail/prison. *Health Care for Women International, 23*, 6-18.

Petersilia, J. (2003). *When prisoners come home: Parole and prisoner reentry.* Oxford: University Press.

Pollock, J. (2002). *Women, prison, and crime* (2nd ed.). Pacific Grove, CA: Brooks/Cole.

Prochaska, J.O., & DiClemente, D.D. (1983). Stages and processes of self-change in smoking: Toward an integrated model of change. *Journal of Consulting and Clinical Psychology, 5,* 390-395.

Schulke, B.B. (1993). Women and criminal recidivism: A study of social constraints. Unpublished doctoral dissertation, George Washington University.

Teplin, L.A., Abram, K.M., & McClelland, G.M. (1996). Prevalence of psychiatric disorders among incarcerated women. *Archives of General Psychiatry, 53*(6), 505-512.

Visher, C.A., & Travis, J. (2003). Transitions from prison to community: Understanding individual pathways. *Annual Review of Sociology, 29,* 89-113.

Young, D.S. (1997). *Health care seeking and service use among incarcerated women.* Unpublished dissertation, University of Washington.

doi:10.1300/J015v29n03_14

Locked Up, Then Locked Out:
Women Coming Out of Prison

Linda Evans

SUMMARY. Women prisoners face tremendous psychological, emotional, and physical hardships inside prison. These include isolation,
separation from their families and children, lack of medical care and
general abuse of their basic human rights. When they are released
from prison, women confront institutional as well as psychological
barriers to a successful return to their communities. doi:10.1300/J015v29n03_15
*[Article copies available for a fee from The Haworth Document Delivery Service:
1-800-HAWORTH. E-mail address: <docdelivery@haworthpress.com> Website:
<http://www.HaworthPress.com> © 2006 by The Haworth Press, Inc. All rights
reserved.]*

KEYWORDS. Re-entry, women and courts, women and trial, women
and sentencing, prison time, families of prisoners, family reunification,
parental rights, child custody, homelessness, housing, voting rights and
prison

INTRODUCTION

I was in prison for 16 years. I was a political prisoner in U.S. federal
prisons, serving a 40-year sentence for actions protesting U.S govern-

---

Linda Evans is a former U.S. political prisoner and currently an organizer for All of
Us or None (E-mail: linda@prisonerswithchildren.org).

[Haworth co-indexing entry note]: "Locked Up, Then Locked Out: Women Coming Out of Prison." Evans,
Linda. Co-published simultaneously in *Women & Therapy* (The Haworth Press, Inc.) Vol. 29, No. 3/4, 2006,
pp. 285-308; and: *Inside and Out: Women, Prison, and Therapy* (ed: Elaine Leeder) The Haworth Press, Inc., 2006,
pp. 285-308. Single or multiple copies of this article are available for a fee from The Haworth Document Delivery
Service [1-800-HAWORTH, 9:00 a.m. - 5:00 p.m. (EST). E-mail address: docdelivery@haworthpress.com].

Available online at http://wt.haworthpress.com
© 2006 by The Haworth Press, Inc. All rights reserved.
doi:10.1300/J015v29n03_15

ment policies. The scars of those 16 years in prison will never go away–that's why I begin this article by recounting how prison conditions affect a prisoner's attitude and emotional life. Since my early release in 2001 through a grant of clemency by President Clinton, I have also experienced many of the same obstacles faced by 64 million men and women who have criminal records.[1] These barriers extend the trauma of imprisonment into the rest of our lives.

This article is an attempt to communicate the harsh and long-lasting impact of prison on women's lives. I will also recount some of the difficulties of coming back from prison to a society which subjects former prisoners to lifelong punishment for the past. It is rare for someone who has been in prison to have the opportunity to discuss these issues from our point of view. I am not a therapist, but I hope my experience and insights will be useful to those of you who are counseling women in prison and women coming back to our communities.

I am not "representative" of women in prison: I am white, middle class, politically radical, and a lesbian with a committed partner who worked to get me free. I was arrested and sentenced to prison as a result of consciously thought-out, social justice activities. But regardless of class, race, sexual preference, or reason for incarceration, I experienced the same prison conditions and many of the same conditions of release that all my sisters in prison go through. So, I will weave my personal story with more general information about women in prison.

Beyond my experiences in prison, I have also gained a lot of knowledge in the four years since I was released. I am a community organizer and a co-founder of All of Us or None, a grassroots movement of formerly incarcerated men and women, prisoners, and our families. We are building a civil rights movement to fight the pervasive discrimination that we face after our release from prison. We advocate for policy changes that will affect the well-being of all communities hit hard by mass imprisonment. My experiences in this movement have enriched me greatly.

WHO ARE THE WOMEN PRISONERS?

Currently in the United States, more than *one million women* are now behind bars or under the control of the criminal justice system (probation, parole, jail, state and federal prisons) (ACLU, Brennan Center, & Break the Chains, 2005). Statistics about women in prison are widely available (see Table 1). But statistics can't tell you who these women re-

TABLE 1

◆ **The majority of women prisoners are women of color.** Nationally, 63% of women in state prison and 67% of women in federal prison are Black or Latino (WPA Focus, 2003). African-American women (with an incarceration rate of 205 per 100,000) are more than three times as likely as Latina women (60 per 100,000) and six times more likely than white women (34 per 100,000) to face imprisonment (Bureau of Justice Statistics, 2001).

◆ **Most women prisoners are mothers.** An estimated 80,000 incarcerated mothers are parents to approximately 200,000 children under 18 (Mumola, 2000). In 1999, over 1.5 million minor children had a parent in prison (Mumola, 2000). Over 10 million children in the United States have parents who were imprisoned at some point in their children's lives. (Hirsch et al., 2002, p. 7). 64% of incarcerated mothers in state prisons and 84% of the mothers in federal custody reported living with their children prior to becoming incarcerated (Mumola, 2000).

◆ **Most women prisoners have suffered physical and/or sexual abuse.** 55% of women in state prisons reported that they had been physically and/or sexually assaulted at some point in their lives (ACLU et al., 2005, p. 18). 79% of women in federal and state prisons reported past physical abuse, and over 60% reported past sexual abuse (ACLU et al., 2005, p. 18).

◆ **Most women in prison are poor.** 22.3% of women in prison held no job prior to incarceration. Of those who had jobs, two-thirds reported never receiving more than $6.50 per hour (Wellisch & Prendergast, 1993). 37% of women in prison earned less than $600 per month prior to their incarceration, and nearly 30% received public assistance (Greenfield & Snell, 2000).

◆ **Most women in prison have problems with drug addiction or other forms of substance abuse.** By 1999, drug offenses accounted for 72% of the women in federal prisons, 34% of the women in state prisons, 24% of those in local jails, and 27% of those on probation (Greenfield & Snell, 2000). Between 1986 and 1999, the number of women in state prisons for drug offenses increased by 888% (ACLU et al., 2005, p. 1).

◆ **Most women in prison have limited education levels.** Over 64% of women in state prisons have not finished high school (WPA Focus, 2003).

ally are as human beings, nor about the trauma they have been through in their lives–usually including drug addiction and physical or sexual abuse from a young age. The statistics don't tell you about the children and family they have left behind, or the worried and often aging grandparents who take care of the children. Nor can statistics convey the incredible vitality, creativity, and intelligence of the women, nor the real pain they suffer every single day.

The women I met in prison were like an extended family to me, and to each other. We took care of each other in times of terrible sickness and the most despicable medical neglect. One of my friends in prison,

Sandi, had been complaining of back pain for several months, but her complaints were ignored by the prison doctors. Finally, we saw a lump developing at the top of her back, and went with her to demand more tests. The tests came back showing that she had advanced and rapidly growing lung cancer. She started chemotherapy. The treatments were debilitating. A whole team of women prisoners took care of her. We developed a schedule of tasks for her care–such as cleaning her cell, keeping her company, making and bringing her food. Sandi's case was unusual–she was released from prison when a judge granted her a compassionate release. She died three months after her release.

In prison, we also comforted each other when someone got news of a family member's death, and on visiting days when children were torn away from their mothers' sides at the end of the allotted hours. Sometimes we fought together when under attack by the prison administration, to assert our basic humanity. And all too often, women fought against each other (sometimes with violence, most often with angry arguments)–a product of racial divisions and misplaced frustrations.

Racism often revealed itself in petty fights about our living space. We had to wait in long lines for a chance to use the telephone–only four phones were available for 300 women in our living unit. Tensions were high about telephone access, and I once witnessed an argument where a white woman called another woman a "Black bitch." The Black woman tipped over the phone booth, and both women were put in the hole. This incident was the catalyst for the formation of the Council Against Racism at FCI–Dublin–a group of women prisoners intent upon lessening the racial tension inside our prison. We advocated for translation of all prison forms into Spanish, for translators to be available at the medical center, and for promotions in the prison factories to be based on job performance instead of supervisors' favoritism. (Many of the white factory supervisors had refused to promote Black or Latina prisoners.) The Council Against Racism also sponsored a Multi-Cultural Festival where prisoners from every country represented in the prison population performed a dance, song, or poem from their country. The Council was unfortunately disbanded after several years when we got a new warden.

Women in prison are aunts and mothers, daughters and grandmothers. We are Black and Latina, Native American, Asian, and Caucasian. In the federal prison in Northern California where I was incarcerated for most of my years, almost 40% of the women were not U.S. citizens (most had been convicted of drug-trafficking related offenses); they came from other countries all over the world, and were being held incredibly far away from their homes and families. Many did not speak English and had no one outside who could advocate for their rights and needs.

Women in prison are diverse in every way, including a wide range of political opinions on every subject. I came to see that the most reactionary, the most revolutionary, and the most mainstream views pervaded the prison–and that generosity and selfishness existed side by side. I was shocked when I discovered, for example, that a number of women prisoners actually support the death penalty!

RIPPING THE SOCIAL FABRIC

Any amount of time in jail or prison–whether a week, a year, or twenty years–disrupts a person's life. Every single arrest results in a criminal record even if charges are later dropped; this record is permanent and easily accessible over the Internet. A single arrest may mean loss of a job, a place to live, public benefits, even custody of one's own children. In any discussion of the psychological impact of imprisonment, it's important to remember that the trauma is long-lasting and affects an individual's entire family and their larger community as well. Vast numbers of Black and Brown men and women are being torn away from their families and communities, often for decades. Communities of color are systematically targeted for arrest and imprisonment, so each family's suffering from generations of imprisonment is magnified by how prison has affected their neighbors. The United States has the longest sentences and the highest rate of incarceration in the entire world. Over 2.2 million people are currently in U.S. prisons, each coming from a community that needs them to come home (Sentencing Project, 2005b).

ARREST AND JAIL

The trauma of imprisonment begins with the nightmare of arrest. Many women are arrested at home, literally torn away from their children by the police. One in five children of incarcerated mothers witnessed their mother's arrest (Women in Prison Project, 2006). Imagine a mother pushed to the floor, handcuffed behind her back, then dragged away with her children screaming, crying, and left in the hands of the police. Very few local police departments allow women to call anyone to care for their children, so women are carted off to jail not knowing what will happen to their children.[2] Neighbors see the arrest–which may reverberate with similar situations in their own family. Many women arrested in the U.S. don't speak English as a first language, so they may not understand what's happening to them, their legal rights, or the charges against them. Due to government budget cut-backs, court-appointed lawyers are not always available, and seldom satisfactory. Young women arrested for drug felonies are urged by these lawyers to plead Guilty rather than bargain down their case–never being informed that having a drug felony on your record brings lifetime consequences: no access to public housing, public assistance, or food stamps, and distinct limits on future employment, student loans, or voting rights.

When a woman is arrested and thrown in jail, even overnight, the humiliation begins. She is stripped and searched in the most private places. To many women this feels like rape and can trigger prior sexual abuse experiences. Women prisoners are forced to submit to strip searches and pat searches every day of their lives during any kind of detention. Searches may be done by either men or women guards, so women are often forced to submit to invasive and humiliating searches by male guards. A high percentage of women prisoners have already suffered from domestic abuse from husbands, fathers, brothers, and others, often from a very young age, so the trauma is further magnified. In most jails and prisons, male guards are routinely able to see women prisoners nude in their cells, using the toilet, or sometimes even in the showers. I remember that while in federal prison, the ONLY place I had any privacy was in the shower. Unlike the gang showers in most prisons and all county jails, our shower had a door that we could close. I coveted my limited time in the shower, always exiting once again to the glare of lights, the constant scrutiny of guards, and the incessant noise of our over-crowded living conditions.

Conditions in county jails are generally terrible. Because they were originally designed only for short-term stays, there is little if any medical care available, and rarely are the limited medical staff experienced in the specific medical needs of women. Women in county jails are often withdrawing from drugs–83% of all women prisoners in New York reported having a substance abuse problem prior to arrest (Women in Prison Project, 2006). Women are forced into withdrawal without any medical treatment: "cold turkey," which is a horrible experience for anyone, anytime. Her cellmates are forced to go through this hell with women sick from withdrawal. Also, mental illness is rarely diagnosed or treated in a county jail, and women with mental problems often go to trial without ever comprehending what's happening to them.

"THE HOLE"

Every jail and prison has isolation cells–often referred to as "the hole." Both men and women prisoners may routinely be kept in isolation cells for years at a time. An ostensible place of "punishment," it often seems that the true purpose of isolation time is "to break the spirit" of those not yet broken. I was sent to the hole several times in several prisons. The worst one was the hole in Louisiana. It was a metal box with no place to stretch out but the concrete slab that served as a bed. Feces and food had been thrown all over the wall. I was sent there for demanding the right to get garbage out of our cells while we were locked down for several days. Whenever there was a demonstration outside the prison, or riots in other prisons, they often sent the political prisoners to the hole for "security reasons." At FCI-Dublin, the hole was far from "solitary." Due to over-crowding, we were often triple-celled with others in the hole, rather than being in isolation. Many times mentally ill women were put in the hole with me, when they were suicidal. Conditions in the hole only made the women's depression worse. In actuality, it was we, the other prisoners, who helped them, and looked after them.

DOING TIME IN THE NEW ORLEANS JAIL

I spent two years waiting for a trial in Orleans Parish Prison (OPP), the New Orleans county jail. There is no guarantee of how long a prisoner will be in a county jail, although these facilities were never designed for long-term imprisonment. Some of my sister prisoners had been incarcerated there up to seven years, waiting for transfer to state prison. (The state prison was so overcrowded that it had been court-ordered not to accept any more prisoners.) Some of the women had such serious dental problems that they had no teeth left. Jail and prison dentists routinely pull teeth out rather than fill them. But there were no provisions for women, even those with absolutely no teeth left, to receive new, false teeth. They literally had to chew using only their gums. Not that there was much to eat–grits at 4 a.m., peanut butter sandwiches on white bread for lunch, maybe beans and rice for supper, gray chicken in grease gravy once a week. We got our food when guards dragged black plastic garbage bags full of sandwiches into the cellblock, and gave us our sandwich from the garbage bag on the floor.

Also at New Orleans jail, there were no eye examinations, eye treatment, or any way for women who needed eye glasses to get them. No newspapers or books were allowed. There was one black-and-white TV. Prisoners had no access to telephones–they were allowed to make one monitored, five-minute call per month. If their family wasn't home on phone call night, there was no chance to call for another whole month. There was no gynecologist although many of the women coming in were pregnant. During cell raids at OPP we were told to strip, and all of us were herded into showers so guards could examine us while others tore up our cells. Even though we tried to joke and laugh about this perverse invasion, parts of this experience felt like a kind of gang-rape.

Mothers in county jails face many challenges: trying to figure out who will take care of their children, how to get them back from the foster care system, trying desperately to stay connected and be a good mother even when you're taken away. Visiting with your family in a county jail is extremely precious but very traumatic. In the New Orleans jail, visits from children under 16 were allowed only for 15 minutes, once a year around Christmas. Only three children per prisoner could visit–so if a woman had more than three children, she had to *choose* which children she would see that year. Visits were through a tiny window, using a heavy phone that young children couldn't hold up. All the women in the jail experienced the pain of women seeing their children, and of not being able to see their own.

I want to emphasize that conditions such as these, and worse, are commonplace in county jails throughout the United States. In most county jails the prisoners are people of color, guards may be of any race, but the majority of higher level staff–lieutenants, captains, and administrators–are white. For prisoners of color, this re-enforces their life experience of subjugation to systematic white supremacy.

COURT, TRIALS, AND SENTENCING

To most women, the criminal justice system seems foreign, unknowable, inaccessible. Many women have no resources to pay a lawyer, and the public defender may pressure her to make a deal, to plead Guilty and get her case off his case load, even if it means she will live with a felony conviction or go to prison. New sentencing laws generally prohibit the

judge from taking into consideration whether or not this is a first offense, whether the women is a parent, has a substance abuse problem, or
anything else about her character or unique situation. It's sentencing by
numbers. Usually the defendant is advised not to speak, and women are
usually too terrified to try. Court just emphasizes that a woman is out of
control of her life, and her ability to influence what happens to her is
extremely limited.

Many of the women arrested are the victims of "conspiracy" laws,
where they are judged guilty of the same crimes as their boyfriends or
husbands, just because they lived with them and "benefited" from drug
money income. Women are judged guilty by association for driving or
renting a car, answering a telephone, or translating a conversation. A
friend of mine in prison got 20 years for signing a FedEx receipt for a
package belonging to her husband. She maintains that she was unaware
of the contents of the package. If that sounds unlikely, ask yourself: do
you know the contents of every package sent to every one of your
family members? Probably not.

Prosecutors often try to force women to testify against their husbands, brothers, or family members with threats of harsh charges and
long sentences. Often women in conspiracy cases wind up with much
harsher sentences than the male leaders of the conspiracy. The women
have no useful information to bargain with, while the men know all the
details of the operation. "Conspiracy" is an unknown concept in many
countries, so many women don't understand why they are being
charged with a crime for doing something their husband demanded of
them, or for living on money that he brought home.

PRISON TIME

When the nightmares of trial and sentencing are over, women con-
victs are transferred to state or federal prison. Draped in chains around
our waists, handcuffed, with shackles around our ankles, we are put on
prison buses or airplanes run by U.S. Marshals. "Con Air" has no pre-
tense of safety procedures or routines for rescue; each prisoner knows
that if the plane goes down, all of us will die. Picture an old jet aircraft,
filled with Black and Brown faces, chained and shackled, mostly men
with some women: a modern-day slave ship.

Upon entering prison, I understood: this is where I will be living for
at least the next ten years of my life, probably much more. (With my
40-year sentence, I could not apply for parole until after ten years at the

earliest.) There was no question I was entering another universe–a tiny world surrounded by double razor-wire fences and high concrete walls, where the guards had absolute control over every aspect of prisoners' lives.

Prisons are designed to make a person feel like a caged animal. Deep depression and suicidal thoughts are often the result. Imagine the effect of living behind bars, in the same small compound of dull gray, concrete, prison buildings, for years and years and years. Nothing ever changes; each day rolls into the sameness of the next. Color is at a minimum. You live with varying numbers of women in a tiny cell, but never alone. Living under these conditions creates tremendous stress and permanent scars for everyone who has ever been locked up. From the beginning you are given your prison number and treated like a commodity. Isolated from family and friends and everything familiar, it feels at first almost like being on another planet.

I personally dealt with the sameness, lack of color, isolation, and inhumanity in several ways. Like many prisoners, I walked around the compound and tried to exercise my body even when I was locked up in the hole. I also became a quilter. I was fortunate that at the federal prison where I stayed for 12 years, one of the women staffers had a big heart. She had been a nurse, now a prison guard. She ran the "recreation" program. She brought in a volunteer quilting teacher, bought sewing machines, and helped us order fabric. Quilting for me was an emotional survival technique. It allowed me to work with beautiful fabrics and be surrounded by color in this drab environment. It gave me something to make that was useful for others: I made quilts to give to my lawyers, family, friends, and other supporters as a way to show my love and appreciation to them. Many, many prisoners are talented artists and develop their creativity while they're locked up. One of the most inhumane trends in recent years is that prisons are now outlawing all craft supplies, even colored pencils.

In prison, it is not safe to show anger. A small spat with a fellow inmate may escalate into a full-scale brawl, with future retaliation. Needless to say, any expression of anger toward the guards or staff results in an immediate trip to the hole–or worse. So I suppressed a lot of the anger I felt. But I decided it was okay to allow myself to cry, to feel my sadness and pain. Keeping those feelings alive in me, rather than suppressed, helped me keep my humanity intact. Although I felt very depressed at times, I was also able to come up from the pain and find what enjoyment I could in life.

There's not much to do that feels productive in prison. Everyone has to work full-time at maintenance or factory jobs at slave wages–literally pennies an hour. Prison education programs are very few, mostly GED level with some vocational skills training. College programs in prisons were drastically cut in 1995 when prisoners were disqualified for the Pell Grant program. Recreation is mostly television and endless card and domino games.

Prison medical care (as in the county jails) is extremely substandard. Doctors and nurses are often poorly paid. Several people I knew in prison died there because of terrible medical care. The treatment of pregnant women is unconscionable. Prenatal care is virtually non-existent, and it is standard procedure for women to be chained to their bed as they give birth. Aging women prisoners, disabled prisoners, HIV+ or Hepatitis C+ prisoners have to struggle hard and long before their most basic medical needs are met. For example, the California prison system denies treatment to prisoners with Hepatitis C, citing the expense of treatment. Although 70% to 85% of state prisoners have drug or alcohol abuse problems, only 13% receive treatment while they are in prison (Criminal Justice Consortium, 2001). Mental health care is generally unavailable, with prison shrinks acting as cops.

Separation from friends and family and isolation from the community outside is a given in prison life. Most prisoners are kept in prisons far from their home. For women, this geographic distance is intensified because there are usually only one or two women's prisons in each state. Most women never see their children or families while they are inside. Visiting is difficult for most families–traveling long distances is expensive, and poor families are dependent on public transportation. Prison sites are usually far from urban centers, which makes it difficult to travel by public transportation even for families living in the general vicinity. When family crises happen, women prisoners feel especially powerless. It's emotionally devastating to be in prison and unable to attend your children's graduations, christenings, and weddings. During any time in prison, distance from family grows and deepens. Family members die, and prisoners are required to pay for several guards to accompany them to the funeral–IF a prisoner receives permission to attend. Many prisoners are denied permission to attend funerals because services will be held in "dangerous" neighborhoods, or because their security classification is too high. My father died while I was in prison. I was denied permission to attend his funeral, even though my friends offered to raise the money to pay for the guards and the expenses of the trip. (Prisoners who attend funerals sleep in local jails and are handcuffed while seeing their family.) I grieved in my cell, comforted by my friends, knowing many of them had also lost loved ones while they were inside.

And what about the children? There is never a way to heal the anger and abandonment that children feel when their mother is not there to care for them. Women try to be long-distance parents, taking classes in parenting if they're available, writing letters and drawing pictures for their kids, struggling with phone call expense to keep in touch–as their children grow up without them. Most prison systems now limit the total number of minutes per month that a prisoner may use the phone, even though phone tolls are being paid through prisoners' own commissary funds. Many women are faced with permanently losing their parental rights because of state laws and poor legal representation in child custody proceedings. Many children of women prisoners are very young–25% of adult women in prison have either given birth at some point during the year prior to their incarceration or are pregnant at the time of their arrest (Mumola, 2000). There is no real counseling available for the trauma of separation experienced by the children left behind.

FAMILY LEGACY

Families bear the burden of the incredible expense of having someone in jail or prison. For example, prison phone systems have uniformly changed to privatized systems where the prisoner must pay for phone calls from her own funds, at a much higher rate than community phone systems charge. A prisoner's family must send in commissary money for women in prison to be able to purchase phone time to talk to their children, or to buy shampoo, clothing, stamps, or commissary food. Families on the outside are often left in financial crisis because their mother or sister's prior income was crucial to family survival. Many women in prison worked hard at 20¢/hour prison factory jobs to send money home to help family members take care of their children. Every prisoner is required to work full-time, to keep the prison functioning. Because I came from a middle-class background, my finances didn't force me to work in the prison factory–instead I collected the prison's garbage for $5.25/month. My friends and family were able to send me money to make phone calls, buy fabric, craft supplies, and food. But I always felt guilty about accepting their support, and I will always be deeply grateful for all the forms of support I received during my years in prison.

Young mothers in many juvenile halls or state juvenile detention generally have no contact visitation with their babies, at a time when bonding is important. The separation is deeply painful for the young mothers and the children. Many young mothers are afraid to reveal that they have children, fearing the label of "negligent mother," which could result in their children being taken away.

THE SHOCK OF FREEDOM

Every year, 600,000 or more people return to their communities after serving time in prison. Seventy thousand of them are women. About 1600 prisoners are released each day nationwide (Sentencing Project, 2005a). Most people come out of prison with few resources and new liabilities caused by years away from their families *and* their convicted felon status. Most are on parole, technically still in custody and subject to the whims of a parole officer. Many will have their parole violated and be returned to prison for technical violations like being late to a parole appointment, visiting a family member who has a past felony conviction, or moving without receiving permission. In California, 67% of prisoners are sent back to prison in the first three years after their release. This is largely because of the discrimination they face because of their criminal record. The few re-entry services and programs that exist are pitifully inadequate to meet the needs of thousands of people returning from prison to face the challenges of re-entry. Most services and programs available for re-entering prisoners are for men–for example, very little transitional or affordable housing exists where women can reunite with their children.

Even for those women who have a support network when coming out of prison, there are tremendous psychological adjustments to make, especially for those who have been in prison for many years. I was in prison from 1985 to 2001. At the time of my release, I had never seen a CD or DVD, had never owned a phone answering machine, and had never seen a cordless phone, much less a cell phone. My computer skills were minimal and I had no experience with the Internet, though I had been unusually fortunate to get a little basic computer training while I was in prison. I felt overwhelmed by the technology, disoriented, as if I were from another planet. I had difficulty communicating what my life had been like to people around me, and I often felt overwhelmed with feelings of sorrow and separation from the friends I had left in prison. I was also immensely happy to be out of prison. Joy and sorrow were all mixed together, and my new freedom felt bittersweet and confusing. The first months I was free, I would burst into tears when I saw any long-distance vista, like the ocean. For so long I had seen only short distances, and the walls of my cell.

I was seriously depressed and disheartened by the poverty, mental illness, and homelessness that I saw everywhere on the streets. Witnessing these conditions was especially hard for me because I had gone to prison due to my efforts to change these kinds of oppression in our society. So on top of everything else, I felt defeated.

Like anyone faced with freedom after many years of prison, I had a lot of trouble making even the smallest decisions. Buying things seemed impossible–everything was so expensive, and there were too many choices in every store. When a good friend of mine got released, she just sat down and wept in the middle of the supermarket because she couldn't comprehend the excess and the choices.

Many prisoners end up abandoned by their families, because of the stigma attached to their imprisonment. This same stigma makes it hard for formerly incarcerated people to accept themselves and start over. For anyone with a drug abuse history, returning home from prison means extremely difficult challenges: suddenly drugs and alcohol are readily available, and getting high seems like a way out of the difficult struggle for survival and a way to dim the pain. Women, especially, often started using drugs to numb the pain of emotional, sexual, or physical violence. It's hard to stay away from old acquaintances who are still "in the life" of drug addiction and crime, and difficult to build new relationships with new people.

RE-ENTRY AND DISCRIMINATION: LOCKED OUT OF SOCIETY

In addition to psychological readjustments and barriers, formerly incarcerated people suffer widespread discrimination. Legal barriers have been established that make it difficult for someone to come out of prison and successfully transition back into a productive life. (It's also important to recognize that the term "re-entry" may be inappropriate. The majority of prisoners probably never felt that they had "entered" mainstream society, even prior to prison. Facing constant discrimination because of your past record is debilitating and depressing. Added to this is the daily burden of racism if you are a person of color, which of course magnifies the obstacles on the road to success.

Whether applying for work, housing, a student loan, or public assistance, nearly every application form has a box or question requiring that we disclose our criminal record. If you have no criminal record, you either mark NO convictions with relief, or just pass it by without a thought.

But when confronted with the box, what are the choices for someone who has been to prison, or anyone with a criminal record?

If it's an employment application, we can lie and say we have NO past convictions. Usually with a "NO" response, the question will be used as a "truth test." If we get the job we'll be fired for lying on the application when a criminal background check is completed, no matter how well we perform on the job.

The other choice is to answer the question truthfully. A former prisoner answering YES about past convictions is usually eliminated outright from consideration for a job. Just the appearance of the box on the application stops many of us from even applying. The always-difficult process of seeking employment is deeply depressing for anyone coming out of prison. Following are examples of other areas which effect all ex-prisoners, and women in particular.

FAMILY REUNIFICATION

Each year approximately 400,000 mothers and fathers finish serving prison or jail sentences and return home, ready to rebuild their families (Hirsch, Dietrich, Landau, Schneider, Ackelsberg, Bernstein-Baker & Hohenstein, 2002, p. 1). When a prisoner comes home, families are often angry and resentful. They have suffered from the burden of imprisonment financially and emotionally. Overcoming this anger is a years-long process, and healing is slow, sometimes impossible. Prison especially affects African-American and Latino families because people of color are sent to prison at such disproportionate rates, and generations of family members are locked up. Black children are nine times more likely than white children to have a parent in prison; Latino children are three times more likely to have a parent in prison than white children (ACLU et al., 2005, p. 49). Children of parents in prison are two to six times more likely to go to prison than their peers (Brenner, 1998). Child welfare laws are more harshly enforced against families of color, resulting in more of these families being permanently torn apart.

Women are more likely than men to have been caretakers of their children before imprisonment. These women face many barriers as they try to re-establish their relationships with children and other family members. Many of these barriers are not quantifiable because they involve stress and psychological trauma to both children and parents as they struggle for family reunification. On the other hand, some of the barriers are all too codified and legal.

CHILD CUSTODY AND PARENTAL RIGHTS

The vast majority of incarcerated mothers wish to resume care of their children when they get out of prison. However, the federal Adoption and Safe Families Act (1997) permanently terminates parental custody rights after a child has been in foster care for 15 of the most recent 22 months. Termination of parental rights dictates that your legal status is that of a "stranger" to your own children, prohibiting any contact between parents and children, including letters, telephone contact, or visiting. In addition, in at least 25 states, statutes provide that a parent's imprisonment is grounds for termination of parental rights. Because women's prison sentences are usually longer than 15 months, thousands of mothers are losing all contact with their children for life. Termination hearings are held while mothers are still in prison, and only very rarely will a prisoner be transported to the hearing where her parental rights could be permanently terminated. Even if parental rights have not been permanently terminated, mothers must find a place to live, get a job or obtain public benefits, and perhaps access drug or alcohol treatment before they will be allowed to reunify with their children. If children are in foster care, foster parents rarely facilitate contact between imprisoned parents and their children. Women coming out experience tremendous anxiety about how to rebuild their families, and how to deal with their children's feelings of abandonment and anger.

Family members often volunteer to care for children whose parents go to prison, but background checks for criminal records may disqualify them from being declared eligible by the state. A friend of mine was disqualified from gaining custody of her granddaughter because of a 20-year-old felony conviction, even though she is working steadily as a registered nurse and supporting six other grandchildren. Twenty years after leaving prison, she and her family are still suffering ongoing trauma and discrimination because of her conviction.

If children are placed in foster care programs while a parent is in prison, state child welfare agencies usually make a claim for child support from one or both parents. Although incarcerated parents have no way to pay child support, failure to pay may be used to terminate their parental rights. Additionally, the state may seize prisoners' savings accounts for back child support payments. A woman I knew in prison saved money throughout her entire ten-year sentence so she could have a way to bring her children back together. Two months before she was due to be released, she was informed that her savings account had been seized. Six months later she was back in prison for forging checks to pay rent, and she was sentenced to five more years in prison for a parole violation.

LIFETIME BAN ON RECEIVING WELFARE AND FOOD STAMPS

Formerly incarcerated women are mostly poor women of color, returning to poor communities without a family support network. Most of them had been unemployed before they went into prison. Some never had a legal job. Almost 30% of all mothers in state prison had been receiving welfare assistance before their arrest (Allard, 2002, p. 19). Public assistance could make it possible for them to survive instead of ending up homeless or going back to prison. But the federal "Personal Responsibility and Work Opportunity Reconciliation Act of 1996" imposes *a lifetime ban* prohibiting people with felony drug convictions from ever again receiving food stamps or TANF (Temporary Aid for Needy Families). Currently, 15 states currently implement this ban in full (Sentencing Project, 2006).

Women coming out of prison want to establish a life for themselves, create a stable home, and reunify their families–but they have no resources to put a life together. Losing public benefits makes it more difficult to pay rent, provide food for a family, have money for transportation in order to look for a job, pay for child care, get new job skills, or go to college. It's so hard to find work that pays enough to live on that women are driven to supplement family income through illegal means, and the cycle of imprisonment starts all over again.

Women are also ineligible for foodstamps, SSI, or TANF if they have any current problem with the criminal justice system (outstanding bench warrants, probation/parole violations). They remain ineligible until those problems are resolved. Work requirements for TANF or foodstamps often conflict with court-ordered requirements: appointments with parole or probation officers, drug and alcohol rehabilitation programming, parenting classes, further court appearances. Absences from welfare-to-work programs may result in dismissal from the program, termination of benefits, or other sanctions. Trying to resolve so many conflicting requirements is extremely stressful, and women often end up in despair, being sent back to prison for parole or probation violations, or losing their eligibility for welfare and ending up homeless.

EMPLOYMENT

A felony conviction subjects a person to an automatic lifetime public employment ban in several states (Love & Kuzma, 1996, p. 5). Most states routinely deny professional licenses to people with felony convictions, including licenses in fields commonly pursued by women–childcare, nursing, social work, dental assistant, physical therapy, teaching, accounting, and real estate. Former prisoners are also excluded from many entry-level jobs that require insurance bonding such as security guards, cashiers, night janitors, and hotel housekeeping. Legal restrictions are widespread, confusing, and vary widely by state and profession.

Steady employment is essential to family reunification and basic survival, particularly because many former prisoners are barred from receiving public assistance even during their transition from prison back into community life. As mentioned earlier, "the box" on employment applications is an employer's first opportunity to disqualify someone with a criminal record. Over 60% of employers surveyed in a recent UC Berkeley study said they would definitely or probably not consider hiring an ex-prisoner (Holzer, Raphael, & Stoll, 2001, p. 38).

NO PLACE TO COME HOME TO: HOUSING AND HOMELESSNESS

The "one-strike eviction" law passed by Congress in 1998 allows local Public Housing Authorities to deny admission or to evict people accused of engaging in criminal activity including convictions, accusations, or simply suspicion. The law extends this eviction policy to residents whose family members, guests, or caretakers participate in those activities. The one-strike eviction policy effectively bars admission to public housing for anyone with a drug record.

One of the problems women face when coming home from prison is that they may not have housing or a support system waiting for them. The one-strike eviction policy means that people coming out of prison cannot return to their families if the families live in any type of subsidized housing. Private landlords also routinely reject rental applications of people who have criminal records. Increasingly, individual cities are enacting "nuisance eviction ordinances," where people can be labeled a "nuisance" and evicted because of a single police report or complaints by neighbors.

VOTING RIGHTS

Nearly 4.7 million Americans, or 1 in 43 adults, have lost their voting rights as a result of a felony conviction. Over 500,000 formerly incarcerated women are disenfranchised. Currently 48 states and the District of Columbia prohibit inmates from voting while incarcerated for a felony. Thirty-six states prohibit felons from voting while on parole. Four states permanently deny the vote to anyone with a felony conviction (Legal Action Center, 2005, p. 14).

Denying them the right to vote means that formerly incarcerated people have no way to change public policy through normal, democratic, electoral methods. This perpetuates alienation with the political system, and disengagement from the democratic process. In most states, a formerly incarcerated person cannot regain the right to vote until after she has completed their full sentence. This means completion of parole and full payment of any fines or restitution fees, which often total thousands of dollars.

STUDENT LOANS

For someone getting out of prison, the chance to go to community college or vocational school means a chance to start over: get a new life, new skills, new friends and associates. School is a positive way to spend your time if you have past addictions, and more education gives you a better chance of future employment. But the Higher Education Act of 1998 makes people convicted of drug-related offenses ineligible for any student grant, loan, or work assistance.

In prison, vocational training is almost non-existent, so when you come out of prison you don't have marketable skills. Some prisons have training programs in barbering or cosmetology, but many states deny licenses in these fields to anyone with a criminal record. Most prisoners have had little access or exposure to computers either before or during prison, so they are unprepared for today's computer-driven workplace. More than 43,000 current college students faced possible denials of federal education aid in 2001 because of the imposition of the ban on student loans for people with past drug felonies (Hirsch et al., 2002, p. 86). Additionally, many campuses ban people with criminal convictions from living in low-cost student housing.

IMMIGRATION

Many of the women I lived with in federal prison were undocumented, although most had lived in the United States for many years. All of them knew they would be deported after serving their sentences. Their children were citizens, sometimes they had worked to bring their parents to the United States, so they were faced with leaving their whole family behind. Very often they knew no one in the country to which they were being deported. After an immigrant prisoner serves her sentence, she is transferred to INS holding facilities for many long months until deportation proceedings are completed. In the INS jail, she has very little access to legal representation, or any kind of law library so she can represent her own interests. Arguing that all of her children are citizens and that her family lives in the U.S. rarely succeeds with an immigration judge.

"Mixed status" families–those with citizen children and non-citizen parents–represent 9% of all American families with children (Hirsch et al., 2002, p. 91). These families are commonly torn apart because of encounters with the INS or criminal justice system. Even if criminal charges are dropped, non-citizens face deportation if they are undocumented, and they can be barred from re-entering the U.S. for three to ten years. For those with children, this separation means family dissolution, economic hardship, trauma, and even permanent loss of parental rights if children are put in the foster care system. If someone has been banned from re-entering the U.S., simply trying to re-join family members is a criminal act that can result in long periods of imprisonment or immigration detention. This aspect of the law disproportionately affects Mexican and Central American immigrants, since many of them have documented relatives living in the U.S. Many of the women I was with in prison had crossed the border illegally many times, just so they could re-join their families or see their children.

HEALTH CARE

Since most prisoners come from poor communities, the problem of marginal health care often begins before a person goes to prison, continues during incarceration, and persists when they return home. Many women coming out of prison have chronic and serious diseases. Tuberculosis, Hepatitis C, HIV and AIDS are all far more prevalent in prisons than in society as a whole. Mental illness is also common, and exacerbated tremendously by the trauma of imprisonment. The prevalence of these diseases in the population of returning prisoners constitutes a significant public health crisis. Prisoners released to the community are not given filled prescriptions of any of their medications, which may leave them in medical or mental crisis as soon as they're out of prison.

A high percentage of formerly incarcerated people also have histories of drug or alcohol abuse. Recovery programs are usually absent from prison settings, so successful reintegration back into society often requires access to drug and alcohol treatment. But there are far too few treatment programs available, particularly for women. The U.S. Substance Abuse and Mental Health Services Administration estimates that 3.9 million more people need treatment than can be provided services (ACLU et al., 2005 p. 13). Women have a lot of difficulty accessing services, especially residential services, and only 8% of all available programs offer childcare (ACLU et al., 2005, p. 13). Existing treatment options are mostly based on male habits and behaviors, and are not effective treatment for women. Most residential treatment facilities require one month to one year residence in the program, making participation impossible for women responsible for caring for children or elders.

Physical, sexual, and emotional abuse have been defining experiences for the majority of women in prison. Mental health care and psychological treatment are necessary for women to recover from these levels of abuse, but treatment isn't available inside prison, and it's largely unavailable to women coming out of prison. Histories of abuse also complicate family reunification and recovery from drug addiction. Free and low-cost psychological counseling services are desperately needed for women, and all prisoners, returning to society.

CONCLUSION

Clearly, the discrimination which women face when coming out of prison only adds to the many psychological and emotional difficulties they already have in their struggle to re-enter society. This situation can lead to debilitating discouragement, lifelong disenfranchisement, community impoverishment, return to drug addiction, homelessness, and prison recidivism.

This article has summarized the barriers women face when released from prison, but it doesn't reflect women's determination to overcome these obstacles, to change and to succeed. *All of Us or None* is a civil and human rights movement which formerly incarcerated people are organizing. We are working to eliminate these barriers, to expand alternatives to incarceration, and to reduce our society's reliance on mass imprisonment as a solution to poverty. We are determined to change public policies about prison conditions and discrimination against formerly incarcerated people, while simultaneously changing long-held prejudices against those who have been in prison. I encourage you to support our policy initiatives, to check out our Website and give us a call: 415-255-7036 x337 or www. AllofUsorNone.org.

Thank you, as always, to my beloved partner Eve Goldberg, who edited this article and helped me remember these stories.

NOTES

1. As of December 2001, the Bureau of Justice Statistics estimated that over 64 million people in the United States had a state rap sheet, about 30% of the nation's adult population. (See "Survey of State Criminal History Information Systems, 2001: A Criminal Justice Information Policy Report" August. 2003, http://www.ojp.usdoj. gov/bjs/pub/pdf/sschis01.pdf) At least 13 million people in the U.S. have past felony convictions. (Uggen, C., Manza, J. & Thompson, M. (2000). *Crime, class and reintegration: The socioeconomic, familial, and civic lives of offenders.* November 18, 2000, American Society of Criminology Meeting, San Francisco.)

2. See *The Bill of Rights for Children of Incarcerated Parents*, San Francisco Partnership for Incarcerated Parents, 2003, for an overview of the need for policy changes in arrest and subsequent criminal justice procedures, focusing on how they affect children with incarcerated parents.

REFERENCES

ACLU, Brennan Center for Justice, Break the Chains. (2005). *Caught in the net: The impact of drug policies on women and families.* New York: Brennan Center for Justice.

Allard, P. (2002). *Life sentences: Denying welfare benefits to women convicted of drug offenses.* Washington, D.C.: The Sentencing Project.

Brenner, E. (1998). *Fathers in prison: A review of the data.* Washington, D.C.: National Center on Fathers and Families.

Bureau of Justice Statistics. (2001, August). *Prisoners in 2000.* Washington, D.C.: US Department of Justice.

Criminal Justice Consortium. (2001). *Los Angeles in lockdown.* PowerPoint presentation.

Greenfield, L.A. & Snell, T.L. (2000). *Women offenders.* Washington, D.C.: U.S. Department of Justice, Bureau of Justice Statistics.

Hirsch, A., Dietrich, S., Landau, R., Schneider, P., Ackelsberg, I., Bernstein-Baker, J., & Hohenstein, J. (2002). *Every door closed: Barriers facing parents with criminal records.* Washington, D.C.: Center for Law and Social Policy, and Philadelphia, PA: Community Legal Services.

Holzer, J.H., Raphael, S., & Stoll, M. (2001). *Will employers hire ex-offenders? Employer checks, background checks, and their determinates.* Berkeley, CA: Berkeley Program on Housing and Urban Policy, University of California.

Legal Action Center. (2005). *After prison: Roadblocks to reentry.* New York: Legal Action Center.

Love, M.C., & Kuzma, S.M. (1996). *Civil disabilities of convicted felons: A state-by-state survey.* Washington, D.C.: US Department of Justice, Office of the Pardon Attorney.

Mumola, C.J. (2000, August). *Incarcerated parents and their children.* Washington, D.C.: U.S. Department of Justice, Bureau of Justice Statistics.

The Sentencing Project. (2005a). *Prisoners re-entering the community.* Washington, D.C.: The Sentencing Project.

The Sentencing Project. (2005b, May). *New incarceration figures: Growth in population continues.* Washington, D.C.: The Sentencing Project.

The Sentencing Project. (April 2006). *Summary-Life Sentences: Denying Welfare Benefits to Women Convicted of Drug Offenses.* Washington, D.C.: The Sentencing Project.

Wellisch, J., Anglin, M.D., & Prendergast, M.L. (1993). Number and characteristics of drug-using women in the criminal justice system: Implications for treatment. *Journal of Drug Issues, 23*(1), 7-30. http://www.aetn.org/mip/html/statistics.html

Women in Prison Project. (2006, March). *Women in Prison Fact Sheet.* New York: Correctional Association of New York.

Women's Prison Association. (2003, December). *WPA Focus on Women & Justice.* New York: Women's Prison Association.

ADDITIONAL READINGS

All of Us or None and The Data Center. (2004). *Policy recommendations and briefing packet.* San Francisco: Legal Services for Prisoners with Children.

Associated Press. (2001, December 29). 43,000 Students with Drug Convictions Face Denial of Aid. *New York Times,* p. A11.

Fix, M., Zimmerman, W., & Passel, J.S. (2000). The integration of immigrant families in the United States. Paper presented at the Strengthening Immigrant Families & American Communities: Strategies for a New Century Conference, sponsored by Annie E. Casey Foundation in Miami, FL. (June 8-10, 2000). Published by Urban Institute.

Harlow, C.W. (1999). *Selected findings: Prisoner abuse reported by inmates and probationers.* Washington, D.C.: U.S. Department of Justice, Bureau of Justice Statistics.

Human Rights Watch. (2005). *No second chance: People with criminal records denied access to public housing.* New York: Human Rights Watch.

Legal Action Center. (2004). *Legal barriers affecting individuals with a criminal record.* New York: Legal Action Center.

Little Hoover Commission, State of California. (2003). *Back to the community: Safe & sound parole policies.* Sacramento, CA: Little Hoover Commission.

Little Hoover Commission, State of California. (2004). *Breaking the barriers for women on parole.* Sacramento, CA: Little Hoover Commission.

Love, M.C. (2005). *Relief from the collateral consequences of a criminal conviction: A state-by-state resource guide.* New York.

RAND Research Brief. (2002). *Prisoner reentry: What are the public health challenges?* Santa Monica, CA: RAND Corporation.

Simmons, C.W. (2000). *Children of incarcerated parents.* Sacramento, CA: California Research Bureau.

The Sentencing Project and Human Rights Watch. (1998). *Losing the vote: The impact of felony disenfranchisement laws in the United States.* Washington, D.C.: The Sentencing Project, and New York, NY: Human Rights Watch.

Women in Prison Project. (2004, March). *Effects of imprisonment on families fact sheet.* New York: Correctional Association of New York.

Women in Prison Project. (2004, March). *Women prisoners and substance abuse fact sheet.* New York: Correctional Association of New York.

doi:10.1300/J015v29n03_15

Index